DIVIDED BY FAITH

DIVIDED BY FAITH

Religious Conflict and the Practice of Toleration
in Early Modern Europe

Benjamin J. Kaplan

The Belknap Press of
Harvard University Press

Cambridge, Massachusetts
London, England

First Harvard University Press paperback edition, 2009

Library of Congress Cataloging-in-Publication Data
Kaplan, Benjamin J.
Divided by faith : religious conflict and the practice of
toleration in early modern Europe /
Benjamin J. Kaplan.
p.   cm.
Includes bibliographical references and index.
ISBN 978-0-674-02430-4 (cloth : alk. paper)
ISBN 978-0-674-03473-0 (pbk.)
1. Religious tolerance—Europe—History.   2. Europe—Church history.
3. Europe—Religion.   I. Title.
BL640.K37 2007
274'.06—dc22   2007011250

Contents

III. INTERACTIONS

IV. CHANGES

List of Maps and Illustrations

Central Europe 1648

BALTIC SEA

NORTH SEA

to Sweden

Hamburg

Franeker

Friesland
DUTCH REPUBLIC

Bremen

Wittenberg

BRANDENBURG

HANOVER

Berlin

Haarlem
Amsterdam
Leiden
The Hague
Utrecht

Lingen

Osnabrück

Nijmegen

Münster

Holland

Zeeland

Sluis

Uden
Kevelaer

Cleves

HOLY ROMAN EMPIRE

Leipzig

SAXONY

Antwerp

Brabant

Brussels

Maastricht

Westphalia

Jülich

Cologne

JÜLICH-CLEVES

Aachen

Erfurt

Dresden

SPANISH

Overmaas

NETH.

Rhine

B. of WÜRZBURG

Prague

BOHEMIA

Worms
Speyer

Würzburg

FRANCE

PALATINATE

Heidelberg

Franconia

Nürnberg

Ansbach

Regensburg

Châlons-sur-Marne

Metz

Dinkelsbühl

Nördlingen

WÜRTTEMBERG

Donauwörth

Alsace

Strasbourg

Ulm

BAVARIA

Linz

Colmar

Swabia

Augsburg

Munich

Salzburg

Biberach

Ravensburg

Basel

Thurgau

Appenzell

Rheintal

SALZBURG

Zurich

Toggenburg

Glarus

TYROL

FRANCHE-COMTÉ

Bern

SWISS CONFEDERATION

Grisons

Geneva

Trent

Lyon

VENETIAN REPUBLIC

SAVOY

Milan

Verona

Padua

Venice

Grenoble

Mantua

Turin

Piedmont

Parma

Ferrara

Adriatic Sea

Gap

Modena

Bologna

Avignon

Liguria

Genoa

Nîmes

Montpellier

Nice

Pisa

Florence

Ancona

Marseille

Toulon

Livorno

TUSCANY

0   100 miles

Europe 1648

SCOTLAND

Glasgow • Edinburgh

Derry •

IRELAND GREAT

Dublin • Newcastle • NORTH
Liverpool Lancaster SEA
Cork • Preston
Manchester York
BRITAIN Lincoln

WALES DENMARK and NORWAY

ENGLAND King's Lynn

Norwich • Hambur •

Oxford • DUTCH

Taunton • Bath London • Amsterdam • REPUBLIC

Plymouth • Canterbury Antwerp •

Portsmouth St. Omer • SPANISH Brussels • HOLY

English Channel Douai NETH. ROMAN

EMPIRE

ATLANTIC Caen • Rouen •

OCEAN Paris • Nürnberg •

Strasbourg •

Nantes • Loire

Berry BAVARI

FRANCE Salzburg •

La Rochelle • Dijon • FRANCHE-

COMTÉ SWISS

Bay of Lausanne • CONFED. TYROL

Biscay Geneva • Trent •

Bordeaux • Lyon • SAVOY Milan • VENETIAN

Grenoble • Padua • Venic

Bayonne • Gap • REP.

Mauvezin • Avignon • Genoa • Bologna

NAVARRE Toulouse • Nîmes • Liguria

Montpellier • Florence •

Marseille • Livorno • TUSCANY Ancona •

Toulon •

PORTUGAL PAPAL

Lisbon • Madrid • CASTILE ARAGON CORSICA STATES

to Genoa Civitavecchia •

S P A I N Barcelona • Rome •

VALENCIA Balearic Napl •

Sea

Seville • SARDINIA

Cadiz • GRANADA to Spain

Malaga Tyrrhenian

Sea

M E D I T E R R A Palermo •

SICIL

Algiers • to Spain

MOROCCO Oran • ALGIERS Tunis •

TUNIS N E A

MALTA

0   100   200   300 miles

DIVIDED BY FAITH

Introduction

In the three centuries of European history sandwiched between the medieval and modern eras—the period known as early modern—no episode is more notorious or horrifying than the Saint Bartholomew's Day massacres of 1572. It began with a botched attempt to assassinate Gaspard de Coligny, political and military leader of France's Calvinists, known as Huguenots. It proceeded, on the order of Charles IX, with the murder of the flower of the Huguenot nobility. By a bitter irony, the latter had gathered in Paris to celebrate the wedding of Henri of Navarre to the king's sister, a match intended to pacify relations between Protestants and Catholics and end a decade of religious wars. Crowds of Parisian Catholics then took the killing a great, unauthorized step further. The episode ended with the wholesale slaughter of Huguenots, first in Paris, then in some dozen other French cities. Thousands of Huguenots died—perhaps two thousand in Paris and another three thousand in the provinces, though we will never know for sure. Many died gruesome, painful deaths, as their killers joyously, almost playfully, mutilated and degraded the bodies of these "heretics." In 1535, France's "Most Christian King" Francis I had declared that he wanted heresy banished from his realm "in such manner that if one of the arms of my body was infected with this corruption, I would cut it off, and if my children were tainted with it, I would myself offer them in sacrifice."[1] In 1572

still more had to reckon with "heretics" living just down the road or across the field. People found themselves divided by faith from their closest companions: friends, neighbors, fellow citizens, even family. And as it turned out, the split was permanent.

How to relate to people of different faiths thus became one of the most urgent concerns of the age. "Tolerance" and "intolerance" became major subjects of European thought for the first time and an issue in daily life for millions. Even in the eighteenth century, after their colonial conquests had brought them face-to-face with a great number of the world's peoples, the form of "otherness" that challenged and engaged Europeans most forcefully was still the religious differences among themselves. Religious tolerance became the paradigmatic, first tolerance in Western history, the matrix out of which emerged the modern concept of tolerance as applied to all forms of difference—ethnic, cultural, and racial as well as religious.

The story we tell about the rise of tolerance has its own history: it is a heritage of the Enlightenment. For those who spearheaded that optimistic movement, history was first and foremost a story of mental progress. It was the story of humanity growing up, casting aside the fears, superstitions, and ignorance of its childhood for the rationality and knowledge of adulthood. Using this metaphor of maturation, Enlightenment "philosophes" projected the course of individual human development, as they understood it, onto that of humanity as a whole. The part of humanity they had specifically in mind, though, was Europe and its colonies. Its final coming-of-age some saw occurring in their own eighteenth century; others spied it just over the temporal horizon. In either case, philosophes like Voltaire, Lessing, Diderot, and Condorcet saw the light of reason (employing another metaphor) banishing the darkness of faith. Not that they believed Enlightenment entailed the abandonment of religion altogether. While some philosophes, especially in France, lashed out fiercely against the perceived dogmatism and tyranny of religious institutions, the majority thought that religion would itself become more rational, less "enthusiastic" and "fanatical." The faith of a mature humanity, they held, would accord fully with the dictates of human reason, as did the revelations of Scripture, properly understood. Tolerance they declared an essential quality of this mature religion, the concrete social manifestation of its reasonableness. As some earlier European thinkers had done, the philosophes declared tolerance an essential mark of genuine Christianity. Unlike any predecessors, they made it the endpoint of an elaborate historical schema, a yardstick to measure human progress.

At the start of the twenty-first century, we still employ this schema to interpret the past. Consider, for example, some modern historians' interpretations of St. Bartholomew's. The forms of brutal killing its perpetrators used, writes Janine Garrisson, "descended from the dawn of time: the collective unconscious had buried them in itself, [and] they reemerged in that month of August 1572. As primitives carry out their purificatory practices, the people subjected all those 'wicked dead' to the action of the requisite elements: water, mud, air, and fire. . . . Anthropologists describe these same rites of purification and of appeasement of the gods among primitive peoples."[2] Robert Kingdon suggests likewise that the massacres could best be explained by the "primitive religious emotions" of the population.[3] What do the powerful adjectives and non-Western parallels employed by these scholars imply? Human societies, they suggest, pass through stages of development, from the primitive to the advanced. Religious conflict is a primitive form of behavior, driven by emotion, ritualism, and tribal loyalties; the more advanced, or civilized, a society is, the greater the tolerance it will practice. Some societies have not proceeded as far along this evolutionary path of development as others and are backward compared to them. Taking temporary setbacks and detours into account, though, all societies are moving in the same direction, toward greater toleration.

The problem with the schema is that it is a myth, in more than one sense of the term. A myth, by one definition, is a statement that one can show to be false or at any rate misleading. Current events are not the subject of this book, but obviously religious violence still occurs on a horrific scale, as ongoing or recent conflicts in Northern Ireland, the Balkans, the Middle East, India, Indonesia, and other parts of the world attest. Are these primitive societies? Are they inevitably moving toward greater tolerance? For that matter, can we count on religious tolerance to endure permanently in Europe and America? On the global stage, religious conflict seems at the moment to be increasing, not decreasing, and it is far from clear that technology, economic development, and other things associated with modernization and progress are having the effect of reducing it. As for early modern Europe, countless studies present facts that do not fit the presumed pattern of a rise of toleration. The Gordon Riots in England, the War of the Camisards, the "Bloodbath of Thorn," the expulsion of twenty thousand Lutherans from Salzburg, the Calas affair in France: these are a few of the episodes testifying to continued conflict and persecution in the eighteenth century. The late seventeenth witnessed in Britain a revolution to remove a Catholic monarch from the throne, and in France the conversion at sword point of three quarters of a million Huguenots. These facts are common knowledge among historians. Yet somehow the story of a rise of tolerance has never lost its credibility. In the nineteenth century it was told with verve by writers such as Thomas Babington Macaulay, John Lothrop Motley, and W. E. H. Lecky—members of the so-called Whig school of historians, who gave it an anti-Catholic twist. In the twentieth century, the story was both told and critiqued. Yet more than ever before, it became conventional wisdom among Europeans and Americans. Discrepancies between fact and myth were dismissed as exceptions, setbacks, or detours.

"Myth" has a second meaning as well, a more literary one. A myth is a symbolic story told about characters who are larger than life, a story with a moral, told about the past in order to explain or justify some present state of affairs. In this sense, too, the "rise of religious tolerance" is a myth. To each historical period it assigns heroes, champions of tolerance who anticipated "modern" values and who eventually triumphed over their "backward" opponents. It is a symbolic story in that it describes change in metaphorical terms—of movement upward and forward ("progress"), of light replacing darkness ("Enlightenment," "le siècle des lumières," "Aufklärung"), of maturation. In telling the story we convey a moral, namely the timeless value of tolerance, and congratulate ourselves for practicing it more than any previous age.

This is not all bad, for like similar ideological constructs, the "rise of tolerance" has a circular, self-confirming power. It provides a standard against which we judge our societies—severely sometimes—and lends moral weight to calls for greater tolerance. On the other hand, its chauvinism can be paralyzing. By blaming intolerance on primitive irrationality it obscures its true causes. And since no people want to consider themselves primitive, it encourages us to view intolerance as someone else's vice, not our own. More subtly, the myth takes for granted the universal validity of a single definition of tolerance, our own, and reduces all differences to a matter of quantity. It asks only *how much* tolerance prevailed in a particular time and place, failing to acknowledge that qualitatively different *kinds* of tolerance may exist. In this way it distorts our vision of the past, as it narrows our thinking about ways to avoid or resolve conflict in the present.

This book takes a fresh look at the history of religious tolerance and conflict in Europe in the centuries between the Reformation and the French Revolution. It neither seeks to establish new facts nor surveys all known ones. Its goal is rather to make people see this history differently by shifting the focus of their attention. Traditional histories of tolerance focus on bold intellectuals who argued for tolerance, like Sebastian Castellio, John Locke, and Voltaire, and on enlightened rulers who instituted tolerant policies, like England's Oliver Cromwell, Prussia's Frederick the Great, and Habsburg emperor Joseph II. In the writings of the first group historians have traditionally discerned the emergence of the modern idea of tolerance, in the decisions of the latter its spreading practice. In the first case, historians have treated tolerance as an abstract concept, in the second they have defined it as a matter of law and government fiat. Tolerance, they have suggested, was first imagined by a visionary few, who offered increasingly robust theoretical justifications for it, then it was institutionalized by a small number of forward-thinking rulers, who let themselves be guided by reason. Two genres of historical writing (often combined with one another) have served as the chief bearers of this story: one traces the genealogy of ideas, the other tells a political narrative. In both, the cast of characters could scarcely be more elite.

In the past ten or fifteen years, an increasing number of historians have grown discontented with this story and, within their subfields, produced studies that depart from it. Their work remains fragmentary, however, and not very accessible to nonspecialists. Meanwhile, other historians continue to write the history of tolerance just as it was written in the 1950s, when Joseph Lecler published his classic on the subject, and even the 1930s, when Wilbur K. Jordan's appeared.[4] Sometimes it seems as if, in the intervening decades, a revolution had not swept the broader field of history. At the heart of that revolution lay a single insight: that elites are not all-powerful and that other sorts of people—peasants and craftsmen, women and minorities—played an active role, too, in shaping the past. Such people, formerly "without history," now receive as much attention as do philosophers and kings.[5] With this change, historians have widened enormously the scope of their subject to include daily life as well as extraordinary events, social groups as well as individual leaders, popular mentalities as well as erudite systems of thought, the local community as well as the national polity. To tackle these new subjects, historians have drawn on such disciplines as demography, anthropology, and literary studies to devise new methodologies. As a result, social and cultural approaches to history have blossomed alongside intellectual and political ones, challenging old verities, opening up new lines of inquiry, and forcing people to reconceptualize the past.

This book draws on some of these approaches to reexamine the history of religious tolerance in early modern Europe. It begins from the crucial premise that tolerance was an issue not just for intellectuals and ruling elites, but for all people who lived in religiously mixed communities. For them tolerance had a very concrete, mundane dimension. It was not just a concept or policy but a form of behavior: peaceful coexistence with others who adhered to a different religion. Let us call this form of behavior "toleration." It was a social practice, a pattern of interaction among people of different faiths. It operated, or failed to, on the local level, and had a complex relationship to both ideals and official policies. In short, this book focuses on toleration, defined as the peaceful coexistence of people of different faiths living together in the same village, town, or city. It asks how such toleration worked in practice and why it prevailed only at certain times and places. And it questions whether such toleration underwent an evolutionary rise.

So defined, religious toleration required no "principle of mutual acceptance," much less an embrace of diversity for its own sake, as our modern concept of tolerance presumes.[6] Despite the arguments of the philosophes, most Europeans continued to the very end of the early modern era to use the word *tolerate* in its traditional meaning: to suffer, endure, or put up with something objectionable. It was a pragmatic move, a grudging acceptance of unpleasant realities, not a positive virtue. In its very enactment the people doing the tolerating made powerful, if implicit, claims about the truth of their own religion and the false, deviant character of others'. The revolutionary pamphleteer Thomas Paine condemned toleration for precisely this reason. He viewed it as an affront to the natural rights of humanity, among which he counted religious freedom. "Toleration," he wrote, "is not the opposite of intolerance but is the counterpart of it. Both are despotisms. The one assumes to itself the right of withholding liberty of conscience and the other of granting it. The one is the Pope armed with fire and faggot and the other the Pope selling and granting indulgences." The poet Goethe put it more succinctly: "To tolerate is to insult."[7]

Paine's denunciation of toleration makes a subtle but critical point: tolerance and intolerance were not, in the ordinary sense, opposites in early modern Europe, and one should not expect to find either one or the other. Rather, the two were "dialectically and symbolically linked."[8] Just as bigotry and discrimination were inherent in tolerance, so was conflict in even the most peaceful coexistence. This paradoxical statement would not surprise social scientists, who recognize conflict as a normal part of human social life. Communities establish rules of engagement and employ a variety of mechanisms, formal and informal, to regulate conflict and keep it within bounds. Peace involves not eliminating conflict but successfully regulating and containing it. This holds doubly when a society's values legitimize and even encourage conflict in a particular sphere. Such was the case for early modern Europe in religious matters. Those who harbored no antagonism toward other faiths were exceptional people, in conflict with the official norms of their communities—at least until the Enlightenment, when a gulf opened dividing elite from popular opinion. By the same token, those willing to kill their neighbors over a religious dispute were exceptional too. Early modern Europe had both its butchers and its martyrs, whose actions stunned contemporaries and left indelible marks on their culture. But the vast majority were neither, nor did their conception of Christian piety oblige them to be. Even when Europe's churches preached intolerance most vehemently, they also taught countervailing values, like love for one's neighbor and respect for the law. Religious obligations and secular commitments were difficult to disentangle in early modern culture. Honor, loyalty, friendship, affection, kinship, civic duty, devotion to the common weal: these bonds had themselves a sacred character that might reinforce or complicate a person's confessional allegiance. And even when most at odds, rival confessions continued to share a common Christian heritage, derived from antiquity and the Middle Ages, just as Christians, Jews, and Muslims shared a common scriptural one. Meanwhile, a variety of institutions, some old, some new, struggled to keep the peace. Thus the seeming inconsistency—the "Janus face"—of early modern tolerance/intolerance, and the volatility of life in religiously mixed communities.[9]

Peaceful coexistence remained always a precarious achievement. It required an elaborate set of arrangements and accommodations for people of opposing faiths to live together peacefully, given how deeply religion was integrated into the social, cultural, and political life of early modern communities. Where would the various groups worship? How would they pay for their churches and pastors? Who would educate their children, and with what curriculum? How would charitable funds be distributed? How would public events be solemnized? Whose holidays would be celebrated? How would the powers and spoils of governance be shared, if at all? What rights and privileges would each group have? Peace depended on resolving these issues in a way that all groups found satisfactory, or at least bearable. Coexistence also raised acute questions about how people of different faiths might interact with one another. Did they intermarry? If so, how would their children be raised? Did they live in the same neighborhoods? employ or buy goods from one another? belong to the same guilds and clubs? drink in the same taverns? attend each other's weddings and funerals? To what extent did they form distinct subcommunities and subcultures? Depending on the answers to these questions, relations between groups could follow very different patterns.

This book does not attempt to treat all the interactions Europeans had with people of different faiths in the sixteenth through eighteenth centuries. If it did, it would have to range around the entire globe, as those centuries famously saw Europeans explore distant lands, trade with countless peoples, and establish vast empires in Asia and the Americas. In the process, they encountered followers of most of the world's religions. However important those encounters were, they do not raise the central question concerning us here: how religious diversity was accommodated within the Christian society of early modern Europe. Accordingly, the book limits its focus to Europe, specifically to the part of it that in the Middle Ages had acknowledged the spiritual leadership of popes and the temporal leadership of Charlemagne's successors, the Holy Roman emperors. Stretching from the British Isles to the Commonwealth of Poland-Lithuania, this part of the Continent is sometimes referred to as "Latin Christendom" or "Western Christendom," and in the early modern era was synonymous with Europe itself: it was what people usually meant when they used the word *Europe*. This restricted usage, which we shall adopt, was cemented when Pope Pius II and others summoned "Europe's" princes to unite in defense against a powerful new threat, the Muslim empire of the Ottoman

Turks, who in 1453 had conquered Constantinople. This epochal event had destroyed the last vestige of the Byzantine Empire, which until then had constituted a second, Eastern Christendom. By the 1520s the Ottomans had extended their conquests into Hungary, and in 1529 their armies would—for the first but not the last time—lay siege to Vienna itself. Forged in the desperate struggle to beat back these "infidels," the early modern definition of Europe equated it with the western lands that for centuries had shared a common cult, a learned language (Latin), and a political tradition. This Europe, this Christendom, was the community torn to pieces, on many levels, by the Protestant and Catholic Reformations; the community whose members now found themselves divided by faith. The subject of this book is how Europeans, when confronted in their own towns and villages by religious differences, grappled with them—how members of rival confessions managed, or failed, to coexist with one another, and how they treated the Jews, Muslims, and Eastern Orthodox Christians who lived (or were prevented from living) among them.

To distinguish between the nitty-gritty practice of toleration, on the one hand, and the ideal of tolerance, on the other, some scholars would prefer to give the first a different name: "confessional coexistence" or "religious pluralism."[10] This book agrees with the point but opts for plain language. It uses the term *toleration* to refer to situations of stable coexistence where conflict was being successfully contained and physical violence avoided. To understand the process of containment, however, it is crucial to understand the conflict. Part I, "Obstacles," examines why it was so difficult for people divided by faith to live together in early modern Europe. It describes the tremendous forces that fueled intolerance: the belief systems that legitimized, even demanded, conflict; the central role that religion played in communal life; and the ways in which religion and politics intertwined. Religious strife, it argues, had two chief causes, the confessional nature of Christian piety in the post-Reformation era and the equation of civic and sacral community, which operated on both local and national levels. In addition to these factors, though, a specific trigger was required to set off popular violence: a public ritual, or an event that sparked fears of subversion.

Part II, "Arrangements," shows how certain mixed communities successfully contained the threat of conflict. It reveals how few communities succeeded in keeping Christians of different beliefs together in the same church, but how many managed to preserve, despite realities, a semblance of religious unity. This they did by maintaining publicly a single official faith but allowing dissenters to worship either outside the borders of the community or inside a newly defined private sphere. Only when forced by circumstances did communities acknowledge and accept their divisions. When they did, religious groups had to share power and sometimes even churches. Official pluralism made a complex and rigid framework of laws and institutions necessary in order to keep the peace. Part III, "Interactions," looks at how people of different faiths got along in daily life. It shows once again that toleration was not just a matter of more or less, but that it took different forms. In some parts of Europe, Protestants and Catholics showed a long-term trend toward mutual segregation, which proved as conducive to peaceful relations as did their earlier integration. Taboos against intermarriage and conversion encouraged this trend. Ironically, Europeans often found it easier to tolerate people of other faiths who were foreigners or outsiders than ones who were full-fledged members of their own community. That applied also to Jews, who began in sixteenth-century Italy to be segregated in ghettos. Except in Venice, no similar arrangement facilitated the toleration of Muslims.

Part IV, "Changes," returns finally to the question of how much changed from the sixteenth to the eighteenth century. It shows how prevalent religious conflict remained, and how tardily and unevenly different segments of European society embraced Enlightenment ideals of tolerance. Basic structures, like the disparity in privileges enjoyed by different religious groups, remained universal until the end of the Old Regime. When they changed, it was through revolution, not evolution.

Today, sadly, religious conflict seems more prevalent around the world than it was a decade or two ago. This fact gives new immediacy and relevance to a question that millions of Europeans, in the wake of the reformations, struggled with: Can people whose basic beliefs are irreconcilably opposed live together peacefully? More often than usually recognized, the answer in that earlier era was yes. To be sure, with our modern commitment to nondiscrimination and individual freedom, few of us today would find acceptable any of the arrangements for peaceful coexistence this book describes. But this should not obscure the fact that in early modern Europe they offered viable alternatives to bloodshed. Then, as perhaps now, people did not have to love each other in order not to kill each other.

I

OBSTACLES

ONE

A Holy Zeal

Hunted Heretic

On October 27, 1553, on the field of Champel in the shadow of Geneva's city walls, the Spanish physician Michael Servetus was tied to a stake and burned for heresy. His execution was one of the most notorious, controversial acts of the sixteenth century, and some book telling the story of it has appeared almost every decade in the 450-odd years since. The chain of events that led Servetus to his excruciating end began with a very ordinary occurrence, a quarrel between cousins. Antoine Arneys, a Roman Catholic, lived in Lyon, the metropolis of southern France; his cousin Guillaume Trie had converted to Protestantism and fled his Catholic homeland for Geneva, workplace of the great reformer John Calvin. Though divided by faith and distance, Trie and Arneys still felt bound to one another, and one way they expressed their familial caring was by arguing. In February 1553, Arneys wrote Trie pleading with him to abandon a religion that would lead to his damnation. As evidence of Protestantism's falsehood he alleged that vices of every kind flourished in Geneva, unchecked by any proper system of "ecclesiastical discipline and order." With the words of scripture etched in his mind, "by their fruits ye shall know them" (Matthew 7:20), Arneys presumed that true religion produced true godliness, and that the truth of

a religion could be judged—not solely, but in a strong, presumptive way—
by the behavior of those who embraced it. Arneys presumed also that his
cousin held the same belief—that it was a piece of common ground shared
by Protestants and Catholics, and a basis for competition between the two.
He was correct. The accusation astounded Trie, who threw it back in his
cousin's face: not Geneva but Lyon lacked good discipline and order:

> I see vice better conquered here than in all your territories. And al-
> though we allow greater liberty in religion and doctrine, we do not suffer
> the name of God to be blasphemed. . . . I can give you an example which
> is greatly to your confusion. . . . You suffer a heretic, who well deserves to
> be burned wherever he may be. I have in mind a man who . . . says that
> the Trinity, which we hold, is a Cerberus and a monster of hell and . . .
> disgorges all possible villanies against the teaching of Scripture concern-
> ing the eternal generation of the Son of God. . . . And this man is in good
> repute among you, and is suffered as if he were not wrong. Where I'd like
> to know is the zeal which you pretend? Where is the police of this fine
> hierarchy of which you so boast?[1]

The man whom Trie went on to denounce by name was Servetus, one of
the most brilliant, iconoclastic thinkers in a generation of iconoclasts. In
1531, at the age of twenty, Servetus had written a book repudiating the doctrine of the Trinity, central to Christianity for over a millennium and one
of the few doctrines on which Protestants and Catholics agreed. Later,
views like Servetus's would be called Socinian, or—a more familiar label—
Unitarian. For expounding them Servetus became a "hunted heretic," surviving by subterfuge and silence.[2] In 1541, under the name of Villeneuve, he
had settled in a suburb of Lyon, where for the next twelve years he supported himself by practicing medicine and editing texts for a publisher. He
even counted the local archbishop among his patients. In January 1553,
however, Servetus published—anonymously, and in extreme secrecy—a
new book entitled *The Restoration of Christianity*. Bolder still than his
youthful writings, it offered a comprehensive new theology that denied
Christ's human nature, reconceptualized God, and recast the relationship
between God and man. Its appearance outraged Trie, who knew its prove-
nance. He knew because, hoping to engage Calvin in a dialogue over its
contents, Servetus had sent the reformer a copy of the manuscript, and

Calvin had shared it with Trie. To support his allegations, Trie now sent the first four leaves of the manuscript to his cousin.

Arneys lost no time presenting them to the inquisitor Matthieu Ory, and a full-scale investigation was soon under way. Embarrassed, of course, and protective of his protégé, the archbishop of Lyon demanded further evidence. The request made its way via Arneys to Trie and finally to Calvin, who, after some hesitation, allowed two dozen letters he had received from Servetus to be sent to France. In this way, the leader of Reformed Protestantism supplied the Roman Catholic Inquisition with the evidence by which it convicted Servetus of heresy.

Assisted by friends, Servetus managed to escape his Lyon prison, and the inquisitor had to content himself with burning him in effigy, along with a pile of his books. Traveling in disguise, Servetus went in search of a new hiding place. Apparently he headed for Italy. Why he chose to pass en route through Geneva remains to this day a mystery. He knew of Calvin's role in his misfortune and could easily have found another route. It proved a fatal mistake: in Geneva, while attending a church service, he was recognized and again seized. Calvin himself composed the thirty-nine charges against Servetus, accusing him of a string of blasphemous heresies. The verdict of Geneva's court was a foregone conclusion, but before deciding on a sentence, the magistrates sounded the opinion of Geneva's sister churches. The ministers of Schaffhausen insisted that Servetus had to be silenced, "lest his blasphemies like a cancer despoil the members of Christ."[3] Zurich's ministers saw the case as a God-given opportunity for the Swiss churches to refute accusations that they condoned radical doctrines. So bolstered, the magistrates acceded to Calvin's demand for the death penalty. And so, following the ancient law code of Justinian, which for the crime of denying the Trinity prescribed burning at the stake, Servetus was subjected to one of the most painful deaths Europeans knew.

His execution for heresy, the first in Geneva since the Reformation, caused an international uproar and sparked Europe's first great debate on the subject of religious toleration. Protests flew in from Italy, France, and elsewhere in Switzerland, especially from Basel, a tolerant town that offered safe haven to many religious dissidents, including one Sebastian Castellio. A poet and philologist from Savoy, Castellio had once been on good terms with Calvin, and in the early 1540s had even served as rector of Geneva's institution of higher learning, the Collège de Rive. Since then,

Castellio's beliefs had moved far away from Reformed orthodoxy. Castellio now led the protests against Geneva's treatment of Servetus—not because he agreed with the latter's teachings, but on the principle that heretics should never be executed. To argue this point he published in 1554 *Concerning Heretics: Whether they are to be persecuted and how they are to be treated.* It was the first major treatise in early modern Europe arguing for religious toleration.

A compilation, Castellio's book brought together passages in favor of toleration from writings by church fathers, Protestant reformers, and others. Strategically, Castellio excerpted most from authors who enjoyed great respect among mainstream Protestants, including Saint Augustine, Martin Luther, and, in an ironic twist, Calvin himself. The longest single excerpt was from a pamphlet written by Luther in 1523 entitled *On Civil Government.* In it Germany's leading reformer had drawn a sharp distinction between two realms, the spiritual and the civic, which he called the "kingdom of God" and the "kingdom of the world." Restricting the authority of magistrates to the latter, Luther had denied them any jurisdiction whatsoever over matters of belief. Castellio also included, under various pseudonyms, several tracts he himself had written. He spoke his mind most clearly and directly, though, in two dedicatory epistles that framed the whole compilation. In these he articulated four chief arguments: First, that there was real uncertainty as to which of the many doctrines in dispute between religious groups were correct. The very diversity of religious beliefs seemed to him proof that the truth was far from obvious. What then was heresy? "I can discover no more than this, that we regard those as heretics with whom we disagree." Second, Castellio noted that all Christians did in fact agree on certain "fundamental" doctrines, modest in number. Subscribing to these, he argued, made a person sufficiently orthodox:

> Religion does not consist in some point which transcends human understanding and concerning which we have no indisputable passages of Scripture, as, for example, in the understanding of the three persons, the Father, Son, and Holy Spirit. It is enough for us to believe that there is one substance in three persons without bothering ourselves unduly as to how one is related to the other. We need not worry whether the body of Christ is in heaven, whether God has created some to be damned and others to be saved, how Christ descended into hell, and the like. On these

points each may be left to his own opinion and to the revelation of the Savior. It is sufficient to accept the fundamental points of true religion which consists in believing that God is the source of all good, [and] that man is condemned because of the disobedience of the first man and saved by the obedience of the second, who is Jesus Christ our Savior.

Within the parameters set by these fundamentals, it was our behavior, moral or immoral, not the doctrines we subscribed to, that marked us as good Christians or bad. Castellio returned to this argument later. "Why has [Calvin] never burned anyone for avarice and envy though he knows many culprits and could accuse and convict them? . . . Are hypocrites better than heretics?" he asked rhetorically. Finally, he argued, Christ himself had augmented and clarified the moral standards that are "engraved and written in the hearts of all men from the foundation of the world," bequeathing to Christians a special model of virtue, his own behavior on earth. To be pious was to imitate it. Christ himself had taught toleration by example, treating even the worst sinners with compassion and mildness. To execute a heretic was "cruel enough, but a more capital offense is added when this conduct is justified under the robe of Christ and is defended as being in accord with his will, when Satan could not devise anything more repugnant to the nature and will of Christ!"[4] In the following centuries, advocates of toleration would echo and elaborate all these arguments.

Calvin, meanwhile, had not waited for the appearance of Castellio's book to offer a defense of the trial and his role in it. Always uncompromising, on this occasion he took a position stunning in its starkness: "Those who would spare heretics and blasphemers are themselves blasphemers. Here we follow not the authority of men but we hear God speaking as in no obscure terms He commands His church forever. Not in vain does He extinguish all those affections by which our hearts are softened: the love of parents, brothers, neighbors and friends. He calls the wedded from their marriage bed and practically denudes men of their nature lest any obstacle impede their holy zeal. Why is such implacable severity demanded unless . . . devotion to God's honor should be preferred to all human concerns and as often as His glory is at stake we should expunge from memory our mutual humanity."[5] Heresy had to be expunged first and foremost because it was an offense to "God's honor," in defense of which Calvin was prepared to dehumanize himself as well as the heretic, and demanded that others do likewise. All Christians were obliged to promote God's honor, but for Christian magistrates it was a sacred duty of office. God had vested them with the "power of the sword" precisely for this end, among others— to prevent that "impure and petulant tongues . . . lacerate the sacred name of God and trample upon His worship."[6] They also had the duty of defending the church, to which heresy was a mortal threat. Nor was there any doubt as to what constituted heresy: Reformed teachings were drawn directly from scripture, whose meaning was clear, and those teachings were essential, defining aspects of Christianity.

This last point was emphasized as well by Theodore Beza, professor of Greek in the town of Lausanne, who enthusiastically supported Calvin and took it upon himself to reply directly to Castellio's *On Heretics*. His refutation, known for short as the *Anti-Bellius,* appeared later in 1554. Beza pointed out that Castellio, in selecting from the writings of Protestant reformers, had drawn solely from the authors' early works. The same reformers had often adopted far less tolerant stances in their later, more mature works, from which Beza offered counterquotations. Concerning the status of dogma he wrote: "There is one way that leads to God, namely, Christ; and one way that leads to Christ, namely, faith; and this faith includes all those dogmas which you reject as unnecessary. . . . If Christ is not true God, coeternal and consubstantial with the Father, how is He our Savior? How is He our sanctifier? How is He victor over sin, death, and the devil? Unless He is true man, save for sin, how is He our mediator?"[7]

Faith, in other words, is empty if it is not faith *in* something specific. Castellio's arguments to the contrary, said Beza, were themselves blasphemous and heretical. In making them, he had betrayed the cause of the Reformation. The license he demanded was worse than "papal tyranny." When a heretic committed blasphemy and impiety, scorning God's Word and resisting all attempts at correction, the death penalty was fully justified. Indeed, it was required, so as to stop heresy from "infecting" other people and destroying the church from within. Magistrates are "guardians and protectors not only of the second table of the [Mosaic] law," that is, the moral code embodied in the second half of the Ten Commandments, "but also, indeed principally, of the pure religion, in matters concerning external discipline." Those who protested against Servetus's trial were "servants of Satan," Beza declared, "mortal enemies of the Christian religion" worthy themselves of capital punishment at the hands of the same magistrates whose sword they would snatch away.[8]

The polemics continued furiously for two years, and in his rebuttal to Calvin's *Defence* Castellio got off his most famous line: "To kill a man is not to defend a doctrine, but to kill a man." Predictably, it failed to convince Calvin and his supporters. On the contrary, several facts emerged from the mid-1550s debate. First, Reformed Protestantism had joined Lutheran and Catholic camps in approving the execution of heretics. Intolerance was henceforth the official teaching of all Europe's governmentally sanctioned churches. Not only was it practiced, it was declared a good thing and toleration bad. John Jewel, an English bishop, declared himself proud that a Protestant authority, not a Catholic, had executed Servetus. Philip Melanchthon, the preeminent Lutheran leader after Luther's death, said the church would owe Calvin its gratitude "now and for all future times" for his role in the proceeding.[9] In the seventeenth century, France's Bishop Bossuet would proudly define Catholicism as "the most severe and least tolerant of all religions."[10] Europe's churches competed with one another to be the most rigorous doctrinally and zealous in combating heresy.

Second, crucial arguments in favor of toleration had been declared tantamount to heresy. For Reformed Protestants, to challenge intolerance became a dangerous act. In 1560 the Scottish reformer John Knox blasted some of his countrymen who dared voice their disapproval of Servetus's execution. They defend, he said, a blasphemer; "therefore ye are blasphemers before God, like abominable as he was."[11] That heretics could rightfully be executed became itself a point of dogma for the Reformed churches, even in places where no executions were carried out. On the Catholic side too, expressing tolerant impulses, or even humanitarian ones, grew perilous. In 1560 a man named Robert Delors was attacked by a Parisian crowd after he showed sympathy for a Huguenot on the scaffold. Delors had not even known the man's religion, but out of compassion had reportedly said, "What's this, my friends? Isn't it enough that he die? Let the executioner do his job. Do you want to torment him even more than the sentence calls for?"[12] Four days later, Delors himself was executed for blasphemy.

Finally, the debate over Servetus's death helped determine the future direction of the Reformed movement. Beza's *Anti-Bellius,* followed by other polemical tracts defending Calvin's doctrines, won him the respect and gratitude of the great reformer, who picked Beza to succeed him as leader of Geneva's church. This made Beza, in a loose sense, leader of Reformed Protestantism as a whole after Calvin's death in 1564. As a consequence, Beza's "scholastic" brand of Calvinist dogma came to set the standard of orthodoxy for the entire movement. It was a brand more rigid and precise than Calvin's own.

Christian Freedom

It was by no means apparent in the first years of the Reformation that Protestants would ever combat heresy with fire and sword. Martin Luther himself initially denied authorities the right to impose their beliefs on anyone. In 1523 he told clergy that they "are neither higher nor better than other Christians" and "should impose no law or decree on others without their will and consent." In the same tract, quoted by Castellio, he told magistrates it was futile as well as wrong for them to encroach on God's kingdom: "The temporal government has laws which extend no further than to life and property and external affairs on earth, for God cannot and will not permit anyone but himself to rule over the soul. . . . Heresy is a spiritual matter which you cannot hack to pieces with iron, consume with fire, or drown in water. God's word alone avails here."[13] The previous year he had scolded the magistrates of Wittenberg for abolishing the Catholic mass; they should have waited, he said, for the Gospel message to "first win the hearts of the people."[14] With supreme confidence, Luther believed that God's Word, unleashed on earth by its preaching and teaching, would itself effect a religious revolution. In their initial optimism, he and his followers did not envisage the need to spread the Gospel by coercion. Persecution was, as yet, a tool only of Catholic authorities and could be rejected out of hand.

Besides, coercion seemed to contradict the whole point of the early evangelical movement, which was to release people from religious oppression. In 1520 Luther had stirred Europe by proclaiming "the freedom of a Christian." By this slogan he meant that Christians did not need to buy indulgences, go on pilgrimages, fast, or perform other "works" to go to heaven. Salvation was a free gift of God's grace, wholly unmerited by the receiver—and a good thing too, argued Luther, for sin was so deep-rooted in human nature that no one could attain the goodness necessary to earn salvation. Strive as he or she might, no one could satisfy the demands laid down by the Law of the Old Testament. But thanks to the sacrifice of Jesus Christ, a Christian did not need to; having faith in that sacrifice and in the Gospel that proclaimed it was enough. All the requirements for salvation mandated by the Catholic Church were "human ordinances," not divine injunctions, which the priestly hierarchy based in Rome had added to scripture in order to tyrannize over the laity. Through them the priests had set impossible standards for salvation, inculcating guilt and fear in pious Christians. At the same time, they had set themselves in God's place as judges, claiming the "power of the keys" to open or slam shut the gates of heaven. Luther wanted to liberate Christians from human ordinances, clerical tyranny, fear, and, above all, from the requirement that they perform works to achieve salvation. Such was "Christian freedom," as Luther defined it.

Luther's idea has often been misunderstood. In the modern era, the temptation has been to impose on it our own belief in progress. In the nineteenth and early twentieth centuries, many people in Britain and America celebrated "Christian freedom" as a great leap forward in the rise of liberty. This interpretation was classically formulated by "Whig" historians such as Macaulay and Motley. In their view, medieval Catholicism was indeed an oppressive religion that subjected the consciences of lay folk to papal dictate and priestly ruse. The Reformation had emancipated Protestants from that subjection, raising the laity to a status equal to priests (creating, in Luther's words, a "priesthood of all believers") and encouraging them to read and interpret scripture for themselves. Protestantism, they claimed, was a more rational, individualistic faith than Catholicism. It taught freedom of conscience as a fundamental principle. That made it the religious counterpart to democracy and the fitting belief system of Anglo-American peoples, who were distinguished by their love of freedom generally. Rising or falling together, religious freedom and political freedom were inseparable parts of an integral whole. Religious tolerance was an expression, or outcome, of its rise.

It is easy for us to see today how the Whig interpretation reflected the political ideology and liberal Protestantism once dominant in the Anglo-American world. It projected back onto the Protestants of early modern Europe the values and principles of their descendants. Such is the danger of all progressive historical schemas: in seeking the roots of the present, they abridge the distance separating it from the past. But in fact, the "Christian freedom" that reformers like Luther and Calvin championed was quite restricted and did not resemble modern "freedom of conscience."

Admittedly, Luther himself used the two terms synonymously. For example, in his 1521 tract *On Monastic Vows* he wrote: "So, Christian, or evangelical, freedom is that freedom of conscience by which the conscience is liberated from works, not in such a manner that no works are performed but such that the conscience does not put its trust in them. . . . God has freed it from works by teaching it through the Gospel not to put its trust in any work and to rely on nothing except his mercy. And it is thus that the faithful conscience adheres solely to the works of Christ in the most complete liberty."[15] As the quotation shows, "freedom of conscience" did not mean to Luther freedom to choose one's own beliefs. In the same breath that he repudiated the authority of popes and councils, Luther declared his conscience "captive to the Word of God," whose instructions to humanity, he thought, were unambiguous: "There exists on earth no clearer book than Holy Writ."[16] Freedom of conscience, as he used the term, did not even free people from the obligation to perform religious works, like attending sermons or giving alms. It only meant that people's salvation was not contingent upon their performing those works, so that in a sense (a crucial one, to Luther's mind) they performed the works freely. In his *Institutes of the Christian Religion*, Calvin likewise defined "freedom of conscience" as an aspect of Christian freedom. Yet when Calvin wrote that by virtue of it we are "released from the power of all men," he was not approving individual autonomy or freedom of choice.[17] Quite the opposite: he meant that we are subject, exclusively and absolutely, to God's will. We should direct our entire lives, Calvin taught, toward serving as God's agents. That required freedom from all religious injunctions that had man, not God, as their source. As late as the 1640s, Calvin's followers sometimes used "freedom of conscience" in this original sense. It meant, as the Puritan John Canne put it, to have "no king but Jesus."[18]

After a brief initial period, Protestantism was no more tolerant of religious deviance than was contemporary Catholicism. In the 1530s, Protestant authorities in Germany, Switzerland, and Austria executed, with the blessing of reformers, hundreds of Anabaptists. This persecution they conducted in parallel, sometimes in cooperation, with their Catholic counterparts. Anabaptists, though, were not merely heretics. Challenging the very basis of Christian community, they rejected the practice of infant baptism and insisted that church membership be voluntary. Most refused to take oaths, serve in government, or perform military service. The social and political implications of their teachings sufficed alone to brand them as dangerous radicals, but authorities saw their worst suspicions confirmed when in 1535 Anabaptists seized the city of Münster and attempted a coup in Amsterdam. At midcentury, what made the Servetus case different was that it involved no sedition or immorality. It made it explicit that, even in the absence of these, Protestant leaders considered "blasphemous heresy" a capital offense.

Protestants and Catholics were both heirs to a heritage of Christian thought that legitimized persecution. Dating back to antiquity, that heritage had been shaped by one individual more than any other, the church father Augustine of Hippo. A reluctant persecutor, for years Augustine had counseled the church against resorting to force in its struggle with the Donatists, and to the end of his days he rejected applying torture or the death penalty to heretics. In his later writings, though, he offered a justification for lesser forms of coercion that became a fixed part of Catholic dogma and was taken over by Protestants as well. For Augustine, persecution was a form of tough love. "Thou shall beat him with the rod, and shall deliver his soul from hell" (Proverbs 23:14), he quoted. Like a father who chastised his son, a shepherd who drove wandering sheep back into the fold, or God who sent tribulations to his chosen people, the church persecuted the wayward for their own good. Skillful application of corrective discipline could return heretics to the church, outside which there was no salvation. Leaving heretics mired in error condemned them to damnation. The one was therefore an act of Christian love, the other of uncaring neglect. In 1582 a Calvinist synod phrased the argument thus: "Regarding Christian love, it does not consist in having to tolerate every person in his disbelief without speaking against it or punishing him. . . . He too uses love who admonishes and instructs with soft and hard words, as the need demands. . . . The Reformed church cannot exempt [a person] from God's law nor teach anything else . . . or promise anyone freedom and salvation except those to whom God has promised them. Therefore, ministers do not neglect love in tolerating and admonishing where proper, and punishing in accord with God's ordinance where it is necessary."[19] Augustine found support for this argument in various passages of scripture, most notably the parable of the banquet in the Gospel of Luke (14:15–24). Spurned by his invited guests, a householder welcomed the poor and maimed to his meal, and when there still remained room around his table ordered his servants to "go out to the highways and hedges, and whomsoever ye shall find, compel them to come in." The banquet Augustine compared to "the unity of the body of Christ," the highways and hedges to "heresies and schisms."

To be sure, Augustine conceded, no one could force a person to believe anything. This principle had been firmly established by earlier church fathers, among them Tertullian. Faith, the latter asserted, was an internal conviction that no coercion could generate. It was therefore "against the nature of religion to force religion."[20] Augustine argued that one could at least make heretics listen to the truth, ponder it, and reconsider their views. Many people remained mired in error out of custom, negligence, or obstinacy. Such persons needed to be "shaken up in a beneficial way by a law bringing upon them inconvenience in worldly things."[21] Persecution could serve a valid pastoral function by making people amenable to instruction. Although it could not convince of its own power, wrote Anglican theologian Jonas Proast in 1690, it could "bring men to consider those reasons and arguments which are proper and sufficient to convince them, but which, without being forced, they would not consider."[22]

Further legitimizing persecution was a definition of heresy that distinguished it from "unbelief." Since they had never accepted Christ as savior, pagans, Jews, and Muslims were considered by Christian theologians unbelievers, "infidels." It was to them that the Tertullian dictum, that one could not force a person to believe, was held to apply most fully. Heretics, by contrast, were the enemy within the Christian fold. They "profess the Christian faith, but corrupt its dogmas."[23] Their crime was one of "treason against the divine majesty." As Tertullian had explained, the term *heresy*, deriving from the Greek αἵρεσις, meant choice: heretics knew the truth but chose to adhere instead to their own fancies. Their error, according to the churches, was less a product of misunderstanding than a sinful act of malicious will. Pride drove them to claim religious authority; the desires of the flesh drove them to fabricate teachings that licensed immorality. From antiquity onward, stereotypes circulated casting heretics as hedonistic revelers whose clandestine, nighttime gatherings were excuses for orgies.

Such accusations will seem absurd to most people today. Why could none of the Christian churches admit the possibility that individuals might disagree in good conscience on basic matters of faith? Part of the answer lies in an irreducible dogmatism—a belief that there *was* something called truth, revealed to us by God and clearly identifiable, and that every other belief was plain wrong. It is also crucial to realize that Christian tradition conceived of the conscience not as an independent judge of right and wrong, as we think of it today, but as a slate upon which God wrote his law. One could not violate that law, it held, without violating one's own conscience. True, people might misunderstand a church teaching or be ignorant of it. They fell into heresy, though, when they "obstinately" maintained their erroneous opinion after being corrected. This rejection of church authority made them rebels against God, against his agents on earth, and even against their own consciences. It was the defining characteristic of heresy.

Persecution also had direct scriptural warrant, found mostly in the Old Testament. Passages in Deuteronomy (13:1–11, 18:20) and Leviticus (24:14) set the death penalty for idolatry, false prophesying, and blasphemy. Christian tradition, going back to Tertullian, Athanasius, and other church fathers, equated heresy with these offenses. The equation receded into the background in the Middle Ages, when the Catholic Church defined heresy as a punishable offense in itself and began in the eleventh century to execute people for it. It took on new life, though, in the hands of Protestants, who relied heavily on it to justify the repression of dissent. Protestants declared Catholicism, with its veneration of images and relics, idolatrous. Catholics threw the accusation back in their faces, denouncing Protestants for "worshipping" their own bodies and for "spiritual idolatries." The charge of false prophesying flew in many directions but seemed to fit especially well those who claimed to receive new revelations from God. Anabaptists and spiritualists made such claims in the sixteenth century; Quakers, among others, did so in the seventeenth. Blasphemy was an even more fluid concept. Although in the Mosaic law it had chiefly meant scorning or cursing God, from the beginning Christians applied it to almost any challenge to fundamental church doctrine. Luther called the mass a "public blasphemy" because it suggested that Christ's onetime sacrifice on the cross did not suffice to save humanity. Protestants blasphemed, according to Catholics, when they denied Christ's real presence in the Eucharist. Above all, in the eyes of contemporaries, Socinians blasphemed by denying the divinity of Christ. Their rejection of the Trinity and Incarnation put them beyond the pale, calling into question whether they were even Christians. It provoked a persecution that in severity matched and in duration exceeded that of any other religious group. Even irenic churchmen like the Calvinist Franciscus Junius approved the death penalty for them. Even Castellio urged that they be punished.

As for the death penalty, which Augustine had rejected, we must remember first that in the world we are considering it was the punishment prescribed for crimes as minor as petty theft. Heretics should be executed, argued Thomas Aquinas in the thirteenth century, since they were guilty of an offense far greater than others, such as forgery, for which criminals were routinely executed. Aquinas also advanced the argument that heretics would influence and corrupt the orthodox, spreading their crime like a communicable disease. He quoted the church father Jerome: "Cut off the decayed flesh, expel the mangy sheep from the fold, lest the whole house, the whole paste, the whole body, the whole flock, burn, perish, rot, die."[24] In the sixteenth century, Catholic theologian Robert Bellarmine explained that, for their own benefit as well, heretics should be prevented from compounding their offense by perverting others. He repeated also the argument that if one could excommunicate heretics, damning them for eternity, one could certainly impose on them the lesser penalty of execution, which only caused physical death.

Confessionalism

All these arguments circulated among Protestants as well as early modern Catholics. They formed part of a heritage common to all the churches that emerged from the sundering of Western Christendom. That sundering, though, created a radically new context for their application. It was not just that new forms of Christianity came into being, or that there broke out among rival churches a conflict such as Christendom had not seen for over a thousand years. For Catholics as well as Protestants, the very nature of Christian piety changed.

No religion is static, and over its two millennia of existence the Roman Catholic Church has transformed itself several times. The so-called Investiture Controversy of the eleventh century precipitated one such transformation; in the 1960s, Vatican II decreed another. So too in the sixteenth century, partly in response to the Protestant challenge, partly driven by internal impulses for renewal and reform, the Catholic Church initiated sweeping changes in everything from ecclesiastic administration and the training of priests to liturgy and forms of private devotion. Conventionally, the drive to enact these changes is referred to as either the Counter-Reformation or the Catholic Reformation, the first term emphasizing its reactive quality, the second its self-generation. Both terms, however, obscure a crucial fact: that changes in Catholicism resembled in some respects the reforms instituted by Protestants. That is, for all the differences and points of contention that bitterly divided them, in some respects the churches of early modern Europe were developing in parallel to one another. Christianity was changing, irrespective of church. The new type of Christianity that resulted from this process is known as "confessional." Its emergence, also called the "rise of confessionalism" or the "formation of confessions," can be charted beginning in the sixteenth century and continuing through the seventeenth.

To dispel any confusion, it must be explained that the term *confession* and its derivatives do not refer in this context to the Catholic sacrament of penance. Rather they refer to a type of document, the "confession of faith," a declaration of the fundamental doctrines held by a church. Perhaps the most famous was the Augsburg Confession of 1530, which came to define Lutheran orthodoxy. All early modern churches issued such documents, which embodied three of the most basic trends then in Christianity: the internalization of church teaching, the drawing of sharp dichotomies, and the quest for "holy uniformity." Each fueled intolerance.

The timing and modalities of these trends varied greatly by church and by region, and in Ireland they had hardly affected the vast majority of peasants (who remained loyal to Catholicism) by the 1660s. According to Englishman Jeremy Taylor, the Irish peasantry could "give no account of their religion what it is: only they believe as their priest bids them and go to mass which they understand not, and reckon their beads to tell the number and the tale of their prayers, and abstain from eggs and flesh in Lent, and visit St. Patrick's well, and leave pins and ribbons, yarn or thread in their holy wells, and pray to God, S. Mary and S. Patrick, S. Columbanus and S. Bridget, and desire to be buried with S. Francis cord about them, and to fast on Saturdays in honour of our Lady."[25]

Granted that Taylor was a hostile outsider, his description not only matches what we know about seventeenth-century Ireland, it captures a state of affairs that was quite the norm across Europe prior to the Reformation. For medieval Christians, religion was as much a set of ritual practices as a set of beliefs. It entailed feasting and fasting on prescribed days; attending mass; reciting prayers in a language (Latin) they scarcely understood; making pilgrimages to holy places, where they offered sacrifices to wonder-working saints; and a wide array of other "works." These had merit, according to theologians, only if performed in a devout frame of mind. In practice, though, priests and laity attributed to them an efficacy as reliable as transubstantiation, the miracle of the mass whereby wafer and wine became Christ's body and blood. The more frequently they were performed, it was said, the more divine grace they conveyed and the better your chances of going to heaven. Many religious acts, in any event, were directed less toward attaining salvation after death than toward escaping misfortune in life. Making the sign of the cross, wearing an amulet containing the words from the Gospel of John, parading images of saints through parish streets: such acts were believed to ward off evil, offering protection from disease, accident, war, and famine.

In medieval Europe, ordinary laypeople knew little church doctrine. They received no formal religious instruction, and their pastors rarely preached. Like Taylor's peasants, they could establish their orthodoxy simply by declaring they "believe as their priest bids them." Such ignorance did not matter greatly in a world where everyone was by default Catholic. It did after Europe split into competing "confessions," each propounding a rival truth. As each church began to define its identity in terms of its unique teachings, doctrine took on an unprecedented importance, and the expectation, echoed in Taylor's disdain, began to build that church members know what their church taught and how it differed from other churches. For Protestants, this expectation was built into the very definition of their religion, which taught that salvation is "by faith alone." All the Protestant churches accepted it as their mission to teach Christians what they needed to believe to be saved. At the same time, a more general dynamic operated: the very existence of alternatives created pressure for Christians to be better informed and more self-conscious in their commitments. Catholic reformers too began to demand that ordinary church members internalize the teachings of their church. Religion itself thus came increasingly to mean belief in a particular creed, and a life lived in accordance with it.

It was easy for churches to enunciate such dramatically raised standards. Implementing them required decades, in some regions as much as two centuries, of strenuous effort. The churches had to undertake massive pedagogic campaigns, which they conducted via preaching, education, printed propaganda, church discipline, and revamped rituals. In all these areas Protestant reformers broke new ground. They made the sermon the centerpiece of Protestant worship. They required that children receive elementary religious instruction, either at school or through special catechism classes. They released torrents of printed propaganda and encouraged ordinary Christians to read scripture. They established new institutions and procedures to supervise parish life. Most famously, Calvinists invented the consistory, an organ of church governance that administered a strict new form of discipline. Finally, they devised rituals that gave visible form to Protestant tenets—including, paradoxically, the idea that salvation was not achieved by the performance of rituals.

Catholic reformers found themselves caught between two imperatives. On the one hand, the very survival of Catholicism depended on their reforming it. This was true in a global sense across all of Europe, but lands that officially went Protestant presented the extreme case. If their inhabitants continued unthinkingly to participate in the regular round of parish rituals, they would be lost to the Catholic Church. They had to be taught that salvation was to be sought not in habitual acts of observance but in the self-conscious adherence to prescribed (and now proscribed) religious tenets. This was the chief message of the polemical literature directed by English priests against "church papists," people who professed loyalty to Catholicism yet attended Church of England services. Ironically, it was the same message that English Puritans directed against "statute Protestants," who attended the same services out of inertia, conformity, and a sense that if they just "be no prophane contemners of the Word and Sacraments: but repayre to the Church every Sabboth day, & heare divine Service & Sermons orderly, as by Law they are enjoyned, they are good Christians, & sure to bee saved."[26] From the perspective of reformers, Puritan or Catholic, little separated the church papist from the statute Protestant. Both were

"Neuter Nullifidian sots"—persons of "no conscience, no fervour, no faith, no religion," whose verbal formalities and external gestures were empty.[27]

Facing many of the same challenges as Protestant reformers, Catholic reformers had no qualms about adopting the former's pedagogic methods (and vice versa). The Jesuits in particular engaged in a range of activities that show striking parallels to those of their enemies. They became renowned preachers, wrote catechisms (that of Peter Canisius was the most popular in Catholic Europe), and founded hundreds of new schools, mostly at the secondary and college level. Using the *Spiritual Exercises* written by their founder, Ignatius of Loyola, they taught people how to examine their own consciences and achieve pious goals through a remarkable self-discipline. As confessors, chaplains, and organizers of a new type of club, the Marian sodality, they encouraged frequent confession and Communion. This disciplinary routine encouraged the internalization of norms even as it provided an external mechanism for enforcing them.

On the other hand, Catholic reformers recognized that much of Catholicism's popular appeal derived from its traditionalism. In particular, peasants—who, outside of heavily urbanized areas like northern Italy and the Netherlands, formed the large majority of Europe's population—showed a strong attachment to the rituals of the old faith and the protection from physical harm they were believed to offer. Many also found comforting the continuity they provided with the lives of their ancestors. Reformers recognized furthermore that the elaborate ritual life of their church and the theology of works it embodied gave their church much of its unique identity. At the Council of Trent, held in twenty-five sessions between 1545 and 1563, church leaders acknowledged they could not abandon either, and in a series of epochal decisions they forcefully reasserted both. Catholic reformers therefore had to proceed more by revising old practices than by replacing them. They often found that their need to maintain the appeal of Catholicism clashed with their desire to reform it.

One example will have to suffice: the pilgrimage to Sharp Hill (Scherpenheuvel) in the Southern Netherlands. Since time immemorial, an oak tree reputed to have powers of healing had stood on the remote hill. Pagans had venerated it, and Christians later had come seeking cures to illnesses. In the fifteenth century, a statue of the Virgin Mary had mysteriously appeared in the tree, and clergy had taught pilgrims that it was the Virgin who performed the wondrous healings there. This typical, obscure pilgrimage site was suddenly transformed around the turn of the seventeenth century by confessional conflict. With the armies of Spain and the Dutch Republic fighting for control of eastern Brabant, Sharp Hill stood just a few hundred yards from the battlefront between Catholic and Protestant Europe. Suddenly, every pilgrimage there became an act of courage that proclaimed one's confessional commitment. After scoring an important military victory they attributed to the Virgin's aid, Archdukes Albert and Isabella, rulers of the Southern Netherlands, began to promote the shrine. Now the miracles the Virgin performed there, within eyeshot of the enemy, became proof that Catholicism was the true faith, supernaturally supported and destined to triumph. The miracles also demonstrated the divine favor enjoyed by the pious archdukes. Once merely a source of healing power, the shrine had become a symbol of militant Catholicism and a focus of patriotic sentiment. Pilgrims flocked to it by the tens of thousands.

The popularity of the site pleased church officials but also made them wary. On the one hand, every miraculous cure there provided ammunition in their fight against Protestantism. On the other hand, they did not approve of the popular obsession with physical well-being, and suspected that some of the cures trumpeted as miraculous were not really so. Increasingly they feared that false miracles could discredit Catholicism as easily as true ones could support it. To prevent abuses, in 1604 the archbishop of Mechelen had the old oak tree chopped down. Its wood was used, under close supervision, to make additional images of the Virgin. A great baroque basilica was built, so that the mass and other liturgical rites could be performed with proper decorum. Over time, church officials verified fewer cures as genuine miracles, and after 1682 they stopped altogether. Appointed to administer the shrine, the ascetically minded order of Oratorians exhorted pilgrims to acts of penance and instructed them to implore the Virgin not just for health but for salvation.

As at Sharp Hill, so elsewhere a positive, Catholic Reformation proved a harder goal to achieve than an anti-Protestant, Counter-Reformation, and required more time. The same was true on the Protestant side: reformers found it easier to secure the loyalty of church members than to raise their level of understanding or transform their behavior. Or, to adopt the perspective of ordinary Christians: a person could form a firm attachment to one of the confessional churches without mastering its theological system or accepting all its demands. That was true in no small part because of a second aspect of the rise of confessionalism, the drawing of dichotomies.

Chalk and Cheese

"We are all Christians," remarked Frenchman Jean Gesse in 1665.[28] As magistrate of Mauvezin, a town of two thousand souls in southwestern France, Gesse dealt every day with Catholics as well as with members of his own Calvinist congregation. Among them he saw many humble, charitable, good people whom he was sure God would receive into heaven. Gesse saw the difference between the two faiths in relative terms. Both, he believed, were bona fide forms of Christianity. Which offered the surer path to salvation? In his heart, silently, Gesse conducted a debate similar to the one the French cousins Trie and Arneys had conducted through letters: Which church was more faithful to God's Law? Which taught proper obedience to it? Precisely because he was a conscientious, pious Christian, Gesse pondered these questions long and hard, and in 1664 he landed in a spiritual crisis that he resolved by converting to Catholicism.

Ironically, Gesse's conversion flew in the face of official Catholic as well as Calvinist teachings, for it was predicated on an aconfessional attitude that both churches repudiated. Like the champions of capitalist and communist ideologies during the cold war, the religious opponents of early modern Europe pictured the world as divided into two camps: truth and falsehood, good and evil, Christ and Antichrist. They saw nothing relative about the differences, no common ground between the two. In 1579 an anonymous Calvinist pamphleteer wrote: "Either the Reformed religion is good or it is bad; there is no middle, since the affairs of heaven permit no averages . . . truth and falsehood are as much at odds as Belial and Christ, and hence there is as little in common between the Reformed teaching and Roman fantasies as there is between white and black."[29] His enemies saw things similarly. Jesuit John Radford called the two faiths "as farre as heaven and hell asunder" and as different as "chalke" and "cheese."[30] Lutheran preacher Tilmann Hesshus declared that his faith and the Reformed "were as diametrically opposed to each other as winter and summer, day and night, light and darkness."[31] Anabaptists, too, shared the viewpoint, their Schleitheim Confession of Faith stating: "All creatures are in but two classes, good and bad, believing and unbelieving, darkness and light, the world and those who [have come] out of the world, God's temple and idols, Christ and Belial; and none can have part with the other."[32] This was a worldview that reduced all differences to binary oppositions and replaced all grey zones with sharp boundary lines. In a sense, it effaced the most fundamental outcome of the reformations: the division of Christianity into rival forms. Those who maintained it portrayed other faiths not as inferior forms of Christianity but as Christianity's opposite, an antireligion embodying everything that true Christianity was against. Between the two there could be no neutrality and no sane choice.

From its beginning, Christianity was distinctive among religions in its tendency to demonize its enemies, especially one type: the enemy within the fold. For the first Christians that enemy was the Jew, but by the late second century it was the heretic, whom church father Irenaeus first identified as the "agent of Satan."[33] Christian theology began to cast heretics not as mere erring humans but as evil incarnate, "the embodiment of transcendent forces."[34] So powerful did early Christians conceive Satan and his minions to be that the pagan philosopher Celsus attacked them for betraying monotheism. In a later age he would have accused them of Manichaeism, that is, of seeing God and Satan as evenly pitted opponents locked in eternal struggle. He was wrong, but only just: Christian theology always asserted God's omnipotence and the ultimate victory of good over evil, but Christians often talked as if Satan wielded on his own account a vast and frightening power.

This too was part of the Christian tradition inherited by the churches of early modern Europe. As they portrayed it, the battle on earth against heresy was just the visible dimension of a great cosmic struggle pitting God against Satan. Catholics considered it obvious that Luther had been inspired by the devil. Huguenot ministers called the Catholic Church "Satan's synagogue." "Satan is guiding both, Calvinists as well as Jesuits," said Hesshus. According to another Lutheran official, the Reformed "pretend to be bright, white angels of light, even though they are actually ugly black disciples of the prince of darkness."[35] Oliver Cromwell, who ruled England as Lord Protector from 1653 to 1658, called Quakers and the other new sects of his day "diabolical," "the height of Satan's wickedness."[36]

At least as often, Protestants employed the motif of the Antichrist (Fig-

the period. Although the original Protestant reformers preferred genres such as exegesis and catechesis, their successors adopted the "scholastic" method of Catholic theologians like Robert Bellarmine. Calvin's successor Beza was on the forefront of this development. An invention of the High Middle Ages, the scholastic method treated theology in a highly technical manner. At its core, it was disputational, raising questions, drawing distinctions, asserting propositions, offering proofs and rebuttals. Defining orthodoxy in negative as well as positive terms, it enabled theologians to develop entire systems of dogma. It was ideally suited to the kind of debate used to instruct students in theology (hence its name) and to defending dogmas against confessional adversaries. Competition and common needs made scholastic theology the dominant genre among Protestant and Catholic theologians alike from the late sixteenth to the end of the seventeenth century.

As the genre matured, it increasingly incorporated polemics against specific foes, but such polemics also constituted a genre of writing unto itself. A flood of these more-focused publications poured from Europe's presses: in France alone, seven thousand different titles appeared between 1598 and 1685. Some were short pamphlets, others quarto or folio tomes. Like a gauntlet thrown down, the appearance of one was taken to demand a response, producing an entire chain of publications. Challenge and response, thrust and parry—these were not mere metaphors but a genuine "war of books," called such at the time.[40] Lengthy titles announced the doctrinal points in dispute and the enemy against whom texts were directed, as, for example, *Demonstration that what the Church teaches about the real presence of the precious body of Jesus Christ in the Holy Sacrament of the altar is merely the pure word of God, in which the pretend-reformed religion* [*religion prétendue réformée*, French Catholics' standard term for the Reformed faith] *could never find a single word to verify what it holds concerning its [Lord's] Supper, to which [God's Word] is diametrically opposed, as is the teaching of all the holy Fathers* (1608).

Of course, to refute their opponents, polemicists had to address their arguments. One of the most remarkable aspects of confessional polemics is the detailed information they provided their audiences about rival groups' teachings. Other ages have tended to deal with challenges to their basic values with silence, making even the mention of some "heresies" taboo. Not the confessional age: just as its churches had high hopes about teaching even simple lay folk to understand their dogmas, so they brought doctrinal controversies directly to the people, through preaching as well as printed matter. Protestant ministers singled out disputed doctrines for extended treatment in their regular sermons. Holidays and Communion services provided them with specific subjects related to the event, while on special occasions like the 1617 centennial of the Reformation they positively spewed invective. On the Catholic side, Jesuits and Capuchins were the pioneers in polemical preaching, developing a new genre, the "controversy sermon." These became common as early as the 1550s in French cities like Paris and Lyon, helping account for the outbreak of popular religious violence soon thereafter. In the German city of Augsburg, they did not reach the peak of their vogue until the turn of the eighteenth century. In general, though, controversy sermons saw their heyday in the early to mid-seventeenth century, when the volume of polemics on all sides was the loudest.

Experts in theology, trained in disputation, clerics introduced this manner of preaching, and in many cases it is clear that through it they fueled or even instigated religious conflict. But confessionalism was by no means an exclusively clerical culture. Evidence appears here and there of popular demand for polemical preaching, to which the clergy was responding. In 1615 the Calvinist minister of Wassenaar, a Dutch village, was hauled before the regional synod for disciplinary action by members of his own flock, who complained that he preached "without rebuking the papacy or other sects, as a result of which the people had the impression they still had their old Catholic pastor."[41] Some even refused to attend his services on this account. In 1709 the Lutheran clergy of Hamburg had to apologize to the city senate for delivering anti-Catholic sermons. Sheepishly they explained that they had to preach thus to keep the respect of their congregants, who demanded to be shown "that they had faithful guardians and not mute dogs, an expression already used by some malcontents."[42]

By their nature, polemics focused on disputed points of doctrine and practice, such as the role of faith and works in salvation, the nature of the Eucharist, the veneration of saints, and the proper form of church governance. This focus had the desired effect of sharply demarcating the line between orthodoxy and heresy. In the process, it elevated the importance of those disputed points to an extraordinarily high level. This had unintended pedagogic consequences: in the German countryside near Lauenburg and

Ulm, for example, Catholic officials noted that some peasants knew points of confessional controversy better than they did the Ten Commandments or Lord's Prayer. It also had substantive consequences, changing the very self-definition of the rival churches.

One example concerns the doctrine of predestination, according to which God in eternity had decided which persons he would save before they were even born. Although John Calvin formulated this doctrine somewhat more strictly than his contemporaries, all the mainstream Protestants of his day accepted some version of it. Indeed, it was implicit in the Protestant assertion that salvation was by faith, a gift of God, not by works. In 1551 the first in a series of controversies turned predestination into a hot-button topic. Over the following decades, Protestant theologians debated the implications of the doctrine, developing through the scholastic method far more precise formulations of it than any their predecessors had proposed. In the Formula of Concord (1577), Lutherans repudiated the stricter Calvinist version. Predestination became a byword for Calvinism.

Of all the contrasts and oppositions distinguishing the churches, it seems that differences in liturgy and ritual stirred the most powerful emotions among the laity. Such differences were visible, concrete markers of confessional identity that everyone recognized and cared about, even people who knew or cared little about doctrine per se. Some prominent ritual practices in fact embodied disputed doctrines. Devotion to the Virgin Mary, for example, enacted the Catholic belief that some humans, by virtue of their purity, were holier than others, and that the holiest of all, the Virgin and saints, could intercede with God on our behalf. The confession of sins to a priest affirmed the priest's divinely given power to absolve and, by implication, all the other sacramental powers that set him above the laity. These were ancient practices that took on an added layer of meaning when promoted by the Jesuits in a divided Europe. The Forty Hours' Devotion, favorite of the Capuchins, was by contrast a new ritual practice. It involved continuous veneration, through day and night, of the "Host"—the consecrated eucharistic wafer. Obviously this devotion affirmed the Catholic doctrine of transubstantiation. Its polemical subtext was barely submerged: in France the Capuchins often arranged to conduct the ceremony in towns where Huguenots were at that moment holding a synod. Moreover, they presented the ceremony as an act of expiation for the outrages that Huguenots had committed against the Holy Sacrament.

The ritual life of Protestants was less elaborate and colorful than Catholics', and in this very quality embodied the diminished importance that Protestant theology attached to ritual actions. Nevertheless, it too provided specific markers of confessional difference. For example, the laity's taking of Communion in both kinds, the wine as well as the wafer or bread, enacted the priesthood of all believers. From the beginning of their movement, Protestants considered this practice, which distinguished their liturgy from the Catholic, essential to true Christianity. Other markers had a more complicated history and status. The Reformed did their utmost to abolish everything that smacked of Catholicism, but Lutherans put themselves in a more ambiguous position. Precisely because the performance of rituals did not contribute to salvation, they considered many rituals neither required nor forbidden. In theology such optional practices were called "adiaphoral" or "indifferent." The choice of whether or not to perform them was considered a crucial part of Christian freedom; one could decide on the basis of circumstances and utility. But when such practices became markers of confessional identity, they took on an importance that doctrine did not assign to them.

One example is the elevation of the Host. Part of the Catholic liturgy of the mass since the twelfth century, it involved a cleric raising a eucharistic wafer above his head when he consecrated it, so that it was visible to all. Luther himself had declared the practice adiaphoral, saying, "Christ does not forbid the elevation, but leaves it to free choice." During Luther's life some Lutheran churches in Germany maintained it, others omitted it. Beginning in the 1550s, though, controversy began to surround the practice. Reformers like Paul Eber, superintendent-general of Saxony's Lutheran church, wanted it abolished because it encouraged old Catholic "superstitions." Such "papal relics," they feared, blurred the distinction between Protestant and Catholic worship, making it easy for Catholic reformers "to draw the people back to their religion." On the other side stood Lutheran reformers more concerned with the Reformed than with the Catholic threat. They wanted the practice retained as an assertion of Christ's physical presence in the Eucharist, which the Reformed denied. Between about 1550 and 1600, as several German territories abandoned Lutheranism in favor of Reformed Protestantism, Lutherans in Germany grew obsessed with the Reformed threat. Co-religionists who adopted practices that seemed Reformed were tarred as crypto-Calvinists. The party of the self-declared orthodox, known as Gnesio-Lutherans, came down firmly on the side of maintaining the elevation. A practice still recognized, in theory, as adiaphoral "had actually become a litmus test of people's confessional orthodoxy."[43]

The same overloaded significance became attached to other Lutheran practices: the exorcism of infants; the celebration of Corpus Christi and other holidays; the use of wafers, not loaves of bread, in the rite of Communion; the preaching of weekly Gospel and Epistle selections rather than entire books of the Bible, verse by verse over successive weeks. Deemed adiaphoral by Luther and his generation, they came to serve as markers enabling later Lutherans "to distinguish true from false doctrine . . . and reveal our sectarian adversaries."[44] Those who deviated from these practices might claim to be Lutherans, but by the end of the sixteenth century they were no longer considered such. In the eyes of the orthodox, they had become one of the Satanic "others."

Holy Uniformity

Out of the crypto-Calvinist controversy, then, emerged a more precise and rigid definition of Lutheran orthodoxy. Those who did not concur with it were disciplined into conformity or expelled from the Lutheran churches, while within those churches beliefs and practices grew more uniform.

A parallel story could be told for Catholicism. When the Council of Trent condemned everything vaguely reminiscent of Protestantism, it threw a good deal of bathwater out with the baby. Several movements that had been perfectly orthodox, even dominant in fifteenth-century Catholicism, were stifled: conciliarism (which vested supreme authority in church councils, not in the pope), nominalism (a school of theology associated with the Franciscans, opposed to the "realism" championed by Dominicans), Renaissance humanism, some forms of mysticism, the reading of vernacular Bibles. In fact, until the reformations the Catholic Church had been a rather loose institution with room, beneath its broad umbrella, for considerable diversity. Only with Trent did it become essentially intolerant. The Council's decisions also closed off alternate paths to reform. As late as the 1560s, powerful Catholic leaders such as Charles de Guise, Cardinal of Lorraine, and Emperor Ferdinand I favored permitting clerical marriage and Communion in both kinds. These practices, widespread in some regions, were condemned to disappear. Empowered by the Council, the Roman Curia produced a series of normative texts whose purpose was to standardize belief and practice in the church. Among them were the Tridentine Profession of Faith, the Tridentine Index of Prohibited Books, the Roman Missal, and the Roman Ritual, which prescribed in detail the form of common ceremonies such as baptism and burial. Catholic confessionalism entailed a suppression of internal tensions and differences, a stifling of variety, and the imposition on the entire church of a narrow new definition of orthodoxy. Even if it took more than a century to impose in some regions, by 1614 that definition was essentially complete.

Uniformity was no mere by-product of polarization but rather a quality that confessional reformers idealized and strove to endow their churches with. When they met in 1568 to lay the groundwork for their churches, Dutch Calvinists articulated this ideal: "The Apostle Paul teaches that in God's church all things should be done decently and with order. Therefore a unanimous agreement not only in church doctrine but also in the office and political governance of the ministry should be established and kept. But in order for these matters to be arranged similarly in all the Netherlandic churches, it seemed fit that we set forth the following points, concerning which we have consulted with the best-reformed churches."[45] Like Tridentine Catholics and Gnesio-Lutherans, Calvinists found harmony and order in uniformity. In its pursuit they agreed not only to teach the same doctrines, but to sing the same psalms, recite the same prayers, decorate their churches similarly, and celebrate the same few holidays. They did not deny that some things were adiaphoral: for example, whether Communion was received standing or sitting, or whether baptized infants were sprinkled once or thrice with water. They severely restricted, though, the scope of such adiaphora and tolerated them with a certain grudgingness. Not only did they suspect variety as an opportunity for deviance, they regarded it in itself as a species of disorder offensive to God. Uniformity, by contrast, they declared "holy." It had for them beauty as well as spiritual worth.

Uniformity was an ideal on the national and international levels as well as the local. Here Catholic reformers had in theory an advantage, for their church was an international institution with a single head. Although they first had to be adopted by regional synods, the canons and decrees of Trent applied to all its members, as did the papal bulls establishing the authority of the Roman Missal, Ritual, and so forth. Reformers could promote uniformity by centralizing authority in Rome and streamlining the chain of command from pope to bishops to priests. In reality this rarely worked, as popes had little control over church personnel or finance. Catholic reformers also faced a unique challenge in the diversity of late medieval Catholicism. To cite an extreme example, we know of about 560 different breviaries (books of prayers for the canonical hours) in use before 1500—and these are just the ones that made it into print.

Lutheran institutions, by contrast, were organized to coincide with political units, so that Lutheran countries like Denmark had a national Lutheran church, territories like Württemberg had a territorial one, and autonomous cities like Danzig, Thorn, and Elbing in Royal Prussia had municipal ones. Uniformity within these units was enforced by a variety of mechanisms. Headed by the ruler, in whom episcopal authority was vested, a hierarchy of church officials passed down orders and conducted inspection tours known as "visitations." By contrast, in most lands the Reformed had a presbyterian form of church governance. Local churches were governed by boards known as consistories, composed of both ministers and lay elders. In Geneva the consistory was the highest organ of church governance; elsewhere local churches consulted regularly with one another and made collective decisions—at the regional level through representative bodies known in English as presbyteries, at higher levels through provincial and national synods. Authority flowed upward through this pyramidal hierarchy, but all churches were bound to obey decisions made by majority vote. Consistories disciplined and, if necessary, excommunicated wayward church members; synods did the same for ministers.

Between territories and countries, Protestants could strive for uniformity only by influencing one another and building consensus. Their successes testify to the power of a shared ideal. The founders of Dutch Calvinism, for example, signed the French Reformed Confession of Faith and adopted the Genevan and Heidelberg Catechisms as instructional material. One of them, Peter Dathenus, based his verse translation of the psalms directly on an earlier one by Beza and Clement Marot. Adopted by all the Dutch congregations, Dathenus's psalms were sung for centuries. In the seventeenth century, the Dutch took over the leadership of international Calvinism. Just as their own students had once flocked to Geneva and

Heidelberg, now they welcomed thousands of foreign students at Leiden, Franeker, and Utrecht. Just as many of them had earlier fled religious persecution, now they hosted Calvinist refugees from abroad. In 1618 they invited representatives from Switzerland, France, England, and Germany to attend the Synod of Dort, whose decrees on the doctrine of predestination defined orthodoxy for all of Calvinist Europe.

"Holy uniformity" appealed also to some Anabaptists, but could not be achieved by them as it could by Catholics, Lutherans, and Calvinists. As a result, an important component of confessionalism was missing, or at least much reduced, among Anabaptists and their descendants, the Mennonites. Anabaptist congregations were self-governing churches that retained their autonomy even when they affiliated with one another. Consensus produced statements like the Schleitheim Confession of Faith (1527), but churches subscribed to them only voluntarily. Membership in a church was equally voluntary, but absolute commitment and conformity were expected of those who joined. Viewing their churches as visible communities of God's elect, Anabaptists and later most Mennonites strove to keep them "without spot or wrinkle" by excluding all who sinned or lacked faith. Those who deviated in doctrine or behavior were quickly "banned," that is, excommunicated. Disagreements produced schisms, with each side banning the other. Strict uniformity within congregations thus came at the expense of unity among them.

[margin note: uniformity not possible for Anabaptists]

Those Christians who did achieve some measure of uniformity found themselves bound together in a powerful new form of community. Identical beliefs and practices produced a spiritual unity much tighter than that of medieval Christendom. Typically, Puritan William Bradshaw felt closer to Calvinists abroad than he did to some of his fellow Englishmen: "Touching the word *forreyne,* those Churches being all the same household of faith that we are, they are not aptly called forreyne. . . . So all Churches and all members of the Church, in what Country so ever they be, are not to be accounted Forreyners one to another, because they are all Citizens of heaven, and we all make one family or body."[46] It was characteristic of the confessional age that a Catholic could say the same thing. In 1624 a Spanish ambassador to Switzerland admonished his co-religionists there "that they should feel a closer kinship to a Catholic Indian or African than to a heretical . . . countryman."[47] The flip side of this new unity was, of course, the enmity people now felt toward those who adhered to a different faith. The one was a force for integration, producing new friendships and alliances, the other a force promoting confrontation, dissolving old ones. Together, the two disrupted high politics and daily life across Europe.

The Servetus affair came at a pivotal moment in European religious history. The Protestant Reformation had translated into action the longing of countless Christians for reform. It had taken a religious scene that was already diverse—for until the Protestant challenge reared its head, the Catholic Church had not scrupled to embrace an abundant variety of pious forms and practices—and expanded vastly its horizons. A generation of geniuses had offered compelling new visions of Christian truth, and decisions about which was right had been thrust into the hands of laypeople. At midcentury, the final outcomes of this upheaval were still far from clear. Christians of different inclinations were not yet polarized into a few irreconcilable camps, and it seemed quite possible that the lost unity of Christendom might still be restored. At that moment, views like those of Castellio were not exceptional but widespread. Castellio questioned the primacy of doctrine over morals. He proposed that a few fundamental principles made a person sufficiently orthodox. And he presented the image of a complicated, pluralistic world in which people of different beliefs could engage in fruitful dialogue with one another. Compared to the blatant heresies of Servetus, such views were a subtle form of dissent. Those who held them did not challenge one orthodoxy in the name of another, but rather resisted all efforts to define a confessional orthodoxy. In short, they rejected confessionalism itself.

By this term we do not mean a belief system, in the sense of a creed maintained by a particular Christian denomination. Confessionalism was, instead, a form of religious culture that developed in the sixteenth and seventeenth centuries in all the sundered branches of Western Christendom. In this respect one might compare it to mysticism, or perhaps more aptly to apocalypticism or modern fundamentalism, forms of religious culture that have been known to fuel intolerance. In part, the rise of confessionalism was a reaction to the division of Western Christendom, which shocked and disoriented many Europeans, sending them in search of new organizing principles for their mental universe. Confessionalism provided the "discipline and order" for which Calvinist Trie and Catholic Arneys both

their inhabitants did not enjoy citizenship rights. Just as their population overflowed city walls into suburbs, so much of their economic activity went on outside the traditional regulating structure of the craft guilds. To be sure, such metropolises were not seas of anomie on which individuals floated but rather mosaics composed of many discrete subcommunities. An urban neighborhood could be as intimate as a village, with its own rhythms, smells, characters, and pride. Nevertheless, big cities offered the possibility, at least, of belonging to what sociologists call "multiple reference groups": people could do business with certain individuals, socialize with others, and worship with still others, defining themselves differently in the various contexts.

Only eight other cities had reached the hundred-thousand mark by 1750. Two centuries earlier, only three had so many inhabitants. Early modern Europe was filled with cities—three to four thousand of them, at the time of the Protestant Reformation—but by modern standards they were tiny. What made them cities was less the size of their population than the walls that set them apart from the countryside and the markets and shops where commerce and manufacturing (in the literal sense of manual production) went on. Above all, they were cities by virtue of the charters that granted them special privileges, including powers of self-governance. Fewer than one in ten had even ten thousand inhabitants. At that size, equivalent to about two thousand families, people could get to know, at least by face, more or less all of their fellow burghers. In such intimate "home towns," there were no multiple reference groups: your friends were your fellow guildsmen, who were also your fellow neighbors, parishioners, and citizens.[7] If you offended them by, say, breaking a law, producing shoddy goods, or marrying an outsider, you could lose your livelihood as well as your voting rights. Law and custom made social honor, citizenship, economic self-sufficiency, and membership in the established church contingent on one another; men enjoyed all or none.

Rural social structures were at least as varied as urban ones. At one extreme stood the type of settlement found high in the Austrian Alps. Family farmsteads there were scattered, not grouped in villages. The peasants who cultivated them visited infrequently the market towns in the valleys, the trip being arduous. In winter especially they seldom saw the inside of a church or the face of a government official. Mostly they worshipped at home as families, praying and reading devotional books. Their settlements were the opposite of big cities in terms of population density, but like those cities they were relatively loose communities. They contrast sharply to the nuclear village, the type of settlement that predominated on the plains of northern Europe. Social control was very tight in such villages, where houses were grouped closely and villagers worked together to till the surrounding open fields. Here village assemblies made life-and-death decisions for the entire community, like what crops would be planted and when they would be harvested. Animals grazed in common meadows, while people drew water and picked firewood from other communally owned resources. Bound by a cohesion as strong as the nuclear forces of modern physics, the nuclear village was the rural counterpart of the home town.

These extremes capture the range of early modern communities but not their diversity. Many a city was neither metropolis nor home town. There were provincial capitals, where judges and other officials presided; centers of long-distance trade, bustling with merchants and markets; mining towns; ports; spas; and centers of textile production, Europe's largest industry. Similarly, large expanses of countryside were neither open plain nor high mountain. In the rugged countryside of Liguria and Piedmont, in northwestern Italy, villages had a fragmented, almost chaotic layout, with peripheral neighborhoods and outlying districts. In the Dutch polderland, reclaimed from the sea, farmsteads lined up in precise rows, looking out on their own strips of fertile soil. Scattered hamlets dotted the wooded *bocage* country of central and western France. Settlement patterns varied as much as natural ecologies and human needs.

Beyond any such categories, individual towns and villages reveled in the irreducible uniqueness of their customs, their institutions, their piece of earth. In the Netherlands alone, over seven hundred communities had their own legal codes in the sixteenth century. The number speaks volumes about the entrenched localism, or "particularism," of early modern society. Jealous of their autonomy, even small local communities liked to see themselves as worlds unto themselves. The difficulty and slowness of travel, especially overland, where the swiftest rider might hope to make eighty-five miles per day, contributed to this sense. Writing of his youth in Northamptonshire in the 1790s, the poet John Clare wrote, "I had never been above eight miles from home in my life and I could not fancy England much larger than the part I know."[8] More telling than any figure or fact is that "fancy," or sense of Clare's, that set the horizons of his mental world and directed his allegiances. These went first and foremost to his local community, while beyond the nearest market town things grew vague. A "foreigner" was someone who did not come from your town or rural district. Your "country" was the county you lived in. Even as it set them apart, particularism was a trait Europe's communities had in common. A heritage of the Middle Ages, it attenuated over time only slowly and unevenly.

Corporate organization was another such trait. Early modern society was composed of corporations, organizations that existed legally as collective entities. Towns, villages, political estates (clergy, nobles, commoners), craft guilds, patrician clubs, militia companies, universities, parishes, cathedral chapters—all were corporations, or aspired to be (full corporate status under the law was rarer in England than on the Continent). As the term suggests, they were conceived of not as concatenations of individuals but as organic units with a body (corps), limbs (members), and even a spirit—whence the term *ésprit de corps*. Corporations could own property, issue bylaws, select officers, sign documents with a unique seal, sue and be sued, tax or fine their members, and arbitrate disputes among them. On some regular basis they assembled to conduct their business and celebrate their unity. They differed from one another in the exclusive rights each possessed, called "privileges" or "liberties." Which corporations people belonged to not only determined their legal rights and social rank, it made them participants in a set of rich, diverse subcultures, as each group had its own clothing, jargon, lore, and rituals.

In the midst of dazzling diversity, corporations shared a common ethos. To the extent possible, they sought to be autonomous and self-governing; at the same time, they cultivated among their members fraternal bonds of friendship and interdependence. In some notional sense, all members were considered equal and all were supposed to subordinate their personal interests to the common good of the group—the "common weal," as the English called it. When the corporation in question is a town or village, this ethos is called "communalism." It provided the founding principle of those towns that began their existence in the Middle Ages as communes. In the early modern period, cities were still, in theory, voluntary associations of free citizens who delegated authority to their magistrates. Some, like Strasbourg, still had the entire citizenry renew its original oath of associa-

greater number were voluntary associations with mixed membership. Like other corporate bodies, they excluded the indigent, undomiciled, and dishonorable elements of society. At the same time, confraternities operated on the principle "that we are all brothers in God and that there is no precedence before him."[11] Dedicated to a saint or an aspect of the divine, like the Trinity or Holy Cross, these devotional clubs venerated their supernatural patron, whose intercession they sought. Some specialized in works of charity, others in penitential devotions like flagellation, popular in Mediterranean regions. All had an annual feast day, when the soul-brothers (and -sisters, in the case of mixed confraternities) marched in procession, attended a special high mass and vespers, and banqueted together. Disputes between members would there be mediated and new members inducted, sometimes exchanging a kiss with their soul-brothers and -sisters "in tokenynge of loue, charite, and pes."[12] The spiritual union thus consummated was deemed a great good in itself—a right ordering of relations between Christians. The ultimate purpose of confraternities, though, was to provide solidarity in the face of death. Each confraternity had a communal grave and an altar—or sometimes an entire side-chapel—in a local church. When members died, they would be laid to rest in the grave and a priest would say masses for their souls at the altar. The group's living members would attend the funerals and pray for the deceased. On as many other occasions as the confraternity could afford, it paid for a priest to say masses for the souls of living and deceased members.

Early modern Catholic reformers felt as ambivalent about confraternities as they did about many medieval practices. On the one hand, these organizations exhibited an alarming independence: organized and run by laymen, they were subject only to the loosest of clerical supervision. Their annual festivities were boisterous, mixing food, alcohol, and games with devotion in a way that seemed to sully the sacred. And the communal, ritualized character of that devotion seemed itself inadequate. As we have seen, Catholic reformers favored a more internalized, individual piety. On the other hand, Catholic reformers recognized the popular appeal of the old devotions and remained wedded to the theology behind them. In this area as in others, reform succeeded chiefly by harnessing the appeal of the old, purging it of perceived excesses, and "grafting orthodoxy onto traditional and popular spirituality."[13] In rural regions in particular, traditional confraternities, now carefully supervised by parish clergy, continued to flourish. In Catholic villages of Westphalia, Speyer, Bavaria, and other German regions, they even experienced a new heyday in the early eighteenth century. Theirs, in miniature, is the story of Catholic piety, which never lost its communal character even as it gained in diversity and depth.

At first consideration, it seems the Protestant Reformation should have put an end, among its adherents, to the corporate quest for salvation. After all, the breakthrough that formed the theological core of the new belief system was the doctrine of justification by faith alone. That doctrine makes nonsense of the idea of transferring or sharing merit, for it asserts that humans have no saving merit. It makes salvation contingent entirely upon an individual's faith, or, more precisely, on God's decision to give some individuals the gift of faith, which he withholds from others. Christian love and charity are merely the fruits of faith. Our prayers for others, as for ourselves, have no inherent power, and leave their fates where they always lay: in the hands of divine providence. We cannot, therefore, help our fellow Christians attain salvation, any more than we can help ourselves. Protestants do not venerate saints or pray for the dead, and where they came to power they dissolved the confraternities.

Yet what Protestant reformers ejected by the front door, they readmitted by the back. For if justification was essentially an individual, spiritual affair, what they called "sanctification" was not. The same Holy Spirit that "gives people faith in Christ," wrote Luther, "sanctifies them . . . that is, he renews heart, soul, body, work, and conduct, inscribing the commandments of God not on tables of stone, but in hearts of flesh." By this unending process, we are given a will to obey God's Ten Commandments and avoid sin. Although we can never do so perfectly in this life, "we constantly strive to attain the goal . . . until we too," like Christ, "shall one day become perfectly holy and no longer stand in need of forgiveness." If that day shall only arrive with our death, still in this life we "need the Decalogue not only to apprise us of our lawful obligations, but we also need it to discern how far the Holy Spirit has advanced us in his work of sanctification and by how much we still fall short of the goal."[14] It teaches us to honor our parents, obey our rulers, help our neighbors, and not steal or overcharge. It commands, and the Holy Spirit enables us more and more, to be "chaste, self-controlled, sober . . . charitable . . . truthful, trustworthy," and to lead "honorable lives."[15]

These passages, from a 1539 treatise on the Church, present a side of Lu-

theran teaching often ignored. Conventionally, scholars associate sanctification with the Reformed, not the Lutheran tradition. Early Reformed
Protestants construed the Gospel itself as a kind of divine law, a rule for
properly ordering communal life. Calvin went even further, arguing that
the New Testament renewed the same covenant God had made with man
in the Old. Calvin bequeathed to his followers a very positive appreciation
for the Jewish scriptures, encouraging them to identify with God's earlier
chosen people, the children of Israel. They did so with great intensity,
naming their children after biblical heroes, building "New Jerusalems," and
telling their life stories in terms of Egyptian slaveries and flights to promised lands. Likewise, it was Calvin who invented the consistory, that unsur-
passed institutional mechanism for combating sin. And it was he, scholars
note, who declared good behavior presumptive (though not certain) proof
that you were among God's elect.

To be sure, the ideal of a holy community living according to God's law
was strong among Reformed Protestants, but it was never their exclusive property. It could be found operating not only in Geneva, but in
France during the French Wars of Religion, wherever the Catholic Holy
League came to power. The same ideal operated in Lutheran cities such as
Nördlingen. The first article of Nördlingen's municipal constitution, codified in 1650, forbade cursing and blasphemy, urging burghers to "warn,
pray for, and admonish one another" not to engage in such, "for the
honor of God's will, for the better appeasement of His righteous and well-
deserved wrath, and for the laudable establishment of Christian discipline
and civic honor in our city and *commune*."[16] Lutherans (and other sorts of
Protestants) appropriated similarly the role models of the Old Testament.
On the first centenary of the Reformation, in 1617, Lutherans in Hamburg
hailed Martin Luther as "the modern Elijah who had led the German people out of the 'Egyptian captivity' of Rome." On the second centenary, they
prayed for the preservation of "Our Hamburg Zion."[17] Fifteen years later,
in 1732, they and their co-religionists across Germany hailed the Lutherans
expelled from the Austrian archbishopric of Salzburg who trekked northward to find a new home in Prussia. An account of their persecution and
flight published the next year (Figure 2.1) made explicit the Old Testament
parallel:

> Thou, oppressed Israel, wert led by fire and cloud
> When thou quittest Egypt's ban, estranged to start anew,

And so to thee, poor folk of Salzburg, was God's Grace allowed,
When thus before thy footsteps, [Prussian King] Frederick William's
  eagle flew.[18]

Perhaps human beings have an innate inclination to believe that virtue deserves to be rewarded and evil punished, by God as well as man. At any rate, Lutherans and all other Christian groups in early modern Europe

Figure 2.1. The emigration of Salzburg Lutherans compared with the exodus of the Israelites from Egypt. Engraving from *Die Getröstete Saltzburger oder Gespräch im Reiche der Lebendigen, zwischen einem . . . Saltzburger . . . und einem Waldenser* (Magdeburg, 1733). Courtesy of the Augsburg State and City Library.

regarded certain moral norms as, in some sense, sacred. All considered the performance of good works an essential part of what it meant to be a good Christian. All shared the presumption of Calvinists like Guillaume Trie and Catholics like Antoine Arneys that true religion produced true godliness and that moral laxity was a mark of false faith. And for them, as for Trie and Arneys, that presumption operated for communities as well as individuals. It was part of Europe's common Christian culture to view the promotion of piety and suppression of sin as corporate responsibilities. Theology aside, holiness remained a communal quest.

The Civic and the Sacral

For Europeans, every town and village had a spiritual dimension: more than a convenient, worldly arrangement for human cohabitation, it was a religious body—a "corpus Christianum." Viewed through the prism of Christian piety, its unity was an expression of Christian love, its peace godly, and its provision of mutual aid an exercise in charity. The communal welfare it existed to promote was spiritual as well as material. Indeed, the word *welfare* and its cognates, like the Latin *salus* and German *Heil,* meant both, for no one dreamed the spiritual and material could be separated. God rewarded those who deserved it, and the blessings he bestowed included peace and prosperity in life as well as salvation after death. The fate of entire communities, not just individuals, depended on divine favor. Gaining it was therefore a collective responsibility. Protestants and Catholics did not differ on this point, except that whereas Protestants focused their prayers and hopes on the divine will, Catholics directed their supplications also to the Virgin and saints.

Of course, since communities had many shapes, the equation had many permutations. It was simplest in concentrated rural settlements, like the nuclear villages that dominated France north of the Loire River. Here there tended to be a one-to-one correspondence between village and parish, so that the territory, members, and leadership of the two were nearly identical. Indeed, parish institutions often predated village ones and helped give birth to them. It was in the parish church or on the sacred ground surrounding it, the churchyard, that villagers swore to keep the peace. This oath began life as a parochial rite and never lost its spiritual overtones, but came to constitute the village as a political entity, a "commune." In this region all heads of household usually belonged to the parish assembly, which had final say over the temporal affairs of the parish and chose parish officers, or at least ratified their selection. In theory, this assembly was distinct from the village assembly of inhabitants, but no one stood on niceties when the members and concerns of the two were the same. In the province of Berry officers known as "procureurs de la fabrique et communauté" headed both parish and commune. Such blurring occurred in finance as well as personnel. Parishes had responsibility for maintaining the physical infrastructure of the parish church—the "church fabric," as it was called. But with meager endowments, rural parishes in northern France had to turn to their communes to finance any major rebuilding. Just as village funds were used to maintain the parish fabric, so parish funds served village needs, helping to pay wartime taxes or for the lodging of soldiers. None of this was unique to the region. In German-speaking lands, the blurring was even linguistic, as the word *Gemeinde* was used interchangeably for both parish and village commune.

Regions with scattered settlements present a more complex picture than ones with concentrated villages. The hamlets of the Cévennes mountains in southern France, for example, did not naturally cohere as larger parochial units. Every parish had a "chef-lieu," where parish church, parsonage, and cemetery were situated, and yet to families living elsewhere that place might be too distant or the road too rough to bring, say, an ailing infant there for baptism. Pastors might balk at visiting the sick and dying for the same reason. And even if the practicalities of travel were not at issue, the chef-lieu might be resented and have rivals to its claims of primacy. Outlying hamlets were often served by chapels subordinate to the parish church, but such chapels neither met all the inhabitants' religious needs nor assuaged their pride. Such was the case for the peasants of Laviolle, nine kilometers distant and two hundred forty meters higher than the parish seat of Antraigues. The result: after building a chapel in 1685, Laviolle's inhabitants waged an epic struggle to have it elevated to the status of parish church. Vested interests and ecclesiastic conservatism frustrated their efforts for more than a century and a half. What is significant, though, is how the particularism of tiny settlements sought a religious counterpart, and how the trend and direction of pressure was to bring units of religious and social community into line with one another.

Civic and sacral community overlapped in equally complex ways in cities. Nuremberg exemplifies the high degree of sacral unity a city could achieve. In the course of the Reformation, the authority of its magistrates expanded and citywide religious institutions were established. So too elsewhere, Protestant reforms usually contributed to urban integration. At the same time, cities always comprised multiple subcommunities. A few cities had only one parish—these included Liverpool, Leeds, and King's Lynn, whose city council functioned also as "vestry," as the English called their parish councils—but more common in England were modest-sized cities with a large number of parishes, like Norwich with forty-six. Such parishes were truly intimate, face-to-face communities of people who lived and worshipped together. By contrast, London counted over a hundred parishes and even still by 1700 St. Martin's-in-the-Fields and St. Giles's, Cripplegate, each numbered twenty thousand souls. In Paris the population of Ste. Marguerite reached forty-two thousand by 1766. Some urban parishes, then, were much too large for all their members to assemble together in church or know one another. Some parishes also had little geographic unity, but were gerrymandered or included swaths of surrounding countryside. Moreover, outside England most cities were divided also into quarters or wards. The Dutch city of Utrecht, for example, had eight quarters, each of which supplied a company to the civic militia, elected its own officers, collected taxes, had a banner and motto, and on extraordinary occasions met in assembly. Cities were divided also into what contemporaries called "neighborhoods." In Utrecht, these tiny units resembled block associations, with their own statutes, finances, officers, rituals, and rules of behavior. Members gathered for festive meals, attended one another's funerals, and collected alms for the poor. City, parish, quarter, neighborhood: all these units of community could complement or compete with one another, or both, turning urban life into a rich counterpoint.

Invariably, though, church buildings stood at the center of communal life. Look at any cityscape drawn or painted in the early modern period: invariably churches stand tallest, defining the city's profile. Just as their bells could be heard from a distance, so their spires could be seen. And if a single church—often a cathedral or ex-cathedral—dominated, it stood as an emblem for the entire city. A parish church could similarly define a village. Cities at least had walls and town halls, alternate embodiments of civic identity. In villages the parish church was far and away the largest, most durable, and most symbolic structure. It had no rival, except perhaps the tavern, that other "public" building that often faced the church across the village commons. Architecturally, though, and as a symbol of human aspirations, the church stood alone, and villagers poured money, labor, and pride into it.

Churches were also practical structures. Not just places of worship, they were communal property with myriad uses:

[The parish church] was schoolhouse, storehouse, arsenal, fire-station, and when necessary fortress. . . . The lantern tower of All Saints, York, was a lighthouse for travellers. Churches served as storehouses and fortifications in New England, and during the English civil war; they also did duty as prisons, hospitals, stables. In Dublin St. Andrew's church was the Lord Deputy's stable even in time of peace. . . . In most parishes the church furnished probably the only library available. . . . The church was also the news agency, the centre where public and private announcements were made (e.g. about strayed sheep and cattle at Luccombe in Somerset in Charles I's reign), and the forum where communal business matters were transacted. Orders of the manor court were published there. Boxes of evidences were kept in "the lobby at the church". Rents were paid in the church porch. . . . Poor relief was distributed, accounts were audited, debtors were ordered to pay their creditors and putative fathers their alimony—all in the church or its porch. . . . The town plough might be kept in church. At Rye "unruly servants" were whipped there. William Ket was hanged from the tower of Wymondham church after the revolt of 1549. Any transaction that required special solemnity was enacted publicly in the church. . . . St. Paul's cathedral was a meeting place for business, where bills were posted; a public highway on which men wore their hats; a place where servants were hired; and a playground for children. . . . In 1602 players were given 1s. not to perform in the church at Syston, Leicestershire. In 1612 at Woburn the curate baited a bear in church; 25 years later, also in Bedfordshire, there were cockfightings on three successive Shrove Tuesdays in Knottingley church, round the communion table. The minister and churchwardens were also present.

In short, the church was a "civic center," not "a single-purpose building used one day a week only."[19]

cess, the walk affirmed the physical and social as well as ecclesiastic boundaries of the community, making clear who was a member of it and who
was not. It thus established which church people should attend, which they
should be married and buried and have their children baptized in, to
which pastor they owed tithes, and from which parish they were entitled to
charity. Many English parishes continued to perform the perambulation,
purged of its specifically Catholic elements, long after the Reformation
(though not usually every year, as before). A celebration of communal
identity, the ritual also affirmed the bonds of faith and charity that united
the community internally. Stressing this aspect, George Herbert in the
1630s saw perambulations as having "4 manifest advantages . . . first, a
blessing of God for the fruits of the field; secondly, justice in the preservation of bounds; thirdly, charity in loving walking and neighbourly accom-
panying one another, with reconciling of differences at that time, if there
be any; fourthly, mercy in releeving the poor by a liberall distribution and
largesse, which at that time is or ought to be used."[22] When catastrophe
threatened, a Catholic community turned to its supernatural patron for
protection and assistance. On these occasions, the patron's relics or image
would once again be paraded. The schoolteacher Pierre Barthès described
one such procession held in August 1738 in the southern French city of
Toulouse:

> The eighteenth in the morning, the season being extremely dry and the
> heat extraordinary, not having rained for more than two months, the
> messieurs the capitouls [the eight members of the city's supreme gov-
> erning council] made a vow to Our Lady of the Daurade and having had
> sung a high mass in the maison de ville [city hall] they did the same at
> the [church of the] Daurade where, after having offered the Virgin their
> vow and the prayers of all the inhabitants of the city, they had the image
> taken down from its place above the altar . . . the church filled with peo-
> ple of every station to ask God by the intercession of his mother for a
> more suitable season for the preservation of the fruits of the earth. . . .
>
> On Sunday the twenty-fourth of the same, all the religious communi-
> ties of the city, having assembled . . . in the church of the Dalbade, left in
> procession from the said church after vespers with the image of Our
> Lady under a magnificent pavilion and dressed in an extraordinarily rich
> robe; the bailles [officers] of the Confraternity of the Assumption . . .
> bore the candles around the image, which was carried by the children of

the parish. . . . Then came the capitouls, their assessors, and the whole bourgeoisie, everyone bearing a candle. The procession was formed by a countless number of people of all stations. It made a station at [the church of] Saint-Etienne and then returned by the street Croix-Baragnon to the Daurade where the image was honorably put back in its place, and with great devotion. She carried the vows of the city in her arms. The next Friday between six and seven in the morning an abundant rain fell without storm of wind.[23]

Several typical features of this procession are noteworthy. The initiative for it came from the city's chief magistrates, the *capitouls,* at whose order masses were said in the chapel of the city hall as well as in church. "All the inhabitants of the city" participated at least symbolically, through prayers and through the diversity of people present in the church; "the whole bourgeoisie," that is, the corporate community of citizens, a more select group, took part in the procession itself. So did the capitouls, some lesser city officials, and all the clergy, organized by corporation. Such rituals did not simply reflect the unity of a community defined by politics or settlement pattern or common interests. They had a unifying power of their own, as an entire community took collective action to secure its welfare and acknowledged its collective dependence on a spiritual patron.

Such solidarity did not efface social hierarchies—on the contrary, religious rituals articulated social distinctions and even helped constitute them in the first place. Rituals were not necessarily placid events; through them people competed for status and power. Typical was the strife in Toulouse over a position of special honor in the procession, as the officers of one confraternity claimed a right to carry the Virgin's image. Similarly, the grandeur of a person's funeral cortège did not simply reflect his or her social status; it contributed to it and perpetuated it beyond death. So too did the location of a family's pew in church, after pews became common in the seventeenth century. These were all declarations of rank. All of which is to say that in its internal articulations, hierarchies, and tensions, just as in its unity, a community was both a civic and a sacral body.

The language of Christian ritual, however, was primarily a language of unity, not division. And the premier Christian symbol of unity was the Eucharist, which (depending on one's theology) either was or represented Christ's physical body. "When we break the bread, is it not a means of sharing in the body of Christ? Because there is one loaf, we, many as we are, are one body; for it is one loaf of which we all partake" (1 Corinthians 10:16–17). Many rituals mobilized eucharistic symbolism to celebrate and affirm Christian *communitas,* but among them two stand out: the eucharistic procession and the sacrament of Communion. The first was specific to Catholics, who might hold several such processions over the course of a year. Invariably, the grandest of them was the one held in June on the festival of Corpus Christi, dedicated to the veneration of the Eucharist. The sacrament of Communion, by contrast, was common to all the confessions, though it took different forms among them.

In all the major confessions, it seems, Easter was the occasion when the largest number of the faithful received the sacrament. The pattern continued a medieval one: in 1215 the Fourth Lateran Council had made annual confession and Communion at Easter mandatory for all Christians. Not that everyone had fulfilled the requirement—on the contrary, its effective enforcement began only with the Catholic Reformation. This, not the more frequent Communion encouraged by Jesuits, was the practice of the majority of early modern Catholics. It made Communion a collective, not individual, rite—all the more so because the Council of Trent required that everyone, on this occasion, receive the sacrament in their parish church from their pastor, not from a chaplain or friar or other priest. On Easter Sunday, or within the space of a few days, an entire parish would take Communion. With parishioners lining up to confess their sins quickly in the preceding week or so, even confession might have a perfunctory, communal quality. Protestants substituted for the Catholic version of it a public confession of sin spoken together by the entire congregation. They insisted on everyone taking Communion together, both at Easter and on the other occasions it was administered.

In fact, the very term *Communion* was (and is) another word for church. "The church is called the communion of saints," wrote Calvinist theologian Lambert Daneau, "not only because the faithful communicate with God, but do so also among themselves."[24] How thoroughly ordinary Christians conceived of the sacrament as a ritual of social unity is testified to by the refusal of some to take Communion if they were in a state of enmity with a fellow parishioner. Rather than take Communion with an enemy, some people would abstain from the rite—for years, if necessary. Such a rupture, though, threatened the integrity of the corpus Christianum, prompting clergy to intervene as mediators and peacemakers. Healing the rift and bringing about reconciliation was one of their oldest and most important pastoral duties. They busied themselves at it especially in the weeks before Communion, and thus especially during Lent, so that the entire parish, or as much of it as possible, could participate in the sacrament.

Much of the discipline administered by Calvinist consistories had the same pastoral function: to bring about reconciliation and restore unity to the body of Christ. Except perhaps in Scotland, it was not as punitive as once thought, as some figures attest from the early years of the Dutch Republic: in Deventer, quarrels between church members accounted for 29 percent of all "disciplinary" cases recorded by the consistory, in Amsterdam 22 percent, in Sluis 30 percent. In a broader sense, even the disciplining of adulterers, drunkards, and other conventional sinners had reconciliation as its goal. In such cases, the reconciliation was not between two individuals but between the sinner and the congregation, whose members had been "offended" or "scandalized" by the former's actions. "Private" sins, known to few, could be repented privately, but, following guidelines set down by Calvin, "public" ones required a public penance. Until it was performed, the sinner was not allowed to take Communion.

There was another reason sinners had to be kept from Communion: their sin was perceived as a form of disease—a "gangrene," a "cancer," a "plague"—that threatened to spread within the corpus Christianum. Protecting other members from infection required surgery, cutting the diseased limb from the body. That meant expelling sinners from the community, or at least excluding them temporarily from Communion. If this was not done, the entire body would be contaminated. For at the transcendent moment when a congregation was most completely fused into a single body, it was also most vulnerable to transmission. This idea explains the superstition among Dutch Calvinists, denied by their theologians, that the participation of a known sinner in the Lord's Supper spoiled the rite, making it ineffective for all who partook.

More was involved than sinners simply setting a bad example for others. Calvinists quoted frequently and with intense feeling the words of the Apostle Paul: "Do not share in another man's sins" (1 Timothy 5:22). In their view, and equally that of their confessional rivals, to admit sinners to one's company was to share in their sin. Translated into modern terms, the idea was that to tolerate unrepentant sinners in one's community and leave them unpunished was to condone their sin, and that to condone was to be complicit. "The evil which others do by our sufferance, is ours," said Edwin Sandys. "We do it, when we suffer it to be done."[25] God's wrath would descend upon a community that was tolerant of sin, punishing its members indiscriminately, as if every one of them were guilty of the evil. As in the Old Testament Achan was stoned (Joshua 7) and Jonah cast overboard (Jonah 1:15), so sinners had to be punished or expelled to avert the Lord's righteous indignation. Otherwise entire villages and cities would be afflicted, as they were perceived to be when fire, epidemic, or war ravaged them. Early modern catastrophes set off a certain line of reasoning among the sufferers: if we are afflicted, we must have done something to provoke God's ire; we must have sinned. Thus were born moral crusades and religious revivals. When fire razed the city of Dorchester in 1613, it produced "a sort of spiritual mass conversion . . . a recognition that what was needed was a total reformation of the town."[26] The city became the most Puritan in all England. Similarly, between the 1580s and 1650s, the cities of the Holy Roman Empire suffered economic depression, plague, and the horrors of the Thirty Years' War. They responded by issuing a flood of ordinances against vice and impiety. Peering anxiously over their shoulders, Dutch Calvinists heeded the same threats: "The examples are fresh, our [German] neighbours are our mirrors, in whose agony and destruction we may see our future misery should we not seek to improve our lives," warned Arnoldus Buchelius.[27] When catastrophe was collective, so was the conceived remedy. Just as communities had to work together in the quest for holiness, it was believed, God held entire communities to account for the behavior of its individual members. As long as this belief persisted, punishing sinners would be an obligatory act of communal self-defense.

"It does me no injury for my neighbour to say there are twenty gods, or no god. It neither picks my pocket nor breaks my leg," wrote Thomas Jefferson in 1781.[28] Today most people would consider the point obvious. That Jefferson needed to make it, though, points to a profound difference in outlook separating modern from early modern. Until some point in the eighteenth century, most Europeans *did* think it picked their pocket, endangered their own souls, if their neighbor was a heretic. For heresy was a species of sin—

a particularly heinous one—and as such threatened the *Heil* of entire communities. Unless checked, it would spread throughout the body of Christ. The Reformed ministers of Schaffhausen had urged Geneva's magistrates to silence Servetus permanently "lest his blasphemies like a cancer despoil the members of Christ." Others used the same language: heresy "like a cancer spreads insidiously and thus must be cut away in a timely fashion," counseled Laevinus Torrentius, bishop of Antwerp.[29] In this respect, Christian heretics were seen as posing a far greater threat than did Jews or Muslims, who stood outside the Christian community. Heresy also provoked God's wrath, endangering the prosperity, health, and success of all who tolerated it. When Protestant soldiers fighting in the Dutch Revolt attacked Catholic priests in Delft, they claimed in justification that their leader, Prince William of Orange, "could not be victorious as long as the aforesaid ecclesiastical persons persisted with their idolatry in the town."[30] Some Europeans still believed as much in Jefferson's day. One spring in the 1760s, the Catholic peasants of Kaufbeuren assaulted their Protestant neighbors because they blamed them for bad weather. They were not accusing them of seeding the clouds.

Erasmus once described the city as "a big monastery" [*magnum monasterium*].[31] It is hardly a metaphor one would expect Protestants to embrace, but in the wake of the reformations both Catholics and Protestants viewed towns—and villages, which the urbane humanist preferred to ignore—as religious communities. And so they behaved, striving collectively to secure the means of salvation and attain a sanctity that would please God. This was just one branch of collective action taken to secure the community's welfare. The tighter the community, the more such activity directed and encompassed the lives of individuals. Large villages and small home towns were the most cohesive; in them civic and sacral community tended to be most neatly aligned. It should not surprise us, therefore, to find that the same communities were among Europe's most intolerant.

Religious unity was not merely the product, though, of settlement patterns or political boundaries. A shared religion had a unifying power of its own. Investigating the complaints of the peasants of Laviolle, a church official observed that in the Cévennes, "religious services . . . are almost the only opportunities for gatherings . . . and . . . prompt in the masses that spirit of community so necessary for public undertakings."[32] He did not expect that spirit from people who did not worship together. Walenty Kuczborski and Peter Skarga, leading figures in the Polish Counter-Reformation, argued similarly that "where people are not held by a common faith no other bond will hold them together."[33] Their observations merely echoed the conventional wisdom of their day: religion was "vinculum societatis," the chain of society that held it together. As long as religious and civic life remained closely intertwined, it was difficult for many people even to imagine a peaceful, well-ordered community that was divided by faith.

THREE

Flashpoints

Donauwörth

In 1607 a crisis struck the imperial city of Donauwörth, on the banks of the
Danube in southern Germany. Textbooks on the Thirty Years' War, which
routinely mention it, call it a "premonitory crisis"—an episode that presaged and almost triggered the conflict that broke out eleven years later. Lutherans in Donauwörth, an officially Protestant city, attacked local Catholics, a small minority that enjoyed protection under imperial law. Their
action prompted Emperor Rudolf II to place a ban on the city. As enforcer
of the ban, Maximilian of Bavaria occupied Donauwörth with an army.
Taking advantage of the situation, he re-Catholicized the city at swordpoint, forcing Lutherans to convert or leave. Protestants across the empire saw their worst nightmare, a militant Counter-Reformation, coming true. In response, they formed an alliance, the Protestant Union, and
in turn German Catholics organized a league. Polarizing the empire, the
Donauwörth crisis set the stage for a showdown. Subsumed in this wider
narrative of politics and warfare, though, the local details of the crisis have
largely been forgotten. Those details reveal much about the nature of popular religious violence in early modern Europe.

The episode began in 1603 when the monks of Donauwörth's Holy

Cross Abbey resolved to alter a pilgrimage procession they organized each year for the Feast of Saint Mark. On that occasion, they and other local Catholics would make their way from the abbey to the village of Auchsesheim, where they would pray and make offerings at a shrine before wending their way home. In the past, the marchers had always kept to back streets, eschewing all pomp and noise until they got out of the city, and the event had always passed peacefully. In 1603, though, the monks decided to fly the banners of the abbey. When the city's Protestant magistrates stopped them from doing so, they complained to one of the supreme courts of the Holy Roman Empire. In October 1605 the court ruled in their favor and Emperor Rudolf II issued a mandate ordering the magistrates not to hinder Catholics from processing as they pleased. The following April the monks declared their intent once again to march with banners flying. Their hands tied, the magistrates agreed to do nothing to prevent them. They warned, though, of popular unrest.

Thus on St. Mark's Day, 1606, Donauwörth's Catholics unfurled banners, hefted crosses, and set off through the town's chief arteries, chanting litanies as they marched. At first Lutheran townsfolk responded only by heckling the procession. "We'll meet these stick-carrying sacrament rogues with sticks [of our own] and give them cudgel-soup to eat," threatened some.[1] But the Catholics made it safely through the city, and once outside its walls they rejoiced in their accomplishment. Too soon, for while they continued on their journey, Lutherans in town mobilized, and when the procession attempted to reenter the city through a gate, they attacked. They ripped the Catholics' banners, smashed their crosses, and pelted them with stones and garbage. Diverting the marchers from their planned route, they forced them to traverse some of the city's foulest alleys to reach once again the safety of the abbey.

The next year, Rudolf threatened to strip the city of its privileges if the procession was hindered again. As a deterrent, he and Maximilian sent legates to march with Donauwörth's Catholics. The city council pleaded with both sides for restraint, but in vain: this time the procession never made it out of the abbey, which was surrounded by troops of guildsmen armed with clubs and arquebuses. Popular sentiment ran so high that two men were beaten simply for refusing to participate in the siege. As in 1606, Lutheran rioters directed their violence chiefly against symbols and routes.

They did not demand that the procession be canceled, merely that it revert to its previous form. It was not the existence of Catholics in the city that provoked them, nor the Catholic worship conducted in the abbey, nor even the procession per se. It was the more ostentatious, public character the procession had taken on.

At first consideration, this is surprising. Did Lutherans in Donauwörth need special provocation to attack people of different faiths? Did Christians anywhere in Europe? After all, their churches taught that heretics were not Christians of another variety but minions of Satan, enemies of Christendom and humanity itself. Sermons and writings portrayed conflict with them as a cosmic war. Heresy was conceived as a disease that would spread if not checked, and an evil that could bring divine retribution on those who tolerated it. "If we grant [them] the slightest pardon," warned a Catholic preacher during the French Wars of Religion, "God will exterminate all of us."[2] So long as the dominant mode of Christian piety was confessional, and so long as every community was defined as a corpus Christianum, it is no wonder there was religious violence. Indeed, one would almost expect that the kind of brutality France witnessed in the 1560s, culminating in the St. Bartholomew's Day massacre, would have repeated itself over and over, and in other countries.

It did not. None of the other religious wars of the early modern era saw neighbor commit violence against neighbor, burgher against fellow burgher, on such a scale. Not even in France did such violence continue after 1572 as before. There were several reasons for this. First was early modern Europeans' allegiance to the rule of law, which invariably proscribed the kinds of violence that erupted in religious riots. Murder, assault, destruction of property: such behavior, after all, was illegal except in times of war, and even then it was deemed the proper business not of civilians but of soldiers, militiamen, and other specialized groups. In the struggle against heresy, it was normally the place of rulers and their designated agents, not common folk, to wield the sword. Popular religious violence thus had, in many cases, an extraordinary character: it was the recourse of ordinary Christians when they felt that authorities were not doing their job, or when they believed the authorities needed their help in performing it. In other cases, crowds acted only after receiving encouragement from authorities, or what they believed to be such, even if mistakenly, as in the

St. Bartholomew's Day events. Then they might feel they were carrying out the law, not violating it—such a feeling of legitimacy could help overcome many inhibitions.[3]

Europeans acknowledged a variety of obligations that dictated against their use of violence: to obey the law, to accept the limits of their calling, also to practice charity and neighborliness toward one another. Hallowed by custom, enjoined by communal statutes, charity and neighborliness were crucial aids to survival in a harsh world. They bound villagers, towns-folk, and even city dwellers in relations of solidarity and mutual depen-dence that were dangerous as well as painful to break. Peace and prosperity might be threatened by behavior that provoked God's wrath, but they were patently destroyed by civil strife. That was true not just on the local but also on the national or territorial level, where again people divided by faith remained bound to one another by common interests, values, and loyalties. Acknowledging these ties, the Polish Jesuit Peter Skarga remarked of Prot-estants that their "heresy is bad, but they are good neighbors and brethren, to whom we are linked by bonds of love in the common fatherland."[4] It was difficult to dehumanize people to whom one felt such links, and even more difficult when one lived together with them in the small, tightly knit communities that were the norm in early modern Europe.

Sanctified by the Christian injunction to "love thy neighbor as thyself," charity and neighborliness also had, finally, a spiritual dimension. To re-fuse to practice them, even toward a heretic, involved a conflict of religious duties. Civil strife was not just harmful, it was evil. Indeed, it was deemed one of the greatest evils that could befall a community, and the suffering it brought was regarded as itself an expression of God's wrath. When tolera-tion was the only alternative to such strife, which was the lesser evil? With the outbreak of Europe's religious wars, this conundrum began to exercise many minds.

For a religious riot to take place, then, ordinary Europeans had to over-come a variety of inhibitions. In fact, in the known religious riots of the early modern era, confessional antagonisms did not usually suffice in them-selves to carry people over this threshold. Riots required specific sparks as well as underlying causes. Certain situations and events were flashpoints for rioting: they provided the impetus for underlying enmities to be trans-lated into violent action.

Natalie Davis, who pioneered the study of religious riots, offers a useful definition of them. For her they encompassed "any violent action, with words or weapons, undertaken against religious targets by people who were not acting *officially and formally* as agents of political and ecclesiastical authority."[5] Their targets could include objects as well as people, so that iconoclasm counts, as well as bloodshed and beatings. This is important, for much Protestant violence was directed against the paraphernalia of Catholic worship. Objects Catholics venerated—images of saints, relics, eucharistic wafers—were prime targets of attack, as one of Protestants' chief aims was to stop Catholics from continuing to commit "idolatry." It was this offense that Protestants most feared would provoke God's ire. Iconoclasm had a pedagogic aspect as well: smashing a statue of a saint, for example, was meant to prove that it had no power, that what Catholics had been venerating was a mere block of wood. On their side, Catholics seem to have feared with special intensity the bodies of "heretics" as carriers of an infectious spiritual disease. Protestants certainly killed Catholics, and Catholics destroyed Protestant objects, above all their churches. But overall there was a difference: Protestants were "the champions in the destruction of religious property," whereas "in bloodshed, the Catholics are the champions."[6]

Words could have their own violent force. They could rob an icon of its sacred aura or terrorize people almost as much as killing. That was particularly true when the words were threats of physical violence, and when the victims felt defenseless, unable to appeal to the law for protection. Such was commonly the lot of religious dissenters. Consider, for example, the trauma suffered in 1715 by Catholics in and around the English town of Preston. In the wake of the Jacobite uprising of that year, English soldiers took vengeance on them for their presumed part in the sedition. Christopher Tootell, a local priest, described vividly the harrowing scene—perhaps exaggerating for effect, but conveying nonetheless a genuine terror: "Nothing was more dreadful and afflicting on this Occasion, than the Soldiers Insolence & Outrage; whereby some Neighbors were frighted out of their Wits, others abused in their Persons, others starved into Distempers that proved Mortal: nor scarce cou'd any Addition have been made to ye Barbarity of their savage Looks & peremptory Demands attended with horrid Oaths, hellish Execreations, cockt Pistols and drawn Swords set to the breasts of men, women & children; unless they had proceeded to a massacre."[7] In this instance, destruction and plundering accompanied the threats. So too in others, verbal assaults spilled over easily into physical violence. The same was true of symbolic attacks, as when Protestant crowds burned effigies of the pope. Such crowd actions differed considerably from when individuals engaged in name-calling or petty harassment. The latter were real forms of intolerance, creating an atmosphere of tension and hostility, but they could go on for weeks and years without sparking a riot.

Davis confines her attention to violence perpetrated by civilians, not soldiers, and so shall we, but the distinction is not absolute. Like students, soldiers and sailors were important participants in some riots. Many of them had fought religious foes abroad and so found it natural to fight them at home. Without deep roots or long habitation in a locale, they found it easier to dehumanize some of its inhabitants than did natives. Trained in arms and habituated in the use of force, they were almost a law unto themselves and difficult for civil authorities to control under any circumstances. Sometimes soldiers did civilians' dirty work for them—that is, civilians used soldiers to accomplish their own goals, inciting them to perpetrate acts they dared not attempt themselves. Such was the case in the Preston episode mentioned above: "Our Whiggish Neighbors . . . directed & conducted the enraged & greedy Soldiers to plunder & disfurnish the Houses of all Catholicks round about the Town & especially our Habitation [the Catholic chapel in Fernyhalgh], their greatest Eyesore in these Parts: and indeed the furious Hurry in wch [sic] they marched Hitherward, time after time, portended nothing less than Destruction to our dwelling place."[8]

If, then, we survey the incidents of religious violence in early modern Europe that fit the above definition, a striking fact emerges: an extraordinary number of them were triggered by just three types of event: processions, holiday celebrations, and funerals. It is impossible to quantify precisely, as no complete tally of such incidents exists. Nor were these the only triggers; a different dynamic operated during political crises and wars, when religious dissenters were suspected of treason. But outside these contexts, processions, holiday celebrations, and funerals accounted for a high proportion of the known incidents. What gave these three types of event their explosive potential? As the Donauwörth episode suggests, it was their public nature. All heresy did not offend equally: beliefs did not offend people as much as behavior, and the more blatant and conspicuous the behavior—in other words, the more public the act—the greater the "offense" or "scandal" it caused. The most public of all religious acts were these three.

Heretic, Greet Your God!

Although Calvinists have a deserved reputation for iconoclasm, they were not the only Protestant group to react violently to Catholic processions. In Poland, Socinians did; in Germany and Austria, Lutherans did. In 1601 there erupted in the Austrian town of Steyr a riot that bears striking resemblance to the ones in Donauwörth a few years later. The close timing was hardly a coincidence: here too the turn of the seventeenth century brought an effort to revive Catholicism in a Protestant-dominated town. Here too it was a St. Mark's Day procession that Catholics grasped as a tool of self-assertion. Again it was Lutherans who responded violently, and just as in Donauwörth, their attack came precisely when marchers reached the city gate. Journeymen and "masterless" soldiers hurled stones, severely injuring the pastor leading the procession, who took one on the head; they threw a nun in the river, tore the Catholics' banners, trampled on their cross, and scattered their liturgical books.

Even when Protestants countered Catholic processions with defiant gestures rather than force, the result could be equally violent. Such a gesture sparked in 1724 the most notorious religious riot in Polish history. Although Poland was mostly a Catholic country by the early eighteenth century, the three great Baltic ports of Danzig, Elbing, and Thorn, in Royal Prussia, had had large Lutheran majorities ever since the Reformation. On July 16, 1724, a Lutheran in Thorn disrupted a local Catholic procession by shouting insults and refusing to remove his hat when marchers carrying a statue of the Virgin Mary passed him. The Lutheran's insolence outraged a group of Jesuit students. One grabbed his hat; others ordered everyone in the street to kneel. The city's Lutheran burgomaster had a student arrested for his part in the fracas. In retaliation, Catholics seized several Lutheran hostages the next day. All hell then broke loose. As Jesuit students tried vainly to defend their college with sword and gun, Lutherans ransacked it and burned its contents in a great bonfire in the market square. According to Catholic report, they also burned a statue of the Virgin, taunting it, saying, "Now, Woman, save thyself."[9] Thorn's Catholics were a weak minority, but they had the eager support of co-religionists elsewhere in Poland. The Crown Tribunal in Warsaw found the citizens of Thorn guilty of sedition and had the burgomaster, his deputy, and fifteen burghers executed. Across Europe, Protestant propagandists made much of the event, calling it "the Bloodbath of Thorn." It helped give Poland an exaggerated reputation for intolerance.

Where they were the smaller or more vulnerable religious party, Protestants usually countered Catholic processions more subtly than in Thorn. Even more subtle gestures, though, could provoke Catholic violence. The refusal of Calvinists to doff their hats and kneel when a eucharistic procession passed them (Figure 3.1) was a specially sore point in France. Believing Christ to be physically present in the Eucharist, Catholics there found the refusal an unbearable offense to the honor of their Lord; Huguenots felt equally strongly about repudiating this principal point of Catholic doctrine. The Frenchman Théophile de Viau tells the story of a typical incident in the southwestern town of Agen, where one day in 1618 he and a Calvinist friend named Clitophon encountered a priest on his way to the home of a dying parishioner in order to perform last rites. Preceded by an assistant ringing a little warning bell, the priest marched solemnly through the street, wearing his vestments and carrying the viaticum with reverent care. On the street the Catholic crowd fell to its knees, its members baring their heads and waiting in silence for the miniature procession to pass by. Out of sheer prudence, De Viau, himself a skeptic, backed away, doffing his hat and bowing a bit. His friend, though, just stood there. Infuriated by his inaction, one man threw his hat to the ground and shouted, "Get the Calvinist!"[10] The whole crowd began to move toward the pair, and, as De Viau tells the story, only the intervention of a magistrate kept the crowd from stoning Clitophon to death.

Inaction, then, was far from neutral. It had a symbolic meaning as clear-cut as any ritual or gesture. But this put Huguenots between a rock and a hard place. Failure to honor the sacrament could provoke a Catholic crowd to violence, but if they did doff their hats or kneel, they violated their own consciences and exposed themselves to censure by their church. In 1645 a Huguenot national synod stipulated that church members who doffed their hats were to be disciplined—as they already were by some consistories. The decision voided a compromise that had emerged in some locales, whereby Catholics would not take too great offense if Huguenots did not kneel, so long as they removed their hats. Huguenots justified the act by saying they were not doing honor to the Host but rather "either to the preacher who carried it, or to the company who followed it" (Lutherans in Augsburg mollified their Catholic neighbors by the same practice).[11] The French synod, though, demanded that Protestants instead withdraw immediately into a building or side street. By defining this other form of neutral behavior, the synod hoped literally to sidestep the problem. But the attempt did not succeed, at least not entirely. For as Huguenots complained, Catholic priests chased after them.

In 1646 a case came before the parlement, or high court, of Bordeaux that revealed the Huguenots' dilemma and exposed the cat-and-mouse game that French priests engaged in. The defendant was a Protestant maidservant named Toinette, convicted for refusing to render due homage to

Figure 3.1. Simon de Kramer refuses to kneel as a Catholic priest passes by carrying the Eucharist (Bergen op Zoom, 1553). Engraving from Thieleman van Braght, *Het Bloedig Tooneel, of Martelaers spiegel* (2nd ed., Amsterdam, 1685), book 2, page 149. Courtesy of the British Library.

the sacrament. But "far from the maidservant refusing to withdraw," her fellow Huguenots explained in an appeal to the king, "the curé pursued her purposefully and maliciously right up to the house of her master." This, they complained, was a pattern: priests carrying the sacrament would often "expressly detour from their regular route" in order to harass them. Some priests even silenced the bell carried before them, the better to surprise their prey. And when they gave chase—now the rings came fast and furious—the priests would cry out, "Huguenot, adore your Savior, heretic greet your God," and the like. Lay Catholics made it more difficult for Protestants to escape by closing the doors of their homes and shops, or chasing out those who had ducked inside. Such chicanery was hardly new: as early as 1597 Huguenots had complained to the king about a parish priest in the town of Furant who, when carrying the Eucharist through the streets, "would run after those who fled before him, and beat them soundly, either with his Fists or even with the Cross-stick." As late as 1673 they still complained of priests who silenced their bells and "forsook the shortest, most convenient route in order to pass by the homes or shops of the Reformed, to surprise them in public places—in fairs, in markets."[12]

Other sorts of processions could be equally aggressive. In the French town of Niort, Catholics made a point in the 1620s of marching past the city's Calvinist "temple" whenever services were being held in it. Marchers would bang on the temple doors to disrupt the services. Similarly, in December 1614 the Catholics of Biberach in Germany conducted a eucharistic procession "with great ringing and tolling" during a Lutheran service. According to a Lutheran witness, the procession was part of a Machiavellian plot: Catholics were purposefully trying to incite his co-religionists to riot, which would then become an excuse for authorities to forcibly re-Catholicize the city. Their goal, he accused, was "to create a Donauwörth-type of situation."[13]

The Bloodiest Season

The most regular occasions for processions, however, were Catholic holidays. On those days, Protestants' gestures of defiance extended from the processions that formed part of the celebration to the holidays themselves. Protestants believed that Christ alone mediated between man and God, so naturally they repudiated the many days in the traditional calendar dedicated to the veneration of saints and the Virgin Mary. Similarly, Protestants rejected the notion that one could become more worthy of salvation by practicing asceticism; they therefore rejected the practice of fasting during Lent, abstaining from meat on Fridays, and depriving themselves on other set days. In 1522 a group of Zwingli's followers in Zurich broke decisively with Catholicism by eating meat during Lent. In subsequent decades, the act remained a profession of faith and form of public demonstration. By the same token, holidays took on a significance for Catholics they had never had in the Middle Ages: celebrating them became a declaration that a person rejected Protestant teaching. Just as emotions ran high over liturgical practices, so did they over holidays: both gave ritualized form to disputed doctrines.

Friction over the observance of holidays arose between Catholics and Protestants who lived and worked together. In the Dutch Republic, complaints came from maidservants whose Protestant masters prevented them from taking off Catholic holidays or observing fast days. Similarly, a Protestant mason named Jan Hugesz complained to the Haarlem magistrates that his Catholic boss prevented his working on saints' days, depriving him of needed income. In Hungary at the court of Count Adam Batthyány, Protestant servants and soldiers threw pieces of meat in Catholics' wine on fast days, to provoke them.

It was public rather than private celebration of holidays, though, that sparked large-scale, violent conflict. Dances, games, fairs, and feasting were all common parts of celebrations that, like processions, took place in outdoor public spaces. They were festive communal activities in which everyone was supposed to participate. And Protestants certainly felt their attraction: consistories in French towns like Agen and Die had to censure Calvinists who joined in the fun. Those who kept their shops open and went about their daily labors—with a special ostentation, sometimes—did more than abstain, they publicly repudiated the holidays and made their own counterclaim for control of public space. Butchering animals and eating meat out of doors on fast days were even stronger symbolic assertions. In 1566 during Lent a group of Protestants in Augsburg seated themselves right in front of the city's cathedral and sank their teeth into some meat every time a priest walked by. One must marvel at the audacity of Ludwig von Sachsen, a young German Lutheran studying law at Bologna. He hung banners with pictures of a butcher's shop on the route of a Good Friday procession. This was like waving a red flag at a bull. The youth was lucky he ended up in a prison of the Inquisition (where eventually he converted), not torn to pieces by the crowd.

Even when Protestants did not try to provoke Catholics, their holiday activities could elicit a violent response. In the summer of 1658, Catholics and Protestants came to blows twice in the town of Altstädten, in the Swiss Rheintal. Protestants here were legally obliged not to work on Catholic holidays, and on John the Baptist's Day and again on Saints Peter and Paul Day they stayed home in the morning. After noon, though, they went out to their fields to gather hay so that the long wet spell would not harm it too severely. To them the situation seemed an emergency that justified bending the rules. Enraged Catholics gathered at the town gate and attacked the Reformed as they returned from the fields, scattering their hay, overturning their carts, and assaulting them.

Holidays presented difficulty wherever populations were religiously mixed, but nowhere more than in France, where both Protestants and Catholics insisted on their right to manifest their faith in full public view. During the French Wars of Religion, "violence escalated around the key holy days of the Christian calendar," making the season between Lent and Corpus Christi, when those holy days were most concentrated, the bloodiest of the year.[14] Five of the seven major religious riots to take place in Rouen between 1563 and 1571 occurred in March or April. Not coincidentally, this had always been a bloody season for Europe's Jews. From the Middle Ages to modern times, Christians have attacked Jews more frequently during Holy Week—the week leading up to Easter—than any other time of the year. Blamed for Christ's death, Jews did not have to do anything to provoke the violence: the annual rehearsal of the event itself sufficed. Likewise, even when Protestants did nothing provocative, Protestant–Catholic violence was more likely to occur on holidays than other days. In Poland, for example, Catholic crowds set fire to the Bróg, Cracow's Protestant church, on Ascension Day in 1574 and again in 1591. In 1606 they torched Pozen's Protestant church on Maundy Thursday. The previous year on All Saints' Day the Lutheran pastor and vicar of Vilnius were beaten by a mob, the vicar later dying of his wounds. In 1598 on Ascension Day, a group of Catholic students forced their way into the Vilnius home of the anti-Trinitarian leader Fausto Sozzini, burned his books and papers, dragged him barefoot to the town's market place, and threatened him with death unless he recanted. (Sozzini escaped this fate thanks to the intervention of a professor.)

Of all the occasions for sectarian violence, though, none seems to have been more incendiary than Corpus Christi, "the crucial moment of the year for the public expression of religious preference, since the Protestants regarded it as the most abominable holiday of all."[15] Corpus Christi was also the occasion of some of the grandest Catholic processions. The latter often had a military component: the firing of guns by militiamen marching in the procession, or of cannons; or marching to the beat of drums and trumpets, "as one does in war," remarked a Lutheran in Augsburg.[16] In Protestants' eyes, the practice could have a menacing edge. Another striking feature was the elaborate decoration of houses along the procession route. In France it was customary to hang tapestries from the houses' façades and to put candles in the windows. The Edict of Nantes did not require Huguenots to do these things, but it did require them to allow Catholics, at their own expense, to hang tapestries from the Huguenots' houses. Huguenots hated this requirement and flouted it wherever they could get away with doing so. For their part, where they had the means Catholics tried to force Huguenots to hang tapestries and light candles themselves. The matter occasioned dozens, perhaps hundreds, of confrontations in France. Houses that were not properly decorated were attacked and looted. Even after the revocation of the edict, former Huguenots would sometimes "forget" to decorate their homes, risking draconian punishment.

In the years between 1650 and 1800, only one religious riot in the city of Augsburg cost human life: it erupted in 1718 around Corpus Christi. On the eve of the holiday, a fight between a Lutheran tavernkeeper and a group of Jesuit students got out of hand. Called in to restore order, the city guard opened fire, killing one student and wounding another. This enraged local Catholics, and after the Corpus Christi procession a rumor began to spread that Protestants had thrown stones at the Host carried in it. According to the rumor, a miracle had then occurred: the Host had begun to bleed. This type of miracle had precedents going back centuries. In the Middle Ages, Christians had accused Jews of making consecrated Hosts bleed by torturing them. In this way, medieval Christians made Jews out to be unwitting witnesses to the faith they rejected, for of course the bleeding proved Christ's real presence in the Host.[17] With the Reformation, accounts of bleeding Hosts took on new meaning, as reaffirming the truth of a specifically Catholic teaching. Implicitly they drew a parallel between Protestants and Jews. Rumors of a bleeding Host thus turned Catholic victimhood into symbolic triumph. For days Augsburg was in an uproar. Catholic journeymen and youths broke into Lutheran homes and looted them. Eventually they threatened city hall itself, prompting the city council to place two cannons in front of it. Peace returned only after the guard opened fire on a Catholic crowd, killing a weaver's journeyman.

Conflicting Calendars

Like the Catholics, Protestants celebrated certain holidays, which likewise became flashpoints for religious conflict. On the Continent, this conflict was chiefly a product of the Gregorian calendar reform—or rather, of the refusal of Protestants to adopt it because of its papal associations. Based on the best astronomic knowledge available, the reform promulgated by Pope Gregory XIII in 1582 carried no anti-Protestant agenda. Leading professors of theology at the Lutheran University of Tübingen declared as much in 1589, affirming that the dates of holidays were not set by scripture and that the pope would not get "a foot in the church," as some feared, if the new calendar were accepted.[18] But many Protestants remained unconvinced. They also nurtured a special hatred of this particular pope, who in 1572 had celebrated the Saint Bartholomew's Day massacre with a Te Deum, a commemorative medal, and frescoes portraying the event, painted in a room adjoining the Sistine Chapel. The Gregorian calendar was thus condemned by association, as confessionalism trumped neutral scholarship and common interests. Catholic Europe adopted the calendar almost immediately, but most Protestant lands came around only in 1700–1701. Britain, with its colonies, and Sweden held out until the 1750s. Until then, Protestants timed their holidays, court days, market days, elections, due dates for bills, and other annual events in accordance with the "old-style," Julian calendar, which ran ten days (eleven after 1700) behind the "new-style" calendar.

The discrepancy presented no problem where an entire country followed the same calendar, but in parts of Switzerland and the empire it produced confusion and confrontation. In Augsburg the city council resolved in 1583 to adopt the new calendar merely to avoid economic disruption. Although dominated by Catholics, it was chiefly concerned that the city's markets not operate on a schedule different from that of its hinterland and its chief trading partners. Repeatedly it claimed the issue was purely secular, but the city's Lutheran majority would have none of it. On old-calendar holidays, Lutheran craftsmen took to marching provocatively through the city while their Catholic colleagues worked. On new-calendar holidays they worked noisily while Catholics rested. The showdown came at Pentecost, 1584, which the Lutherans celebrated according to the old calendar, against the express order of the council. To break the back of this resistance, the council jailed and then banished the senior minister of the city's Lutheran church. This provoked a full-scale revolt. In the tumult and negotiations that followed, the calendar issue was quickly eclipsed by constitutional ones. The confrontation never lost its religious character, though, as Protestant burghers demanded safeguards against the power of Catholic magistrates. More than any other event before the Thirty Years' War, this notorious "Calendar Fight" *(Kalenderstreit)* turned Protestant and Catholic Augsburgers into confessionally conscious, mutually antagonistic parties.

At least in Augsburg the calendar issue was resolved relatively quickly. Conflict continued into the seventeenth century in the towns of Dinkelsbühl and Biberach, whose Lutheran burghers would sometimes travel to Protestant territories to celebrate holidays on the day they deemed correct. In the bishoprics of Speyer and Würzburg, discordant calendars kept Protestants and Catholics at odds with one another well into the eighteenth century. And in Switzerland, strife only began after the Protestant cantons officially adopted the new calendar in 1700. Until then, Protestants living in the religiously mixed Rheintal had followed the new calendar in economic and political matters but worshipped according to the old. When the highest authorities of the Swiss Confederacy, Protestant and Catholic jointly, tried to force them to abandon the old calendar altogether, some turned to armed resistance. In Glarus, another mixed region, Protestants held fast to the old calendar until 1798.

Holiday violence was not limited to clashes between Catholics and Protestants. In Berlin, for example, riots erupted in 1615 during Holy Week in protest against the decision of Johann Sigismund, elector of Brandenburg, to impose Calvinism on his overwhelmingly Lutheran territory. What pro-

voked Berliners' ire most immediately was the removal of epitaphs, cruci-
fixes, pictures, altars, and other objects from the city cathedral, done at the
elector's order so that Easter could be celebrated there in the Calvinist
manner. On Palm Sunday, after hearing an enraged sermon by a preacher
who opposed this "further Reformation," a hundred burghers took an oath
swearing "that they would strangle the Reformed priests and all other Calvinists."[19] The next day a much larger crowd stormed the homes of those
"Reformed priests," smashing what they did not steal. Even accompanied
by troops, the regent Johann Georg found himself impotent to stop them.
For his attempt he was roundly cursed and received a wound on his thigh.

A similar move toward "further Reformation" provoked riots in 1647 in
the English counties of Suffolk and Kent. Here the conflict was between
Puritans, on the one side, and Protestants who hewed closer to old Catholic traditions, on the other. The issue that triggered their clash was Christmas. This holiday was especially popular in England, and some Puritans
took correspondingly great offense at the revels and "pagan" symbols—
"holly, ivy, rosemary, and bays"—that accompanied it.[20] In 1647 the Puritans who controlled Parliament outlawed its celebration in the usual manner. In Canterbury, townsmen who shared their outlook kept their shops
open on the day, but conservative farmers from nearby villages came into
town, smashing shop windows and assaulting their owners. In Bury St.
Edmunds a group of apprentices led a similar attack.

Actually, in the British Isles most religious violence coincided not with
holidays but with political crises, and in particular with wars—actual,
looming, or just feared—against Catholic powers. Even here, though, religious tensions rose on holidays. Post-Reformation England developed a
calendar unique in early modern Europe, filled with newly invented holidays (Figure 3.2). These commemorated royal birthdays, accessions, and
especially "providential deliverances"—moments of peril when divine intervention, it was said, had saved the Protestant nation from Catholic tyranny. The most prominent of these days were November 5 and November
17. The first commemorated the discovery of the Gunpowder Plot of 1605:
the Catholic Guy Fawkes caught red-handed in the cellar of Westminster
Palace, torch in hand, with enough powder to demolish the building and
kill the entire assemblage in it. In 1688, William of Orange landed at Torbay
on the same date, beginning the Glorious Revolution that removed the

Catholic James II from the throne. Thereafter, the holiday commemorated both events. November 17 was Queen Elizabeth's "Crownation Day," the day on which she had ascended to the throne, succeeding her Catholic half-sister, "bloody Mary." On both holidays parishes across England held special thanksgiving services. Typical sermons on these occasions attacked "popery," painting it as a satanic force ever striving to subdue or destroy the Protestant nation. The holidays were celebrated with bonfires, bell ringing, parades, pageants, the firing of guns, distribution of doles to the poor, feasting, and drinking. With this mix of devotion and festivity the English celebrated "the emergence and safety of the English Protestant regime" and reaffirmed their status as an elect nation, specially favored by God.[21]

Intended to promote unity, these holidays nevertheless took on partisan meanings as English Protestantism fractured over the course of the seventeenth century. The process began in the 1630s when Puritans faced off against Arminians. With one group of Protestants accusing the other of being crypto-Catholics, subverting the Church of England from within, vilifying popery became a divisive act. Moreover, the objects of this Puritan accusation included the king himself. Puritan preachers took November 5 as an opportunity to challenge his philo-Catholic policies and to call for further reformation. Predictably, Charles I and his government discouraged celebration of the holiday. In the 1660s the government of his son, Charles II, introduced two new holidays that antagonized Puritans: that of King Charles the Martyr (January 30) and Royal Oak Day (May 29). The first, a solemn day of fasting, commemorated the 1649 execution of Charles I by "cruel and bloody men."[22] The second was the birthday of Charles II and also the date of his formal accession. Its name evoked the story of his escape from death at the hands of Puritan soldiers, after the battle of Worcester, by hiding in an oak tree. Both holidays repudiated the English Revolution and the Puritan ascendancy it had brought. Both celebrated the restoration in 1660 of the Stuart monarchy and, by implication, the reestablishment of the episcopal Church of England.

During the Exclusion Crisis of 1678–1681, those who wished to keep the Catholic James from succeeding his brother Charles turned the November 17 holiday to their own ends. This group of politicians became known as Whigs, their opponents as Tories, party labels that survived into the twen-

holiday celebrations. Indeed, anti-Whig sentiment "transformed the annual round of anniversaries into a calendar of riot and sedition" in the years immediately following the succession in 1714 of George I.[26] As opponents of the Hanoverian succession, Tories celebrated the June 10 birthday of the Pretender, James Stuart, and that of another hero, the Duke of Ormonde; they disrupted Whig celebrations of the new king's birthday and coronation day. November 5, now doubly significant, retained its anti-Tory as well as anti-Catholic overtones. Party and religious affiliation remained closely intertwined. On the king's birthday in 1715, Tory crowds gutted Protestant dissenters' chapels in Highgate, Manchester, and Oxford. They destroyed roughly forty other chapels, mostly in Lancashire and the West Midlands, in the weeks that followed.

Ireland too had its holidays, some distinctive, others shared with England. Again, they had the power to unite or to divide. Donning shamrocks, some Protestants joined Catholics in celebrating St. Patrick's Day as a sort of national birthday. By contrast, October 23 was a purely Protestant affair commemorating the Catholic uprising of 1641 and the massacres that accompanied it. Sermons whipped up anti-Catholic sentiment by recounting in ghoulish detail the atrocities supposedly perpetrated. They declared the event divine punishment for the sins of the Irish Protestants and warned that a similar fate might be visited upon them again should they fail to repent and reform. At the same time, preachers thanked God for the ultimate failure of the uprising, a providential deliverance on the order of November 5. Both holidays were occasions of anti-Catholic violence in the 1670s and 1680s, met sometimes by Catholic retaliation. William of Orange's landing on November 5, 1688, made that holiday even dearer to Irish Protestants than it was to English. Subsequent celebrations conflated this event with William's birthday on November 4. In the early eighteenth century, they became occasions for anti-Tory harassment as well as anti-Catholic tirades. Today, of course, the marches held by Protestant "Orangemen" to celebrate William's victory over James II at the Battle of the Boyne spark annual bouts of sectarian violence.

In the eighteenth century Irish Catholics celebrated June 10, the birthday of the Pretender, James Stuart. In Dublin they did so with a boisterous gathering on St. Stephen's Green, which many years degenerated into a street battle between Protestant and Catholic gangs. Protestant "Liberty Boys" and Catholic "Ormond Boys" both had a penchant for pelting their enemies with dead dogs and cats.[27] At the peak of their feud, in the summer of 1748, the two gangs went at each other most every Sunday.

Vile Bodies

As for funerals, Elie Benoist, Calvinist minister and chronicler of the persecution suffered by his fellow Huguenots, called them "the fatal Spring of innumerable Vexations and Injustices."[28] His words apply not just to seventeenth-century France: funerals had the potential to provoke violent responses in religiously mixed communities elsewhere too. To be precise, it was not wakes, "watchings," or funeral dinners, conducted inside the home of the deceased, nor funeral rites performed inside churches, that were subject to violent disruption. Rather, it was the most public components of funerals, the mourners' procession from the home of the deceased to the burial site, and the burial site itself.

Funeral processions had several divisive traits in common with other sorts of processions. At least until the eighteenth century, they were communal events inviting wide participation. Guilds and other corporations often required their members to take part when one of their own was to be buried. The role of neighbors was almost as obligatory. The more mourners, the greater the honor shown to the deceased. Symbolically too—as through the bell ringing that accompanied it—the ritual claimed to express the sentiments of the entire community. Funeral processions were also spectacles. Traversing public space, they maximized encounters with nonparticipants, inviting spectators. And finally, they were forceful assertions of group solidarity. Wearing the mourner's uniform of black, marchers formed a company united in grief, proclaiming publicly its respect for the deceased.

Unlike the Catholic processions discussed earlier, though, funeral processions did not always bear a sharply confessional character. Funerals were above all "rituals of honour," their details calibrated to convey the social status of the deceased and their families. The chief distinction they were intended to draw was not between faiths but between "honourable and criminal, rich and poor, *Bürger* and foreigner."[29] To be sure, the funerary rites favored by different confessions varied. But in no confession were funerals a sacrament, unlike weddings and baptisms. From an official ecclesiastic perspective, that fact made it less serious an offense for a church member to attend a nonmember's funeral. Calvinists and radical Protestant groups like the Mennonites and Quakers even desacralized funerals, largely. Processions were to be conducted "without either singing or reading, yea without all kind of ceremony heretofore used," the Scottish Book of Discipline (1560) instructed.[30] These groups' processions were so stripped of religious symbols that they had a kind of neutrality, comparable to modern-day schools where no prayers are said, no crosses or Ten Commandments hung on the walls. In the Dutch Republic, where Calvinism was the official religion, funeral processions had a stripped-down, Calvinist cast. With few modifications, Catholics and others conducted their own processions in the same manner as Calvinists, and people of all faiths took part in one another's funerals. Utrecht's minister Johannes Gerobulus noted in 1603 how "difference of religious conviction holds no one back and makes no one unwilling, so that it has often been a wonder and a joy for me to observe the good order which is maintained."[31]

Even where funeral processions did have a markedly confessional cast, their social aspect may have been more important, in the eyes of many, than their religious. In Maastricht, for example, Catholic funeral processions were led by priests sprinkling holy water and joined by monks. Invoking the saints, marchers carried crosses, banners, and candles. Local Calvinists nevertheless participated (for which their consistory censured them). Similarly, when Catholic patricians died in the German city of Ulm, the Lutheran burgomaster and city council marched in their funerals. When the son of a Catholic count died, they sent their condolences and lent a coach, horse, and convoy for the procession. Lutheran women in Ulm did not shy even from attending a funeral mass: when the secretary of the local Augustinian abbey died in 1670, they carried candles through the church during the ceremony. Funerals thus could unite as well as divide people of different faiths. When death came knocking, class, neighborhood, and other solidarities sometimes bridged the clearest confessional divides.

Not everyone, though, separated faith from honor. Funeral processions paid tribute to a person whose heresy, in the eyes of some, made them supremely dishonorable. So did burial in hallowed ground. Indeed, it sealed their status for eternity as members in good standing of the local community. Outside church precincts only criminals, excommunicates, and those who had committed suicide found their resting places, if their graves could be called that, for it was popularly believed that neither body nor soul would rest peacefully if the corpse was not given a proper, "Christian" burial. To treat people of other faiths in like manner was to degrade them and cast them out equally permanently. An early incident in Dijon presaged a conflict that was to drag out for over a century in France. In 1560 "some women of honor and good Catholics" disinterred the corpse of a Protestant mason buried the previous day in the churchyard of Saint Pierre. They put a rope around the corpse's neck and dragged it from the tomb, shouting "this Lutheran, this Huguenot, this dog does not deserve to be buried with good Christians."[32] The women's deeds—the noose they made—equated the man with a criminal, their words equated him with an animal. In northwestern Germany, burial outside church precincts was called "a donkey's burial." Stories underscored its unsatisfactory nature: animals disturbed the corpse, weather or traffic exposed it. In 1611, in Lancashire, "there died in the parish a woman, and because she was a Catholic they would not bury her in the church but in a great common, so nigh the highway that the horses travelling along did almost dig the dead corpse up again."[33]

Huguenots wanted to be buried in parish churches and churchyards with their Catholic countrymen. Calvinists in Brandenburg and Saxony wanted to be buried in the same, alongside Lutherans. English Catholics desired burial likewise in the consecrated ground of their local Anglican parishes. In all these places clashes occurred when members of the majority faith tried to exclude or eject the corpses of religious dissenters. We have no tally, but in France hundreds of corpses must have been exhumed. For dissenters the same was always at stake: honor versus dishonor, inclusion versus exclusion, acceptance versus stigmatization. As in death, so in life: "If we were separated in our graves from one another once dead, then one would equally have no fellowship among the living," feared Swiss Protestants.[34] Benoist put it still more forcefully: "Indeed, there was little Appearance that the *Reformed* could ever enjoy a quiet Life or a happy Society with them, who were taught to hate their Countrymen in their very Graves, and to deny them the Honour of a Common Burial; and who could not see without Scorn, nor frequent without Horror those Men, whose dead Bodies, in their Opinion, would prophane and sully the Places where they lay buried."[35]

As Benoist suggests, there was an additional issue for those of the majority faith: purity versus pollution. In the eyes of some, the corpses of heretics profaned and polluted hallowed burial ground. Catholic teaching was explicit: churches and churchyards had to be cleansed and reconsecrated once desecrated in this way. Catholic majorities were especially prone to using violence to prevent this horror, but Catholics did not have a monopoly over the violence. In the 1580s and 1590s Lutheran crowds in northern Germany attacked the funeral processions of prominent crypto-Calvinists. These attacks reveal much the same sensibilities as those launched by Catholics elsewhere. Consider, for example, the Dresden funeral of Christian Schütz, court preacher to the elector of Saxony. At it a crowd of hundreds demanded that the body be taken out to the gallows, that ravens be allowed to pick at his body, as they did those of criminals hung there, and that his remains be buried there, not in the communal cemetery. Two youths attacked the most distinguished mourner, a Frau Rappolt, one of them wiping her mouth with a "shitty broom." By such symbolic actions, crowds dishonored the dead and their mourners, expelled them from the community, and profaned them as they felt threatened by profanation. Describing the Dresden incident, a Lutheran pamphleteer urged that Calvinists be "cleansed" or "one must throw them out with the filth."[36] The parallel to France, where Catholic crowds sometimes deposited Huguenot corpses on piles of garbage or dung, was indeed close.

It seems, then, that there were at least three reasons why processions, holidays, and funerals occasioned so much popular religious violence. In the first place, these public rituals brought together crowds for the express purpose of making assertive statements of group identity and group belief. The rituals themselves were one such statement, and the more pomp, noise, and publicity they had, the more assertive the statement they made. One purpose of their enactment, especially in a religiously divided Europe, was to fortify the resolve of participants and convey a feeling of strength in numbers. Such events did not per se license violence, but they did impart a sense of power that could embolden groups to do what might feel too risky for individuals. Many processions had a semi-martial cast, through either the wearing of uniforms, firing of guns, sounding of trumpets, and beating of drums, or the simple act of marching in ordered ranks. Perhaps they encouraged people—spectators as well as participants—to see religious groups as opposing armies. In this way perhaps they contributed to the dehumanization that turned people of other faiths into Satan's minions.

In the second place, such public ritual acts were hard for nonparticipants to avoid or ignore. By taking place in spaces designated as stages for social interaction—street, square, commons, churchyard—they attracted witnesses and invited reaction. Indeed, they forced witnesses to respond in an equally public manner, making evasion or neutrality well nigh impossible. As the story told by Théophile de Viau suggests, even doing nothing was a statement of rejection and defiance. And just as circumstances forced his friend into making a public declaration of his disbelief, so they left the crowd to choose between attacking the Calvinist and condoning his blatant disrespect toward their God.

Finally, contemporaries endowed public rituals of all sorts with representative powers. That is, they viewed such rituals as enacting the will not just of individual participants but of the entire community in whose space they occurred. Every member of the community was believed "to participate in the collective rite at least as citizens [*par civisme*] and in a passive manner."[37] So, when a religious group enacted its beliefs in a public space, it was claiming possession not just of that space but of the entire community, appropriating the authority to speak and act for everyone, and making those of other faiths accomplices in rituals they rejected or even abhorred. By the same token, when individuals disrupted or refused ostentatiously to participate in such rituals, their acts were believed to undermine the entire proceedings and their spiritual efficacy for everyone—as if everyone were an accomplice to their sacrilege. Such was the force of communalism. The belief that the burial of a single heretic in a communal cemetery defiled all the corpses buried there rested on the same assumptions.

For all these reasons, processions, holiday celebrations, and funerals triggered a great deal of religious violence. They were not the only such occasions. Other riots can be traced back to ordinary Sunday services, tavern-room brawls, even the circulation of mere rumors. Still, the explosive potential of public religious acts was unmatched. In 1659 the Capuchin friar Antoine Le Quieu triggered a riot when he erected a cross in a central square of the French town of Mérindol. As he anticipated, the townspeople, who were almost all Huguenots, did not interpret his act merely as providing Catholics with an object of veneration. They saw it as an aggression, similar to planting a flag and declaring a territory to be the property of one's own country. It was, in their eyes, a direct challenge, intended "to humiliate and confound them."[38] As the missionary had hoped would happen, a crowd smashed the cross to pieces and burned its splintered remnants in a mock-Catholic procession. Le Quieu then had no difficulty convincing the authorities to punish those responsible. He *had* created a "Donauwörth-type of situation."

Perhaps we should not be surprised to discover that provocative behavior sparked violent incidents. But the pattern is strikingly specific. It suggests that the religious riots and massacres of early modern Europe cannot simply be blamed on an intolerant culture. Popular religious violence was not "natural" to early modern society. It usually required a specific trigger as well as ideological fuel to set it off. That meant it was neither inevitable nor universal.

Each of the flashpoints discussed above was capable of being at least partially defused. Dutch Catholics, for example, made regular pilgrimage processions to Kevelaer, Uden, Handel, and other sites outside the United Provinces without provoking a violent response from the country's dominant Calvinists. They simply did what Donauwörth's Catholics refused to do: they hid their banners and crosses and refrained from song until outside Dutch territory. An agreement reached in 1759 had some success resolving the holiday issue in the bishopric of Würzburg. It stipulated that on Catholic holidays Lutherans might perform their usual labor, but until the morning's mass is over "all noise from smithy-, coach-, key-work and similar ear-piercing manual labor, as well as from threshing, breaking flax, knocking, splitting wood, and from travel by cart, coach, [and] plough over the streets is to be put off until after twelve o'clock noon"; Catholics were enjoined to refrain similarly on Protestant days of fasting and prayer.[39] Ultimately, though, this kind of piecemeal approach had limited potential. So long as a sacral act occurred in public space, it remained an offense to those of other religions. This fundamental problem demanded a systemic solution.

FOUR

One Faith, One Law, One King

The Sins of This Land

In May 1661, rain fell in buckets on the English countryside. Streams overflowed, fields became lakes, and the seeds of wheat and barley planted earlier that spring washed away or rotted. The country's entire grain harvest threatened to fail, portending "Famine, and Pestilence" in the year to come. When the rain let up (only briefly, it turned out) in the first week of June, the government of Charles II promptly issued a royal proclamation ordering "a general and public fast to be kept throughout this whole kingdom, in such manner as hereafter is directed and prescribed, that so both prince and people, even the whole kingdom, as one man, may send up their prayers and supplications to Almighty God, to divert those judgements which the sins of this land have worthily deserved, and to continue the blessed change of weather now begun, and to offer up to him their hearty and unfeigned thanks for this, and other abundant mercies formerly vouchsafed unto them, and to beseech his blessing upon that great assembly of this nation."[1] According to the proclamation, the rains were divine punishment for England's sins. Preaching before the House of Commons, Thomas Grenfield enumerated the offenses that, in his estimation, had provoked God's ire: Sabbath breaking, swearing, adultery, intemperance, luxury, and "want of Justice and Charity."[2] Attentive MPs must have agreed, for the House quickly ordered the sermon published. Inasmuch as these sins were rampant, guilt for them was collective. As if it were "one man," the entire kingdom had to repent and reform its ways in order to avoid national catastrophe. Such were the assumptions, echoed in countless prayers and sermons, behind the fast day decreed by the government. On the occasion of another storm, in 1703, Richard Willis, dean of Lincoln, made them explicit: "National sins," he explained, "deserve national judgements"; "the best Service we can do our Country is, to endeavour, by a general Reformation, to appease the Wrath of God."[3]

Just as the welfare of towns and villages depended on God's favor, Europeans believed, so did that of countries. A kingdom such as England was not, in Christian teaching, merely an arrangement of convenience, fashioned by humans for purposes of dominance or defense. Rather, it was part of the divinely appointed order of this world. As all human affairs were directed by divine providence, so were the formation and fate of states. "Ordained" in their office by God, acting as his "vicars" and "lieutenants," their rulers preserved the peace and dispensed divine justice—or, if they were wicked, inflicted divine retribution. They, as heads of state, and their subjects, as "members" of the state, formed a single "body politic." Mystically united, head and members formed a Christian community that would prosper or suffer, depending on whether it earned God's blessing or wrath. In that recurrent encounter with divine justice, the fate of the realm hinged on the piety and virtue of its ruler and all its people. In short, like a town or village, a Christian state was a corpus Christianum.

So too, on a vast scale, was Christendom, which Europeans still on occasion saw God's hand stretching out to punish. When Servetus stood on trial in Geneva, a popular rumor spread that if the anti-Trinitarian did not receive proper punishment, God would let the Turks overrun the Continent (they, like he, rejected the Christian Trinity, making them a suitable scourge). In 1663, when Ottoman armies launched an offensive into central Europe, prayers went up across the Continent. One pietist preacher warned his Dutch congregation that the Turks would conquer all unless lax, indifferent Christians put into practice the teachings they mouthed. Two decades later the Turks attacked again, this time reaching the walls of Vienna. At this critical juncture, Pope Innocent XI marshaled an international alliance to relieve the imperial capital. Protestant as well as Catholic princes of Germany sent troops to fight alongside Poles and Austrians. After the combined Christian army broke the Turks' siege, Innocent organized a "Holy League" whose forces drove the Turks once and for all back to the Balkans. This crusade was the last hurrah for the medieval concept of a united Christendom led by pope and emperor.

By then, two developments had made the concept almost completely anachronistic. One we have already examined: the division of Christendom into competing confessions. The other was the emergence of political units resembling modern nation-states. Particularism did not disappear, either as a set of power relationships or as a mentality. Increasingly, though, Europe's rulers asserted an impersonal authority that can be called sovereignty, rather than (or, perhaps better, in addition to) the personal suzerainty of the feudal Middle Ages. They codified laws, issued regulations, raised taxes, formalized institutions, and mobilized networks of officials, casting in this way a tighter net of control over society. One must not exaggerate the control rulers achieved, for early modern governments never had the tools of law enforcement modern ones take for granted. More than is often realized, their authority depended on the consent of the governed. Nevertheless, by the late seventeenth century some princes had achieved what at the time was called "absolute" authority: they could wage war, issue laws, and impose taxes without the approval of representative institutions, or with sure knowledge of their rubber stamp. "Absolutism" vested all sovereign power in a single individual, but even in polities that remained fragmented, like those of the Dutch and Swiss, there developed "a more encompassing, more systematic, and more literate articulation of power and authority."[4] The development took as many forms as there were forms of polity, but across Europe it was clear: the state grew stronger as an institution and more cohesive as a political community.

The fusion of these two developments, confessionalism and state formation, was explosive. The fictional Irishman Dooley, creation of modern humorist Finley Peter Dunne, once observed: "Rellijon is a quare thing. Be itself it's all right. But sprinkle a little pollyticks into it an' dinnymit is bran flour compared with it. Alone it prepares a man f'r a better life. Combined with polyticks it hurries him to it."[5] The observation has a special ring of truth in the mouth of an Irishman, for in modern Ireland, religious and political causes—Protestantism and Union with Britain, Catholicism and Irish Nationalism—have become inseparable. In the sixteenth century, religion and politics combined similarly across Europe. Religious enemies, their hatreds fanned by confessional ideology, became political enemies, and vice versa, as people at odds with one another for social or political reasons tended to choose opposing sides religiously as well. In this way, Europe's religious divisions not only created new conflicts, they threw ideological fuel on the fires of existing ones. Competitions for power, wealth, or land became cosmic struggles between the forces of God and Satan. Inversely, the bonds of a common confession brought people together in equally powerful ways. When they cut across social or political lines, they could make friends of strangers or even former enemies. On every level, from the local to the international, co-religionists felt an impulse to make common cause with one another.

To Europe's rulers, then, the rise of confessionalism held out both perils and promises. A difference in religion could alienate their subjects from them and undermine their authority. As the French Wars of Religion demonstrated, to the horror of contemporaries, it could set citizen against fellow citizen and tear states apart in civil war. A shared religion, on the other hand, could bolster rulers' authority, binding their subjects to them and to one another more firmly. Given these starkly contrasting possibilities, it is no wonder rulers tried to impose religious uniformity on their territories. Their personal piety impelled many to do the same. Since the thirteenth century, the Catholic Church had asked them to swear they would "strive in good faith and to the best of their ability to exterminate in the territories subject to their jurisdiction all heretics pointed out by the Church."[6] The division of Western Christendom gave them compelling new reasons to do so.

In its wake, Europe's rulers tried to make their personal choice of faith official for their state. Most succeeded, though, as we shall see, not all. Either way, the resulting confessional allegiance eventually became a defining aspect of political identity. Whether or not it initially had wide support, the allegiance was institutionalized and sank popular roots. In some essential and irreversible way, England became a Protestant country, Poland a Catholic one, Sweden Lutheran, the Dutch Republic Calvinist, and so forth. This fusion of religious and political identity, piety and patriotism, was (after confessionalism and the communal quest for holiness) the third great cause of religious intolerance in early modern Europe. Forged in the course of Europe's religious wars, it led both rulers and ordinary people to equate orthodoxy with loyalty and religious dissent with sedition. It gave national politics and even foreign affairs the power to spark waves of religious riots as well as official persecution.

Cuius Regio?

From the moment the evangelical movement began to spread in Germany and Switzerland, princes and magistrates faced a momentous choice of whether to support it. It was a choice they felt bound to make not only for themselves but for all those subject to their authority. "For in matters concerning God's honor and the salvation of our citizenry and community," declared Nuremberg's city council, it bore ultimate responsibility. "As a duty of the office entrusted to them and upon pain of losing their souls," the councillors had an obligation "to provide for their subjects, over whom they are placed, not only in temporal . . . but also in spiritual [affairs] . . . , that is, with the holy gospel and word of God, from which human souls and consciences live."[7] The obligation was not new. As "Christian magistrates," they had always understood it as their duty, as their colleagues in Isny once declared "that we shall seek, before all [other] things, God's kingdom and works of divine virtue, and [that we] shall increase and promote divine service."[8] Accordingly, in the previous century they had led their community in an intensive quest for "Heil," issuing moral regulations, coordinating charity, reforming schools, funding preacherships, and cracking down—as best they could, given the clergy's broad autonomy—on clerical abuses. Now, with the Reformation, they also decided how Christianity would be practiced and professed in their city. Henceforth, they would appoint and dismiss Nuremberg's pastors, administer church finances, issue ordinances to replace canon law, and supervise religious life. For them the Reformation brought sweeping new powers to fulfill an old responsibility. It was an eminently satisfying change.

In the following years, rulers across Europe did the same as Nuremberg's magistrates: with pope and emperor impotent to stop them, they chose among faiths and imposed their choice on their subjects. In the process, they turned religious choice into an attribute of sovereignty; indeed, rulers such as Count Ottheinrich of the Palatinate called it the "highest" such attribute *(höchstes Regal).*[9] In the empire, this novel power was ratified legally by the Peace of Augsburg, signed in 1555. The famous catch-phrase *cuius regio, eius religio* was coined decades later by a Lutheran jurist to summarize the central clauses of this treaty. "Cuius regio" meant that "he whose territory" it was had the right to impose his faith (Catholic or Lutheran) on his subjects, free from outside interference. If subjects dissented from their ruler's choice, they had only the right to emigrate *(jus emigrandi)*. Sealing the defeat of Emperor Charles V, who abdicated his throne and retreated to a monastery, the Peace vested the German princes with the *jus reformandi,* the right to reform, and with it sweeping authority over religious affairs within their lands.

Württemberg

Whether established de jure or simply de facto, "cuius regio" offered Europe's rulers unprecedented opportunities to expand their power. The German duchy of Württemberg exemplifies how rulers could use these opportunities for state-building. It is in some respects an extreme example, for Württemberg was a Lutheran territory, and of all the confessions Lutheranism promoted the closest integration of church and state. In fact, it tended to incorporate the church into the structure of the state, turning it practically into a department of government. Württemberg was a pioneer in this regard, developing in the 1550s under Duke Christoph a "church order," or structure of ecclesiastic governance, that other Lutheran territories in Germany copied. At the top of this structure were two bodies, the Consistory and the Synod. Unlike Calvinist consistories in western Europe, Württemberg's was a single, centralized institution, based in the capital, Stuttgart. It consisted of theologians and jurists, all appointed directly by the duke. The jurists controlled church finances; the theologians made appointments to lower church offices, assigned pastors to parishes, and stood as highest doctrinal authority. Twice a year (four times, initially), the members of the Consistory joined four "general superintendents" appointed by the duke to form the Synod. The latter was in charge of disciplinary matters. General superintendents supervised twenty-three special superintendents, who in turn conducted parish visitations. Anyone who refused to take Communion or attend services in their parish church violated the law; if found guilty of heresy, they could be banished or imprisoned and their property could be confiscated. Pastors were required to report suspicious cases, along with those of "notorious," unrepentant sinners, to their superiors. Serious cases were passed up by the special to the general superintendents, and if necessary to the Synod.

Established by ducal edict, the structure was a model of bureaucracy. Comprehensive, it covered all Württembergers. Strictly hierarchic, it robbed the parishes of almost all autonomy and required a great quantity of paperwork (by the standards of the day) to flow up the chain of command. With the appointment of top church officials in his hands, it gave the duke firm control over the church. Since those officials also constituted one of two estates in Württemberg's territorial assembly, it also made the latter body more docile. The chief disadvantage of the structure, at least in the eyes of theologians like Jacob Andreae and his grandson Johann Valentin Andreae, was that it could not enforce morals very strictly. When members of their flock sinned, pastors could do little more than privately admonish the guilty parties and report them to the superintendent. In practice, the Synod was too distant and too busy to handle many cases, which were left to the discretion of local government officials. And that suited the latter just fine: for the time being, they preferred their unrivaled hegemony to moral rigor. Attitudes changed with the Thirty Years' War, whose horrors and depredations were widely interpreted as punishment for Germany's sins. The need to appease God in order to restore peace and prosperity tipped the balance of elite opinion, and in the 1640s authorities finally accepted Johann Valentin Andreae's proposal for the creation of local morals courts, called "Kirchenkonvente."

Andreae's proposal was inspired by his vision of an ideal Christian community, which he described in a work of utopian fiction entitled *Christianopolis*. At the center of this miniature city, surrounded by its symmetrical walls and buildings, embodiments of harmony and order, stood a temple—religion. The citizens of this holy "commonwealth" were of course fervent Lutherans. The judge who presided over them, wrote Andreae, "thinks that the best arrangement for a community is this, that it approximate as closely as possible to heaven; and since he is extremely pious he believes that the salvation of a community lies in the good disposition of God, while His wrath means its destruction. And so he exerts himself in this, that God may not be offended by the sins of the people, and may be appeased by the distinguishing marks of faith. . . . Nothing from Satan, however small, is allowed in; and they have no fear of the growth of evil, for they root it out as quickly as possible."[10] Christianopolis, then, was a theocracy: a society in which church and state cooperated to realize, as best they could, the kingdom of God on earth. In it, religious precepts and values took priority over secular concerns, serving as a blueprint for all spheres of life. Moved by an inner piety, its citizens obeyed freely the community's strict moral code; faith and compulsion joined to produce a perfect conformity to God's will. Far from unique to Andreae or to Lutheranism, this theocratic ideal was another aspect of confessionalism. In fact, Andreae drew his inspiration partly from Calvinist Geneva, which he visited in 1611; in his autobiography he gushed over the moral rigor he observed there.

Few were the cities, never mind territories, that lived up to this ideal. Certainly the morals courts never transformed Württemberg as thoroughly as Andreae hoped. They did, though, crack down on cursing, swearing, adultery, fornication, cardplaying, dancing, and other offenses long forbidden by law. With jurisdiction over education, charity, and public health as well, these local courts subjected peasants and townsmen to a new social discipline. Run jointly by church and secular officials, they not only gave institutional form to a religious ideal, they turned Württembergers into more obedient, orderly subjects, "civilizing" their behavior.

Religious reform, state-building, and social discipline were mutually dependent, mutually reinforcing processes in Württemberg. So interconnected were they that we can even speak of them as three aspects of a single, overarching process that was at once religious, political, and social. Called "confessionalization," this process was at work in many European lands in the late sixteenth and seventeenth centuries.[11] If Württemberg underwent a classic process of confessionalization, though, it was not simply because the dukes willed it. Early in the Reformation, Lutheranism had gained a popular following in the duchy, so that Duke Christoph had broad support for his reforms. It was at the initiative of the estates that the 1559 Church Order was incorporated into statute law and declared unalterable. And it was only when local officials dropped their resistance that morals courts were formed. Like elsewhere in Europe, in Württemberg a crucial part of state-building involved forming strategic alliances with local power brokers. Rulers could not simply ignore the religious inclinations of their subjects, nor could they wipe away at a stroke the medieval heritage

of particularism. Those who tried courted disaster. For just as religious reform and state-building could fuse, so could religious dissent and political
opposition. That is exactly what happened in three of Europe's great religious wars, the Dutch Revolt against Spain, the Thirty Years' War, and the
English Civil War. In all three cases, rulers triggered massive revolts when
they combined abrupt moves toward absolutist government with a crack-
down on beliefs and practices widespread among their subjects.

The Netherlands

The confessionalizing initiatives of Philip II triggered the Dutch Revolt.
In 1555 Philip inherited from his father Charles V the seventeen provinces of the Habsburg Netherlands. Charles had done his best to suppress
Protestantism in them, but had never succeeded in stopping the flow of
books, ideas, and religious refugees. Devoutly Catholic, Philip swore that
he would not be a ruler over heretics. He also saw, and no one could really
dispute, the need to revamp the administrative structure of the Catholic
Church in the Netherlands. Woefully inadequate for pastoral care and
oversight, four bishops presided there over a flock of almost three million
people. Philip therefore had his Brussels advisors draft a plan known as the
"new bishoprics scheme." Receiving papal approval in 1559, it increased the
number of bishops to eighteen, strengthened their powers, and provided
for two inquisitors in each bishopric. Not coincidentally, the plan brought
church and government into line with one another by making the borders
of the bishoprics contiguous with those of the Habsburg territories. Philip
also obtained from the pope the right to appoint all bishops and archbish-
ops. These prelates would take the place of more independent ones in the
States of Brabant, the most powerful province. Philip went on to name several inquisitors as bishops. They exemplified the kind of fervent, efficient
administrators Philip wanted for both church and state. In defense of Catholicism they did not hesitate to violate cherished local privileges such as
the "jus de non evocando," the right of citizens to be tried for criminal offenses in a local court. The new bishoprics scheme would violate other
privileges the Netherlanders claimed as well. It illustrates how Catholic reforms, like Protestant ones, could serve political and religious ends simultaneously.

In the 1560s a broad coalition of noblemen and burghers emerged in opposition to this plan. Crucially, Catholics as well as Calvinists, the leading Protestant group, joined the coalition. They shared many values and viewpoints as well as interests with their Protestant countrymen, and Philip's intolerant, confessional faith little resembled the Catholicism they had been raised in. Indeed, it would be difficult to classify many Netherlanders at the time as either Catholic or Protestant, for their piety combined a variety of influences. In 1566 this coalition forced regent Margaret of Parma to suspend the antiheresy laws. Protestants took advantage of the opportunity to hold public sermons, and in August bands of them began to commit acts of iconoclasm, destroying altars and images in hundreds of churches. Philip's response was equally extreme: he dispatched the Duke of Alba at the head of Europe's biggest, best-trained army to restore order. The duke fulfilled his orders with a vengeance, implementing the decrees of the Council of Trent along with the new bishoprics scheme, executing Protestants, abrogating privileges, and imposing heavy new taxes without the assent of provincial estates. These acts, and the predatory behavior of the Spanish soldiers, alienated more Netherlanders than ever before. Thus, when rebels who had taken refuge abroad, known as "Sea Beggars," launched in 1572 an invasion of Holland and Zeeland, few burghers resisted; many welcomed them with open arms.

For most Netherlanders, the Revolt was a struggle for freedom, both political and religious—freedom from "tyranny" and from what they called the "Spanish inquisition." Around this cause Netherlanders could rally, regardless of religion. For Calvinists, though, the Revolt was something far grander and more desperate: a struggle of good against evil, Christ against Antichrist. For them, fighting Philip was an act of piety on which depended their salvation, as well as their very survival. They could admit no compromise or defeat. Meanwhile, Catholics who supported the Revolt found themselves taking sides with Protestants against the champion of their own faith. Viewed from a confessional perspective, their stance made no sense. Philip concluded that their commitment to Catholicism must be insincere; Calvinists concluded the same about their commitment to the Revolt. In fact, few Catholics in Holland or Zeeland favored Philip's victory in the war, and most of these "malcontents" eventually fled. Nothing, though, could break the association of Catholicism with Philip's regime. Calvinists claimed that Catholics' religious allegiance would drive them to betray their homeland. In the perilous, often desperate straits in which the Dutch found themselves, this false accusation found wide acceptance. Fear of subversion—of a fifth column of Catholic traitors ready to throw open the gates to besieging Spanish troops—gripped cities. Calvinists claimed in addition that God would not grant the rebels military success unless they fulfilled their sacred obligation to eradicate Catholicism. As one group of soldiers put it, justifying a rampage in Delft, their leader William of Orange "could not be victorious as long as the aforesaid [priests] persisted with their idolatry in the town."[12] Reluctantly, in 1573 the estates of Holland and Zeeland outlawed Catholic worship.

The same dynamic repeated itself in other provinces after they joined the Revolt in 1576. Every one of them intended initially to maintain the monopoly of the Roman Catholic Church, but the association of Catholicism with loyalty to Philip generated irresistible pressures. Pope Gregory XIII added to them in 1578 when he threatened Catholics with excommunication if they supported the Revolt. The decisive event came in March 1580, when the Catholic Count of Rennenberg, stadholder of the northeastern provinces, abandoned the Revolt, calling on his fellow Catholics to rise up against its leaders. "Rennenberg's treason" seemed to confirm Protestants' worst fears about the disloyalty of Dutch Catholics. In scores of cities from Friesland to Holland, a wave of iconoclastic rioting erupted, as Protestants demanded the immediate suspension of Catholic worship. By the end of 1581, Catholic worship was illegal throughout the rebel provinces.

In the end, the seven provinces north of the Maas and Waal rivers abjured their allegiance to Spain and formed the United Provinces of the Netherlands, also known as the Dutch Republic. Thanks to its association with patriotism, Calvinism became the official religion of the newly independent country, and those who served in government were required, at least in their official capacity, to support it. It was an ironic turn of events, given that the southern provinces that returned to the Spanish fold had had more Calvinists at the beginning of the Revolt than had northern ones. Even in the 1580s it was estimated that only one in ten Hollanders were members of the Reformed Church. It comes then as no surprise that Dutch society was never thoroughly Calvinized. To the contrary, no other land in seventeenth-century Europe would have as many different churches and sects, and advocates of toleration would hail the Republic as

Prussia for patronage and protection. And the defense of their co-religionists gave those neighbors, as it did Russia, an excuse to intervene repeatedly in Polish affairs. By the eighteenth century, Catholicism seemed to most Poles the only religion compatible with patriotism and loyalty.

Fifth Column

These case studies only begin to capture the variety of ways confessionalism and state formation intersected. What they have in common, though, points to a wider truth: that Europeans drew an equation between civic and sacral community on the national or territorial level, just as they did on the local. They presumed that a shared religion was a crucial cement holding states together, and that religious divisions undermined social and political unity. The French put this common wisdom into the form of an adage: "Une foi, une loi, un roi"—one faith, one law, one king. Theodor Sprenger, author of a 1655 manual for princes, explained the adage by relating it to the concept of a body politic: "For just as it is fitting for one body to have one soul, so it is for one commonwealth to have one religion."[16]

Religious dissenters were perceived as threatening states in two ways. First, their actions and very presence offended God, arousing his wrath against those who tolerated them. Dutchman Arnoldus Buchelius, himself a Calvinist, feared that the "scandalous idolatry" of Catholics and their "denial of the only sacrifice made by Christ on the Cross" would "do nothing but aggravate the wrath of God towards our lands."[17] Emperor Rudolf II blamed himself for the plague that struck Bohemia in 1606, believing God angry over his tolerance of Protestants. England's Parliament hoped in 1656 to escape divine wrath by passing legislation against Socinians and Quakers; MPs urged the house to "vindicate the honour of God" as the only way to "divert the judgement from the nation."[18] Peter Pázmány, archbishop of Gran/Esztergom, suggested that the Turkish conquest of Hungary was divine punishment for the spread there of Lutheranism. Protestants in Hungary claimed the opposite, that it was punishment for Catholic idolatry. As late as 1763, when an earthquake flattened the Hungarian city of Comorn, a Lutheran preacher in nearby Vienna felt compelled to refute Catholic claims that God was punishing Hungary for its Protestants.

Religious dissenters were also perceived as potential, if not actual, traitors. People assumed that their enmity extended from a state's official church to the state itself and to the entire established order of which the church was part. Even when dissenters behaved like obedient subjects and good citizens, their loyalty was often questioned. People suspected it was a pretense, a strategy for biding time while they hatched plots. That some dissenters did in fact hatch plots, and that, in many parts of Europe, they dissimulated on a regular basis, holding clandestine religious services behind closed doors, only fueled these suspicions. Even if dissenters' loyalty was genuine, people feared it would falter if ever there appeared a tempting prospect of a new regime favorable to their faith. What if there were a political crisis—would they seek to overturn the religious establishment? If a foreign army invaded, would they side with the invaders? At such moments, when establishments felt most vulnerable, dissenters turned from chronic into acute threats.

What made dissenters so frightening, ultimately, was their position as outsiders *within* the community. Operating covertly, they could attack without warning where the state was most vulnerable. Worst of all, they could conspire with external foes. They constituted a potential fifth column, a Trojan horse whose soldiers could throw open the gates, literally or figuratively, to foreign armies. This kind of enemy has always evoked paranoia. It did so with special intensity in England, our last case study. Here *most* popular religious violence can be linked, directly or indirectly, to fears of a fifth column.

England

By 1603, when Elizabeth I died, England was a Protestant country. After Henry VIII's break with Rome, Edward VI's Reformed faith, and Mary Tudor's restoration of Catholicism, the religious compromise the queen had fashioned at the beginning of her reign had taken on positive identity and won the allegiance of millions. Granted, its nature remained in dispute, and Puritans saw it only as a starting point for further reforms. But decades of sermons and of war with Spain had had a decisive effect, turning English men and women into confirmed enemies of "popery." The number of English who refused to conform to the national church out of allegiance to Rome never rose in the seventeenth century beyond about sixty thousand—barely more than 1 percent of the population. "Popery," though, was an abstract entity far more fearsome than these few "recusants," and at times English Protestants even dissociated the two. (In 1780 a group of rioters in London were "called upon to go to such a house, as there were *Catholics* there. They replied, 'What are Catholics to us? We are only against *Popery!*'")[19] "Popery" was the imagined foe against which England defined itself as a nation. "Bloody," it persecuted with inhuman cruelty; "superstitious," it kept its adherents ignorant and debased; "tyrannical," it subjected people to the spiritual despotism of popes and priests. Later it would be associated also with the political despotism of absolutist kings such as Louis XIV. These qualities made it the "outlandish" faith of foreigners, antithetical to the temperament and traditions of the freedom-loving English. Disciplined, implacable, and without scruple, the forces of "popery" were imagined as striving in unison to destroy the prosperous, free, Protestant nation.

England, though, had God on its side—at least provisionally. English preachers proclaimed their nation a New Israel, bound to God by a special covenant. Every threat to it, every misfortune, they interpreted as God's way of testing his chosen people to see if they would maintain their piety and faith. So long as they did, God would see that the nation prospered. The Spanish sponsored plots to assassinate Elizabeth and place her Catholic cousin Mary on the throne, but each one providentially failed. Then in 1588 the Spanish king sent the great Armada—130 ships carrying twenty-five thousand men, defeated not by force of English arms but by a "Protestant wind." Its destruction was "a miracle of mighty magnitude, done by the dreadful power of God's right hand." But the greatest of all "miraculous deliverances" that God vouchsafed his people was the discovery of the Gunpowder Plot. It confirmed that Protestant England was an elect nation, destined to prevail. "It is our Passover, it is our Purim," pronounced Bishop Lancelot Andrewes of its annual commemoration.[20]

Yet English Protestants never felt wholly secure. Throughout the seventeenth and into the eighteenth century, fear of popery was a driving force in English politics. The nightmare scenario involved a rebellion by native Catholics and simultaneous invasion by one of England's inveterate enemies, Spain or France. In some versions, Irish Catholics rose up—as they did in 1641—invading from the west and encircling "this beleaguered isle."[21] But the internal threat did not come only or even principally from recusants. This was one of the peculiar side effects of the Elizabethan religious settlement: such were its ambiguities and inconsistencies that people with a spectrum of beliefs and sensibilities, from Puritan to Catholic-leaning, could attend services in their parish church without too many pangs of conscience. This comprehensiveness helped make the Church of England a truly national religious establishment. The same factors, however, gave church members real grounds for suspecting their fellows. Puritans in particular asserted that for every overt papist in England there were five covert ones, conforming only to protect their families and property from the law. These crypto-Catholics and backsliders within the Church formed the ultimate fifth column. They gave the threat of popery a power that England's few recusants could not have done—especially because, for much of the seventeenth century, they included the kings of England.

The power of monarchs to overthrow religious establishments was nothing abstract to the English, for they had already experienced it in the sixteenth century. The flip-flops of successive Tudors left the English feeling vulnerable to new alterations. Protestants remembered Mary Tudor's reign, above all, as a national trauma. Every parish church was required to own a copy of the book that celebrated its victims, John Foxe's *Book of Martyrs*. Its reading and the annual celebration of Elizabeth's Crownation Day kept fresh the memory of the horrors a Catholic ruler could perpetrate. It came therefore as a shock in the early 1620s when James I (who was Calvinist but wished to play the role of peacemaker, reuniting Protestants and Catholics) relaxed enforcement of the laws against recusancy. Even more shocking, his son Charles went to Spain to woo the Spanish infanta. So began the Stuart dynasty's flirtation with Catholicism. Charles I did marry a Catholic princess, though not the infanta. He favored Catholics at court and supported the anti-Puritan offensive of Archbishop William Laud. For these policies and for striving after "absolute" power Charles paid in 1649 with his life. His son Charles II married a Catholic too and on his deathbed actually converted to Catholicism. The Stuarts flirted with Catholicism also through their foreign policy, James I making peace with Spain, Charles II allying with France's Louis XIV. The dynastic courtship was consummated, though, only with the succession of James II, an openly Catholic king. To this day, it is debated whether James II intended to restore Catholicism as England's official religion or merely grant Catholics toleration. In any event, his maneuvers triggered the Glorious Revolution of 1688–1689, in which he was deposed. In 1689 Catholics were excluded from the throne, and in 1701 an Act of Settlement vested a princess of Hanover and her descendants with the right of succession. Thus in 1714 Parliament passed over more than fifty candidates with a better hereditary claim to declare as king George I, a German Lutheran. Until 1766, though, there was always a Stuart "pretender" to the throne living in exile. He attracted the loyalty, or at least nostalgia, not only of Catholics but of all who hated the dominant Whigs.

In Puritan propaganda, all Laudians were papists; in Parliamentary propaganda, all Royalists were; in Whig propaganda, all Tories. Cooler heads, of course, saw reality as more complicated, and ironically, sometimes the clash of armies did more than anything else to clarify them. Most royalists, for example, offered ample evidence during the Revolution that they remained committed to the Protestant Church of England, and Charles I himself died an "impeccably Anglican" death.[22] For that matter, most recusants remained loyal to their country through all crises. Yet fear of Catholics continued to supply "the basis of the popular political vocabulary" in early modern England; "serious occurrences in national politics [were generally] understood at popular level in terms of a papist/anti-papist dichotomy."[23] That fear remained acute, the dichotomy convincing, as long as English men and women suspected their own king of Catholicism and, beyond that, as long as there lived a Catholic Stuart with a claim to the throne.

Much of the religious violence in early modern England was triggered by the threat, real or imagined, of a Catholic restoration. Its timing coincided with specific crises: the face-off between king and Parliament in 1640–1642, the Exclusion Crisis of 1678–1681, the Glorious Revolution of 1688–1689, and the Jacobite rebellions of 1715 and 1745. In each of these instances, domestic turmoil was accompanied by threat of foreign invasion, and in each of them, waves of "panic fears" swept the country. Wild rumors circulated, typically about "Irish and Roman Catholics . . . who burn, kill, and destroy all they meet with."[24] Protestant crowds attacked recusants, searched their homes for arms, vandalized their shops, destroyed their clandestine chapels. Recusants served as scapegoats for a threat that came, to the extent it was real, from kings and armies.

They were not the only victims, though. As some Protestants perceived the matter, anyone who undermined the unity and strength of the Church of England weakened the nation in its struggle against the papal Antichrist; anyone who sharpened the differences and contradictions within the Protestant camp handed the enemy a victory in the war of polemics. Paradoxically, then, some of the most radical as well as conservative English Protestants were accused of popery: Quakers and Baptists in the seventeenth century, Methodists in the eighteenth. Superficial similarities, like the Quakers' refusal to take the oaths of supremacy and allegiance, lent a veneer of plausibility to the sectarian–papist equation. These groups were at best scorned as unwitting papist dupes, at worst denounced as "Jesuits in disguise." In Hogarth's engraving *Credulity, Superstition, and Fanaticism* (Figure 4.1), a Methodist preacher's wig pops off to reveal a monastic tonsure. Methodism, to its misfortune, first spread in many parts of England in the 1740s, around the same time as the Jacobite rising of 1745 and during the War of Austrian Succession. Paranoia about possible spies and traitors triggered anti-Methodist riots. Today it seems incredible that anyone believed the wild rumors that circulated about the early Methodists—for example, that their revival meetings were covers for papist plotting, or that the Wesley brothers had taken Spanish money to raise an army. The very outrageousness of the accusations suggests how powerful fears of popery remained among some segments of the populace.

Given the pain and terror caused by such riots, it seems a bitter irony that, in at least two cases, real Jacobites were among their perpetrators. In fact, Methodists had to take Anglican blows on both cheeks. Whigs and Low Churchmen accused them of popery; Tories and High Churchmen accused them of being radical Puritans—"commonwealthmen," levelers, enemies of all political and social hierarchy. Methodists were objects of violent attack on both counts, as Quakers, Baptists, and other Protestant dissenters had been before them. In the wake of the Civil War, all forms of religious "enthusiasm" posed, in the eyes of conservative Anglicans, a threat to the establishment. Memories of that national trauma left a fear of Protestant dissent almost as abiding as the fear of popery. As if they had been alive in the 1640s and 1650s, latter-day dissenters were called regicides and revolutionaries, blamed for the Civil War, and accused of having desecrated Anglican churches. "Down with the Rump"—the Parliament that had executed Charles I—shouted Tories in 1715, as they sacked dissenters' chapels, and in the 1740s as they assaulted Methodists. Just as recusants were scapegoated for a broader papist threat, so these Protestant groups served as convenient surrogates for their more powerful Whig allies. "If the Ministry and Secret Committee and their Friends will not let the country have Peace and Trade," declared one Staffordshire Tory, "the Dissenters shall not have a quiet Toleration."[25] Dissenters might openly reject Anglicanism, but Tories feared greater damage to the Church of England from

Figure 4.1. William Hogarth, *Credulity, Superstition, and Fanaticism.* Engraving, 1762. Courtesy of the Ashmolean Museum, Oxford.

the Whigs and Low Churchmen within it. Mutatis mutandis, they too constituted a fearsome fifth column.

A nation-state is not just an apparatus of government exercising sovereign authority, nor is it just the geographic area or people over whom a government holds sway. It is also an "imagined community" whose members feel a loyalty and affinity to one another.[26] Their feeling is based on a sense of sharing certain things: ancestors, interests, values, a language, culture, history—perhaps too a common destiny. In Europe, where political units resembling nation-states developed in the early modern era, religion played an indispensable role in creating that feeling of community. The varieties of confessional Christianity not only supplied governments with official ideologies, they provided large, geographically dispersed communities with common symbols and values. They set the shared experience of those communities in a cosmic framework, infusing it with deeper meaning. They gave states spiritual identities. National and territorial churches embodied those identities institutionally. Coordinating worship and belief across entire lands, they united subjects of a state as members of a single corpus Christianum.

For all the alliances that co-religionists made across political boundaries, confession marked states off from one another more strongly than it linked them. This was a contribution of Europe's religious wars, which coincided with a crucial phase of identity formation. As political enemies became religious ones, and vice versa, countries defined themselves in opposition to specific foes. For the Dutch, Catholic Spain was the evil "other"; for England it was Spain, then France, and more generally the Protestant island versus the Catholic continent. Poland defined itself initially as the "outpost" or "bastion" of Christendom, defending Europe against the infidel Turks. Its tradition of toleration was undermined, though, by war with its various neighbors: Orthodox Russia, Lutheran Sweden, Calvinist Transylvania, and Brandenburg. Increasingly it saw itself as a fortress beset on all sides by enemies of Catholicism.

A ruler's choice determined the confessional identity of most states, as it did Württemberg's. Indeed, some rulers were able to make their personal piety the very centerpiece of national identity. The acknowledged mas-

Christians, it was fueled by fears of sedition—of the overthrow of a political regime and with it a religious establishment. Ultimately, the fear of conforming Christians was that the faith of dissenters might become the official one and their own faith the persecuted. It tended therefore to be those dissenters whose church constituted a plausible alternative establishment whose sedition was most feared. The plausibility usually had some basis in fact: a ruler's support for that church, or a previous regime's, or a foreign enemy's. Elaborate myths, though, were built on scant basis. Furthermore, it was during political crises and wars that overturning the establishment seemed most possible. In those periods dominant religious groups felt most vulnerable and "beleaguered," lashing out at dissenters in an aggression born of defensiveness.

The irony was that the equation of heresy and sedition was a self-fulfilling prophecy. By persecuting dissent, states did run the risk of alienating dissenters, and sometimes they practically pushed them into the arms of foreign enemies. In the 1550s, Castellio already saw the problem, and the cure for it. More than a century later, John Locke offered the same prescription:

> The magistrate is afraid of other churches, but not of his own, because he is kind and favorable to the one, but severe and cruel to the other. . . . These he cherishes and defends; those he continually scourges and oppresses. Let him turn the tables. Or let those dissenters enjoy but the same privileges in civils as his other subjects, and he will quickly find that these religious meetings will be no longer dangerous. For if men enter into seditious conspiracies, it is not religion inspires them to it in their meetings, but their sufferings and oppressions that make them willing to ease themselves. . . . Neighborhood joins some, and religion others. But there is only one thing which gathers people into seditious commotions, and that is oppression.[28]

II

ARRANGEMENTS

FIVE

The Gold Coin

To those who lived through Europe's reformations, the idea that Christians might forevermore be divided by faith was unimaginable. After all, from their perspective, the unity of Western Christendom had been a basic principle and continuous fact for more than a millennium. Its shattering seemed nothing short of catastrophic. "Tis all in pieces, all coherence gone," wrote John Donne, lamenting the collapse of an ancient, comforting cosmology.[1] But nothing, not even the discovery of the Americas or of moons around Jupiter, caused Europeans more profound shock than their new religious divisions. It took monumental changes for Europeans to accept them fully, and rather than do so, many clung tenaciously to a hope that the divisions were temporary.

Time and again over its history, the Roman Catholic Church had managed to suppress heresies, resolve schisms, and absorb reform movements. Why, reasoned its supporters, should the new challenge it faced be any different? Many Catholics, failing to appreciate its theological depth, regarded Protestantism as merely a reaction to the "abuses" in their church, which even its staunchest defenders admitted. As long as those abuses remained, Catholics like Etienne de la Boétie, the French jurist and poet, could hope that "when our [church] is regulated and reformed, it will appear entirely new and give [Protestants] a perfect occasion for returning to it without scruple."[2] Francis de Sales called this strategy "cutting the aqueduct": deprived of "water," that is, scandals in the Church, Protestants would lose their reason for rejecting Catholicism.[3] By this means, the saintly missionary stationed in Savoy hoped vainly to recapture Geneva itself.

For their part, mainstream Protestants never sought to establish alternate churches alongside the Roman Catholic. Just as Catholics did, they thought of Christianity as a single religion that bound all Christians together. Their goal was to purge this religion of accretions and restore it—everywhere—to its pristine form. The transformation might not come easily or soon. No reformer was as sanguine as Luther himself about the power of the devil, who, Luther expected, would only rampage more wildly as his defeat approached. But the Gospel was God's own word, its spread his own work. As surely as good would vanquish evil, Protestants believed, the true faith would triumph, as Jesus had foretold: "And this gospel of the Kingdom shall be preached in all the world for a witness unto all nations; and then shall the end come" (Matthew 24:14). On this point of eschatology Protestants and Catholics agreed. For both, the ultimate restoration of unity was an article of faith, guaranteed by divine providence. The errant would hear Christ's voice and there would be just "one flock, one shepherd" (John 10:16).

The only questions, then, were how God would establish true Christianity everywhere, and how soon. Preaching and teaching, moral discipline, and the building of sound ecclesiastic institutions were the first recourse of all parties. By these means, acting as God's instruments, reformers hoped to educate the ignorant and convert the misguided. Inevitably they learned the limits of peaceful suasion. And when it failed? Catholic authorities in Brussels executed the first martyrs of the Reformation in 1523. Within a few years, Protestants also accepted governments' use of coercion for religious ends. But the magistrate's ordinary "sword," the law, stretched only so far. Catholics and Protestants soon found certain of their enemies—God's enemies—too powerful to be vanquished except by military force. Switzerland was the site of Europe's first religious wars, fought between 1529 and 1531. Next came the Holy Roman Empire, where the Schmalkaldic War erupted in 1546, followed by the so-called Princes' War, which came to a definitive end in 1555 with the Peace of Augsburg. Tragic as they were, these conflicts were mere skirmishes compared to the French Wars of Religion, the Dutch Revolt, the English Civil War, the Polish Deluge, and, most destructive of all, the Thirty Years' War. Invariably the militants who launched these conflicts did so believing that God would grant them total victory over their foes. Invariably they were disappointed.

From the beginning, though, there were others who counseled a different path to unity. "It behoves the wise man to try all things rather than weapons," wrote Georg Witzel, a German priest who in 1524 declared his support for Luther, only to return nine years later to the Catholic fold. Advisor to princes, Witzel helped shape the course of the Reformation in Brandenburg, Jülich-Cleves, and other German territories; later in life he enjoyed the confidence of Emperor Ferdinand I. As early as 1533, Witzel predicted that the "remedy" of religious war would be "worse than the disease" of disunity. Such war he declared a betrayal of Christianity: "Those who want to reduce all to smoke and cinders, to cover the home-fires with the blood of the godless, and to soil Christian hands with parricide—those would be unable to bear witness to the spirit by which they claim to be moved (Luke 9:55)."[4]

Witzel devoted much of his life to overcoming the empire's religious divisions through conciliation and compromise. In more than 130 writings, he charted a "middle road" to religious reform, one that ran between the positions of Catholic and Lutheran adversaries. That "royal road," that "old and sound way," Witzel argued, "was that of the Fathers of the Church, more than a thousand years ago." A Christian humanist in the tradition of Erasmus, whom he idolized, Witzel looked to the early years of Christianity for a model of the pristine religion he wished all parties to embrace. This was a religion stripped of superstitions and scholastic quibbles, of ceremonies and abstruse doctrines added in later centuries. "If modern theologians would be content with ancient theology rather than continuing to concoct novelties," he huffed, "the Church would not be afflicted with so many heresies."[5] Witzel proposed a liturgy based on that of the second century A.D. It included many Protestant features: weekly Gospel sermons, Communion for the laity in both kinds (wine as well as wafer), vernacular prayers, no private masses. Yet once he returned to Rome, Witzel remained a faithful son. For all its present-day abuses and corruptions, he believed the Catholic Church of his day was the same church as had been around in Justin Martyr's.

True Christianity, in Witzel's view, could not be reduced to the dogmas of any one religious "faction," as he called the emerging confessions.

Rather, it was a universal religion that defied party labels: "Let us not hear any more, dear brethren, those words: 'I am of Paul, I of Apollo, I of Cephas' (1 Cor. 1:12), or as it is put today: 'I am of the Pope; I of Luther; I of Zwingli; I of [the Anabaptist Melchior] Rink; I of Calvin.' Is Christ divided? Has the Pope been crucified for us? Have we been baptized in the name of Luther, Zwingli, Rink, or Calvin?"[6] With this appeal, Witzel issued a fundamental dissent against the division of Christendom. He did not see the differences between competing confessions in black-and-white contrasts but in shades of grey. Not all confessions were equal, in his view, but none were Satanic antireligions. With a common belief in the same savior, all were bona fide forms of Christianity and those who professed them were all Christians. If they would only engage in constructive dialogue, abandoning their "ambition and the wish to rule," he was sure they could once again unite as members of a single church that was "Catholic" in the truest, original meaning of the term: universal.

Witzel was not alone. In his day, most Europeans still thought it possible that the disputes plaguing Christendom might be resolved through dialogue. Such a resolution seemed especially urgent where religious war threatened, and in central Europe where the onslaughts of the Turks demanded that Christians present a united front if they were to escape a common doom. Urged by their political patrons, churchmen entered repeatedly into theological discussions, or "colloquies," with one another. One of these colloquies achieved a notable success: at Regensburg in 1541, Philip Melanchthon and Martin Bucer, negotiating for the Protestants, and Cardinal Contarini and Johannes Gropper, for the Catholics, agreed on a formula for the doctrine of justification. Adopting a proposal of Erasmus, they acknowledged a need for both faith and works to achieve salvation. The most essential difference between Catholic and Protestant theology, as modern experts have always cast it—works righteousness versus salvation by faith alone—did not prove, on this occasion, the most difficult to bridge. Nor, on later occasions, did clerical marriage, Communion in both kinds, or the use of vernacular in the liturgy: on all these points there were preeminent Catholics, such as Charles de Guise, Cardinal of Lorraine, and Emperor Ferdinand I, prepared to make concessions, and medieval precedents for their doing so. Rather, papal authority and the doctrine of the Eucharist proved the most difficult issues. On these two rocks every ship of compromise foundered. In 1561, at the Colloquy of Poissy, a few rash words on the Eucharist from Theodore Beza ended all meaningful dialogue before it had begun.

Colloquies might be held and national gatherings proposed, but ultimate authority for resolving religious disputes lay with a general council of the entire church. Only a "free, general" council, it was agreed, could make decisions that were binding for all Christians. But the council that, after long delay, finally convened in 1545 did not, in the eyes of many, meet this qualification. When Protestants were invited to send a delegation to Trent, their representatives were treated as accused heretics rather than partners in discussion. Even Germany's Catholic princes later acknowledged that the council had been anything but "free." In fact, Trent was intended by its papal conveners as an alternative to the more open, ecumenical type of council that northern Europeans, Germans and French in particular, were calling for; among those who attended, Italian prelates and Spanish theologians dominated overwhelmingly. Thus it surprised no one when the Council concluded its last session in 1563 with delegates shouting "anathema" to all Protestant heresies. In hindsight it is clear that Trent sealed the permanent division of Western Christendom.

At the time, however, this fact was anything but obvious. In the following decades, those who longed for peace continued to echo Witzel's appeal. Even as Europe's religious scene grew more bitter and polarized, they called for ecclesiastic reunion, and if the current disputes over theology could not be resolved immediately, they called on Christians to join together anyway. For how important, they asked, were the points in dispute really? The irenic emphasized how much confessional enemies actually shared: not just a common humanity, but a common Christian faith. No one expressed such appreciation more eloquently, perhaps, than the anonymous author of a 1579 Dutch pamphlet: "We have been told that these people [Protestants] are monsters. We have been sent after them as after dogs. [Yet] if we consider them, they are men of the same nature and condition as ourselves . . . worshipping the same God as us, seeking salvation in the same Christ, believing in the same Bible, children of the same father, asking a share of the same heritage by virtue of the same Testament."[7] An anonymous French Catholic was more blunt, asserting in 1589 that "Catholics . . . and Huguenots agree in doctrine so [much] that they are of one and the same faith and religion." This man assigned scant importance to the doctrinal points dividing the two groups. They are, he said, so complex, so beyond the comprehension of nontheologians, that ordinary people understand none of them. If an informed agreement on them were necessary, one would have to conclude that "Catholics themselves were not of the Roman Church" and were destined for damnation.[8]

Theology offered a technical vocabulary to formulate such views, distinguishing between the *fundamenta* of Christianity and adiaphora. All varieties of Christianity drew this distinction. But while the trend-setting theologians and dominant churchmen of the confessional age declared all manner of disputed points fundamental, the irenic did the opposite. Reunion depended on defining the fundamentals narrowly, restricting them to points of agreement between the confessions, and relegating everything else to the adiaphoral. Erasmus advocated this approach as early as 1523, and Castellio did so as well, briefly and suggestively, in his famous work of 1554, *Concerning Heretics*, where he used a monetary metaphor. Different lands, he explained, have different coins, and each rejects the other's "unless indeed the money be gold, which is valid everywhere regardless of the imprint." So rival churches have given Christian teaching "different imprints and images," yet all accept the Ten Commandments and the Trinity. These beliefs, according to Castellio, are "the gold coin which is everywhere acceptable no matter what the image."[9] No one who holds them should be condemned. In the following century, eminent scholars of every confession—Catholic George Cassander, Lutheran George Calixtus, Remonstrant Hugo Grotius, Calvinists David Paraeus and John Dury, Socinian Daniel Zwicker, and Anglican William Chillingworth, among others—adopted this approach. In learned treatises, they proposed definitions of the fundamentals that they hoped would enable Christians to reunite.

This goal was known in the sixteenth century as "concord" or "peace"; in the seventeenth, it was called "comprehension," "latitude," or "ecclesiastic toleration." It should not be confused with toleration in the usual modern sense, which went by various other names: "indulgence," "civil toleration," or just plain "toleration." John Locke explained the distinction. Reporting in 1689 to his Dutch friend Philip van Limborch about legislation under consideration in England, he wrote, "In Parliament the subject of toleration is now discussed under two forms, 'comprehension' and 'indulgence'. By the first it is proposed to enlarge the bounds of the church, so that by the abolition of some ceremonies, many [people] may be induced to conform. By the other is designed [*sic*] the toleration of those who are either unwilling or unable to unite with the Church of England, even on the proposed conditions."[10] "Comprehension," then, involved admitting people with a variety of beliefs to membership in a single church. "Indulgence" involved accepting the existence of multiple churches. The two, comprehension and indulgence, were usually conceived as alternatives— after all, there was no need to "indulge" religious dissenters if one could bring them into the fold of the established church. As Locke's words suggest, though, "comprehension" also deserves recognition as a form of toleration. Indeed, it was the most ambitious and charitable of all forms, requiring a genuine acceptance of beliefs different from one's own as valid and a willingness to take Holy Communion with those who maintained them.

Comprehension in Practice

In the middle decades of the sixteenth century, comprehension still seemed a viable solution to the problem of Europe's new divisions. That was because confessional modes of piety had not yet developed fully or spread too widely, at least in some parts of Europe. This is not to say that Catholicism, Lutheranism, Reformed Protestantism, and Anabaptism did not yet exist as distinct, definable forms of Christianity. But some of the points on which they later differed had not yet been articulated, and others had been articulated but not yet declared essential aspects of "true" Christianity. Even more importantly, the pedagogic and disciplinary enterprises of rival confessions were still just getting under way. Millions of Europeans were still malleable, open to considering the merits of different beliefs and practices, and prepared to shift their views as experience revealed their political, social, and cultural as well as spiritual implications. Which confession would emerge as the official one of many states was still unclear, while the subjects of some, notably England and the Palatinate, were being expected to change their confession with each new ruler. Most of these subjects were able to adapt: for every religious exile or martyr in the sixteenth century, there were at least ten Christians prepared to conform. Some were uncertain what the "true faith" was; others were genuinely receptive to the instruction they received from persons they regarded as more expert in theology than themselves. Some believed they had a duty to obey their rulers in religious as in other matters, and others succumbed simply to pressure. As long as confessional orthodoxies remained imprecise, and as long as religious commitments remained fluid, inducing people of different beliefs to worship together in the same church was a realistic goal.

One of the places where these circumstances prevailed was the northern Netherlands, where as late as the 1570s and 1580s both committed Calvinists and militant Catholics formed small minorities. In those years, clergy in Leiden, Gouda, Utrecht, and other Dutch cities attempted to reform their churches in such a way as to accommodate as many members as possible of the local community. The most successful was Hubert Duifhuis.

Duifhuis was pastor of one of Utrecht's parish churches, the Jacobskerk, when in 1576 the city joined the Revolt against Spain. Over the next two years, he stopped hearing confessions or performing masses. Denouncing the veneration of images and other "superstitions," he had altars and other paraphernalia of Catholic worship removed. Taking off his surplice, he ceased to administer any sacraments other than baptism and Communion, which he offered the laity in both kinds. And he introduced a vernacular liturgy that had as its centerpiece a sermon based on Gospel texts. Essentially, the new Jacobskerk was a Protestant institution, and Duifhuis spoke of Catholics as a distinct group—one he wished, by gentle means, to win over. In other respects, though, the church was aconfessional. Duifhuis subscribed to no confession of faith and taught no catechism. He did not ask parents to promise they would raise their infants in a particular way. He refused to establish a consistory, so the church had no system of ecclesiastic discipline. He put no value on uniformity, rejecting the authority of the presbyteries and synods Dutch Calvinists were establishing. And most crucially, he offered Communion to all comers without examining them or asking them to make a public profession of faith. No one was excluded from the Lord's Supper in the Jacobskerk. This infuriated Utrecht's Calvinists, who denounced the Jacobskerk as a "dissolute, Libertine church." For Duifhuis, though, the kind of discipline Calvinist ministers and elders wished to exercise smacked of the same clerical tyranny Catholic priests had previously exercised. It was a "remnant" of that "papal yoke" the Protestant Reformation, with its call for Christian freedom, was supposed to overthrow.[11]

Duifhuis's church was probably as comprehensive as any ever established. For almost a decade, it welcomed all Christians to Communion, regardless of their beliefs. Behind this comprehension, motivating it in large part, was a spiritualist form of piety. Inspired by the heritage of medieval mysticism, Duifhuis believed that to attain salvation Christians had to undergo an inner spiritual rebirth, achieving a communion with God so intimate that their souls were filled and replaced by God's Holy Spirit. What dogmas Christians held, what ceremonies they practiced, even what church they belonged to were irrelevant to this process. Spiritualist beliefs seem to have been widespread in the Netherlands, as was the Erasmian belief, shared by Duifhuis, that a pious Christian was someone who practiced the virtues that Christ himself exemplified in his life: humility, compassion, self-denial, and brotherly love. Such beliefs could be shared—or rejected—by members of any church. Indeed, in dismissing as unimportant all those marks of orthodoxy that Calvinists deemed so fundamental, "Libertines" repudiated confessionalism itself. Like humanism, spiritualism not only encouraged Christians to tolerate those who belonged to other churches, it inspired people of diverse doctrines to sit in church with one another.

From the beginning, the Jacobskerk had the support of Utrecht's magistrates. For them, the church appealed not only for its teachings but also because it offered a solution to their greatest dilemma: how to keep Utrechters united and maintain peace in the face of widening confessional divisions. If they could apply the model of the Jacobskerk to the entire city, they could keep all Utrechters, or at least most of them, in the same church, preserving in the post-Reformation era the old equation of civic and sacral community. That was the magistrates' ardent desire, and for a time they almost achieved it. This arrangement brought them many practical advantages, not least the control they exercised over this municipal, communal church. But Utrecht's Calvinists, just like its more militant Catholics, could never countenance such an arrangement. Refusing to recognize the Jacobskerk as a legitimate, properly reformed church, Calvinists organized their own congregation alongside it, so that from the beginning Utrecht had two rival Reformed churches. When in 1590 the Jacobskerk model was applied to all local parishes, Utrecht's Calvinists boycotted services in the city. Given the crucial role this group played in the Revolt, given their fervor and the advances their co-religionists were making elsewhere in the Republic, and given the Calvinist education the city's future ministers were receiving at Dutch universities, this anomalous local situa-

England's kings, Calvinist William III and Lutheran George I, did so. A
Tory law of 1711 banning the practice was repealed by Whigs only eight
years later.

In hindsight, the unity of Christendom looks like Humpty-Dumpty: once
shattered, it could never be put back together. Certainly after Trent, fundamental differences between Protestant and Catholic were set in stone. In
fact, the turning point came even earlier, in the year or two after the Colloquy of Regensburg, when the papal Curia repudiated Erasmian humanism
and began to condemn anything that smacked even faintly of Protestantism. In any event, Protestantism itself was irrepressibly fissile. Luther
may have taught his followers to do as he said, not as he did, but his defiance of authority set an epoch-making precedent. The "Christian freedom" he proclaimed did not mean what "freedom of conscience" means to
us today, but it did authorize individuals to repudiate the authority of tyrannical clergymen. To their outrage, Luther and other Protestant reformers discovered that they too were considered tyrants by some people.

The repeated failure of comprehension forced Europeans to face, very
reluctantly, a painful dilemma: If they could not accept one another's beliefs as valid and remain in communion, if their towns and villages, territories and countries, really were divided irreconcilably by faith, could they
still live together? The only way was through some arrangement that enabled people to belong to different churches and worship separately—in
short, "toleration." Such an arrangement did not require necessarily the
abandonment of hopes for eventual reunion. When Henri IV, for example,
issued in 1598 the Edict of Nantes, ending the French Wars of Religion, he
expressed regret that "it has not yet pleased" God to establish "one and the
same form of religion" among all his subjects.[19] Like his predecessors,
Henri framed the question as one of strategy: what war had failed to
achieve, a temporary grant of toleration could assist. As his supporter Pierre de Beloy explained to a skeptical parlement, the king intended to permit Protestant worship "until the need [for it] ceases and those who profess it are better instructed, or convinced in their consciences by the Holy
Spirit of their error and heresy."[20] Henri's sincerity (which many historians
question) is beside the point, namely that the future restoration of religious unity was one of the few justifications for toleration early modern

authorities were not ashamed to cite publicly. It even appears in the Peace of Westphalia, which in 1648 ended the Thirty Years' War and sealed, by most interpretations, the permanent religious division of the Holy Roman Empire. In fact, several clauses of the treaty declare its terms provisional "until, through God's grace, agreement is reached over religion."[21] The princes who negotiated the treaty knew well how faint prospects were for such an agreement. "Unless God . . . allowed a miracle to occur," remarked Landgrave Ernst of Hesse-Rheinfels, German Protestants and Catholics would never reunite.[22] That did not take away the princes' need to express a desire for reunion, if only as a wish whose fulfillment, by a psychological sleight of hand, they postponed into a vague, indefinite future.

Toleration—allowing people of a different faith to live peacefully in one's community—was an embarrassment. From a confessional standpoint, it was even a sin, though perhaps, as some figured, a lesser sin than the bloody alternatives. Framed as a temporary concession, part of a longterm strategy for the restoration of unity, it might be acceptable. But to the extent that it entailed the abandonment of hopes for the triumph of the one true faith, it clashed directly with the eschatological teachings of all the Christian churches. Until Christianity itself changed, toleration would suffer from a basic illegitimacy. Its very forms would be shaped by the embarrassment and denial of those who practiced it.

shrine became a symbol of Austria's devotion to the Catholic faith and the focus of an intense cult. For Catholic pilgrims, who followed the same route to it from Vienna as Protestants had once taken, a visit to the Holy Sepulchre in Hernals became an act of atonement for the mass apostasy their countrymen had committed. It was a "cathartic ritual" intended to wipe out the memory of that earlier abomination.[6]

However, it proved far more difficult to extirpate Austrian Protestantism in practice than in symbol. Habsburg officials reserved their harshest measures for the Inner and Upper lands, where "Reformation Commissions" toured the country, requiring inhabitants to confess, take Communion, and swear to maintain Catholic orthodoxy, on pain of banishment. Troops were quartered on the recalcitrant (a technique Louis XIV would later use, with devastating effectiveness, on France's Huguenots). By contrast, in Lower Austria the Counter-Reformation proceeded piecemeal and relatively peacefully. This was because the Protestant nobles of Lower Austria had wisely secured their religious freedoms in writing, and because most had remained loyal to the Habsburgs. They retained their estates and continued to live on them. They could not organize Protestant services, though, even for their own families. To worship, they had to travel to Hungary or Germany. Of course, it was impractical for most to undertake such an expedition weekly or even monthly, but for baptisms, weddings, and each year at Easter for their annual Communion some made the journey, especially to Pressburg or Ödenburg, just across the Hungarian border. This was another form of Auslauf.

All in all, some hundred thousand Austrian Protestants went permanently into exile, or so their descendants have claimed; in any event, there was a large-scale emigration. The only large groups of Protestants to remain by the 1680s were peasants and miners who inhabited the uplands of Styria, Carintha, and Salzburg. These groups had no ministers, organized no services, and when necessary made a show of being Catholics. But as officials eventually discovered, in secret they maintained a fierce loyalty to Protestantism. Some of these mountaineers—the young male farmworkers among them—were perforce great travelers, descending each summer to the flatlands of southern Germany, where they found seasonal employment. There, in the environs of Regensburg and Nuremberg, they could practice their religion freely and buy books such as Arndt's *True Christianity* and Luther's catechisms. These they smuggled back with them to their alpine homes, providing material that nourished the Protestant identities of their families and preserved a knowledge of the faith. Crossing and recrossing borders, they were migrant worshippers as well as workers.

Early modern Europe was crisscrossed by such borders, political boundaries that the Protestant and Catholic Reformations turned into religious frontiers. Yet, as the story of Hernals and Austrian Protestantism shows, these borders did not hermetically seal communities—towns, villages, noble estates, sovereign territories—off from one another. On the contrary, they were invariably porous. Like many other frontiers in history, early modern borders were "areas of exchange" as much as they were sites of confrontation.[7] People, books, and ideas all crossed them. This fact had deep and paradoxical implications for the history of religious toleration.

On the one hand, Protestantism could never be fully suppressed in Vienna as long as it was practiced at Hernals and other nearby estates. Later, Protestant nobles could continue to live in Lower Austria, and Protestant mountain peasants could have their faith continually renewed, because there were officially Protestant lands to which they could travel periodically. The very existence of a neighboring jurisdiction or land with a different official religion made it impossible to eradicate religious dissent entirely. That was of course frustrating, and not just for authorities: ordinary conforming Christians often took offense at the presence of dissenters in their midst and feared its consequences if God too should take offense. Yet wasn't there also something convenient about this state of affairs? For half a century, Austrian officials could not exclude Protestants from Vienna— but they could, for the most part, prevent them from worshipping in it. If Hernals and other places of worship had not lain just outside the city, Protestants would surely have agitated harder for adequate places of worship within it. The existence of Hernals made it easier for authorities to suppress Protestant worship, if not belief, in Vienna itself. It removed the Protestant rituals that Catholics found offensive to a space outside the city walls. Similarly, while Auslauf and seasonal migration ensured the survival of Protestant belief in parts of Austria, they obviated, to some degree, the need for Protestant worship within its borders. And what would have happened if no land of refuge had existed to which Protestant exiles could flee? If they had stayed put, wouldn't authorities have found it even more difficult to win Austria back for Catholicism? Might not Protestants, Catholics, or both have resorted more to violence? Of course, no one knows the

Switzerland, law and custom dictated that a great many decisions be made by majority vote. In most cases, the canton itself was defined as the principal unit of community, the "Gemeinde," and cantonwide votes were held. In Appenzell, however, a citizens' assembly resolved in 1525 to leave the decision in local hands: "In every parish a vote shall be taken which faith the inhabitants wish to accept, and whichever faith gets the majority of hands, the minority shall accept it."[10] Similarly, in the Swiss Grisons each parish was left to determine for itself which faith (Reformed or Catholic) it would practice. Apparently the villagers of Fellers counted every inhabitant, male and female, young and old: the village embraced Catholicism only after the birth of a baby to a Catholic family broke an earlier tie. In Transylvania, following a 1564 law, parishes chose their faith similarly by vote, with the majority winning use of the old parish church.

In most parts of Europe, towns and villages could not determine their own religious fates without deferring to a higher authority. But those that did contributed to the creation of a religious map so detailed and intricate that it defies plotting. Europe's religious borders ran not just between major states, but around petty principalities, enclaves and exclaves, cantons, noble estates, cities, ecclesiastic immunities, and even, in a few regions, parishes. These borders divided European society in a new and fundamental way. At the same time, they created a vast inner frontier land where religious contact and exchange were inevitable.

Babylon or Exile

In 1532 a gold miner named Martin Lodinger, from the town of Gastein in the archbishopric of Salzburg, wrote to Martin Luther posing what was to become an urgent question of conscience in the post-Reformation era. Lodinger was an evangelical living in a territory whose Catholic ruler was determined to suppress Protestantism, by force if necessary. Lodinger wished to take Communion in both kinds and, as he wrote Luther, he felt certain the Catholic form of the sacrament was wrong. Yet that was the only form available in his land. What should he do? In response, Luther suggested that Lodinger might content himself by abstaining from the sacrament entirely, in a physical sense, receiving it only "spiritually." But the solution Luther favored was emigration: "You must leave the land, and seek another place, as Christ said: Fly to another town, if they persecute you in one, for here there is no other way."[11] Over the following centuries, hundreds of thousands of religious dissenters would follow this advice and "flee Babylon."[12]

Dissenters who faced persecution had in theory a range of options. They could work to change the official religion of their homeland by persuasion and proselytizing. But what if that strategy stood no realistic chance of success? Was it then a religious duty to accept martyrdom and die trying? The "rhetorical thrust" of most post-Reformation literature was to answer in the affirmative.[13] Yet in private few church leaders were so uncompromising, so compassionless, as to condemn to damnation those who did not make the ultimate sacrifice. Dissenters could rebel and seek to change the religious establishment by force. But this flew in the face of every teaching (including the fourth commandment, as commonly interpreted), every custom, law, and habit of thought that invested rulers not just with power but with legitimate, God-given authority. To violate these required a justification that, even in the midst of Europe's religious wars, went beyond a denunciation of heresy. Calvin and other leaders of the Reformed churches urged followers to organize secretly their own, illegal services. But this too was a form of disobedience, condemned as such by Luther, and its risks did not fall only on individuals: for the heresy or treason of a member, whole families could be dishonored and stripped of their property. As an alternative, Luther suggested that dissenters abstain from attending religious services, in particular Communion. But repressive regimes required their subjects to attend services and take Communion, inventing new bureaucratic mechanisms to enforce these requirements. Thus in Lodinger's Salzburg, many Protestants got away with absenting themselves in the sixteenth century but they could no longer do so in the seventeenth. Instead they fell back on a more desperate recourse, dissimulation.

In the Middle Ages, Waldensian and Lollard heretics had survived persecution by conforming to the Catholic Church publicly while maintaining their own beliefs in secret. Some Spanish Jews forcibly converted to Catholicism had behaved similarly. With the Reformation, dissimulation spread, especially among would-be Protestants in Catholic lands. Perhaps some interpreted the concept of salvation by faith alone as justifying this behavior. Others, moved by a mystical piety, denied that rituals and church institutions had any bearing on salvation. On these grounds, a group called the Family of Love embraced dissimulation wholeheartedly. Calvin, vehemently denouncing it, called it Nicodemism, after the biblical character who feared to visit Jesus except at night. Used in a derogatory sense, the label stuck. In the mountains of Salzburg and Upper Austria, Nicodemism became a way of life for generations of dissenters who read and prayed at home as Protestants but were prepared, if necessary, to swear they would "live and die" in the Catholic faith. Contrary to Luther's advice, some were more than willing to receive the physical sacraments from a Catholic priest, if he was their only means of access to them. Even so, there were certain things none would do, like recite the rosary or wear a scapulary. When authorities began in the 1680s to confront them with these further demands, some refused. Those who did saw their children taken from them, to be raised as Catholics, and were banished from the territory.

Between Babylon and exile the choice could be excruciating. Travel could be impossible for the aged, the sick, or disabled. Young children might not survive its rigors. Were parents to subject their offspring to its risks? Could dutiful children leave behind elderly parents? How were the poor to acquire the cash necessary to set out on a long journey in the first place? Where would emigrants find a community that would take them in, and how would they earn a living there? Merchants could usually settle in a new city and continue their trade. Artisans had a tougher time, but at least they had skills, tools, and perhaps a bit of capital they could take with them. What remained, though, for peasants who left their fields? Except under extreme duress, they did not.

Despite countless difficulties, emigration for religious reasons was a mass phenomenon in early modern Europe. Acting as a powerful demographic force, persecution drove dissenters to seek refuge, temporarily or permanently, in other lands. Some dissenters left home more or less of their own accord, preempting difficulties by moving to a place where their faith was permitted. Others fled to escape imminent peril, while still others were expelled. Today we might distinguish between emigrants, refugees, and exiles, but contemporaries—those who allowed them to settle in their midst—did not, calling them all "strangers." As is well known, the phenomenon was not limited to Christians: perhaps a hundred thousand Jews left Spain in 1492 rather than accept baptism. The single largest emigration was of Moriscos, nominal Christians of Muslim ancestry and belief, three hundred thousand of whom were deported, mostly to North Africa, by

Spanish authorities between 1609 and 1614. An equal number of Huguenots probably fled France after the 1685 revocation of the Edict of Nantes, but only over decades: two hundred thousand in the 1680s and 1690s, another hundred thousand in the eighteenth century. Habsburg lands produced more than their share of Christian as well as non-Christian emigrants. When the Spanish army reconquered the southern provinces of the Netherlands in the 1580s, up to 150,000 people departed, leaving Antwerp and other cities depopulated; most ended up settling in the Dutch Republic. It has been suggested that an equal number of Protestants fled Bohemia, mostly to Saxony or Poland, in the wake of their disastrous defeat in the Thirty Years' War. Up to a hundred thousand may have left Austria as the Counter-Reformation progressed there, moving to Hungary or southern Germany. Twenty thousand Protestants were driven from Salzburg in 1731–1732, when the archbishop's government cracked down on the remaining crypto-Protestants of his territory; seven districts, including Lodinger's Gastein, were left almost empty. Protestant lands did not produce as many emigrants as Catholic ones, with the exception of Britain, which used its American colonies to absorb many of them; some 21,000 English Puritans fled there in the 1620s to 1640s. This list, including only the largest migrations, should leave no doubt that some rulers were prepared to cause massive upheaval and inflict terrible suffering in order to rid their lands of dissenters. On this point, our modern conventional wisdom is wrong: the presence of large religious minorities did not, in itself, make toleration a practical necessity.

To be sure, rulers—urban magistrates as well as princes—rarely lost sight of the economic cost of emigration. They counted the number of people working the land and producing goods as assets that increased the wealth of their state and society; John Toland called them "the true riches and power of any country."[14] This equation became a point of dogma in the mercantilist theories that gained currency around the middle of the seventeenth century, when it became commonplace to ascribe the extraordinary prosperity of the Dutch Republic to the tolerant welcome it extended to immigrants of all faiths. By the same token, Spain's decline from its position as one of Europe's great powers was attributed partly to the economic loss it suffered from the expulsion of its Jews and Moriscos. Concern to avoid economic loss is one reason Portugal's King Manuel did not imitate his Spanish in-laws in 1497 by expelling the Jews from his king-

strained. In short, one could eliminate the offending acts rather than the person.

Moreover, one did not have to wipe the acts, any more than the person, from the face of the earth. To be sure, the Christian confessions taught their adherents to hope for, and eventually expect, the triumph of their faith throughout the world. All Christians had a notional duty to promote this goal, and at certain moments—the 1570s and 1580s in western Europe, the 1620s and 1630s in the empire—both rulers and people translated their eschatological hopes and fears into violent action. But in general, what Christians felt primary responsibility for was not Christendom as a whole but their own community. Perhaps they did not escape all culpability, but they did not feel personally implicated in what heretics did on the other side of a border, beyond the boundaries of their own town, village, estate, or territory. However those boundaries were defined, they marked the spatial limits of a spiritual community, a corpus Christianum. To excise the offending behavior from that body, one only had to abolish it within those limits. That is precisely what Auslauf accomplished: it removed dissenting worship from communal space. While leaving the community mixed in its beliefs, it preserved it, with regard to worship, as the exclusive enclave of a single religion.

Unlike emigration, Auslauf enabled people of different faiths to live together in the same towns and villages. That makes it, by our definition, a bona fide form of toleration. It can be documented as early as 1528, when Reformed ministers preached just beyond the border of the Swiss Rheintal. By the 1530s, Catholics in Strasbourg, Ulm, and Biberach were traveling to attend services in nearby villages. In different periods and varied forms, dissenters can be found performing Auslauf in Switzerland, Germany, Austria, Poland, Transylvania, Hungary, the northern and southern Netherlands, France, and Ireland. It was not that the inhabitants of these lands copied or learned from one another: rather, facing a common predicament, they lighted on a common solution.

Like other forms of toleration, Auslauf entailed an agreement between dissenters, authorities, and members of the official church. Occasionally the agreement was written in a contract or ratified in an exchange of verbal promises. In 1647, for example, the Bishop of Würzburg, Johan Philipp von Schönborn (one of the architects of the Peace of Westphalia), gave written permission for Lutherans in Kitzingen to attend services in the neighboring territory of Ansbach. In so doing he admonished the town's Catholic citizens "in no wise to block or stop [the Lutherans] at the gates at their departure and return, but rather always to let them come and go untroubled to their services, as long as those who attend the services show themselves to be modest and obedient."[17] Even when the agreement was implicit, its terms can be inferred from the behavior of the parties. Dissenters agreed not to worship in their own town or village, but to undertake the trouble and expense of traveling to services. Authorities agreed not to persecute them for doing so or for their beliefs. For their part, conforming Christians agreed not to take offense, or at least not to lash out with violence, so long as the monopoly of their church over worship in their town or village was not challenged. Auslauf also required the cooperation of a neighboring community, who had to permit the dissenters to join them for worship. It was a delicate arrangement requiring the cooperation of many parties, and predictably it did not always command everyone's assent.

How Auslauf worked in practice varied considerably. It might be very ad hoc, like the so-called hedge preaching (Figure 6.2) that swept the Netherlands in the summer of 1566. This was one of the first episodes in the Dutch Revolt against Spain. With the authority of the Habsburg government in Brussels collapsing, Protestant preachers—many of them untrained laymen—seized an opportunity to proclaim the Gospel publicly. Preaching outside the walls of cities, in nearby woods and fields, they attracted crowds of urban folk who streamed out through city gates by the hundreds and even thousands to hear them. No one instructed the first preachers to avoid the cities proper, nor did local magistrates give them permission to preach. But by tacit agreement, magistrates did not obstruct these illegal assemblies so long as they were held outside city limits. The agreement held for over two months, as the preaching spread from province to province, the assemblies growing larger and better organized. Eventually Calvinists grew discontented with hedge preaching alone, and in August they began to attack city churches, stripping them of images, altars, and other Catholic objects, and seizing them for their own use. At a crucial time, though, Auslauf gave their movement space in which to grow, and as long as it continued, no violence occurred.

Of course, open-air services were rudimentary at best. They might do in a pinch, either as a temporary arrangement or in response to heavy persecution, when the only way dissenters could worship might be to gather se-

cretly in an obscure location. That is what many Huguenots did in southern France in the eighteenth century, and what some Irish Catholics did in the seventeenth and eighteenth. In the days of Cromwell's regime, in the 1650s, the tradition developed in Ireland of the "mass-rock," a large stone used as primitive rural altar. In Silesia, too, where from the 1650s the Habsburgs made worship increasingly difficult for Protestants, Lutheran "bush preachers" would slip in from neighboring Saxony, giving sermons by moonlight in forests and upland glens. More commonly, though, Auslauf involved travel to a nearby town or village where one's faith was exercised in a proper church, or at least in a secure and suitable building. In the Grisons in the sixteenth century, Christians who found themselves out-voted in their own village simply went to services in a neighboring one. In Transylvania, minorities had a legal right to do the same. Such Sunday commuting was obviously practical where official religions varied from parish to parish. It was well suited also to regions like Little Poland, near Cracow, whose swarm of petty gentry lorded over tiny estates. But Auslauf was eminently feasible also in regions like Swabia and Franconia, with their intricate patchwork of sovereign territories. By the late sixteenth century, Auslauf was a pervasive practice in these parts of the Holy Roman Empire. Calvinists in the bishopric of Speyer, for example, commuted on Sundays to neighboring villages in the Calvinist Palatinate; Catholics in the Palatinate made the same trip, only in reverse. For Lutherans who lived in the Catholic imperial city of Weil der Stadt, all roads led to orthodoxy: their town, with its tiny territory, formed an enclave surrounded by the Lutheran duchy of Württemberg, where the urbanites became regular visitors. The princes and diplomats who negotiated the Peace of Westphalia were simply formalizing a long-standing practice when in 1648 they granted those who lived as dissidents in one German territory a constitutional right to attend services in amenable neighboring ones. Legitimized and extended, Auslauf remained common in the empire to the end of the Old Regime.

So large-scale was Auslauf in some parts of Europe that special churches had to be built to accommodate those practicing it. Lutherans in Silesia, for

Figure 6.2 (opposite page). Protestant hedge preaching outside Antwerp in 1566. Detail of engraving by Frans Hogenberg, circa 1566. Courtesy of Museum Plantin-Moretus / Antwerp Print Collection.

example, could scarcely make do with occasional bush sermons. Thousands of them, from the 1650s, trekked regularly across the border to attend services in Saxony, and a string of churches was constructed along the border for their use. Thanks to Swedish intervention, a treaty known as the Convention of Altranstadt guaranteed in 1707 the rights of Silesia's Lutherans to perform this Auslauf, which the Habsburgs had attempted to halt. The county of Lingen offered a similar picture. Catholics formed a majority of the population in this German territory, yet from 1674 they found their ruler, William III of Orange (who was simultaneously stadholder in the Dutch Republic and later king of England), taking drastic steps to suppress their faith, requiring them to attend Reformed services and going so far as to bar them, under some circumstances, from inheriting property. In response, Lingen's Catholics began to travel to the neighboring bishoprics of Münster and Osnabrück, where, along the border, churches were built to accommodate them. The need to perform Auslauf could even shape settlement patterns. When in 1688 the Duke of Württemberg gave permission for Huguenots and Waldensians to take refuge in his Lutheran territory, he stipulated that they could worship only outside it. By mutual agreement, the refugees established colonies close to the borders of the duchy.

All this raises a key question: From what space did Auslauf remove dissenting worship? In the eyes of conforming Christians, what domain had to be kept pure? Since official religions could vary only between legal jurisdictions, it is hardly surprising to find dissenters commuting between jurisdictions; that is simply what they had to do to find churches where their own faith was practiced. Inevitably, most Auslauf involved traveling to a different territory, estate, or parish. Such commuting also had practical advantages: by utilizing the ecclesiastic infrastructure at hand in a nearby locale, groups avoided having to provide for themselves a place of worship, a priest or minister, and the appurtenances necessary for services. These could be very expensive, and the smaller the group of dissenters, the more heavily such costs would weigh on them. For their part, authorities might feel their duty discharged if they removed the offending behavior from the territory over which they had jurisdiction.

Ordinary Christians did not attach the same importance to legal jurisdictions as did authorities. In some instances, intolerant crowds pursued dissenters across borders, attacking their places of worship. In 1716, for ex-

ample, a group of sixty to seventy students from the Catholic city of Cologne went to Frechen, in the Duchy of Jülich, where many of Cologne's
Calvinists worshipped; there they destroyed a church and parsonage that
were being constructed. In other cases, religious majorities submitted petitions asking local authorities to assign dissenters sites for worship; by
definition, such sites were within the authorities' jurisdiction. In 1576, for
example, Catholics in the French town of Châlons-sur-Marne asked magistrates to restrict Protestant worship to some place outside the city gates.
Even authorities did not always care as much about jurisdiction as they did
about the symbolic meaning of sites and the social interactions that were
likely to arise from their use. This can be seen in the Netherlands, where in
1566 some magistrates permitted hedge preaching on sites that lay within
the jurisdiction, or "freedom," of their cities. Such preaching was always,
though, kept outside city walls.

For urban folk, the walls that encompassed their city had immense importance. Iconic like church towers, embracing like church bells, they were
sources of pride as well as security, defining symbolically the boundaries of
their community. What took place within those walls involved every member of the community, at least indirectly—or so it was felt; what transpired
outside them, even in a suburb, did not. Just as morally dubious activities
did not stain a community as darkly, so the deviant rituals of dissenters did
not threaten as much the purity of a community, or challenge as directly its
religious establishment, when performed outside its walls. The pattern was
very notable in France: it was the space within city walls that constituted
the "arena of conflict" par excellence between Catholics and Huguenots,
and the most urgent of all Catholic demands was that Protestant worship
be removed from that space.[18] The French crown paid close attention to
this Catholic sensitivity in the edicts by which it attempted, first to forestall, then to end, the religious wars. In the Edict of Nantes, Huguenots
were permitted "by concession" to worship in the suburbs of two towns
per administrative district. As authorities across Europe were keenly aware,
for practical as well as symbolic reasons dissenting worship was less likely
to trigger clashes if it took place outside city walls, removed from the centers of social interaction where conforming Christians were most likely to
encounter it. Moreover, the less centrally located the site was, the less convenient it would be for dissenters and the smaller the group that would
likely attend. For all the same reasons that processions, holidays, and fu-

nerals sparked violence, removing dissenting rituals from communal space made them less incendiary.

Still, in the tacit agreement between dissenters and conforming Christians there remained a fundamental ambiguity: How far precisely did the former have to go to be outside the latter's sacred space? This was a matter for negotiation—a negotiation often conducted through actions rather than words. Dissenters always wanted to worship close to home; their fellow citizens preferred their rites far away. In practice, dissenters picked places of worship or were assigned ones by authorities, then their fellow citizens either protested or did not. The case of Paris offers an example. To placate the city's militant Catholics and in recognition of the city's symbolic import as capital of France, the Edict of Nantes stipulated that Huguenots could not worship within five leagues—fifteen statute miles—of the city. Henri IV assigned them accordingly a site in the village of Ablon where they could build a "temple." Huguenots could not possibly make it there and back in a day, and eventually they convinced Henri that Ablon was impractical. In 1606, therefore, the king permitted them to build a temple in Charenton, which lay just under two leagues from the capital. Whereas previously there had been no violence, Henri's decision precipitated a riot: the very next Sunday a Catholic crowd attacked the Huguenots as they returned to town through St. Anthony's Gate. Not coincidentally, the violence occurred precisely where Huguenots penetrated the inner sanctum of the city. Clearly, though, Catholics felt that even Charenton impinged on its sacral space.

Distant sites could make weekly worship impossible, but for more occasional rites dissenters sometimes traveled far. Catholics in the Dutch Republic, for example, made long trips to participate in processions. Forbidden to conduct such public rituals at home, they crossed the border into the Southern Netherlands or journeyed to one of the Catholic enclaves within the Republic's territory, such as the Land of Ravenstein. These enclaves were bursting with Catholic clergy, after entire monasteries and convents fled to them in 1629 when the Dutch army captured northern Brabant. Bringing their precious images and relics with them, these clerical refugees established new shrines or, as in Uden and Handel, took over old ones (they also set up Latin schools where Dutch Catholics sent their boys to study—another sort of travel that might be considered a form of Auslauf). The most popular of all pilgrimage destinations for Dutch

Catholics from the late seventeenth through the eighteenth century was Kevelaer. Lay Catholics founded confraternities devoted to Our Lady of Kevelaer and, as groups, made their way to her shrine there on the chief Marian holidays. Traveling by barge and foot, they went as quietly and discreetly as possible as long as they were in republican territory. But once they crossed the border into the Southern Netherlands, they pulled out their banners and traversed the rest of the route in the form of a procession, with hearty singing and ostentatious praying. Such annual processions offered Dutch Catholics a liberating escape from the restrictions they experienced at home.

Auslauf, then, could take a variety of forms. It could be ad hoc or institutionalized, frequent or occasional, short- or long-distance, and could provide for a variety of dissenters' religious and social needs. As a mechanism for accommodating religious dissent, it functioned without regard to the beliefs of the groups involved. As dissenters, Catholics, Calvinists, and Lutherans all performed it, while as establishments they all tolerated it. Other groups too were accommodated in this way. Socinians in the Baltic port of Danzig (until they were expelled in 1643) performed regular Auslauf to the villages of Busków and Straszyn. From Hamburg, Mennonites trekked a few miles west to Altona, on an estuary of the river Elbe. Founded by the counts of Schaumburg and belonging, from 1640, to the kings of Denmark, Altona was intended to attract commerce away from Hamburg by offering non-Lutheran merchants a more tolerant home. Ironically, Altona ended up aiding Hamburg's growth, helping it to become by 1700 the chief commercial center in northern Germany while remaining a bastion of Lutheran orthodoxy. One usually expects such commercial metropolises to incline toward toleration. Hamburg did not, but thanks to Altona, Christian dissenters could worship in dignity and comfort while living and doing business in the city. Alternatively, they could live in Altona, near their places of worship, and travel into Hamburg to conduct business. Enough dissenters and Jews did this to transform the former fishing village into a veritable suburb. This pattern, which resembled the commuting of the modern suburban resident, was the opposite of Auslauf. The logic behind it, though, was the same. In similar fashion, Lutheran Nuremberg developed two satellite communities: Fürth, populated by Jews, and Erlangen, by Huguenots. Lutheran Frankfurt had a similarly symbiotic relationship with Hanau, as did Catholic Cologne in the eighteenth century with Mülheim, in the county of Berg. By virtue of their satellites, these major cities could have their cake and eat it too, maintaining religious uniformity internally while profiting from people of other faiths.

What made Auslauf, in all its forms, an effective solution to the problem of religious dissent was that it respected borders even as it violated them. Every time dissenters commuted to or from their place of worship, they accepted a distinction between two spaces, one where their religion was forbidden and another where it was permitted. Through their travel, they conceded the dearest wish of conforming Christians, that their own form of worship be the only one practiced within the borders of their community. As long as those borders were respected, conforming Christians were usually willing to live alongside dissenters and even to allow them to practice an aberrant faith. Every time they allowed dissenters to pass peacefully, without harassment, out and back again on a journey whose purpose everyone knew, they were practicing a form of toleration. Officials did the same when they suppressed dissenting worship within their jurisdictions but allowed Auslauf. True, they had little effective control over territorial borders, which bore little resemblance to the borders of modern states: there were no sentries or customs inspectors ranged along them. Difficult as it is for modern states to control their borders effectively, early modern ones lacked any apparatus for doing so. Cities, though, were enclosed by walls: magistrates could have ordered guards to note the names of those coming and going through the gates on Sundays and holidays, as did those of Ulm in the 1530s to 1540s. They could even have closed the gates: as the Calvinist consistory of Bergen op Zoom noted in frustration, it was a conscious decision on magistrates' part not to do so. In the Grisons, village officials had the power to strip dissenters of their citizenship if they performed Auslauf, but few exercised it. Through their inaction, officials and conforming Christians colluded with dissenters in affirming the limits of communal space.

Like emigration, Auslauf was based on a paradox: it enabled communities to achieve uniformity of worship thanks to another community with a different form of worship. All the parties who colluded in Auslauf accepted, at least implicitly, the existence of that other community with its other form of worship. In other words, they accepted religious variety, so long as it was organized in accord with the principle of cuius regio or one of its variants. This point is crucial: accepting religious variety between communities helped make uniformity possible within communities. Cities, for example, did not eliminate dissent, they merely shunted it off to a space outside their walls. In their case too, local uniformity was achieved by relying on a wider pluralism. Viewed in this light, cuius regio appears not as the epitome of intolerance, as sometimes portrayed, but as a basis for a limited form of toleration.

Auslauf addressed the problem of religious dissent by regulating where dissenters worshipped. It involved an agreement: dissenters could believe as they wished, as long as they did not challenge the local monopoly of the official church. The agreement was ambiguous, however, on how far that monopoly extended, and thus how far dissenters had to travel. This ambiguity, and the jockeying for advantage that dissenters and conforming Christians engaged in, produced violence: conforming Christians pronounced their verdict on sites they found unacceptable by attacking dissenters or burning down their edifices. The agreement had another ambiguity as well. By removing dissenting worship from communal space, Auslauf was meant to create a semblance of religious unity, and through that semblance to preserve the traditional equation of civic and sacral community. But the semblance was never perfect, for Auslauf was not invisible. When dissenters traveled to services in large groups, they could have a formidable presence en route. Recall the scene in Vienna: thousands of Protestants packed the main roads, passing through the city gates like a procession. On the way, they sang Luther's hymn, "Maintain us, Lord, within thy word, / And fend off murd'rous Pope and Turk."[19] Their Auslauf made as strong a statement as did any public ritual. It was itself a form of demonstration, a collective protest against Catholicism. Auslauf was not usually as aggressive as this, yet it always had an ambiguity, for even as dissenters respected the local monopoly of the official church, the very travel they performed demonstrated also their rejection of that church.

For all these limitations and contradictions, Auslauf was one of the most common arrangements for the practice of toleration in early modern Europe. It owed its success to a little-noticed aspect of religious life: by and large, people found dissenting religious practices tolerable as long as they occurred outside communal space. That fact made another arrangement possible as well.

SEVEN

Fictions of Privacy

Our Lord in the Attic

In Amsterdam's red light district, on the corner of the Oudezijds Voorburgwal and the Heintje Hoekssteeg, there stands today a unique museum. Despite the banner hanging in front, tourists—on foot or in boats—often pass right by it, mistaking it for an ordinary house. Tall and thin, in the manner typical of Dutch residential architecture, the building dates from circa 1629 and was extensively rebuilt in 1661–1663, when its owner, a stocking merchant named Jan Hartman, had a figure of a hart set atop the front façade and renamed the building after himself. A drawing from around 1805 (Figure 7.1) shows how it looked, with three bays and a neck gable. Its exposed right flank reveals the unusual depth of the structure, which consists of a canal house plus two "rear houses" facing the alley, all under a single roof and connected internally. Rows of windows indicate five stories; steps lead down to a basement door, while a staircase parallel to the front façade gives access to the main door. Entering, modern visitors to the Amstelkring Museum find themselves in a well-preserved seventeenth-century merchant's house. Hartman used the airy front room, with its double tier of windows and high ceiling, to display his wares, the one behind it to keep his books. Following the museum's suggested route, visitors work their way upward, passing through a series of domestic chambers, among them the *Sael* (sitting room), a pristine model of neoclassicism and monument to Hartman's social pretensions. Only when they reach the third floor do they see what inspired a group of prominent Dutch Catholics in 1887 to purchase the building and make it a museum. There they find themselves suddenly in a church.

It was named "Our Lord in the Attic" *(Ons' Lieve Heer op Solder)* in the nineteenth century; before, it was simply called the Hart, or the Haantje. Invisible from the street, this place of Roman Catholic worship could accommodate over 150 congregants. To reach it, worshippers entered a side door facing the alley and then climbed some thirty stairs. Narrow and deep, its main hall occupies almost the entire third floor; large rectangular holes in the fourth and fifth floors create two sets of galleries (Figure 7.2). Along the side walls are two pews reserved for prominent men. At one end

Figure 7.1. House called "The Hart," corner of Oudezijds Voorburgwal and Heintje Hoekssteeg, Amsterdam, exterior view. It is the farthest right of the three houses. Detail from J. L. van Beek after C. van Waardt, *De Bloei der R. C. Kerk te Amsterdam*, etching, circa 1805. Courtesy of the Amsterdam City Archives.

of the hall stands the main altar, on it a rosewood tabernacle, behind it an altarpiece set in a high baroque frame rising two stories high. The painting, which dates from around 1716, is a *Baptism of Christ in the Jordan* by Jacob de Wit; formerly it hung for only part of the liturgical year, taking turns on display with several other altarpieces. Inside the base of the altar frame's left column nestles a small pulpit, built in the late eighteenth century, pivoting out into the left aisle for use. Behind the altar frame is a door to an ancillary chapel; opposite it, on the first gallery level, an organ.

The Hart is one of the best preserved examples of what the Dutch call a *schuilkerk,* or clandestine church. In its day, it had counterparts throughout the northern Netherlands. In Amsterdam alone, Catholics had twenty of these illegal places of worship in 1700 and Mennonites six; at least four other groups had one each. In Utrecht there were fifteen: eleven Catholic, two Mennonite, one Lutheran, one Remonstrant. As early as 1620 Haarlem had eleven: seven Catholic, three Mennonite, and one Lutheran. In certain towns, groups perceived as foreigners had splendid places of worship that were not at all clandestine, such as Amsterdam's Portuguese synagogue, built in 1675, or the eighteenth-century Lutheran church in Middelburg, whose congregation consisted largely of German immigrants. Non-Calvinists of native descent, though, worshipped overwhelmingly in schuilkerken. In the Generality Lands—the southern strip of territory captured by the Dutch army that belonged to no one of the seven provinces—the large majority of the population, being Catholic, relied on schuilkerken for services.

Buildings like the Hart played a crucial role in the religious life of the Dutch Republic. For political reasons, the Calvinist or Reformed Church emerged from the Revolt against Spain as the official church of the Republic, with unique powers and privileges. Religious dissenters, however, enjoyed a de facto tolerance that made Dutch society religiously the most diverse and pluralistic in seventeenth-century Europe. The schuilkerk was the chief accommodation, or arrangement, whereby dissenters worshipped in what was officially a Calvinist country. Behind closed doors, they operated churches with permanent clergy and regular services, in violation of scores of placards; what harassment they suffered from authorities was sporadic and local, and in any event dropped sharply over time. Moreover, the secrecy in which these churches operated was never very strict. Neighbors and even strangers knew about their existence, and magistrates often had a significant, if informal, say in the appointment of their pastors. For this reason a few scholars reject the very use of the term *schuilkerk*, which goes back only to the nineteenth century, when Catholics, caught up in their emancipation movement, exaggerated the oppression under which their ancestors lived.

If schuilkerken were not genuinely clandestine, though, why the pre-

Figure 7.2. Clandestine church in the Hart, called "Our Lord in the Attic" *(Ons' Lieve Heer op Solder).* Modern photograph by G. J. van Rooij, taken from the main floor. Courtesy of Museum Amstelkring.

tense of secrecy at all? Under what restrictions did they operate, and how were those restrictions set? Why did magistrates so often condone them? Why did neighbors of other faiths not react violently to their presence? And why did dissenters settle for such cramped, inconvenient, inglorious places of worship, leaving the privileged position of the Reformed Church essentially unchallenged? These questions gain additional urgency when one realizes that the Dutch schuilkerk had thousands of counterparts elsewhere in Europe. Such edifices went by a variety of names: house churches, prayer houses, meetinghouses, mass houses, house chapels, oratories, assembly places. They could be found in France, Austria, Switzerland, the British Isles, and the Holy Roman Empire. There, as in the Dutch Republic, they served as a crucial mechanism for the accommodation of religious dissent.

As these architectural artifacts attest, one way tolerance worked in the early modern era was through a new distinction between public and private worship. In one sense this distinction came to be set literally in stone, embodied in the architecture of buildings. In a more important sense, though, its boundaries were constantly being negotiated. Parties to this process included not just governing authorities and religious dissenters but also neighbors and fellow citizens, to whose opinion both authorities and dissenters were sensitive. Defined chiefly in symbolic and visual terms, the resulting boundaries were fundamentally different from the legal ones distinguishing public from private in the modern world. Examining them sheds new light on the broader distinction between public and private life in the early modern era.

Ultimately, the early modern distinction between public and private was as much cultural fiction as it was social reality. The schuilkerk and its equivalents were bona fide churches, places where large assemblies took place, not without the knowledge of magistrates and neighbors. Both the religious dissenters who attended their services and the orthodox who tolerated them were engaging in a pretense. Nevertheless, this pretense provided a crucial detour, as it were, around one of the chief obstacles to religious pluralism: the central role of religion in defining communal identity. By containing religious dissent within spaces demarcated as private, schuilkerken accomplished much the same trick that Auslauf did, only better: they preserved the monopoly of a community's official church in the public sphere. By maintaining a semblance of religious unity, they neutralized the threat posed by dissent to the identity and thus to the very integrity of communities.

For the Sake of Conscience

As we have seen, the purpose of Auslauf was to keep the rituals of religious dissenters outside the communal space whose purity conforming Christians were committed to preserving. By removing those rituals to a site that was peripheral, beyond city walls, or in a different community altogether, Auslauf made the rituals symbolically less offensive. It also kept conforming Christians from having to witness them. If the rituals took place outside their jurisdiction, local officials lost authority over them, so they did not have to take responsibility for either permitting or preventing them. For these groups Auslauf had a certain convenience. For dissenters, on the other hand, Auslauf could be highly inconvenient. Time-consuming at best, it exposed them to all the rigors and dangers of travel in early modern Europe. Not surprisingly, the numbers performing it went down in winter. Tender infants, complained Huguenots, died on the way to baptism. The greatest limitation of Auslauf, though, was that it required proximity. Whereas emigrants traveled great distances when necessary, even across seas, to find new homes, dissenters could commute only so far, at least for regular services. Small territories, fragmented jurisdictions, and irregular boundaries made Auslauf easier. That is why it proved such a common and enduring arrangement in central and eastern Europe, while farther west its usefulness was more limited.

Yet if dissenting religious practices were tolerable as long as they occurred outside communal space, the question arose what the boundaries of that space precisely were. Crucially, the confessional age saw the emergence of a new sort of boundary, internal rather than external, delimiting that contested space: a line was drawn around the family home separating it from the public areas surrounding it. Public and private, communal and family spheres grew more distinct, and within the latter, by common consent, dissenters were allowed some freedom of worship.

This distinction between public and private supplied the key to religious toleration in the Dutch Republic. It was a cultural distinction there, not a legal one; it does not appear as such in the Union of Utrecht (1579) or in other defining documents of the polity. These drew a different contrast, between freedom of conscience and freedom of worship. By virtue of Article 13 of the Union, all Netherlanders enjoyed freedom of conscience—but that is the only religious freedom the law ever guaranteed them. What did it entail? First, that people could believe as they wished; magistrates had no authority to examine or judge religious convictions. Second, no one could be required to attend Calvinist services; the Dutch Reformed Church would not assume the role of "established" church, with membership in it required by law. In theory, that was all freedom of conscience guaranteed. It made no provision for dissenters' acting on their beliefs by worshipping God in their own manner. In practice, though, much more ensued. The distinction between conscience and worship was recast into one between private and public piety, and the line between the two was drawn not around the conscience but around the family house.

Although never established, the Reformed Church played a unique role in Dutch society. Secular authorities sanctioned its teachings, paid its ministers, and watched over its meetings. The Church provided pastoral care to the Republic's soldiers and sailors, as it did to orphans and residents of other public institutions. It enjoyed exclusive use of the old parish churches and had an important say in educational, charitable, and marital matters. On Sundays its ministers read mundane announcements from their pulpits, and in times of crisis they led the community in penitential prayer. In their sermons, they called not just church members but the entire nation to account for its sins. The official spiritual organ of society, yet unestablished, the Dutch Reformed Church required a new label: Netherlanders called it the "public church." It monopolized public religious life in their land.

It was forbidden for non-Calvinists to challenge that monopoly. As individuals, they might manifest their piety in daily interactions with friends and neighbors, but as groups they could not assume a public profile. They could not worship in buildings that looked like churches, nor could they organize open-air services. Indeed, Dutch law defined any worship that involved a gathering of different families as a public event, a "conventicle," and proscribed it. But within the confines of their own home, it permitted individuals and single families to do as they pleased. Catholics, for instance, could say prayers or recite the hours to themselves, and for this purpose they could use any devotional paraphernalia they desired, including books, paintings, and furniture. Neither the production and sale nor the purchase and ownership of such objects was illegal. Indeed, an early seventeenth-century Catholic chronicler reported "that almost every house belonging to a Catholic had a small room used as a place of prayer, [outfitted] with a pretty little altar and devout images, where [the family] went to read and pray."[1] Thus "freedom of conscience" really meant freedom of private, domestic worship. It meant, as the States General explained in a letter of 1644, that "for the sake of conscience every inhabitant could remain unmolested in his private home and family."[2] In this context, "family" meant not a unit of kinship so much as a household—a co-resident group that could include servants, apprentices, wards, and even long-term guests, as well as relatives.

Such freedom of conscience did not license dissenters to meet in groups larger than a single family—to have, in other words, a church. In practice, however, domestic devotions served as a cover for something much more robust and elaborate, namely the schuilkerk. At their simplest, clandestine places of worship resembled the prayer room described by our chronicler. In Leiden, the Catholic sisters Van Santhorst described theirs as a cramped attic room with some candles, a picture of the Virgin, and a chest that doubled as an altar; whenever a priest came around to perform a mass, they would send word to their Catholic neighbors to attend. In the early years of the Republic, such places of worship were legion: in 1619 Catholics in The Hague met in some fifty different houses, most with room for only a few worshippers at a time; in 1641 Leiden's 3,500 Catholics met in thirty. Such dispersion maximized invisibility but made it exceedingly difficult for a small number of priests to serve the entire membership. So while the number of places of worship a denomination had in any particular locale varied with the number of its members there, it was also an inverse indicator of the degree of security it enjoyed. The trend over the seventeenth century was for consolidation to reduce the number of places of worship, as ad hoc prayer rooms and one-room chapels were replaced by larger, permanent schuilkerken with resident pastors. Catholics called these "stations," replacements for the parish churches lost with the Reformation.

In the cities, such schuilkerken typically resembled the Hart, an adapted attic able to accommodate large numbers of people, with galleries creating multiple levels and proper accoutrements for worship. A report prepared in 1643 by the provincial court of Holland noted that such "formal chapels" usually had "very expensive altars, galleries [supported] on pillars, vaulted roofs, pews, organs, musicians and all sorts of musical instruments and, in sum, everything that might be asked of a chartered chapel." They were "of so large a size and capacity that if the exercise of their religion were allowed publicly, they [the Catholics] could not ask for them to be larger or more decorous."[3] Recent reconstructions of schuilkerk interiors in Gouda and Amsterdam show that the report, though wishful in its thinking, was not indulging in hyperbole: by the middle of the seventeenth century such interiors tended already to be richly decorated. In cities, warehouses too provided readily adaptable space; in rural districts, converted barns offered enough room for huge assemblies. Most schuilkerken, though, were located inside houses.

Some schuilkerken were separate structures newly built to function as churches. Typically they were erected between rows of houses on ground formerly occupied by their back gardens. One, named Vrijburg, still stands. Used by Amsterdam's Remonstrants, it was built in 1629–1631 behind a row of houses facing the Keizersgracht. A large brick-faced structure with a wooden frame (Figure 7.3), it had an elegant neoclassical interior with nave, side aisles, and two sets of galleries supported on columns. Eventually the congregation bought most of the houses immediately surrounding it, using one as a parsonage and renting out the others. Some Catholic congregations, like St. Jan Baptist in Gouda or St. Marie in Utrecht, built entire ecclesiastic complexes by accumulating real estate in this manner, providing housing not only for their pastor but for women known as *geestelijke maagden,* or *kloppen,* who lived together in the manner of a noncloistered religious order and provided crucial services to the Catholic community.

Grand or humble, what all schuilkerken had in common was invisibility: they could not be identified as churches from any public thoroughfare. Their outsides lacked all the symbolic markers of a church: crosses, bells, icons, tower, splendor. The degree of difference between a schuilkerk and a proper church varied by denomination, depending on its attachment to such symbols: for baroque Catholicism it could not have been greater, while at the other extreme Mennonites preferred very simple, plain structures. Schuilkerken, though, not only lacked public presence as churches, they literally hid behind the façade of a different sort of structure. They did the same legally as well, appearing in deeds and mortgages as houses or barns or warehouses, and remaining the property of a private individual, usually an eminent member of the congregation. The congregation did not exist as a legal entity, nor did the larger ecclesiastic organization to which it belonged. Its physical disguise, though, not its legal one, was the most essential mark of a schuilkerk and the key to its functional success. It avoided causing "offense" or "scandal" by not signaling its presence through visual and auditory symbols. Dutch authorities who informally authorized schuilkerken always insisted on such self-effacement. A committee of Amsterdam regents was unusually specific when in 1691 it set conditions under which one of the city's Catholic congregations could abandon its old schuilkerk for a newly built one. The former had grown so dilapidated that it threatened to collapse under the weight of the crowds squeezing into it. Fearing disaster, the regents approved the move on con-

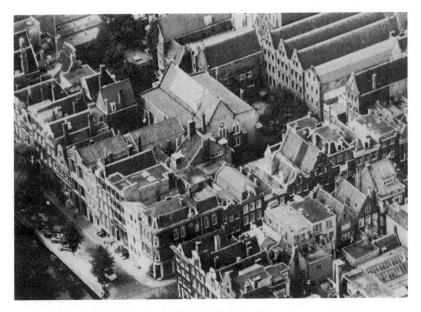

Figure 7.3. Aerial photograph of the schuilkerk Vrijburg, the former Remonstrant Church in Amsterdam, built 1629–1631, located between rows of houses. Size approximately 18 by 20 meters. Courtesy of Aviodrome Luchtfotografie, Lelystad, Holland.

dition that the pastor of the congregation, the Franciscan friar Egidius de Glabbais, agree to eleven points, including:

(4) To avoid giving any offense, [Glabbais] promises that the entrance to the new permitted assembly place shall no longer be on the Joodebreestraat but behind, on the Burgwal, where it is less offensive

(5) [Glabbais] promises not to tolerate any sleds being parked in front of the assembly place

(6) [Glabbais is] to see to it that at the end of services no one stands around in front of the assembly place waiting for another person, nor shall [he] in any manner tolerate any poor people waiting around for alms in front of the assembly place

(7) The undersigned shall take great care that his services begin and end at such times that no offense will be given by [Catholics and Reformed Protestants] meeting each other when coming from and going to church

(8) The undersigned shall see to it that Catholics not pass through the street in a troop, nor with rosary, church book, or other offensive objects apparent, when going to or coming from the permitted assembly place.[4]

All these stipulations were directed toward stripping the church of any presence *as church* in the public sphere.

Such invisibility, though, was never more than superficial. In a society that exalted and demanded intimate relations between neighbors, unusual comings and goings could scarcely escape notice, no matter how hard one tried to conceal them. And many congregations felt secure enough that they did not try too hard; at times, passersby in the street even could hear music emanating from services indoors. When compiling information for their many remonstrances to secular authorities, Calvinist ministers never had difficulty ascertaining the precise location of the schuilkerken in their community. And their remonstrances offered no surprises to authorities. In fact, everyone either knew where they were or could find out easily enough. Guidebooks, such as Philip von Zesen's *Amsterdam* (1664), even indicated their locations for the benefit of tourists, on whose itinerary they regularly figured. Jan Wagenaar gave a complete rundown of them in his 1765 description of the city.[5] Nevertheless, the pretense of privacy and domesticity embodied in the schuilkerk offered a working solution to the dilemma posed by religious diversity. Keeping dissent out of sight, stripped of any symbolic presence, preserved the monopoly of the Reformed Church over public religious life. It thus maintained a semblance, or fiction, of religious unity.

The arrangement did subject dissenters to burdens and harassments. They still had to pay "recognition fees" to local law enforcement officials, the price the latter charged for going along with the fiction. It also did not spare them from having their services raided by zealous, anxious, or extortionate officials. Particularly when the war against Spain went poorly, fears rose of a fifth column of Catholic traitors, prompting officials to crack down on Catholic worship. After the conclusion in 1609 of the Twelve Years' Truce, though, such crackdowns became less frequent, and after the Peace of Westphalia ended the long conflict in 1648, they were rare indeed. As a mechanism for the practice of religious tolerance—not the only, but the most important such mechanism in the Republic—the schuilkerk worked.

Different Domiciles

While the schuilkerk is a well-known Dutch phenomenon, few scholars have paid attention to its many counterparts elsewhere in Europe. Regardless of the religious groups involved, the formula for tolerance it embodied proved capable of application wherever local communities struggled to reconcile an official orthodoxy with religious diversity. Catholic majorities might tolerate Protestant minorities through this formula just as easily as the reverse. In Catholic Cologne, for example, Lutherans worshipped from the late sixteenth century onward in a "secret, oppressed house-church," as did Reformed Protestants.[6] The latter, in fact, had two and sometimes three congregations—for speakers of German, Dutch, and French. The existence of these groups was an open secret. When the writer P. de Blainville, visiting Cologne in 1705, attended a service, he "was completely amazed to see such a crowd of people there, for the hall was entirely full, above and below—as many people there as was room for, their number reaching at least five to six hundred."[7] Yet discretion remained crucial: riots broke out in 1708 when Brandenburg's ambassador sent written invitations to Protestants to attend services in his home. They broke out again in 1787 when the city council gave permission for Protestants to build a big new "prayer-, school- and preacher-house."[8] Elsewhere in the empire, clandestine churches accommodated groups other than the three recognized confessions. Remonstrants in Glückstadt received official permission in 1624 "to exercise and practice their religion . . . behind closed doors." Mennonites in Königsberg were told in 1722 by the Prussian government they "could hold their gatherings for their worship in a private house, but only in complete quiet, without [causing] rumor."[9]

Perhaps the most extraordinary case of reliance on clandestine churches was Ireland, where the religion of the majority of the population was illegal. Except in the 1640s and 1650s, when persecution peaked, Irish Catholics were widely able to operate semisecret chapels, which the English called "mass houses." In the countryside these were mostly cottages, barns, or sheds, built of mud, thatch-roofed, and often still used for their original purpose. In cities they were more commodious. The interior of the Jesuit chapel that operated in Dublin in the 1620s made a grand impression on visiting Englishman Sir William Brereton: "The pulpit in this church was richly adorned with pictures, and so was the high altar, which was advanced with steps, and railed out like cathedrals; upon either side thereof was there erected places for confession; no fastened seats were in the middle or body hereof, nor was there any chancel; but that it might be more capacious, there was a gallery erected on both sides and at the lower end."[10] Such galleries, making the most of a restricted space, were a feature common to urban schuilkerken across Europe. The eighteenth century witnessed a proliferation of Irish mass houses and general improvement in their quality, yet care was still taken to keep them unobtrusive. Most of those in Dublin were converted stables or warehouses located on narrow lanes behind other buildings. In County Cork, the magistrates of Cloyne and Charleville blocked the erection of mass houses "within view of the churches in those towns." A Kildare rector had a mass house torn down because it stood "in the direct road to my church, and not far from it."[11] Like the 1691 Amsterdam instructions, these actions demonstrate that location as well as appearance determined how public or private a clandestine place of worship was perceived to be. They highlight again, though, the special power of the visual: even disguised, a mass house in plain sight of a church was viewed as a challenge to the latter.

In addition to close parallels like the mass house, three variants on the schuilkerk also emerged outside the Netherlands. All three were obscured by an architectural façade, located within residential space, and built on a foundation of domestic devotional practices. At the same time, they differed from ordinary schuilkerken as the domiciles in which they were situated differed from the homes of ordinary burghers and peasants.

One was the manorial chapel. Well before the Reformation, Europe's landed elites had developed a tradition of domestic worship. Medieval custom and canon law had permitted them, and with them their households, to worship at home on condition that they attend their parish church on major festivals. After the Reformation, some elites extended this seigneurial privilege in an unprecedented way, using it as a vehicle for dissident devotions. In England and Scotland, recusant gentry and peers established Catholic chapels in their manor houses. These illegal chapels were served by missionary priests who resided on the manor semipermanently. As of 1701, Bishop Leyburn counted 219 peers and gentry who kept such resident chaplains. The latter provided pastoral care first and foremost to the manor's household, usually a larger unit than non-elite households, but recusant elites commonly invited tenants and other dependents to attend their services as well. These were the only Catholic services conducted in some regions, especially in the rural south of both countries. Carved out of residential rooms, the chapels themselves tended to grow larger and less hidden over time. In the early seventeenth century, they usually sheltered in some cramped attic. By 1700 the norm was for a suite of commodious second-floor rooms to serve as chapel, sacristy, and lodgings for the priest. By 1750 the chapel had completed its descent to ground level.

Reliance on manorial chapels had far-reaching consequences for the social character of English Catholicism. Among others, it left priests captive to the needs and desires of the gentry, on whom they depended for lodgings, funds, protection, and places to conduct services. In this way it shifted fundamentally the balance of power between clergy and laity. By the same token, it gave female members of the gentry—the women who ran such recusant households—an unusual leadership role within the Catholic community, at least until the 1620s. Women were similarly empowered in the early phases of Scottish and Irish recusancy. In the Dutch Republic, it took a few decades for the Catholic Church hierarchy to establish effective control over schuilkerk congregations, and priests always remained dependent on the financial and practical assistance of kloppen. Such shifts in power away from the usual wielders of religious authority tended, however, to be reversed or at least mitigated over time.

Unlike British recusants, the Calvinist nobility of France had a legal right to their chapels, known as *églises de fief*. Compared to those in Britain, these chapels played only a secondary role in sustaining religious dissent; for outside regions like the Cévennes, French Calvinism was primarily an urban movement. Until its revocation in 1685, the Edict of Nantes, like earlier toleration edicts, permitted Huguenots to have public places of worship in the suburbs of certain cities. The edict underlined the public quality of worship in them by specifying that "the people may be summoned [to services], even by the ringing of bells." The edict also, though, extended to Huguenot nobles the right "to have in . . . their houses . . . the exercise of the said [Reformed] religion as long as they are resident there, and in their absence, their wives or families."[12] Nobles with powers of high justice could invite as many people as they wished to these domestic services. Nobles without such powers were limited in theory to a maximum of thirty guests, but in practice they often ignored the restriction, welcoming tenants, clients, friends, and others.

In the Middle Ages, Europe's nobles had modeled their chapels after those of their rulers. In the early modern era, most rulers still had court chapels, and in those exceptional lands where their religion differed from the official one, these too became protected centers of religious dissent. They constituted a second variant on the schuilkerk. In England it was not kings, strictly speaking, but their consorts who had the first such private chapels. Queen Henrietta Maria, wife of Charles I, had two, both designed by Inigo Jones: Somerset House Chapel and, at St. James's Palace, Marlborough House Chapel. In the Holy Roman Empire, the Peace of Westphalia allowed a Lutheran ruler of a Reformed territory, and vice versa, "to have court preachers of his confession . . . with him and in his residence."[13] When in 1697 Friedrich August I of Saxony converted to Catholicism, he extended this provision to the Protestant–Catholic divide, arranging for Catholic services in his various residences. Prince Karl Alexander of Württemberg did likewise, establishing private Catholic chapels in Stuttgart and Ludwigsburg when in 1733 he succeeded to the Lutheran duchy. Württemberg's estates, which paid for construction of the two chapels, stipulated that Catholic services be held nowhere else and that no "symbols and activities associated with public worship" accompany them.[14]

Embassy chapels constituted a third variant on the schuilkerk. In the wake of the Reformation, a new rule of diplomacy emerged allowing ambassadors serving in lands whose religion differed from their own to maintain within their residence a chapel for their family's use. Because ambassadorial residences, following the early modern norm, served both as lodgings and workplace, such chapels came to be called embassy chapels. Their legitimacy, though, remained rooted in the domestic: in theory, they and their chaplains could serve only the ambassador and his household. Fuss was rarely made if compatriots of the ambassador—merchants abroad on business, for example—also attended services. Whether foreigners from other countries might do the same was a more sensitive point. But by far the most contentious issue was whether native dissidents could attend embassy services, and whether such services could be conducted in the local language by native clerics. In London this issue provoked repeated clashes, some of them violent, in the streets surrounding the Spanish, French, and Venetian embassies. In several of these incidents, local officials tried to arrest natives emerging at the end of services, setting off diplomatic protests and embarrassing the royal government. Yet despite occasional skirmishes and a more constant tension, London's embassy chapels (Figure 7.4) functioned effectively as places of worship and points of protection for English Catholics. So it went on the Continent as well. The Dutch alone sponsored embassy chapels in twelve different capitals. For Emperor Leopold I the whole point of maintaining ambassadors in various Protestant cities was "that Catholic services might be held to comfort the Catholics of that area, and to promote the further growth of this religion."[15]

In the eighteenth century there emerged a new legal principle, "extraterritoriality," that legitimized embassy chapels. It stipulated that one was to "assume or pretend that the ambassador and the precincts of his embassy stood as if on the soil of his homeland, subject only to its laws." By this principle, an embassy chapel did not violate the religious laws of its host country because it did not stand on the host country's territory. But neither court rulings nor treaty stipulations nor established legal principles lent protection to embassy chapels at the time of their proliferation. Extraterritoriality was an ex post facto justification, developed in no small part to rationalize the already established practice of tolerating embassy chapels. Indeed, the embassy chapel question was "the largest single factor in preparing men's minds to accept this extraordinary fiction."[16]

The schuilkerk formula proved applicable to Jews as well as dissenting Christians. Operating under the cover of domesticity, scores of clandestine synagogues functioned in Alsace from the late seventeenth century. These synagogues consisted initially of rooms in private homes. Often upstairs, the rooms were usually richly appointed, with separate spaces for men and women. A rare survival, the remains of one dating from 1723 can still be seen in Traenheim (Figure 7.5). The private character of these "oratories" was underlined in 1701 by the intendant of Alsace, Le Pelletier de

Figure 7.4. The Sardinian Embassy Chapel, in Lincoln's Inn, London. Called by Bishop Richard Challoner "the chief support of religion in London," it served in the late eighteenth century as ersatz cathedral for the Roman Catholic Church in England. Etching from R. Ackermann, *The Microcosm of London,* vol. 1 (London, 1808). Courtesy of the Library of Congress.

la Houssaye. Investigating a complaint made by an abbé that the Jews of Reichshoffen were practicing their religion publicly, the intendant found precisely the opposite: "The worship which the Jews established in Reichshoffen perform is not as public as one would have you believe. There is no synagogue per se, only, by a custom long established in this province, when there are seven Jewish families in one locale, those who compose them assemble, without scandal, in a house of their sect for readings and prayers."[17] As the Jewish population increased, oratories multiplied and a certain number of houses were renovated internally to function as community centers, incorporating a synagogue and school. Externally they continued to look like the houses in their neighborhood. But in Alsace, like elsewhere, the line between public and private was more a matter of perception and negotiation than of bricks and timber, as a conflict that erupted in 1725 shows. The Jews of three villages, Biesheim, Wintzenheim, and Hagenthal, were accused of building illegal new synagogues. They claimed in response to have merely enlarged or "moved" their existing places of prayer.[18] In the end, the Conseil Souverain of Alsace ordered that the structures be demolished.

In Hamburg, negotiations between Christians and Jews involved threats

Figure 7.5. Attic synagogue in Traenheim, Alsace, interior view. Size 5.5 by 4.5 meters. The space was adapted to serve as synagogue in 1723 despite the vociferous objections of the local pastor. Modern photograph, courtesy of Prof. Bernard Keller.

of violence as well as appeals to authority. Worshipping initially in private homes, Hamburg's Sephardic community dated to the 1580s. In 1650 it received permission to hold prayer gatherings of up to fifteen families, although, to avoid notice, only four or five families were to enter or leave at a time. This license emboldened the community, which began to consider building a larger, more formal place of worship. Its intentions evoked howls of protest from Hamburg's Lutheran clergy, who stirred up popular sentiment with anti-Semitic sermons. In 1672 the community went ahead anyway with plans to enlarge an existing prayer house. Riots immediately threatened to break out, and the captains of the city's militia warned the government that their men could not be counted on to suppress them. Taking preemptive action, the senate soon closed the synagogue, forcing the Sephardim to content themselves once again with small unofficial prayer houses.

A similar drama unfolded in the eighteenth century with the city's Ashkenazic community. A *Judenreglement* issued by the senate in 1710 forbade the Ashkenazim to have any "public buildings" but permitted them to worship privately "as long as they refrained from ostentatiously provoking their neighbours by using ceremonial horns or trumpets [a reference to the shofar] or by publicly displaying liturgical lanterns."[19] This almost transparent cloak sufficed to keep the peace, and by 1732 the growing community had fourteen clandestine synagogues. In 1746, however, the building of a large new synagogue provoked disturbances. Hamburg's senate had tacitly approved the construction, and a strategically unobtrusive site had been chosen in a narrow alley on the periphery of town, but the work of construction inevitably attracted attention. When formal remonstrances by the citizenry failed to sway the senate, an angry crowd gathered around the half-completed building, threatening to demolish it. Cowed, the senate ordered its dismantling.

Looking through the Fingers

By giving Jews permission to build a larger clandestine synagogue, Hamburg's senate was colluding with a religious minority to redraw the line between private and public worship. By mobilizing and threatening violence, Hamburg's Lutheran crowds restored the line to its earlier position.

As was typical, the negotiation involved not just religious dissidents and local authorities but also orthodox citizens and clergy. In rural areas and less autonomous cities, such negotiations involved other actors as well: princes, estates, nobles. Such popular mobilization as occurred in Hamburg, though, marked a failure of official policy. Rulers generally sought to preempt it and the challenge it entailed to their authority by regulating carefully the activity of dissenting religious congregations. Silently gauging what the orthodox of their community might, if only grudgingly, assent to, they set boundaries to the private sphere within which those congregations operated. For example, Amsterdam's regents sought to ensure that Glabbais's Catholic congregation would "avoid giving any offense" to Calvinists; Prussia's government stipulated that Mennonite worship had to be conducted "in complete quiet, without [causing] rumor"; in approving Jewish worship, the Alsatian intendant noted that it caused no "scandal." This vocabulary reveals the sensitivity of officials to popular opinion. It signals a negotiation conducted, in the usual course of events, discursively rather than physically.

The points in dispute in these negotiations indicate the criteria early modern Europeans applied to distinguish public from private worship: how many people attended the services; what sort of persons attended; when services were held; the size of the chapel; its location and appearance; the presence of beggars or parked vehicles outside it; the number of people entering or leaving at a time, and how they conducted themselves; whether bells rang or invitations were sent to announce services. Some of these criteria have the same valence in modern Western culture as they did in early modern, but others do not. Invitations are today deemed markers of a private, not public, function, and hundreds of people being in attendance does not make a service any more public. Similarly, churches today look like churches, synagogues like synagogues, and mosques like mosques, yet they remain private organizations. They are considered private above all because of their status as nongovernmental, voluntary associations, a status they share with business corporations and similar bodies.

Some intellectuals formulated such a definition of privacy as early as the seventeenth century. Among the first, Roger Williams argued in 1644 that a church or any other "*company* of *worshippers*" was "like unto a Body or Colledge of *Physitians* in a *Citie;* like unto a *Corporation, Society, or Company* of *East-Indie* or *Turkie-Merchants,* or any other *Societie* or *Com-*

pany. . . . The *essence* or being of the *Citie*, and so the *well-being* and *peace* thereof is essentially distinct from those particular *Societies*."[20] John Locke similarly emphasized the voluntary, associative nature of churches. Yet even most Enlightenment philosophes saw a need for some sort of religious establishment, civil if not Christian. Eighteenth-century practice, more even than theory, shows the continued functioning of an older definition of private worship, based on symbols and other sensory signals, especially visual ones. Throughout that century, schuilkerken and their equivalents continued to function, new ones were built, and contests occurred over the boundaries of the private sphere they constituted.

Britain formed a partial exception. In the wake of the Glorious Revolution, Protestant dissenters there enjoyed increasing social acceptance, and the Toleration Act of 1689 offered licenses for their meetinghouses, which formerly had remained clandestine. Some of their new places of worship, with imposing façades and central locations, made bold public statements. For British Catholics, by contrast, change occurred only within parameters set long before: their places of worship grew grander and less secret too, but retained the essential quality of a schuilkerk, invisibility. The impact of Catholic emancipation at the end of the eighteenth century was correspondingly dramatic, as a Scottish comparison reveals (Figure 7.6). Constructed in the 1750s, St. Ninian's Chapel, Tynet, was "a small little house wher a poor woman had lived for some time, to which Tynet proposed making an additione as a cot for his sheep, but in effect for our use." St. Gregory's, Preshome, built on the eve of emancipation, had a western façade in the Italian baroque style that proclaimed its identity as a Catholic church. Its pedimented gable, complete with urn finials, was inscribed "DEO 1788."[21]

Exceptions can be found outside Britain as well, but what is striking overall is the continued vigor of the schuilkerk tradition. In the short run, at least, Enlightenment influence produced a broadening of toleration within that tradition more often than its repudiation. Emperor Joseph II's Patent of Toleration (1781), hailed as a milestone in the rise of tolerance, offers a telling example. The freedom it granted Austrian Protestants was to have "private religious exercise" *(exercitium religionis privatum)*. This differed from "public" religious exercise, the edict specified, in the appearance of the building where it was conducted. Protestant churches were to have "no chimes, no bells, towers or any public entrance from the street as might signify a church."[22] However revolutionary it was in granting full citizenship to religious dissenters, the edict remained conservative with regard to the spatial accommodation of their worship. It allowed Vienna's Protestants, the largest group in the land, merely to trade one schuilkerk for another—or three, to be precise, for two. Protestant worship had been thriv-

St Ninian's, Tynet (1755).

St Gregory's, Preshome (1788).

Figure 7.6. Clandestine church versus public church: St. Ninian's, Tynet, and St. Gregory's, Preshome, in Scotland. Modern drawings by Peter F. Anson. Courtesy of Dom Donald McGlynn, Sancta Maria Abbey—Nunraw, Haddington, Scotland.

ing in the capital for well over half a century under the auspices of the Danish, Swedish, and Dutch embassies. Upon issuance of the edict, the two Lutheran congregations merged and, together with the Reformed, purchased an abandoned convent belonging formerly to the Poor Clares. The complex had to be modified extensively to meet the terms of the edict. The convent church, used by the Lutherans, was hidden from street view by a new row of two-story houses; access to it was from a courtyard reached via the entrance to one of the houses. Only in the 1880s did either the Lutheran or the Reformed *Bethaus* take on the external appearance of a church.

Exercitium religionis privatum: Joseph II's government borrowed the term from a document that predated the Enlightenment by half a century, the Treaty of Osnabrück (1648), part of the Peace of Westphalia. There it stands as one of three recognized types of religious worship. One is called "domestic devotion" *(devotio domestica):* Lutheran subjects of Catholic princes, and vice versa, "are to be patiently endured and not hindered from applying themselves to their devotions with a free conscience privately at home, without investigation or disturbance."[23] The treaty also permits the three major confessions to operate proper churches wherever they were doing so in 1624—to have what it calls *exercitium religionis publicum.* But it also recognizes an intermediate category of worship that people could likewise continue (or resume), *exercitium religionis privatum,* which it describes as led by clergy and practiced not "in churches at set hours" but rather "in their [the worshippers'] own houses or in other houses designated for the purpose."[24] In other words, *exercitium privatum* was worship in a schuilkerk.

With this tripartite distinction the diplomats in Westphalia acknowledged that much more than family prayers went on in private "houses." Joseph's government was even more explicit, describing "churches" that lacked the external signs of a church. How paradoxical—an institution whose sole value lies in its invisibility is acknowledged in epochal documents and written into the very constitution of the empire. The paradox, though, reflects two crucial truths about the schuilkerk: first, that its physical, not legal, invisibility was chiefly responsible for its effectiveness; and, second, that the pretense to privacy and domesticity it embodied was a very thin one. Indeed, the distinction in early modern Europe between public and private worship was as much cultural fiction as it was social reality. It was a story that enabled Europeans to accommodate dissent without confronting it directly, to tolerate knowingly what they could not bring themselves to accept fully. It preserved a public semblance of religious unity, and thus contained the threat of religious conflict. It allowed people to go on living as if civic and sacral community were still one and the same. This was patently a fiction, and was recognized as such. The Dutch spoke of "looking through the fingers"; the metaphor captures the self-imposed character of the blindness as well as its incompleteness. "Turning a blind eye" to dissent carried a similar sense. Even more common was the term *connivance,* used from Ireland to Prussia. This language captures a tolerance that was grudging and partial, but self-conscious. For their part, dissenters participated in the fiction by refraining from challenging the monopoly over public religious life enjoyed by the official church of their community. Their assertiveness usually took a different form: expanding the private space within which they worshipped.

The distinction between public and private worship that emerged in early modern Europe was not an isolated phenomenon. It formed part of, and indeed helped give rise to, a new distinction between public and private spheres generally. In the wake of the Protestant and Catholic Reformations, Europe's new religious divisions threatened to destroy the cohesion of communities; distinguishing public from private was a way to save it. By redefining freedom of conscience to mean freedom of devotion for families within their homes, Europeans designated the family home as something it had never previously been, a space safe for practices otherwise forbidden. No longer did every act performed within the boundaries of town or village impinge on the salvation of all inhabitants. Communal space was split. Every time dissenters met for worship in a schuilkerk, and every time the orthodox turned a blind eye to their services, the line separating private sphere from public was reinforced.

As the location and architectural form of schuilkerken suggests, this new private sphere was located first and foremost in the family home, which by the eighteenth century became, at least for some people, a refuge not just from demands for religious conformity but from the demands of society generally, a protected space for informality and emotional intimacy. Although other structures served also as disguises, most schuilkerken were tolerated by pretending they were family homes. The Edict of Nantes,

Peace of Westphalia, and other official documents spoke of them explicitly as located inside houses. Several of the terms used to denote them—house church, prayer house, meetinghouse, mass house, house chapel—emphasized likewise their domestic character.

Schuilkerken shed light also on the nature of the public sphere. Philosopher Jürgen Habermas saw emerging in the eighteenth century a new, "authentic, bourgeois" public sphere, in which individuals engaged in rational discussion and debate, first about literary matters, then politics.[25] Did schuilkerken help give birth to such a sphere? Habermas saw the new sphere crystallizing in salons, coffeehouses, Freemason lodges, and other social forums. Schuilkerken bear a certain similarity to these. Religious controversy stimulated public debate and appeals to "public opinion" of the kind Habermas describes. Obviously schuilkerken were forums for the expression of religious dissent. Yet there are good reasons not to conflate the schuilkerk or religious dissent generally with the phenomenon that concerned Habermas. Schuilkerk congregations may indeed be regarded as components of a civil society separate from the state, but, with members of widely different social status and degrees of education, they did not form a unitary, enlightened public. Affiliated with every Christian denomination and both branches of European Jewry, they shared no common set of beliefs or practices. Some engaged in "rational-critical debate"; others gathered principally to enact rituals. Some allowed women and lay men to play leadership roles, but over time clerical authority tended to rise, not fall. Nor were such congregations hosted only in "bourgeois" homes.

Habermas contrasted his modern public sphere to an earlier one characterized by "representative publicness."[26] In the latter, self-display and self-representation to others were what gave a person or thing its public quality. Such publicness, he argues, was achieved through the use of insignia, clothing, demeanor, rhetoric, festivities, and other symbolic vocabularies. It was in itself an assertion of status and power. Although brief and merely suggestive, Habermas's description of "representative publicness" does seem to capture the difference between public and private worship in early modern Europe. Symbolic self-representation to an external audience was precisely what distinguished an ordinary parish, cathedral, or monastic church from a schuilkerk, and the publicness of the former was indeed an assertion of the status and power that distinguished a community's official faith from that of dissenters. Contrary, though, to Habermas's claim that this sort of publicness yielded to a new, modern version in the eighteenth century, the continued operation of schuilkerken suggests that "representative publicness" survived to the very end of the Old Regime and, fragmentarily, even beyond. While the trend was for them to grow in size and lose their concern about secrecy, schuilkerken always maintained at least a superficial invisibility. In the final analysis their privacy was a widely acknowledged fiction, and an increasingly thin one at that. Yet as late as the 1780s that fiction was still being maintained. As a concession to popular opinion—the prejudice of the orthodox—it bears a striking resemblance to the "Don't ask, don't tell" policy that President Bill Clinton introduced for gays and lesbians in the U.S. military. Such pieces of social hypocrisy belie both the rationality and the openness that Habermas attributed to the "authentic" public sphere. At the same time, they reveal how "unstable and elusive" the boundaries between public and private really were, and still are.[27]

EIGHT

Sharing Churches, Sharing Power

St. Martin's, Biberach

In the picturesque town of Biberach (Figure 8.1), in Germany's Upper Swabia, a modern tourist can visit the antithesis of a schuilkerk. Standing tall at the center of town, its iconic tower visible from the surrounding hills, the Church of St. Martin was for centuries the sole parish church for all of Biberach's inhabitants, who in the town's late medieval heyday, when its weavers produced a fashionable fustian, numbered some six thousand souls. Biberach was a classic German "home town," and its inhabitants perforce lived their lives together. Commerce and festivity took place on the central *Marktplatz*, deliberation and governance in the adjacent town halls. Still small, by modern standards, Biberach today retains its intimate atmosphere, and many traces of its past survive. Massive medieval houses ob-

---

Figure. 8.1 (opposite page). An intimate German "home town," early modern Biberach was dominated by the parish church of St. Martin, a shared church used jointly by Catholics and Protestants. Engraving from Matthaeus Merian the Elder, *Topographia Sveviae, das ist Beschreib- und Aigentliche Abcontrafeitung der furnembste[n] Stätt und Plätz . . .* (Frankfurt am Main, 1643). Courtesy of Edinburgh University Library, shelfmark JY993.

Biberach.

1. S. Martini Pfarrkirch.
2. Das Gotts Hs. Spital.
3. Schusters Clausa.
4. S. Nicolai Capell.
5. Das Rathhauß.
6. Greda oder Kornhauß.
7. Der Zehend Stadel.
8. Der Saltz Stadel.
9. Der Statt Cantzley.
10. Der Statt Eich.
11. Der Pfarrhoff.

12. Geschlechter Stuben.
13. Das Ober thor.
14. Graben thor.
15. Spittel thor.
16. Süchen thor.
17. Der Einlaß.
18. Rechthor.
19. Burger thurn.
20. Die Blaichinen.
21. Schützenhauß.

Figure 8.2. Clock with one face toward Protestant nave, another toward Catholic choir, in the parish church of St. Martin, Biberach. Modern photographs, courtesy of Frau Andrea Riotte.

scure the entrance to St. Martin's, whose gothic interior was given in the 1740s a rococo face-lift.

If you enter the church and look around, you may be struck by the oddity of a large clock embedded in its vaulting, with faces visible from both nave and choir (Figure 8.2). You may also notice that the nave is decorated less richly than the choir, with its resplendent gilding, imitation marble, and stucco. If you then examine the church's ceiling frescos (Figure 8.3), which enjoy some artistic fame, you will find a discrepancy. On the one hand, from the western portal to the apse of the choir, the frescos are unified in style, as well they should be, given that a single artist painted them. On the other hand, they have two distinct iconographic programs. The fresco above the nave is appropriate for a Lutheran church: it represents scenes from the life of Jesus—the adoration of the shepherds and wise men, the circumcision, the presentation in the temple, the boy Jesus among the scribes, the miracles of Easter and Pentecost. The side aisles are bedecked similarly with scenes from the New Testament. By contrast, in the vaulting of the choir, as if in heaven, rises the Church Triumphant, with apostles, church fathers, evangelists, the archangel Michael, the apocalyptic lamb, and a choir of angels. Personifying the Church is the Virgin Mary, whom angels crown with a papal tiara—an emphatically Catholic representation. This discrepancy offers the clearest clue to St. Martin's peculiarity: it is a "Simultankirche," a church used by both Lutherans and Catholics.

St. Martin's is the oldest functioning shared church *(Simultankirche)* in Germany. It has been in almost constant use as such since 1548, when Charles V, flushed with his (temporary) victory in the Schmalkaldic War, ordered the resumption of Catholic worship in Biberach, which had officially embraced the evangelical cause. At the time, the vast majority of the town's inhabitants were Protestant. Short of occupying the town with troops, which Charles did not have available, the emperor could not simply suppress Protestantism in Biberach. He did, though, see to it that Catholics enjoyed privileges and powers out of all proportion to their number. He abrogated the town's constitution, installing a new government dominated by Catholic patricians, and he forced Protestants to share use of St. Martin's. Beginning in 1553 both Protestants and Catholics held a full panoply of services in the church, each group following its own liturgy under the leadership of its own clergy. Soon afterward, the Peace of Augsburg froze

this arrangement in place, declaring that in imperial cities where "both religions" had been "for some time in practice and use," they would "hereafter remain so and be maintained." Citizens of both religions were to "live
peacefully and quietly with and alongside one another," each enjoying their
property and privileges.[1] Along with seven other imperial cities in Swabia,

Figure 8.3. A shared church (Simultankirche): the parish church of St. Martin,
Biberach—interior, decorated in 1740s with ceiling frescos by Johannes Zick.
Modern photograph from southwest corner, courtesy of Verlag Schnell und Steiner.

Biberach thus became officially biconfessional, with two forms of Christianity practiced publicly with full legal sanction. In the sixteenth century, this arrangement was called "Simultaneum."

In following centuries, this term took on a more specialized meaning, being reserved for when religious groups shared use of a building or other property, as in Biberach. St. Martin's, moreover, was not just any church. It had always embodied the town's spiritual aspirations and its sense of being a single sacral community. Now the church embodied the town's division by faith and became a site where its split was regularly enacted. On Sundays and common holidays, Catholics and Protestants held services in alternation. An imperial commission of 1649 specified that Catholics could use St. Martin's from 5 to 6 A.M., Lutherans from 6 to 8, Catholics from 8 to 11, Lutherans from 11 to 12, and Catholics again from 12 to 1 P.M.—hence the need for a clock. Afternoons were similarly divided, the precise hours varying with the season. The bells of St. Martin's rang to announce both sets of services. Catholics had free rein of the church, while Lutherans were normally restricted to the nave, being allowed into the choir only when their pastor administered Communion. Entering and exiting the church the two groups rubbed shoulders with one another, sometimes literally. Thus were Protestant and Catholic Biberachers required to share a building charged with symbolism. They had to let one another proclaim beliefs and perform rituals they considered perverse, even satanic, in a space that both groups, in different ways, deemed sacred.

Biconfessionalism was never the preferred solution in early modern Europe to the problem of religious diversity—to the contrary, it was usually a product of circumstances that made it impossible for rulers to maintain even a thin pretense that they and their subjects were religiously united. In many ways, it was the opposite of Auslauf or of worship in a schuilkerk; based on evasion and denial, these enabled people to accommodate religious diversity without acknowledging or coming fully to terms with it. In contrast, biconfessionalism was based on a full and open recognition of religious divisions. It required opponents to face one another, acknowledge publicly one another's existence, share resources, and cooperate. Simultaneum, in the modern sense of two or more groups worshipping separately in a shared church, was even more an arrangement of last resort. That it caused tension is scarcely surprising; what is remarkable is how stable, long-lasting, and essentially peaceful it was in communities like Biberach. By comparing times and places where biconfessional communities saw much conflict with ones where they did not, we can draw valuable lessons about toleration generally. Above all, we can see that its practice did not depend on eradicating tensions or resolving conflicts between religious groups—an impossible task, often—but on managing and containing them.

Dual and Multiple Establishments

With the rarest of exceptions, Europe's rulers did their utmost to avoid recognizing religious divisions among their subjects. This is not surprising, given the momentous implications such recognition carried. In an age when separation of church and state, in the modern sense, was inconceivable, rulers could not abstain from involvement in religious affairs. To adopt a neutral stance was therefore not an option. To accept religious diversity required them to sanction, protect, and possibly even give material assistance to more than one faith. Such acceptance led not to disestablishment, but to the founding of "dual" or "multiple" establishments, with more than one church receiving state support. In such an arrangement, all members of the community had to belong to one or another of the established churches, while other churches were banned, or at best tolerated by connivance. Such was the situation, for example, in the Palatinate, where in the eighteenth century inhabitants were required by law to attend either a Calvinist, Lutheran, or Catholic church, and could be asked by magistrates to supply written proof that they took Communion at Easter.

This type of arrangement did not mean necessarily that people of different faiths lived and worshipped in the same towns and villages. The Swiss Confederation, for example, had a dual establishment, yet in most cantons only one faith was practiced. Similarly, after 1555 the Holy Roman Empire had a dual establishment, and after 1648 a triple one (Catholic, Lutheran, Calvinist), yet most territories had a single official faith. What interests us, rather, are the instances where local communities were bi- or multiconfessional. Even a partial list of these would not be short. For Switzerland it would include, from 1531, towns and villages in the so-called Mandated Territories, as well as in the canton of Glarus and slightly later the Grisons. It would include many communities in Transylvania, where from 1568 four religions—Calvinist, Catholic, Lutheran, and Unitarian—

were officially "received," that is, approved. It would include the same in Royal Hungary in the early seventeenth century, fewer later—just two towns per county after 1681. In the Holy Roman Empire there were biconfessional communities in Jülich-Cleves, the bishopric of Osnabrück, and other territories in the seventeenth and eighteenth centuries. As we have seen, Biberach and seven other imperial cities—Ulm, Donauwörth, Kaufbeuren, Leutkirch, Ravensburg, Dinkelsbühl, and the great commercial center of Augsburg—were biconfessional from the 1540s or 1550s, and several territorial cities—Colmar, Hagenau, Essen, Dortmund, Aachen, and Aalen—became so in the following decades. The Palatinate had an increasing number of biconfessional communities after it gained a Catholic ruler in 1685. So did Alsace after it was "reunited" with France in 1673. In the Dutch Republic, the city of Maastricht was biconfessional. Also, the Lands of Overmaas had biconfessional towns and villages after being conquered in 1632 by Dutch troops. Vilnius, in Lithuania, was biconfessional—arguably it had been so since the Middle Ages, when Catholics and Eastern Orthodox Christians had lived as fellow citizens. It was in France, though, that the largest number of biconfessional communities could be found, some dating to the 1560s, others to the Edict of Nantes in 1598. They included all the French cities where Huguenots were allowed, by virtue of "possession," to have a church within the city walls. By a slightly broader definition, they also included cities where by "concession" Huguenots were allowed a church in a suburb.

For a community to become bi- or multiconfessional, it required of course a religiously mixed population, though not an evenly mixed one: members of one confession could vastly outnumber another. But something else was involved as well: a formal, legally sanctioned division of authority along confessional lines. Such a division was the outcome of religious wars fought to inconclusive stalemates in the sixteenth century in Switzerland, the Holy Roman Empire, and France.[2] Unlike the "religious peace" treaties that ended the Swiss and German wars, though, the Edict of Nantes established in France (as previous edicts had done) the biconfessionalism, not just of the polity as a whole, but of hundreds of local communities. Wherever the edict permitted Protestant worship, the result in theory, and usually also in practice, was a biconfessional community, since under the edict's terms, Catholic worship was supposed to be reestablished wherever Huguenots had previously suppressed it. Even cities overwhelmingly dominated by Protestants, like Nîmes and La Rochelle, thus became biconfessional.

It did not always require war to produce a legal division of authority. In 1573, in the wake of the St. Bartholomew's Day massacres, Polish nobles concluded the Confederation of Warsaw to preempt the kind of horrible strife they saw raging in France. The Confederation, though, was more like the Swiss and German treaties than the French edict: a noninterference agreement between members of a ruling elite, it created a patchwork of estates each with a single official faith. Other agreements, by contrast, produced biconfessionalism on the local level as well as higher ones. In 1614, for example, rulers with rival claims to inherit the northwest German lands of Jülich-Cleves agreed to partition them. One ruler was the Calvinist elector of Brandenburg, the other the Catholic duke of Pfalz-Neuburg. A series of treaties between them and their successors guaranteed an extraordinary mix of publicly practiced faiths in the lands they had divided, particularly in Cleves and Mark, which belonged to Brandenburg. A similar dispute led to an even more remarkable compromise concerning the bishopric of Osnabrück, which from 1650 was ruled in alternating succession by a Catholic bishop, whom the local cathedral chapter elected, and a Lutheran prince of the house of Braunschweig-Lüneburg. Of the bishopric's fifty-nine parishes, thirty-one ended up having Catholic pastors, twenty Lutheran, and eight both. The Holy Roman Empire was full of such anomalies.

Sometimes official religious pluralism was the product of legal and political arrangements that long predated the Reformation. In Transylvania, for example, it resulted when ethnic groups who for centuries had enjoyed broad political autonomy embraced different faiths. Most Magyars (ethnic Hungarians) converted in the sixteenth century to Calvinism. "Saxons" (ethnic Germans) chose overwhelmingly for Lutheranism, while Szeklers, descendants of the guards brought in to defend the land's eastern borders, mostly went Unitarian or remained Catholic. In 1437 these three groups had confederated, forming a "Union of Three Nations." In the 1560s, gathered together in the Transylvanian diet, they simply extended the powers of self-government each nation enjoyed, approving the religions each had embraced and allowing each to regulate its own religious affairs.

A more common arrangement inherited from the Middle Ages was "condominium," in which sovereignty over a territory was held as common property and exercised jointly by two or more rulers. After the Reformation, these rulers might well be of different faiths, as the inhabitants of Maastricht, in the Netherlands, experienced. Since the early Middle Ages the city had had two lords, the dukes of Brabant and the prince-bishops of Liège. When the Dutch army conquered Maastricht in 1632, the Dutch States General took over the powers of the former dukes. Henceforth they ruled the city jointly with the Catholic prince-bishop. So likewise Protestant and Catholic cantons ruled jointly over the Swiss *Gemeine Herrschaften.* Conventionally these territories are called in English "Mandated Territories," although a better translation would be "Common Lordships." They included the Thurgau, the Rheintal, and some sixteen other regions. Neither cantons themselves nor associate members of the Swiss Confederation (like Geneva or the Grisons), they were dependent territories subject to the cantons' rule. In fact, the situation was even more complicated, for different Mandated Territories had different combinations of cantons over them. The Thurgau, for example, was ruled by the Catholic "five cantons" *(V. Orte),* their archenemy Zurich, religiously divided Glarus, and from 1712 Protestant Bern. Echallans, in the Pays de Vaud, was subject to Bern and to Catholic Freiburg.

Citadels of Faith

Official religious pluralism raised on the local level a host of practical difficulties, especially when the faiths in question were Catholic and Protestant. The most acute difficulty, though, was the most immediate: Where would rival groups worship? Many small towns and villages, especially nuclear ones with houses bunched closely together, had just one church or chapel. Unless the confessions shared use of the existing structure, one of them would have to build a new church for itself. That was a huge financial burden for a minority to bear. When Ulm's Protestants took this step between 1617 and 1621, it cost them some twenty thousand florins. Biberach's Protestants would have imitated the Ulmers, but they found it impossible to raise sufficient funds. They were prepared to cede use of St. Martin's to their Catholic fellow burghers but could not afford to do so. When deciding to approve several faiths, the estates of Transylvania grappled with this difficulty and proposed an unusual solution to it. While granting the majority confession in each parish exclusive use of the parish church, they required the majority to contribute funds to help the local minority build its own place of worship. It is not known whether this extraordinary stipulation was carried out in practice.

In any event, the financial burden of a new church did not consist solely in a onetime expense: even after it was built and properly outfitted, a church had to be maintained and its clergy paid. For existing churches, such ongoing costs were generally covered, or at least subsidized, by medieval endowments—funds that in the first case were part of the "church fabric," and in the second case constituted benefices. New churches had no such endowments attached to them. Would old endowments be divided between confessions? If so, they might not suffice to cover the expenses of either group, a difficulty that led to endless conflicts in Glarus and other mixed parts of Switzerland. What about tithes and *jura stolae,* the fees local pastors received for registering baptisms, marriages, and deaths: would these too be divided? Doing so could undermine the fiscal foundations of existing institutions. To prevent this, some religious groups, even ones with rights of public worship, found themselves required to make payments to the clergy of another, more privileged church. In France, for example, Huguenots were obliged by the Edict of Nantes to pay Catholic tithes, a requirement they found intensely galling.

These difficulties did not weigh as heavily in cities as they did in towns and villages, for several reasons. First, most cities inherited from their medieval past a number of church buildings, sometimes a great number, so that Protestant cities usually found it expedient to convert some of them to other uses, or even demolish them. In religiously mixed cities rival confessions could potentially use different churches. This is what happened in Erfurt, Hildesheim, Minden, Breslau, Strasbourg, Regensburg, Isny, Kempten, and many other cities of the Holy Roman Empire. These cities all went officially Protestant but failed, for legal and political reasons, to impose their will on some of the Catholic institutions within their walls (monasteries and cathedrals, most commonly) before the signing of the Peace of Augsburg. Under the latter's enduring protection, these institutions became enclaves within which Catholic worship continued, and Catholic laypeople had recourse to them for services. This arrangement was very convenient in some respects, as it allowed cities to preserve, just as Auslauf and schuilkerken did, a semblance of religious unity.

Cities had a concentration not only of church buildings but of people, which meant that religious groups in them, even minority ones, tended to be bigger than in towns or villages. And just as they traveled to cities to attend markets or fairs, so villagers might do the same for worship, swelling the ranks of urban congregations. Three Silesian cities, Glogau, Jauer, and Schweidnitz, offer extreme examples of this phenomenon. Under the terms of Westphalia, Lutherans were not allowed to use any of the existing churches in them but were permitted to build a "Friedenskirche" just outside the walls of each. These were the only Lutheran churches after 1648 in the Habsburgs' hereditary duchies in Silesia, which once had been centers of Protestantism. Villagers from as far away as seventy kilometers traveled to Jauer to attend services, which, although the massive wooden church could hold five thousand people, had to be conducted three times on Sundays in order to accommodate all the worshippers. (As one might guess, a great number of inns sprang up in Jauer.) Between the concentration of worshippers in cities and the wealth that commerce yielded, urban congregations were far more likely than rural to have the financial resources necessary to build, equip, and staff a new church. For this reason, too, freedom of worship was easier to arrange in cities than in smaller communities.

But of course, in the confessional age no issue concerning religion was purely practical. Where a group worshipped had the greatest symbolic importance. Like citadels in an age of siege warfare, churches were among the highest prizes in the struggle between confessions, and the larger the church, the more prominent its location, the stronger its association with the civic community, the higher the prize it represented. This was the other reason so many parish churches in early modern Europe came to be shared: religious opponents unwilling to abandon their claim not just to a community's resources, but to its spiritual heart. This was also the reason members of one confession were so likely to find another group's public worship both offensive and threatening. For to the extent that a church was visible and had a presence in the public sphere, so did the group that worshipped in it. The sensibilities stirred were much the same as when a procession, holiday celebration, or funeral sparked a clash. In public worship, individual heretics became assertive groups. The stronger a church's presence, the harder it was benignly to ignore the services held in it. And by knowingly allowing those services to proceed, one tolerated them.

No wonder certain churches became objects of attack. Such violence was recurrent in the royal cities of Poland, whereas in France, Protestants as well as Catholics had (for a time) the right to worship in proper churches; while Catholics retained use of the parish churches, Protestants were allowed to build new ones of wood. Catholic crowds torched the latter repeatedly. Its royal privilege did not protect the Bróg, a shared church in Cracow where Lutherans and Calvinists worshipped: it was despoiled and damaged by arson in 1574, burned to the ground in 1587, and again destroyed in 1591. The Lutheran church in Posen was attacked by students of the local Jesuit college every year beginning in 1603, until in 1606 it was destroyed. Twice it was rebuilt, and twice it was burned to the ground again. In 1627 a Catholic crowd destroyed the Calvinist and Socinian churches of Lublin. In Warsaw Lutherans began to build a church but gave up after a crowd tore down what they had erected. Protestants were most persistent where they were strongest, in the Lithuanian capital Vilnius. The Lutheran church there, invisible from the street except for its tower, was damaged or destroyed by fire six times between 1610 and 1737; each time it was rebuilt. The Reformed church there was likewise destroyed and rebuilt four times.

Two features above all gave churches a powerful presence in the public sphere: their towers and bells. Dominating neighborhoods, even whole cities, the sight of the one and sound of the other could be more difficult to avoid than a procession. They thrust an awareness of a church's presence upon all within their orbit, while the ringing of bells called attention specifically to the services they announced. Nothing was more unwelcome to members of other confessions, and a prohibition against tower and bells was one of the most common restrictions placed on the worship of dissenters. As late as 1781, Joseph II's famous Patent of Toleration insisted that the "churches" that Austrian Protestants could now build were to have no towers or bells. In 1791 England's Second Catholic Relief Act stipulated similarly that Catholic chapels could have no steeples or bells. In both cases, the restriction had a dual purpose: to mark the minority's lesser status, and to make its churches less "offensive" to the conforming majority, whose backlash authorities feared. By contrast, the Edict of Nantes emphasized the right of Huguenots to worship publicly by agreeing that their "temples" could have bells. Despite this concession, the Catholics of Gap, in Dauphiné, complained loudly in the 1620s when local Huguenots added a tower to their temple and began ringing its bells to announce services. In 1605 the magistrates of Strasbourg (then still a Lutheran city in the Holy

Roman Empire) forbade the nuns of the Sainte-Marguerite convent to ring the bells of their chapel; they feared that violence would erupt between Catholic laity going to services and Protestants who, alerted by the bells, might try to stop them from doing so. A century later, bell ringing occasioned conflict in the Alsatian countryside: Catholics there wanted to stop Lutherans from ringing church bells during holy week, when Catholic bells hung silent. In 1704 the curé of Muntzenheim made sure no one would ring the parish bell by climbing the church tower and cutting the bell's rope. He then stood guard in the belfry, threatening to knife any Lutheran who approached. Bell ringing during processions, holidays, and funerals was contentious too. In 1687 a "battle of the bells" erupted in the Palatinate after its new Catholic ruler permitted his co-religionists to ring the bells of local parish churches, which were in Reformed hands. The government found it necessary in 1696 to send troops into the town of Bacharach to enforce the decree.

Simultaneum

Simultaneum was the ultimate form of public worship. Where rival confessions shared use of a church, there was no averting of eyes, or ears: the other group was in your face. Every time you went to services you confronted it. There was an element of sacrilege to the arrangement, letting God's house be used by God's enemies. Such, at least, was the sentiment of religious authorities in the seventeenth century. The Reformed ministers of Maastricht described Simultaneum as allowing "God and the devil from hell" to be served "in one and the same church."[3] In Rome, the Congregation for the Propagation of the Faith issued between 1627 and 1631 three decrees against it. These, in the strongest possible terms, forbade missionary priests from celebrating mass in a church "in which heretics too hold their profane and sacrilegious exercises."[4] Rather than do so, declared the Congregation, priests should set up portable altars in private homes. In other words, a schuilkerk was preferable to a shared church.

Naturally, such objections were weaker, the less bitterly opposed religious groups were to one another. Lutherans and Calvinists happily shared use of the Bróg and other churches in Poland. Presbyterians and Episcopalians shared St. Columbine's in Derry, Ireland, before 1661 and again dur-

ing the 1689 siege of the city. In the early eighteenth century, they did likewise in a few Scottish cities. Protestants and Catholics tended to have
stronger misgivings about sharing churches with one another than did
Protestants of different confessional stripes. Yet paradoxically, Protestant–
Catholic shared churches always outnumbered the other sort. Two circumstances accounted for this fact. First, a ruler of one faith might inherit or
conquer a territory whose inhabitants were of another faith. This was essentially the situation in Biberach and the other imperial cities forced to
become biconfessional in the 1540s. This was the situation also in the
Dutch-held Lands of Overmaas, where Catholic natives were forced to
share their churches with Calvinist carpetbaggers and converts. Similarly
in the Grisons, Protestant authorities forced Catholics in the villages of the
Valtelline to share their churches. But the largest concentration of shared
churches in early modern Europe was along the upper Rhine, in Alsace and
the Palatinate. Here Simultaneum was brutally imposed toward the end
of the seventeenth century by princes determined to promote their faith
against massive opposition.

Rome had strong reservations about Louis XIV's policy of imposing
Simultaneum on the Lutheran churches of Alsace; so did French bishops.
Typically, the Sun King ignored them. Barred by treaty from simply sup-
pressing Protestant worship (as part of the empire, Alsace fell under the
Peace of Westphalia, even after it was incorporated into France), Louis did
the next best thing: in 1684 a royal order required Lutherans to surrender
the choir of their church if seven or more Catholic families lived in their
parish. Lutherans were to retain use of the nave, and a wall was to be
erected separating the two spaces. Within four years, the choirs of more
than fifty churches were appropriated; by 1697, over one hundred. It did
not matter that many parishes lacked the requisite seven families: Jesuit
and Capuchin missionaries encouraged the immigration of Catholic day-
workers who were counted as families. Nor did it matter that there weren't
enough priests available for each of these churches to be given a Catholic
pastor; that came later. In the meantime, Louis established a Catholic
beachhead, as it were, in each parish. Equally important, he seized the holiest part of each church back from "heretics" and established in principle
the primacy of Catholicism.

The Electoral Palatinate, whose population had predominantly been Reformed since the late sixteenth century, gained its first few shared churches

when it was occupied by a Spanish army during the Thirty Years' War. In the 1680s, Louis XIV's army imposed Simultaneum on all the palatine communities situated on the left bank of the Rhine, plus a few on the right. The key turning point came in the fateful year 1685, when the last Reformed elector died and was succeeded by a Catholic branch of the family. Without abrogating earlier treaties, the electors from the house of Pfalz-Neuburg began to promote their faith. Finally in 1698 Elector Johann Wilhelm declared that all churches hitherto exclusively in Reformed hands would be shared in a three-way Simultaneum by Catholics, Lutherans, and the Reformed. A storm of protest greeted his move, and in 1705 the elector stepped back, conceding that the right-bank churches be assigned either to the Reformed or to Catholics in a ratio of 5-to-2 (Lutherans got none). In fact, 212 churches ended up Reformed, 113 Catholic, and 130 remained shared churches. Among the latter was the Church of the Holy Spirit, the principal church in the capital city, Heidelberg.

The other circumstance that led many churches to be shared between Protestants and Catholics was condominium. For rulers of different faiths who jointly held sovereignty over a territory, Simultaneum was an obvious recourse, based on firmly established legal rights. This explains why shared churches were so numerous in some of the Mandated Territories, like the Thurgau. Protestantism there had spread rapidly in the 1520s, and from around 1526 Protestants had been able to reform worship in many parishes. The 1531 defeat of Zurich on the battlefield, however, reversed the situation. Under the terms of the Second Peace of Kappel, Protestants in the Mandated Territories could not introduce reforms where they had not done so already. Where they had, they could continue to worship as they were doing. However, if a Catholic minority as small as three families ever wished to use the church as well, the two groups would have to share it. In the seventeenth century, the number of shared churches in the Thurgau alone reached about thirty-five.

While Catholics and Protestants in the Mandated Territories were equal in civil matters, their two faiths were not. Catholicism enjoyed a privileged, normative position under the terms of the 1531 treaty, while Protestants were left with limited exemptions. This legal imbalance had wide-ranging implications for their shared use of churches. In theory Catholics could always establish new confraternities, erect new altars, and introduce new services, while Protestants could only continue their old ones. In theory,

Catholics could also alter or decorate shared churches as they pleased. The treaty stated explicitly that Protestants could not hinder conversions to Catholicism, but it said nothing about the opposite. Realities on the ground were quite different, for in most mixed parishes Protestants formed a majority of the population, often a large one. This discrepancy between Protestants' inferior legal position and their de facto dominance of towns and villages led to countless lawsuits.

Even where confessions were equal, Simultaneum created infinite opportunities for squabbling and petty forms of harassment. The Calvinist minister of Valk, in the Lands of Overmaas, complained in 1687 of local Catholics "that they hang around in the portal to the church and disquiet us with their mocking and otherwise, shoving their way into the church before we can exit, etc."[5] In the Swiss town of Glarus, a Protestant stuck a playing card in the tabernacle where Catholics kept consecrated wafers. In Augsburg's Church of Saints Ulrich and Afra, Protestants left dog feces in front of the altar; another time Catholics tore down the soundboard above the Protestants' pulpit. In Biberach, tensions flared during the Thirty Years' War. Catholics there were scandalized in 1638 when they found someone had blown their nose into the vessel containing holy water. They retaliated by locking the metal door to the church choir, preventing Lutherans from celebrating Communion in their customary way. The next year, a Catholic disturbed the wedding of a Lutheran apothecary, a prominent man in town, by ringing the great alarm bell that hung in the church tower. In response a crowd gathered. Catholics claimed the ringing was a simple mistake, but Lutherans darkly construed the act as an effort to provoke a riot. The episode escalated into a political showdown, with both parties mobilizing the support of regional allies. It took an imperial commission to resolve the dispute.

Many conflicts involved members of one religious group disrupting or hindering the other's services. In March 1607 a priest disturbed Protestant Biberachers with loud chattering, "unseemly gesticulations," and running back and forth.[6] When he did it a second day in a row, the minister stopped the service and several members of the congregation seized the priest, punched him, and threw him out of the church. The men were jailed for assaulting a priest. In the Alsatian village of Hunawihr, the Lutheran schoolmaster, accompanied sometimes by youths, would walk through the choir in the middle of Catholic services and ring the bells to call students to catechism class.[7] Other conflicts focused on furniture and ritual objects. In the Toggenburg, a Swiss territory where Protestants clashed repeatedly with their Catholic lord, the Abbot of St. Gall, an arbitration panel established that only Catholics could use the baptismal fonts in shared churches. Protestants, however, were allowed to baptize infants in ewers placed on the lids of the fonts. In reaction, the abbot's officers had lids made with pointed spikes at the center, so that ewers could not be placed on them. In the Alsatian lordship of Horbourg-Riquewihr, Catholic curés complained in 1754 that Lutherans had filled churches with benches, tables, and chairs that hampered processions. One night in 1759 the curé and Catholic schoolmaster of Hunawihr removed some of this wooden furniture, chopped it up, and burned it as firewood. The way groups decorated churches could also cause offense. In 1691, Catholics in Biberach hung a painting of purgatory in the chapel of the city hospital, which Protestants and Catholics shared. Magistrates ordered the painting's removal after Protestants threatened "to put [a picture of] Martin Luther in there as well."[8] In 1742, when the interior of St. Martin's began to be redecorated, Biberach's Protestants protested a wall fresco showing the Apostle Peter with triple tiara, triple cross, and keys, symbols of papal authority. Such conflicts did not grow rarer in the eighteenth century. In fact, Simultaneum occasioned a great deal more conflict in that age than in previous ones, if only because it was more common. While in the empire the number of shared churches peaked at the beginning of the century, in Alsace it continued to rise, reaching about 160 on the eve of the French Revolution.

However frequent these conflicts were, though, and however intense the passions they aroused, they remained limited in scope. For them to occasion violence was not unknown—in the Palatinate one priest shot a bystander when the Protestant minister's service ran overtime—but it was exceptional. For them to cause a riot was almost unheard of. Rather, glancing confrontations, surreptitious acts of minor destruction, and mockery were the rule. Such harassment did not threaten the existence or fundamental rights of those who were its object. Neither did legal suits that challenged the details of how Simultaneum was arranged but not the basic fact of it. On the contrary, the very pettiness of the harassment indicates that more violent, destabilizing strife was being avoided. Quarrels over the use of churches were common, but they focused on relative trivia.

Viewed from an anthropological perspective, the conflicts that accompanied Simultaneum might even be regarded as functional. In this respect, they resembled some of the violence perpetrated by Christians against Jews in medieval Spain. The peaceful coexistence of religious groups, known as *convivencia,* that prevailed in Spain until the end of the fourteenth century involved regular episodes of minor violence. Every year during Holy Week, prior to Easter, Christian clerics and children would stone the walls and gates of the Jewish quarter in their city. In the process, a Jew might occasionally be killed, but this was not the agitators' goal. Their violence was completely different from the pogroms suffered by Jews in the modern era. Limited in scale, it had a strong element of ritual and even of play. Through it, Christians did not seek to eliminate a Jewish presence in their community. Rather, they sought to put Jews in their place and to emphasize the boundaries separating Christians from Jews. Through their actions, those who by profession or status had a special duty to enunciate the spiritual values of the Christian community proclaimed, on behalf of the community, their loathing and rejection of Judaism. Through a reenactment of the conquest of Jerusalem in A.D. 70, they reasserted the subjection of the Jewish people. In one sense, their violence was a protest, "a warning that the toleration of Jews in a Christian society was not without its dangers and costs." But in another sense, by expressing the proper relationship between Christians and Jews, it stabilized that relationship, contributing to the "conditions that made possible the continued existence of Jews in a Christian society."[9]

The mutual harassment that accompanied Simultaneum in the early modern era may likewise have contributed to the stability of biconfessional communities. To be sure, it could not have been pleasant, and the atmosphere it created must often have been tense. Religious conflict was very visible in such communities, much more so than in ones with a single official faith. For where rival confessions practiced their faith publicly, they also acted out their antagonisms publicly. They could not turn a blind eye to one another, as could conforming Christians when dissenters traveled elsewhere or worshipped privately. To the contrary, where rival confessions shared use of a church, their confrontations were as frequent as their worship. Such conflict, though, was utterly unlike the riots in which rival confessions fought for control of the public sphere. With limited and largely symbolic goals, the conflict was itself a form of essentially peaceful engagement. Instigated frequently (though by no means always) by clergy, it reasserted the rivalry and mutual rejection that defined official relations between the confessions. At the same time, it served as a relatively harmless outlet for antagonisms. This was obviously true in the case of legal suits, which channeled conflict into a designated forum where it was conducted according to strict rules. Far from challenging peaceful coexistence, such limited forms of conflict may even have helped make coexistence possible. They were the least one might expect from people who tolerated—in their place of worship, no less—what on some level they deemed intolerable.

For all its travails, then, Simultaneum worked. When other arrangements were impossible or unacceptable, it enabled rival confessions to worship publicly in the same community, managing and limiting the conflict between them.

The Letter of the Law

It is true, of all the cities I have ever seen, in none are the two religions so embittered toward one another as they are here. Yet this hurts no man. Our security comes from the letter of the law. The bitterness, though, is extreme; it influences everything. . . . It rules in city hall, in the churches, in the marital bed; it pumps our blood. We are born antagonists—it is unbelievable, to what extent. . . . In the morning, in city hall, the fathers of the state are the warmest patriots, work hand-in-hand for the state's preservation, and are all cast in the same mould. After noon, however, after the council meeting has ended, they are enemies. You would not believe what enlightened men Augsburg has within its walls. In this respect, however, there is not a single one.[10]

So described an inhabitant the religious situation in Augsburg in the late eighteenth century. A century and a half after the Peace of Westphalia, Germany's greatest biconfessional city was still riven by antagonism. Here the "Age of Enlightenment" saw no rise of secularism; no willingness, even on the part of the educated, to elide religious differences or consider the different confessions equally valid; no relegation of faith and worship to the private sphere. On the contrary, confessional rivalry continued to permeate public life. Catholic and Lutheran Augsburgers showed a "mania" for differentiating themselves from one another, and a zest for certain

forms of confrontation. Confessional allegiance determined what names
they bore, how they decorated the façades of their houses, and how women
dressed. It determined which schools they attended, which hospitals cared
for them, in which prison they were incarcerated, and ultimately in which
cemetery they were buried. It divided Augsburgers into two distinct, opposing groups, separated by an "invisible border." And yet these "two peoples" lived with one another in almost uninterrupted peace.[11]

If toleration had depended on a friendly acceptance of other religions, if
it had required an acknowledgment that people had a right to believe and
worship as they pleased, there would have been precious little of it in early
modern Europe. Paradoxically, for coexistence to be peaceful, it had to be
compatible with confessional antagonisms and take them into account.
This is nowhere clearer than in biconfessional cities like Augsburg, where
religious divisions were legally acknowledged and publicly displayed. The
remark of our anonymous contemporary about the "letter of the law" suggests how toleration worked in such communities: through a complex
framework of laws and institutions that contained religious conflict and
rendered it relatively innocuous. That framework involved much more
than a set of arrangements for worship. Extending far beyond the religious
sphere, it structured a community's politics and institutions as well.

The most basic component of such a framework consisted of assurances. The single thing most conducive to peace in multiconfessional communities was what today we would call security guarantees, firm and reliable pledges to all the religious groups that their worship would not be
suppressed and they themselves would not be persecuted. Such guarantees
had an effect on both the weak and the strong. By quieting the apprehen-
sions of weaker groups—the nightmare scenarios that haunted all who had
experienced religious war, or had heard about atrocities committed in earlier days and other lands—they reduced the aggressive behavior so often
born of fear. At the same time, they dashed any hopes the strong may have
entertained of gaining a religious monopoly. By denying them the prospect
of all-out victory, they robbed them of incentive to press home their advantage.

Who or what could provide such guarantees? To a limited extent, fellow citizens could assure one another. In the 1560s, on the eve of the second French War of Religion, Catholics and Huguenots in Caen, Montélimar,
Annonay, Nyons, and some half-dozen other towns concluded "solemn

pacts of friendship." Gathering at general assemblies, the citizens of these towns swore to live "without difference of religion . . . in perpetual peace, friendship, and fraternity, like true citizens all of one city."[12] They agreed not to provoke or offend one another, not to take part in the upcoming conflict, and even in some cases to share its financial and military burdens with one another.

Purely local ententes, however, could not stay the force of armies, nor could they offer fellow citizens permanent guarantees about one another. Even if civic traditions and loyalties were strong, would they continue always to trump confessional allegiances? For security, people turned naturally to their co-religionists elsewhere, building networks of allies and courting the patronage of the powerful. Through such relationships, they sought to harness the kind of political and military clout that could deter aggression. Inevitably, though, they found themselves embedded in a wider set of relations between the confessions, one that extended far beyond their immediate environs. In that case, local peace depended to no small degree on the balance of power between confessions on the regional, national, and even international stages. When the balance was relatively even, the deterrent usually worked, raising the cost of conflict for both groups, and for their allies and patrons as well, who had an incentive to keep local tensions in check. But if the balance tipped heavily to one side, it was profoundly destabilizing. When a confession triumphed on one of these wider stages, its adherents might feel emboldened to act aggressively in their own towns and villages. Alternatively, it might be the weaker party that struck first, seeking safety in a preemptive defense, retribution for the losses of their co-religionists, or a vent simply for their anger and fear.

War not only brought destruction and depredation from outside, it also gave victory to one party in a community's internal struggles. By the same token, peace laid the basis for local accommodations. That is one reason Augsburg's Protestants held an annual holiday to celebrate the Peace of Westphalia, and why they and their counterparts in Biberach, Worms, Hamburg, and other German cities held centennial jubilees to commemorate Westphalia and the Peace of Augsburg. Augsburg's Protestants regarded Westphalia as an act of divine providence. Not only did it lift the threat of annihilation by armies, it brought the "miracle of parity," that set of institutional arrangements that kept the peace so successfully within the city. In France, even though Huguenots did not create holidays to commemorate the Edict of Nantes, they did totemize it, exaggerate its power to bind even kings, and seek their safety in the punctilious enforcement of its terms. In Poland similarly, the Warsaw Confederation took on a mythical aura among Polish nobles, who came to regard it as one of the foundations of their "golden liberty." In the grand scheme, these treaties were Protestant victories, securing for them legal rights that Catholics had enjoyed without question since before the Reformation. But for Catholics as well as Protestants, they brought a degree of real security, formalizing a balance of power and giving it force of law.

One of the ways treaties brought security was by freezing the status quo. Transylvanian law did so in an unusual way, forbidding forms of Christianity that had not been "received" as of 1572. This was the legal basis in Transylvania for the persecution of Sabbatarians, a group that split off from the Unitarians. More commonly, laws and treaties used the notion of a status quo to fix where groups could worship. The first major treaty to do so was the Second Peace of Kappel in 1531, for the Swiss Mandated Territories. Like some of its predecessors, the royal "edicts of pacification" that had punctuated the French Wars of Religion, the Edict of Nantes confirmed the Huguenots' right of "possession," that is, their right to worship wherever they had a church as of 1577 or 1596–1597. The Peace of Westphalia established 1624 as the normative date *(Normaljahr)* for the empire: wherever Calvinists or Lutherans had worshipped in officially Catholic territories as of that date, they could continue or resume doing so, and vice versa for Catholics in Protestant territories. If the worship had been public, so could it be in future; if only private, then it had to remain so. Many lesser treaties decreed similarly the freezing of some aspect or version of the status quo.

In fact, determining any "status quo" was an act of creative interpretation, especially when the normative date was sometime in the past. If the fortunes of the confessions had undergone any dramatic swings, choice of date was crucial. To restore the supremacy of the Reformed faith in the Palatinate, negotiators at Westphalia agreed to set 1618, before the territory was occupied by a Spanish army, rather than 1624 as the normative year there. For the Reformed in Lutheran territories and vice versa, they set 1648. Opposing sides could propose different dates: for almost sixty years the rulers of Brandenburg and Pfalz-Neuburg could not agree on one for the lands of Jülich-Cleves, until in 1672 they largely abandoned the attempt, instead specifying ecclesiastic arrangements village by village, in a painstaking and contentious procedure. Even when princes and diplomats agreed on a date, members of rival confessions frequently offered conflicting portraits of the state of affairs that prevailed then in their town or village. Resolving competing claims on this score was one of the chief tasks of the royal commissioners who toured the French provinces in the wake of Nantes, determining how its terms applied to specific local situations. "Implementation commissions" were charged with the same task in the empire after Westphalia.

However a status quo was determined, though, freezing it had a comforting, stabilizing effect: a religious minority need no longer fear that it might lose the churches it had. By the same token, a majority could no longer hope to seize or close its opponents' churches. Even if the minority dwindled to a handful of families or if it doubled in size, the allocation of churches could not be altered. In a sense, then, the status quo became a straitjacket, preventing arrangements for worship from changing with circumstances. Paradoxically, though, in constraining the confessions, it liberated them from conflict. The harder a status quo was frozen, the more it had this effect.

If we consider the regulations that divided other assets and resources between the confessions, we see the same paradox at work: the more detailed and rigid those regulations, the more conducive they were to peace. This is not mere hindsight: ruling elites in France, Switzerland, and the empire drew this lesson from experience and applied it in writing laws and treaties. The sheer length of such documents grew correspondingly: whereas the French Edict of Amboise in 1563 had only seven points, that of Beaulieu in 1576 had sixty-three, while Nantes had ninety-two public articles plus fifty-six secret ones, not including the secret brevets. As government officials experimented with clarifications and additions, the French edict of pacification evolved into a summa covering the entire range of issues raised by Protestant–Catholic coexistence, from the decoration of houses on holidays to the conversion of children. On the core issue of where Huguenots might worship, it came to include long lists of exceptions and special dispensations. The text of the Peace of Osnabrück (the relevant part of Westphalia) was similarly more than four times as long as the Peace of Augsburg, which it amended and supplemented.

Only one paragraph in the Peace of Augsburg addressed the situation in religiously mixed cities, and critically, it said nothing about public offices. This omission reflected the desire of Charles V to pack the governments of biconfessional cities with as many Catholics as possible. He succeeded well enough that, in the years between the Peace of Augsburg and the outbreak of the Thirty Years' War, Catholics tended to dominate the magistracies and councils of Biberach, Augsburg, Ravensburg, and Dinkelsbühl, all four of them cities with Lutheran majorities. Predictably, this proved to be a formula for conflict. Next to churches, positions in city government were the most sensitive resource that had to be divided between the confessions. They were the key to sharing all the other resources that magistrates disposed over, such as public funds. It was magistrates who in the first instance were charged with enforcing the terms of any religious peace. A group whose sentiments were so far out of line with those of the town's citizens would not be trusted to do so fairly. Nor could it play effectively the mediating role expected of all local authorities, resolving disputes within the local community. Indeed, in the absence of a reasonable power-sharing arrangement, religious peace was a "dead letter."[13] Local government not only mediated disputes among citizens, it provided an essential forum for the peaceful conduct of those disputes. In the chambers of city hall, antagonists were bound to obey strict protocols and rules of engagement. They could confront one another directly there in an institutional setting that forbade violence, encouraged negotiation, and elevated the common good of the civic community over other interests.

Yet for people of different faiths to be eligible for public office did little in itself to promote stability. True, it opened the possibility that members of rival confessions might share power and even forge alliances with one another. But it could equally unleash fierce struggles, as each confession formed in effect a political party and sought to win for itself as many offices as possible. This is what happened in Aachen in 1581 when Protestants gained a majority on the city council. Refusing to sit on the council any longer, Catholic leaders fled the city, electing a rival council-in-exile that, seventeen years later, was installed in power with the help of Spanish troops. Laws and decrees requiring candidates for office to be chosen without regard to their confessional affiliation also had limited effect. They worked only if the confessions were not too polarized, and in any event they were practically unenforceable. So Biberach's Lutherans learned in 1563 when the emperor insisted that Protestants as well as Catholics were eligible for all municipal offices: it was another thirteen years before the first Lutheran gained a seat on Biberach's privy council, and another nine before one was elected burgomaster. In fact, the only way to ensure that rival confessions would be adequately represented in government was to allocate a certain number of offices to each. This could be done proportionately, so that the confessional ratio in government mirrored, at least roughly, that in the broader population. Alternatively, government offices could be divided evenly, in a fifty-fifty split between two confessions. This was the system known as "parity."

Parity

The root meaning of parity, of course, is equality. Long before the Peace of Westphalia used the term itself, many partial and de facto forms of parity could be found in the empire, and the same is true for Switzerland and France. Indeed, the first cities in Europe to experiment with it, arguably, were French. In 1563–1564, in the wake of France's first religious war, magistrates in more than a half-dozen French cities created a consulate that was "mi-partie," that is, they arranged for an equal number of Catholics and Huguenots to hold the highest post in city government, that of consul. Not coincidentally, the cities included Caen, Nyons, and Montélimar, where just a few years later pacts of friendship would be sworn. In effect, the Huguenot majorities in these cities agreed to relinquish a degree of power for the sake of peace. These early experiments were ad hoc local initiatives, and most were short-lived. By contrast, the best-known, most studied parity-regimes were instituted by treaty and kept the peace for more than a century and a half. These were the governments of four German cities, Augsburg, Biberach, Ravensburg, and Dinkelsbühl, as constituted under the Peace of Westphalia.

In its full-blown, mature form, parity was an arrangement of baroque complexity. The basic principle, as stated in Westphalia, was "equality and equal number" of offices for the two confessions. That applied to councils, courts, and all other municipal bodies. In one respect, such a principle was easy to implement, since in the early modern era even positions like burgomaster were collegial, held not by a single man but by a group who made decisions jointly. Many such bodies, though, had an odd number of members. In those cases, the treaty was specific: in Augsburg, for example, Catholics were to hold four seats on the privy council, Protestants three. To maintain balance, Protestants were to outnumber Catholics by one among the other city councillors, so that their numbers would balance on the city's "small council." Because Augsburg had three treasurers, the treaty stipulated that there was to be an alternation, so that two of them would be Catholic one year, two Protestant the next. The numbers were to alternate similarly among the administrators in charge of city defenses, taxes, commerce, and construction, and on all other bodies with an odd number of members; and all was to be calibrated and coordinated so that in any one year the number of bodies with two Catholics was to equal the number with two Protestants. The same was to be done with offices that had only one incumbent at a time: alternation, coordinated such that the number of Catholics and Protestants was always equal.

In fact, parity could be, and was, applied to any number of institutions. The French town of Niort, for example, had twelve militia companies in the seventeenth century; six had a Catholic captain and ensign and a Protestant lieutenant and sergeant, the other six companies had the opposite. In La Rochelle, Protestant and Catholic merchants sat in equal numbers in the city's chamber of commerce. A royal order imposed parity in 1633 on the college of Nîmes: Jesuits taught first-, third-, and fifth-graders and the physics class, while Protestants taught second-, fourth-, and sixth-graders, plus logic (first grade was highest, sixth lowest). In 1680 a similar order assigned one Protestant and one Catholic to head each of the guilds in Colmar. Even convents could be divided in this fashion. That of Schildesche in the county of Ravensberg included in the eighteenth century Lutheran and Reformed as well as Catholic "nuns": each confession got one-third of the places, and the abbess was chosen in turns from each. In all these cases, members of rival confessions participated jointly in common institutions. But parity could also take the form of separate institutions—separate, equal in number, and receiving equal funds from government. In Augsburg, for example, Lutherans were entitled under the Peace of Westphalia to control the original city orphanage. An imperial commission determined therefore that a separate orphanage had to be established for Catholic children, and saw to it that half the furniture, clothing, and other movable property in the Lutheran orphanage was transferred to it. In Switzerland, the canton of Glarus adopted in 1683 a form of parity that divided the government itself: Catholics and Protestants continued to live side by side, but from then on they were governed by their own courts and councils, had their own treasuries and military companies, and sent their own representatives to meetings of the Swiss Confederation. A few organs of government remained common, but in the eighteenth century they even had their own postmasters and mail carriers.

Parity in general, and full-blown, numeric parity in particular, had several great virtues. First, it deflected attention away from fundamental, and thus dangerous, issues, such as the right of each confession to worship in a town and participate in its government. Those who lived under regimes of parity tended to show obsessive concern that their confession held precisely the same number of offices, received precisely the same funds, was shown precisely the same honors, and so forth, as the other. In this respect parity resembled Simultaneum: while it practically encouraged squabbling, it imposed rigid, narrow parameters on conflict. Second, it eliminated uncertainty. Like treaty clauses defining a status quo, parity froze into place a specific state of affairs that could be defined precisely and policed fairly easily. Numeric parity created a balance of power between the confessions that did not depend on their relative numbers in the population, their wealth, princely patrons, or any other factor. Augsburg's population, for example, underwent a sea change between 1650 and 1800: Protestants initially outnumbered Catholics by two to one, but by the end of the Old Regime, Catholics outnumbered Protestants by roughly three to two. Yet the number of offices each confession held remained the same. By ruling out any change in that balance of power, parity assured the confessions they would never lose their current assets and resources, or be able to seize their opponents'. Finally and most obviously, numeric parity ensured that neither confession could get its way simply by outvoting the other. No law could be passed or decision taken without the consent of members of both.

Proportional division of offices did not have these virtues. Even though it guaranteed a minority representation in government, it did nothing to prevent a majority from tyrannizing over the minority. Such power on one side and vulnerability on the other were not conducive to peace, and in the town of Kaufbeuren they led twice to a breakdown of local government. These breakdowns prompted intervention, and in 1721 an imperial commission finally resolved the issue by imposing a set of practices known by their Latin tags as "itio in partes" (division into parties) and "amicabilis compositio" (friendly agreement). When a religious issue arose that concerned only one confession, the city councillors of that confession would meet and decide the matter by themselves, exercising the same authority as if they were the entire council. If the issue concerned both confessions, Protestant and Catholic councillors would caucus separately and each group would formulate a position. Then the two groups would meet together in a joint session where each held one vote. Decisions required the approval of both. *Itio in partes* and *amicabilis compositio* thus gave the confessions, irrespective of their numbers on the council, equal voting power, and ensured that disputes between them would be resolved only by negotiated agreement. In and by themselves they established a form of parity between the confessions. By the same token, they liberated each confession to handle its own internal affairs without interference from the other party. In its own way this autonomy was as crucial as parity itself, for one must remember that early modern magistrates had extensive authority over religious affairs. The scope of this authority ranged from oversight over church wardens, at a minimum, to the appointment of clergy and even the adjudication of doctrinal disputes. It seemed illegitimate and prejudicial for Catholic magistrates to exercise such authority over Protestant churches, or vice versa, but without *itio in partes* that was precisely what happened.

Historically, it was mostly Protestants who objected to the use of majority voting by religiously mixed governing bodies. *Itio in partes* was the fulfillment of demands of theirs going back to the 1520s. Indeed, Protestants got their very name from the "Protestation" they submitted in 1529 against a decision taken by majority vote at the imperial diet of Speyer requiring them to return to the Catholic fold. In matters of conscience, they argued then, the decision of a majority cannot bind a minority, since "in matters concerning God's honor and the welfare and salvation of our souls, each person must stand before God and account for himself."[14] They also cited the Roman law principle, "Quod omnes tangit, ab omnibus debet approbari" (what affects all, should be approved by all).[15] By no coincidence, a parallel confrontation had taken place just the year before in Switzerland, at a *Tagsatzung*, or assembly of representatives of the cantons. There, supported by Bern, Zurich had declared that, in religious matters, it would no longer recognize the binding power of a majority vote. These

were momentous episodes in the constitutional history of empire and confederation, throwing into doubt their unity and very existence. In both
cases, the eventual solution was the same: *itio in partes* and *amicabilis
compositio.* In the empire, the solution came at the end of the Thirty Years'
War, when under the terms of Westphalia the imperial diet adopted these
practices. In Switzerland, it came more gradually.

For almost two hundred years, the validity of the "majority principle"
was the chief point of constitutional conflict among the Swiss. Year in, year
out, it arose every time the confederal assembly dealt with the Thurgau, the
Rheintal, and other religiously mixed Mandated Territories. Protestants
enjoyed citizenship and rights of worship in those territories but not parity. Their inequality was cemented by the fact that Catholic cantons outnumbered Protestant ones in the Confederation—or to be precise, in the
groups of cantons that ruled these condominia, appointing administrators
and setting policy for them. Majority voting gave Catholics dominance
over the Mandated Territories. Calling it a "fundamental law of our free
status as Swiss," Catholic cantons insisted "that a majority must remain a
majority."[16] Protestant cantons, on the other hand, tried to draw a distinction between secular matters, where the majority should prevail, and religious ones, where it should not. In 1632 they won a major concession from
the Catholic cantons when the latter agreed that in matters of religion and
"matters necessarily pertaining thereto [*dero notwendigen Anhang*]" only
unanimous decisions would have force, and that if the cantons could not
reach such agreement, the matter would be decided by a court of arbitration (*Schiedsgericht*) that had an equal number of Protestant and Catholic
judges.[17] The problem with the treaty was its vagueness: it did not define
what counted as religious. Protestants subsequently claimed its protection in every dispute that had the slightest religious dimension; Catholics argued that only a majority vote of the cantons could grant a dispute
this special status. It took a religious war to resolve this deadlock. In
1656, under the terms of the Third National Peace (*Landfrieden*), the Swiss
agreed that another court of arbitration (also half Protestant, half Catholic) would hold what they, in dead earnest, called the "jurisdiction of jurisdiction" *(Kompetenzkompetenz):* it would adjudicate whether a dispute
counted as religious and thus whether it would be decided by majority vote
or go to arbitration. Religious war almost broke out again in the early
1680s when the issue of majority voting arose with respect to Glarus. Final

resolution was achieved only in 1712 after a fourth religious war, which Zurich and its allies decisively won, enabling them at long last to reverse the consequences of their 1531 military defeat. On the confederal level, the Fourth National Peace prescribed what in effect was *itio in partes* and *amicabilis compositio* for all of the most weighty deliberations, whether the matter at hand was religious or not. The very protocols of the confederal assemblies, in which the latter's decisions were registered, were to be agreed by these procedures, with a Catholic and a Protestant secretary taking down separate minutes of the meetings and then conferring to reach an agreed text. On the ground, in the churches and cemeteries, schools and government of the Mandated Territories, the Peace triggered a peaceful revolution, granting Protestants full parity.

From the lowest levels of government to the highest, then, majority voting did not contribute to peaceful coexistence. Its demise in the assemblies of the Swiss Confederation was doubly important because those assemblies had a dual function vis-à-vis the Mandated Territories. On the one hand, they were an executive body, appointing administrators and setting policy for them; on the other, they were a judicial body, a court of last instance that decided all serious conflicts between the Territories' Protestant and Catholic inhabitants. The case of Switzerland thus directs our attention to a final set of mechanisms for managing and containing religious conflict: the judicial system. That system was all the more important because, like in Switzerland, in early modern Europe the boundaries between justice and administration were fluid. Courts not only rendered judgments, they enforced them, and on the local level the same person commonly served both as sheriff and as public prosecutor. It has been said that court cases—suits for noncompliance with the law, appeals for favorable rulings in jurisdictional disputes, cases concerning financial accounting, challenges to the authority claimed by individuals and institutions—were the very essence of early modern government and its principal tool for regulation and law enforcement. This made it absolutely crucial that, in their personnel, procedures, and legal standards, courts respect the principle of confessional parity. Courts were also, in a way more familiar to us, the principal institution to which parties turned for a resolution of serious disputes, and for a remedy if they felt wronged. And again like today, a great many suits were not pursued to their conclusion, ending not with a formal verdict but with a negotiated settlement. To fulfill effectively their function as arbitrators, courts had to hold a mediating position between the conflicting parties. They had to be perceived as a recourse for the weak, offering them protection against the strong. In short, they had to be nonpartisan. If they blatantly favored one confession over another, they could not help keep the peace between them; indeed, they could even encourage aggression by assuring members of the favored confession that they would not be punished for it. Impartial justice, by the same token, offered not only a remedy to quell conflict but a preventive medicine of valuable, if limited, efficacy.

On this score, the judicial systems of Europe's multiconfessional states offer some striking contrasts. France's was a failure. As early as 1564 Huguenots called for the creation of religiously mixed "chambers"—courts—to adjudicate conflicts between Protestants and Catholics. Such chambers, established after 1576 and again after the Edict of Nantes, were known as "chambers of the edict." Those of Bordeaux, Castres, and Grenoble had an equal number of Protestant and Catholic judges and were therefore called "chambres mi-parties." By contrast, Rouen's, established later, had a Catholic majority, and that of Paris, whose jurisdiction stretched over most of northern France, included only one Protestant judge. Studying the chamber in Castres, one scholar has found that its activity did help pacify the province of Languedoc after the last religious war, preventing local disputes, concerning such matters as cemeteries, processions, and the sites where Huguenots worshipped, from turning into violent conflicts.[18] By 1612, however, Huguenots were complaining to the king that the power of the chambers was being undercut by the parlements, most of whose judges were vehemently anti-Huguenot and unhappy to see their authority diluted by these rival courts. By contesting the jurisdiction of the chambers, the parlements severely undermined their authority. Such jurisdictional disputes often ended up before the king's royal council, which under Louis XIII and Louis XIV colluded in undermining the chambers. Specific cases went to the royal council whenever the judges of the *chambres mi-parties* split evenly along confessional lines, and in addition whenever it pleased the king, who retained the right to hear any religious case. Bipartisan justice was thus severely hobbled in France by majority voting, hostile courts, and the blatant partisanship of the crown. These factors undoubtedly help explain why low-level popular religious violence continued sporadically in seventeenth-century France: Catholics could count on it that the highest judicial organs would be predisposed to sympathize with them. One suspects a similar dynamic was behind the violence of Catholic crowds in the royal cities of Poland. Through their regional assemblies, Polish nobles issued complaint after complaint that the courts were not prosecuting the perpetrators of such violence and were thereby giving them a green light. In France it is clear also that the partisanship of the judicial system encouraged Catholics to use the law itself as a weapon of confessional conflict. It assured them that any suits they brought in the parlements against their religious foes were likely to receive a favorable hearing.

Things worked differently in the Holy Roman Empire: here the judicial system was on the forefront of promoting parity. The crucial institution in this development was the Imperial Cameral Court *(Reichskammergericht)* (Figure 8.4). Instructed under the Peace of Augsburg to dispense justice "without regard to which of the said religions the [parties] may be," the court developed a nonsectarian jurisprudence that treated the Peace of Augsburg as a constitution for the empire.[19] Parity between the empire's two official confessions was implicit in its rulings long before the Peace of Westphalia codified it. From 1560 on, the panels of jurists that handled religious cases for the court always included an equal number of Protestant and Catholic members. Anticipating the later procedures of *itio in partes* and *amicabilis compositio,* these "assessors" were required to respect one another's positions and seek consensus. Contrary to expectations, this experiment proved largely successful. The court did not become, for the most part, a forum for the waging of religious war by peaceful means; on the contrary, it issued writs protecting the weak and vulnerable of both confessions against religiously motivated arrests and acts of violence. Though the court broke down in 1601, the princes and diplomats who negotiated the Peace of Westphalia looked on it as a model, spelling out in detail the procedures it had pioneered and extending them, along with parity, much more broadly—to its sibling institution, the Aulic Council *(Reichshofrat);* to the judicial appeals process; and, most crucially, to the imperial diet itself.

Biconfessional cities like Biberach and Augsburg were peculiar kinds of places. Three things set them apart from other communities in early modern Europe that were religiously mixed. First, people of different faiths worshipped openly in them—openly in the sense of worshipping in full public view, without the slightest clandestinity; openly also in the sense that their worship was authorized, their faith having been legally recognized and approved. Second, people of different faiths enjoyed full civil rights (though not necessarily equal religious ones). And third, power was somehow divided so that members of rival confessions shared political authority. In such communities, Christians divided by faith had to face one

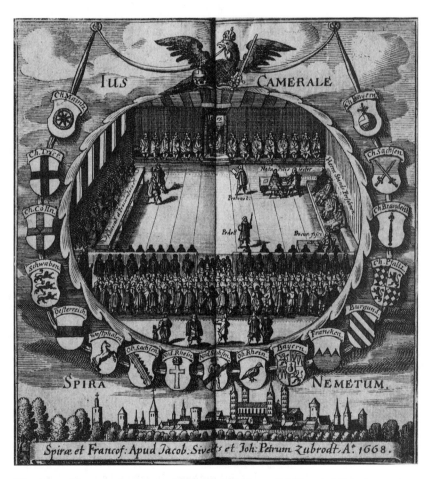

Figure 8.4. Pioneer of nonsectarian justice: the Imperial Cameral Court *(Reichskammergericht),* one of two supreme courts for the Holy Roman Empire. Anonymous engraving showing a session, or "audience," of the court. Courtesy of the State Library Center / Palatinate State Library.

another squarely, acknowledge one another's existence, and put up with one another's activities. Such a full and frank recognition of religious difference demanded, in a sense, the highest degree of mutual toleration. It raised in acute form all the thorniest questions to which confessional coexistence could give rise: not just about churches and government offices, but about every aspect of communal life that was informed by religion—education, charity, burial, oaths, calendars, marriage law. All became, potentially, fields of contestation.

In such communities, five things proved conducive to peace: (1) security guarantees that eliminated both the threat of persecution and the prospect of persecuting others; (2) rigid, detailed regulations that limited what the confessions could fight over; (3) parity between confessions, so that one could not rule over the other(s); (4) autonomy for each confession to govern its internal affairs without interference; and (5) legal mechanisms for adjudicating disputes impartially. As edicts and treaties attest, the value of all these factors became increasingly clear over time to ruling elites in France, the empire, and Switzerland. The French, one might say, learned the lesson most quickly but least well. The Edict of Nantes offered security, regulations, autonomy, and mixed courts. The royal commissioners who saw to its implementation instituted systems of proportional representation in numerous French cities, and of parity in a few. All these arrangements, though, depended on the good will of the king, and after the death of Henri IV that will was, on the contrary, intent on reducing the Huguenots to obedience. Ultimately, the centralized structure of the French state itself made true parity between the confessions, and with it an impartial judiciary, impossible. Also, as French kings made increasingly strong claims to "absolute" power, they were bound to find the Huguenots' autonomy and their *places de sûreté* unacceptable. Looser state structures, like those of the empire and confederation, could accommodate multiconfessionalism more easily.[20] Because their sovereign territories and cantons stood in a relationship of legal equality to one another, they had the potential to strike among themselves a genuine balance of power. (The same was true in Poland, but only vis-à-vis the nobility, not in the royal cities.) Parity arrangements at the local level could therefore be echoed and reinforced at higher ones. Such states also inherited from before the Reformation institutions and procedures for arbitrating disputes that could be adapted to new circumstances. In the empire, these developments culminated in the Peace of Westphalia, to whose terms Germans clung rigidly for the next century and a half. The Swiss cited Westphalia as a model for themselves in the 1680s, and its principles informed the more general peace they struck in 1712. In fact, the ruling elites of all three lands had their eyes on one another and learned vicariously from their neighbors' experiences.

Equally important, though, was the acceptance of peaceful coexistence by townsfolk and villagers themselves. Local ad hoc experiments with parity began as early as 1563 in some French cities. In the empire the first explicit demand for numeric parity came from Biberach's Lutherans in 1562, a demand they repeated more than once. In all four of what became the empire's parity cities, burghers implemented, of their own accord, some aspect of parity for a shorter or longer period before 1648, anticipating what was later codified by treaty. Even though biconfessionalism had been imposed on them by Charles V, they came to accept it and groped for ways to make it work. The provisions of Westphalia fulfilled most directly the demands of Protestants, but by 1648 the Catholics in these cities were prepared to welcome them too. Thus it is no wonder that both Protestants and Catholics were quick to accept the parity arrangement prescribed by treaty and to extend it to education, charity, and other areas of social life. On their own, they had already begun to internalize its norms.

The same was true of Simultaneum. Imposed commonly by rulers of one faith on subjects of another, it nevertheless won popular acceptance as an objectionable but, if necessary, acceptable arrangement for worship. Townsfolk and villagers in the Thurgau even figured out a way to improve the arrangement. As in other Mandated Territories, Catholics had a legal right to use the nave as well as choir for their services. Nevertheless, over the seventeenth century they permitted physical partitions to be erected separating the two spaces in an increasing number of churches, conceding Protestants exclusive use of the nave. Similarly, Protestants in the Dutch Lands of Overmaas began in the latter half of the century to hang great curtains between nave and choir, which they pulled closed during their services so they would not have to look at the most offensive to them of all objects, the Catholics' high altar. Authorities took up the innovation: shared churches in Alsace and the Palatinate had partition walls from the beginning. And in 1757 the Congregation for the Propagation of the Faith

NINE

A Friend to the Person

The Syndics

Known to every cigar smoker, Rembrandt's 1662 painting *The Syndics of the Clothmakers' Guild* (Figure 9.1) is a pop icon of seventeenth-century Dutch art. When we look at it, it is as if we ourselves, transported back to that time, have entered a room where six sober Dutchmen are working. Interrupted, they look up from their book and peer at us, as do we at them. Assisted by the hatless servant behind them, the syndics had the duty of assessing the quality of cloth sold in Amsterdam, Europe's great emporium of trade. It was a duty with a moral edge, ensuring that no shoddy wares were passed off as good. Wearing a modest black with flat white collars, the officers exude unity and seriousness of purpose. One would never imagine from this image that they were divided from one another in any fundamental way. Yet these five men belonged to four different confessions. The chairman, seated with the book directly before him, was Calvinist. The second man from the left, half standing, was a Mennonite of the strict Old Frisian variety and probably a deacon of his congregation. Two other syndics had Catholic schuilkerken in their homes. The fifth was Remonstrant.

To those who know its details, Rembrandt's painting has come to symbolize the religious toleration of Dutch society in its Golden Age, a society where, according to English ambassador William Temple, "differences in [religious] Opinion make none in Affections, and little in Conversation"; where people of different faiths "live together like Citizens of the World, associated by the common ties of Humanity, and by the bonds of Peace, Under the impartial protection of indifferent Laws, With equal encouragement of all Art and Industry, and equal freedom of Speculation and Enquiry."[1] Here is an ideal of toleration most of us today would heartily endorse. It is an ideal of perfect integration, with no walls of prejudice or discrimination dividing society. In it, people of different faiths live, work, play, trade, learn, share, sacrifice, and even make love with one another. United by common interests, they share common tastes and values as well. Religious differences are relegated to the private sphere, where every individual enjoys freedom of conscience. People worship voluntarily or not at all, and the people with whom they worship aren't necessarily the same ones they live next door to or—like the syndics—work with. To the extent its reality matched this ideal, the Dutch Golden Age seems a precursor of modern liberal society. That is one reason why we still celebrate it.

Figure 9.1. Rembrandt, *The Syndics [Staalmeesters] of the Clothmakers' Guild* (1662). Canvas, 191.5 x 279 cm. Courtesy of the Rijksmuseum, Amsterdam.

As do many people today, Temple believed that integration was the key to toleration. According to him, it was "the force of Commerce, Alliances, and Acquaintance, spreading so far as they do in small circuits" that made "conversation, and all the offices of common life, so easie, among so different Opinions."[2] Was he right? Did social integration grease the wheels of coexistence in the Dutch Republic? Should we expect to find it wherever religious groups lived together peacefully in the early modern era? Unfortunately, historians have not yet done the kind of nuts-and-bolts research that would enable them to say, for most parts of Europe, whether people of different faiths had friendships, went to school, did business, intermarried, and so forth with one another. Nor will their verdict likely take the form of a simple yes or no. In sixteenth-century Paris, for example, Huguenots "dealt by preference with one another," intermarrying, lending one another money, taking in one another's children as servants and apprentices, the elites among them offering patronage and protection to their co-religionists.[3] This was just a preference, though, and Huguenots continued to do the same things with Catholics as well. Alternatively, religious groups could be integrated in some respects but not others. In the German town of Wesel, for example, Calvinists and Lutherans attended church and even took Communion together in the sixteenth century, in comprehensive parish churches. At the same time, they kept their schools and charitable systems separate.

For all these complexities and uncertainties, though, one thing is clear: toleration in early modern Europe did not depend, as Temple suggested, on the public sphere being religiously neutral or on groups being thoroughly integrated. Just as there were different ways of arranging worship in religiously mixed communities, so there were different patterns of interaction between people of different faiths. In this respect too, toleration took different forms.

Two Models

More than we often recognize, our model of toleration is based on a radical individualism. In the ideology we have inherited from the Enlightenment, every individual human being has been vested, by God or nature, with certain inalienable rights, among them religious freedom. Each one of us may believe as we wish and worship accordingly, revising our beliefs and changing our practices as we please. We may convert; we may proselytize to convert others; we may switch our affiliation from one religious community to another; and if none of the existing communities satisfies us, we may found new ones. We have a choice not only between faiths, but between belief and disbelief, practice and nonpractice. However much our choices are influenced by the people surrounding us and the culture in which we are raised, religion is ultimately a voluntary matter for each individual.

Contrast this model to one in which groups are the primary units of society. Imagine a world in which religious communities enjoy broad autonomy but individuals do not—in which toleration extends to communities as communities, not to individual members of those communities. In a thought-provoking exercise, philosopher Will Kymlicka does precisely this, except that he does not rely entirely upon his imagination; he takes the former Ottoman Empire as an example of such a world.[4] Famous for their toleration of Jews and Christians, those two other "peoples of the book," the Ottomans developed what is known as the "millet" system. Islam was their established religion, and only those who practiced it enjoyed full citizenship. But in exchange for paying a special tax, Jews and the two main Christian groups, Greek and Armenian Orthodox, were treated as protected subjects (dhimmis) and allowed to organize as communities. Each protected group, or millet, had its own laws, courts, and officials as well as places of worship. Religious leaders also functioned as secular leaders, with the power to tax their followers and to punish them for offenses. Every non-Muslim had to belong to one of the millets and submit to its leaders. Members had no rights of conscience—no right to deviate from their millet's official teachings or disobey its rules. Nor could they proselytize; convert, except to Islam; or marry outside their faith (except that Muslim men could marry dhimmi women). Jews and Christians endured a host of humiliating restrictions. But each millet was largely self-governing, and within its confines Jews and Christians enjoyed legal protection for their worship and way of life.

These two models tend to produce very different kinds of societies. The first, liberal model (liberal in the original sense of vesting autonomy in the individual) encourages a religious melting pot. Allegiances are fluid, as people of different faiths consort with and influence one another. As they move in and out of religious institutions, congregations and whole religions may wax and wane. Because individuals can decide what role religion will play in their lives, their faith may form a large or only a small part of their identities. At work, at play, and in most other spheres, they participate in a common society and culture, regardless of religious difference. By contrast, in the second model, religious groups tend to be sharply bounded, self-contained bodies, with little movement among them. Society is segregated, not integrated. At the same time, each group is a comprehensive community with dimensions that extend far beyond the strictly religious. Like the millets of the Ottoman Empire, each group has its own laws and customs, schools and charities, networks, clubs, festivities, and even government. To be sure, if we judge this second model by the standards of the first, it seems to offer less toleration. And it is our prerogative to make such a judgment, based on our values. But it is important to see that what the second model really offers is a different kind of toleration from the first, with advantages as well as disadvantages. In it, religious groups form strong, cohesive communities. Enjoying great autonomy, they can regulate their entire lives—public as well as private, communal as well as individual—in accord with their faith.

These models, like the "ideal types" of Max Weber, are of course abstractions. They represent in very simplified, pure form what in real life are only tendencies. Still, they can help us make sense of the variety of patterns found in the religiously mixed communities of early modern Europe, for both models had real-life approximations there. The Dutch Republic resembled very roughly the first. Not that the ideology informing its toleration was that of human rights, in the Enlightenment sense. But in the course of their Revolt against Spain, the Dutch embraced "freedom of conscience" as a fundamental principle. That freedom was vested in the individual. Translated into practice, it took the form, as we have seen, of a distinction between public and private spheres. To be sure, public and private had different meanings in the seventeenth century than they do now, and the public sphere was not neutral. Behind closed doors, though, in their schuilkerken, non-Calvinists could worship as they pleased, as magistrates turned a blind eye. While the Republic had an official Church, no law required people to attend its services or those of any other church. Ironically, this arrangement was more conducive to *individual* religious freedom than if multiple churches had been recognized and granted privileges. A national church like the Dutch Reformed, with sharply restricted powers, was the closest thing in early modern Europe to a disestablishment of religion. It left Netherlanders free not only to choose among churches, but to decide whether to join any, and the most striking religious characteristic of the Republic in its early years was the number of people who exercised this option. In Haarlem, Delft, Gouda, Utrecht, and other major cities, those who declined membership in any church formed a majority until at least the 1620s, when our knowledge trails off. In the northeastern provinces of Friesland, Groningen, and Drenthe, a substantial minority continued to belong to no church through the seventeenth and into the eighteenth century. Some of these nonmembers had no confessional affiliation and never attended church services. These people were not atheists in the modern sense; the vast majority, if not all, believed in God and thought of themselves as Christian. For one reason or another, though, they preferred to have an individual, purely private relation to the divine rather than join groups for worship. In some cases they held mystical beliefs similar to those of Hubert Duifhuis, or like Erasmus (though without necessarily reading him) thought the essence of Christian piety lay in upright, moral behavior.

Unless they chose for a strict Mennonite congregation, Netherlanders who did affiliate with a church could determine for themselves how closely they wished to do so. A great many of those who attended weekly services in the Reformed Church, for example, were not actual members of the church. They declined to submit to the church's moral and doctrinal discipline, and hence were barred from Communion, which was offered three or four times a year. That seems to have suited very well those Protestants known as "sympathizers" who wished to pray and sing together with church members, as a congregation, and to listen to the sermons of the Reformed ministers. In similar fashion, Catholic congregations included people who confessed and took Communion frequently, others who did so just once a year at Easter, and still others who turned to priests only to solemnize with ecclesiastic rites life's great passages of birth, marriage, and death. Officials of the Catholic Church called these groups, respectively, the devout, "good," and "nominal" Catholics. Even among the devout, though, the very presence of rival churches, and the option of belonging to no church, gave laypeople a leverage that Christians in confessionally homogeneous lands scarcely knew. The records of Dutch Reformed consistories are full of disciplinary cases in which church members refuse to accept censure. Some Reformed church members, like many "sympathizers," were skeptical of clerical authority, believing that laypeople could understand and interpret scripture themselves. In Rotterdam in the 1640s to 1660s, some organized clubs where they discussed religious questions with Mennonites and Remonstrants. A few even attended Mennonite or Collegiant Communion services, in addition to Reformed ones. Such cases, though exceptional, are indicative of the eclecticism, experiment, and fluidity of the Dutch religious scene.

As for social integration, anecdotal evidence suggests a high degree of it, at least through the first half of the seventeenth century. Culturally too, while the confessions were not identical, they shared common tastes. Those who bought Rembrandt's paintings, for example, like the people he painted, were of all religious persuasions. Even an artist such as Pieter Saenredam, whose paintings of whitewashed church interiors used to be understood as Calvinist in aesthetic, turns out to have produced them for Catholic as well as Protestant buyers. The most popular writer of the Dutch Golden Age was Jacob, affectionately known as "Father," Cats. A pious Calvinist, he wrote didactic moralizing books that found an audience among all confessions. The most lauded, prestigious writer of the Golden Age was Joost van den Vondel, a poet and playwright who converted at the age of fifty-three from Mennonite to Catholic faith.

For a sharp contrast to the Netherlands, consider the German city of Augsburg, which conforms in many respects, especially after 1648, to our second model. Only two faiths, Lutheran and Catholic, were legal in the city, and every inhabitant belonged to one of them. Movement between the two faiths was rare, and dissent from both was a criminal offense. Each faith had its magistrates, who caucused separately whenever a matter concerned only their community *(itio in partes)*. In civil affairs government was conducted jointly; in religious affairs each community was autonomous. Catholics and Lutherans had separate, parallel sets of institutions—each confession its own schools, hospitals, orphanages, prisons, cemeteries. As a visiting philosophe scornfully observed in the eighteenth century, Augsburg even had two pigsties, one for Lutheran pigs, the other for Catholic ones.

Augsburg was by no means segregated in every respect (neither, in fact, was Ottoman society). Of sixty neighborhoods in 1711, only three had no Lutheran households and only four no Catholic ones. Catholics commonly worked as servants in Lutheran households, and merchants of the two faiths undertook joint ventures. Every guild, at least in the eighteenth century, included members of both. At the same time, certain occupations were dominated overwhelmingly by one group: most butchers, brewers, and goldsmiths, for example, were Lutheran, whereas most gardeners and construction workers were Catholic. Craftsmen almost never took on apprentices or journeymen of the other faith, while Lutheran and Catholic journeymen socialized separately in different taverns.

Culturally, Augsburg could scarcely have been more sharply polarized, as Catholics and Lutherans showed a "mania" for differentiating themselves from one another. They decorated the façades of their houses differently, Catholics using images of monstrance and host and other highly charged confessional motifs. They dressed differently—at least the women did, Catholics wearing "bolt" bonnets, Protestants "wing" ones. They bore different names. Catholics gave their boys names such as Franz Joseph or Joseph Ignaz, after saints and other figures whom they venerated. Lutherans named their boys after heroes of a very different sort, such as Friedrich Wilhelm, Prussia's great elector. They also continued to use many traditional Germanic names, such as Heinrich, which Catholics increasingly avoided. Little else remained neutral, either, in this *Kulturkampf,* which stamped the mentalities and practices of Augsburg's two religious communities so deeply that they seemed to become two distinct "peoples," divided by an "invisible border."[5]

Yet these two communities were not separate "peoples," in the sense of ethnic groups. In this respect, Augsburg differed from the model we began with, the Ottoman millet system. At least initially, the division between Catholics and Lutherans in the city was purely and exclusively religious. That is one reason Augsburgers found it so hard originally to accept the division. Another reason was that the split struck the very core of the community, its citizens. In the Ottoman Empire, by contrast, religious groups also had ethnic identities. Muslims, to be sure, were a diverse, multinational group, and so on a lesser scale were the members of the Jewish and Christian millets. Still, there was a clear sense in the Ottoman Empire that dhimmis constituted distinct peoples, with their own ancestors, customs, and sometimes languages, as well as beliefs. Moreover, only one group, Muslims, were full citizens; the rest remained tolerated subjects—outsiders in "the territory of Islam," regardless of how permanently they resided in it. In Europe, too, it proved easier and more common for people to tolerate other faiths when those who practiced them were not citizens but foreigners who belonged to an alien "nation."

Foreign Nations

Long before the splintering of Western Christendom, the idea that different nations practiced different religions had gained a degree of acceptance among some Europeans. A counterpoint to the crusading ideal, this idea was conveyed in works of medieval literature such as Boccaccio's *Decameron,* which contains a story about a father who had three sons and a precious ring. Whichever son the father gave his ring to would, by family tradition, be his heir. But this father loved all his sons equally, and so he had two other rings made, so similar to the first as to be indistinguishable, and gave one ring to each son. As the narrator, a Jew, explains, the father is God and his sons are the Jew, the "Sarazen," and the Christian, each believing he alone has "the heritage of God, and his true Law."[6] The story circulated widely in sixteenth-century Italy. It was recounted in 1580 by a Venetian goldsmith and in 1599 by a miller named Menocchio, who concluded from it, "Every person considers his faith to be right, and we do not know which is the right one: but because my grandfather, my father, and my people have been Christians, I want to remain a Christian, and believe that this is the right one." Boccaccio's text helped Menocchio formulate a relativistic view of faith. The miller drew similar conclusions from another fourteenth-century text, *The Travels of Sir John Mandeville,* which told of encounters with strange peoples on a fabulous journey to the Far East. From it, said Menocchio, "I got my opinion that when the body dies, the soul dies too, since out of many different kinds of nations, some believe in one way and some in another."[7] In Spain, where Christians, Muslims, and Jews lived for centuries in close proximity, there were "many Menocchios." Come the Reformation, some applied the same wisdom to the new brand of Christianity from northern Europe: "Each can save himself in his own law," testified one, "the Moor in his, the Jew in his, the Christian in his, and the Lutheran in his."[8] This use of the word *law* as synonym for religion implied in itself the possibility of toleration, for after all, it was accepted as normal that laws varied among peoples.

Around the Mediterranean, the inhabitants of port cities were accustomed to the presence of foreigners. Typically, these foreigners lived in special quarters, grouped together by language and place of origin. In Venice and other European ports, they constituted "nations," self-governing corporate bodies with their own laws, finances, and officials. Venice hosted nations of Turks and Albanians, both Muslim; Jews, legally subdivided into "Levantines" (from the Ottoman Empire), Ponentines (from Iberia), and Germans (that is, Ashkenazim); and Orthodox Greeks. Germans constituted another nation in Venice, and when most of them embraced Protestantism, the existing arrangement accommodated them with ease. Inside the Fondaco dei Tedeschi, the edifice where Germans traded and sometimes lived, they could worship as they pleased, and from at least the 1640s they had a full-fledged Lutheran congregation with its own minister. The same organization of foreigners into "nations" could be found on Venice's terra firma at the University of Padua. Here, as at other European universities, students had long been divided into nations, and with the Reformation, Padua's German nations became mostly Protestant. As long as their members were discreet and did not express their faith publicly, they were not harassed. The easy treatment of these Protestants contrasted sharply to the persecution faced by native dissenters. The difference was that "foreign nations," while residing in a Christian city, were "manifestly . . . not of it."[9]

Politically as well as religiously, members of foreign nations were outsiders. That too made them less threatening, both to local elites and to native artisans, who showed an antipathy to outsiders that bordered at times on xenophobia. Artisans in particular were jealous guardians of the privileges they enjoyed as citizens and were loath to share them with newcomers. To them doctrinal orthodoxy seemed inseparable from, even a prerequisite for, certain qualities on which they set great store: social honor, moral propriety, economic self-sufficiency, civic responsibility. Cities where they had a voice in governance, such as Hamburg, tended to be less tolerant than ones where merchants held all the reins of power. Yet while artisans often wished to keep dissenters from becoming citizens, they had fewer objections to dissenters' living in their cities as noncitizens. In fact, many cities distinguished between two types of noncitizen, denizens and foreigners. The first resembled the group known today as resident aliens. Long-term residents, they enjoyed a variety of rights that in some cases amounted to a lesser form of citizenship and was sometimes called such, but they were always excluded from formal political participation. "Foreigners" were only temporary visitors, at least in theory. They had no rights, unless magistrates drew up a contract *(Fremdenkontrakt, condotte)* with a group of them. They were allowed to remain in a community on sufferance for as long as they were useful, or unobtrusive. Paradoxically, many cities were more tolerant of religious dissent among these groups than among their citizens. In Worms, for example, Catholics constituted in the late sixteenth century less than 10 percent of the citizenry but roughly 20 percent of the total population. Strasbourg, previously a Lutheran town, developed an extreme imbalance after it became part of France: as of 1783, 71 percent of its citizens were Protestant and 68 percent of its denizens were Catholic.

The explanation for this pattern is partly economic. In hard times especially, artisans feared immigrants, regardless of religion, as economic competitors. Because only citizens of a town could join a guild, this fear could be assuaged somewhat by preventing immigrants from gaining citizenship, as doing so barred them from practicing most crafts or keeping a retail shop. The dissenting faith of some immigrants offered townsfolk a ready justification for excluding them from citizenship. To be sure, such exclusions were often relaxed by self-interested elites or simply evaded. Still, they had a pervasive influence on the occupation, wealth, and status of religious dissenters as a group, pushing them out of the middle strata of urban society into its upper and lower reaches. Forced to make livings in occupations open to noncitizens, dissenters could, on the one hand, be merchants, nobles, princely officials, university students, physicians, or priests—all elite positions that carried no citizenship requirement. On the other hand, they could be soldiers, sailors, servants, peddlers, day laborers, migrant workers, or vagabonds. A similar bifurcation can be observed, for the same reason, among Europe's Jews.

Much more was at work, though, than economic interests. Because they were excluded from politics, noncitizens could not challenge a government or alter an ecclesiastic establishment. They did not belong to a city's (or a nation's) corpus Christianum, so they could not rupture its unity. And since they were not full-fledged members of a community, their presence was not perceived as tainting its holiness as much as if they had been citizens, just as dissenting worship did not taint it if kept out of communal space. Politically and religiously, dissenters actually threatened a community less as outsiders than as citizens, and the more they were outsiders, the less threatening they were. This scale of sensibilities inverted the civic order. It explains why in the Dutch Republic Lutherans and Jews, unlike Catholics and other dissenters, had very public, resplendent places of worship. While non-Calvinists of native descent worshipped overwhelmingly in schuilkerken, these groups consisted—the former largely, the latter entirely—of foreign immigrants and their descendants. The same considerations help explain why, after having just brutally suppressed French Protestantism, in January 1686 Louis XIV reassured German and other foreign Protestant merchants and artisans that they could enter and leave France as they wished: Louis found the presence of foreign Protestants in his kingdom more acceptable than that of native ones, and in the following years—even when Huguenots were being severely persecuted—he permitted Lutheran and Reformed embassy chapels to operate in Paris. Across Europe, ambassadors resident in a country whose official faith was different from their own could admit their countrymen to services in their embassy chapels without controversy. By contrast, admitting native dissenters from the local community to embassy chapel services often aroused protest. In London, where violent clashes broke out repeatedly in the seventeenth century around the Spanish and Portuguese embassies, citizens and local officials made it clear that they did not think native dissenters should enjoy the same freedom as foreign ones. The latter were even easier to tolerate if they were only visiting temporarily, as was the case in theory for all foreigners (as opposed to denizens), but it was true especially of ambassadors, merchants, university students, and soldiers. Some communities tolerated only dissenters who they felt sure would not settle. Thus, for example, the magistrates of Mainz decided in 1662 to allow Protestant merchants to reside in their city only as long as they remained unmarried.

Western Europeans always had a clear sense, at least, of who were "foreigners"—whose language, customs, and religion were normative, and whose alien. The distinction was more complex in eastern Europe, where waves of ethnic migrations had created settlement patterns of exceeding intricacy. Here "nations" coexisted on terms that in some cases approached equality, as did the Saxon, Szekler, and "Hungarian" nation (which in fact included Slovaks, Croats, and Ruthenians as well as Magyars) in Transylvania. Even in the Middle Ages, many national divisions in eastern Europe were at the same time religious: Tatars were Muslim; Armenians, Monophysite; Jews, of course, Jewish, though Karaites, of Turkish origin, considered themselves the only true Jews. Greeks and Ruthenians, a huge and exploited group, were Orthodox; many Czechs were, from the fifteenth century, Hussite; while even at that late date some Lithuanians remained pagan. With the Reformation, some ethnic splits that had previously lacked a religious dimension gained one. Why and to what extent this was so are vexed questions, and to this day nationalists continue to mythologize correspondences between ethnicity and religion in eastern Europe. Still, one can safely say that, from the Baltic Sea to the Carpathian Mountains, most "Saxons" (ethnic Germans) became Protestant, and as lines hardened between Protestant confessions, they chose overwhelmingly for Lutheranism. Most Szekler communities embraced Unitarianism, while some remained Catholic. In Transylvania, most Calvinists were Magyars.

Correspondences between "nation" and religion continued after the Reformation to facilitate toleration in eastern Europe. They gave religious pluralism well-established precedents. "There is nothing new about diversity of religion in Poland," observed the Lutheran Swietoslaw Orzelski in a 1592 speech. "Aside from the Greek, which is Christian, pagans and Jews were known for a long time and faiths other than Roman Catholic [that is, the Hussite] have existed for centuries."[10] If these groups could live together peacefully, Orzelski argued, why couldn't Protestants and Catholics now? Arrangements that, before the Reformation, had kept the peace between "nations" continued to do so now that the latter were divided also by faith. The three nations of Transylvania, for example, had long been autonomous and self-governing. It seemed natural to give each the power to regulate its own religious affairs, and to "receive" (formally approve) the religions each had embraced. Arrangements that in the past had applied to one religious group could also be extended to new ones. This is what happened, for example, in the Lithuanian capital of Vilnius. Since the 1430s, Ruthenians in Vilnius had enjoyed full citizenship alongside Lithuanians— Orthodox Christians alongside Catholics, thus—and the city's constitution had guaranteed that the Ruthenian minority would always be represented by a burgomaster and three city councillors. Guilds had likewise reserved for Ruthenians a fixed share of offices—in the case of the cobblers' guild, half, a medieval instance of parity. With the Reformation, Vilnius's guilds extended this model to Lutherans—but not to Calvinists, because as Germans the Lutherans constituted a "nation," whereas the city's Calvinists were fellow Lithuanians. Thus the cobblers henceforth had two Catholic, two Orthodox, and two Lutheran deacons; other guilds did likewise. Because they differed from Catholics only in religion, Calvinists were not allocated any offices. Ruthenians who belonged to the Uniate Church (created in 1596 by the Union of Brest) were treated as Calvinists were: because they did not constitute a "nation" separate from the Orthodox (known henceforth as "Disuniates"), they were not recognized as a distinct group or allocated any offices. The arrangement for toleration that Vilnius inherited from the Middle Ages was applicable only to religious divisions that followed ethnic lines.

Intimate Relations

How was coexistence to work, though, when groups were not divided by anything *but* faith—when they shared the same ancestry, customs, language, and privileges, and were accustomed to thinking of themselves as one people, one community? Ironically, this situation was more problematic. While our two models suggest answers, they also oversimplify. Even the extreme cases of the Dutch Republic and Augsburg do not match them perfectly. For the rest of Europe there was too much variety and too little is known to offer more than the most tentative, limited generalizations. Certain patterns, though, seem to recur frequently.

First, neighborhoods tended not to be segregated. Unlike Jews, Christian dissenters were nowhere forced to live in ghettos. In some cities, like Cologne, they were barred from citizenship and so could not own property, but that did not prevent them from renting. Elsewhere they could not keep shops within the city walls, as in Paris, where most Huguenot artisans ended up living in a suburb, the Faubourg St. Marcel. Merchants and professionals were not hampered by this restriction, though. Dissenters might have to worship outside city walls or even farther, beyond the boundaries of the community. Rather than perform a long Auslauf, some found it convenient to live near their place of worship. Similarly, within the walls of biconfessional cities such as Augsburg, Colmar, and (until 1607) Donauwörth, minorities tended to cluster around their places of worship, which naturally were centers of communal life for them. By this kind of elective affinity, religious groups often came to dominate certain neighborhoods, where they found comfort, conviviality, and sometimes security in numbers. But such patterns did not amount to segregation: in all cities we know about, most neighborhoods were religiously mixed to a greater or lesser degree. Peace between the confessions was not contingent upon their living in separate spaces.

To the contrary, neighborhoods themselves had the capacity to promote toleration. Early modern neighborhoods were (by modern standards) cohesive social organizations. In many Dutch cities, they were corporate bodies with their own statutes, finances, officers, and festivities. Promoting harmony among members was their avowed raison d'être. Typically, their statutes forbade neighbors "in any way to offend, injure, or speak any contemptuous words . . . to one another, or . . . do any violence or make any threats." According to an English visitor, many specifically prohibited "any discourse about Religion, for fear of falling out."[11] Even where neighborhoods lacked formal structure, neighbors had extensive obligations toward one another and were intimately involved in each other's lives. Regardless of faith, residents were expected to attend their neighbors' weddings and funerals, a custom that some clergy—Calvinist in France, Catholic in the Netherlands—struggled to combat. They were expected to help neighbors in need with small loans and other forms of charity. When domestic quarrels turned violent, they were supposed to intervene. Neighbors vouched for—or against—one another in court cases; in a sense the opinion of neighbors was a court in which every person was tried and their honor judged.

"Love thy neighbor as thyself," commanded Jesus (Matthew 22:39). Neighborliness was an ethos that overlapped with notions of Christian charity and love. As such, it could counterbalance the centrifugal force of religious differences. In 1592 the Polish Jesuit Peter Skarga wrote of Protestants that their "heresy is bad, but they are good neighbors and brethren."[12] In 1572, during the St. Bartholomew's Day massacre, and again during riots in 1621, some Parisian Huguenots were hidden by Catholics "with whom they had contracted a friendship either upon the score of Kindred, or Neighborhood, or some tie of Interest."[13] When in 1650 the bishop of Würzburg ordered the Lutherans of Kitzingen to tolerate the Catholic minority in their city, he enjoined them to live "peacefully, amicably, modestly, and as good neighbors." For their part, the Lutherans promised to live "with their Catholic fellow-burghers . . . in Christian love and unity."[14] In

England, a man who refused to help a magistrate persecute Quakers explained in 1670, "tears tricklin dowen his Cheekes," that that he was "loath to wrong his peacabl nibours."[15] Visiting Dorchester in 1724, Daniel Defoe was delighted to find Anglican and dissenting clergy taking tea together, "conversing with civility and good neighbourhood, like . . . men of a catholic and extensive charity."[16]

Compared to the neighborhood, the market was a volatile and variable place. Economic interactions between religious groups show little consistency, but seem to have been sensitive both to economic conditions and to the wider atmosphere of confessional relations. At one extreme stood (as usual) the Netherlands, and in particular Holland, where the picture in the seventeenth century resembled that in Rembrandt's *Syndics*. Even here, given how many commercial ties were based on family connections, people may well have tended to work and trade with their co-religionists disproportionately. That may have been the case especially among Mennonites, a relatively small group, as it was in England with Quakers. But just as the Dutch traded enthusiastically with nations of all faiths, in their trade-driven cities they did the same with one another. One should distinguish, though, between maritime and inland Dutch cities: in many of the latter, Calvinist burghers campaigned successfully to restrict citizenship and with it guild membership. Between the 1620s and 1650s, Arnhem, Nijmegen, Deventer, and Zwolle all declared Catholic immigrants ineligible. Unlike their maritime counterparts, ruled by oligarchies, these cities had relatively open, communal constitutions that gave guildsmen a voice in such matters. In this respect they resembled cities in nearby Germany, where ordinances likewise restricted the ability of dissenting immigrants to gain citizenship. By the 1650s, Strasbourg, Regensburg, Ulm, Frankfurt, Cologne, Gmünd, and Rottweil had all adopted such measures. At the insistence of guildsmen, most major Polish cities had done so even earlier.

In the struggle between confessions, opponents sometimes took up economic arms. Excluding people of other faiths from guilds, refusing to take them on as apprentices or journeymen, boycotting their shops, not trading with them: cases are known of all these behaviors, and even more cases of clergy exhorting their flocks to them. These tactics, though, are not all compatible. Excluding religious opponents from a trade or craft, for example, did relieve one of the need to bond fraternally or work with them. But when different religious groups controlled different sectors of the economy, they had to buy goods from or sell goods to one another. One way or another, it seems, religious groups were always interacting in the economic sphere.

Another striking fact is how broadly that sphere was defined, extending even to goods and services needed for religious worship. In the Dutch village of Graft, for example, a Mennonite carpenter—son of an elder, no less—was hired to repair the Calvinist minister's parsonage, while in the Frisian village of Dronrijp a Calvinist carpenter built a Catholic schuilkerk. In the French city of Nîmes, a Calvinist apothecary sold candles to Catholics, a Calvinist goldsmith produced a chalice, and Calvinist ironsmiths placed a cross on top of a Catholic church tower. To the Nîmes consistory, who called these men to account in the 1590s and 1600s, their actions made them accomplices to idolatry. But church authorities struggled, usually in vain, against such behavior. Calvinist synods in France forbade the production of Catholic books and art, yet in the 1650s the Calvinist engraver Jean-Jacques Thurneysen in Lyon produced portraits of saints and scenes from the life of the Virgin Mary. Other Calvinist publishing houses in Lyon published Catholic liturgical books and compendia of canon law. In Augsburg, too, Lutheran goldsmiths, engravers, printers, and painters produced objects for Catholic worship and devotion. In the eighteenth century, when Catholic painters dominated Augsburg's artistic scene, they produced work for Lutheran churches (and shared churches) as well as Catholic ones. None of which is to say that it wasn't more common for Catholic art to be produced by Catholic artists, Catholic books by Catholic publishers, and Protestant materials likewise by Protestants. The exceptions, though, are numerous.

In sensitive personal and familial matters, people of different faiths similarly relied on one another's services. In seventeenth-century Montpellier, Catholics and Huguenots tended to use notaries of their own faith, but all notaries had clients of the other faith as well. In Lyon, Huguenots had to use Catholic notaries, as none were Calvinist. Lyon's notaries were careful to respect the beliefs of their Calvinist clientele: in the will of one woman, a notary even used the phrase "Jesus-Christ nostre seul médiateur," calling the church she belonged to "l'église réformée de Lyon"—not "prétendue réformée" as French law dictated.[17] Europeans in mixed communities relied on people of other faiths even more commonly for medical care. As a profession open to Christian dissenters and to Jews, physicians came disproportionately from the ranks of these groups. In a way, the position of midwife was even more sensitive, as among Catholics it carried a semi-priestly function: when newborn infants were in danger of dying, Catholic midwives were supposed to perform emergency baptisms. The refusal of Protestant midwives to perform the ritual gave the French crown an excuse in 1680 to bar them altogether. Protestants protested the decree vehemently, fearing Catholic midwives would baptize their infants against their will. But even Catholics "murmured" against it, preferring, at this moment of extreme peril for mother and child, to employ the most skilled midwives regardless of faith. In fact, there were Catholics who preferred Reformed midwives, believing them to be "more sage, more reliable, [and] more experienced than the others."[18] In the Rhineland town of Oppenheim, midwives showed a remarkable willingness to accommodate their clients: at the insistence of the town council, Protestant midwives agreed to perform emergency baptisms, when necessary, for Catholic parents, while Catholic midwives agreed not to perform them if the parents were Protestant.

The position of domestic servant was sensitive and intimate in a different way. When servants were taken into a household, they became members of a family, subject to the authority of its paterfamilias. A difference of religion raised a host of issues: could servants be present at family prayers? Could they accompany the family to church? Could Catholic servants prepare meat for Protestant families to eat on Catholic fast days? Could they eat with their families on such days and partake of the same food? Could they work at all on Catholic holy days? In the view of many clergy, for religious difference to penetrate the inner sanctum of the household seemed perilous. On the one hand, clergy feared that orthodox servants might be enticed or pressured by heretical masters into converting. The bishop of La Rochelle was one of many in France who complained in the 1660 and 1670s of such behavior by Huguenot masters. On the other hand, clergy feared that heretical servants might infect orthodox families. In the 1600s a major controversy erupted in Germany's biconfessional cities when Lutheran ministers demanded that laypeople dismiss their Catholic servants, who, the ministers claimed, were trying to convert innocent children. Even in Holland clergy were concerned about this threat. In 1652 a Reformed synod issued a warning that church members should use caution about hiring "papist" servants, so as to guard their families against "their freedom being spied upon, [and] especially their religious purity being infected."[19]

Despite such admonitions, it was not uncommon in religiously mixed communities for families to hire domestic servants of other faiths. And it was particularly common in Dutch, French, and German cities for Protestant families to have Catholic servants. The reason was demographic. Many domestic servants were rural girls who went to a nearby city to find work that would enable them to save money for a dowry. Those who hired them tended to be established, middling or well-to-do urban families. From the beginning of the Reformation, city people proved more receptive to Protestantism than country folk, and that pattern persisted throughout the early modern period. The result was a statistical imbalance: those who migrated to cities from the surrounding countryside tended to be Catholic, while families who hired them tended to be Protestant—though of course the opposite occurred as well.

If clergy feared that servants might pervert children, they had little doubt that teachers of a different faith would do so. Education in early modern Europe had almost invariably a strong religious component, especially at the elementary level, where children learned their ABCs by piecing their way through the text of prayers and catechisms. It seems remarkable, therefore, that any parents sent their children to schools of a different confession. In the late sixteenth and early seventeenth centuries, the practice seems to have been widespread in Poland and France, where Jesuit colleges had a reputation for excellence that attracted many Protestant students. In Poland their only rivals were the Lutheran academies in the cities of Royal Prussia (Danzig, Elbing, Thorn) and the Socinian Academy in Rakow, which counted the famous educational reformer Comenius among its professors. Founded in 1602, it attracted the sons of gentry of all faiths until its destruction in 1638. As they do today, some parents were prepared to overlook a school's confessional affiliation if it offered their children the best education available. According to a minister in 1618, most Protestant notables in the French city of Nîmes sent their boys to Jesuit schools. When hauled before the local consistory for doing so, one Huguenot mother complained that the local Reformed college "is not as well regulated as is required" and declared defiantly that she had an obligation to "advance" her sons.[20]

For their part, some schools took pains to accommodate students of other faiths. Polish Jesuits, for example, required Protestant students to listen to sermons and take courses in religious subjects, but exempted them from attending mass and other services. This was a none-too-subtle strategy for attracting potential converts. It worked only because Polish Jesuits abstained from exerting too much pressure on their charges. Other teachers took a pluralistic approach, using different materials to teach children of different faiths. In the 1670s, for example, the Catholic schoolmaster of one French village taught Huguenot children the Reformed catechism; his counterpart in another village taught Huguenot children to sing the psalms of David in Clément Marot's impeccably Calvinist version. In the French town of Pont-le-Veyle, students at the local college were taught "to say their prayers, each according to the form used in their religion."[21]

Such cases were the exception, not the rule. Sending children to study with masters of another faith meant accepting that they would be exposed to a rival version of Christian truth, and that they would mingle and make friends with its adherents. It is no wonder the practice was anathema to church leaders, and in France Huguenot ministers waged a fierce campaign to end it. Synods issued prohibitions, consistories disciplined parents. But the frequency of their efforts, repeated over decades, shows how limited their success was. In striking contrast, such effort was unnecessary in England, whose Catholic gentry dispatched their boys across the channel to study at Douai, St. Omer, and other colleges where they would be formed into pious Catholics. Some Dutch Catholic families similarly broke the law by sending their boys across the borders of the Republic to schools in Catholic enclaves such as the County of Megen and Land of Ravenstein, or to the Catholic provinces of the south.

Integration vs. Segregation

Clergy feared the effects that intermingling and intimacy—"the dwellinge together and familiar conversacion of the godly with the godles, the faithfull withe the faythles"—might have on their flocks.[22] They saw the difference between confessions as a matter of sharp, unchanging, black-and-white contrasts, and they saw Christians as divided into opposing camps. Ambiguities of allegiance—indifference, uncertainty, eclecticism, experiment, changeability—fit uneasily into their confessional worldview. And while they greatly desired defections from their enemies, by some point in the seventeenth century they all took it as their first order of business to consolidate and strengthen the allegiance of their existing flocks. From that point on, clergy tended to prefer the safety of segregation to the exposure and potential for loss that integration brought. The pressure they exerted in this direction may have contributed in the long run to a general trend in which communities that were relatively integrated in the sixteenth century became more segregated along confessional lines.

The trend was most evident in officially bi- or multiconfessional communities, where the explicit recognition of confessional differences was the very basis of peaceful coexistence. In such communities, recognition of difference tended increasingly to translate into forms of institutional segregation. An example was the introduction of *itio in partes* as a mechanism of government. Another was the erection in shared churches of physical partitions that divided choir from nave, reserving the former for Catholic use, the latter for Protestant. Cemeteries (churchyards) offer another very concrete example. In the Swiss Thurgau, Protestants and Catholics continued to be buried together until the eighteenth century. When full parity was instituted, however, existing cemeteries were divided into separate sections. So were many in France, where in the sixteenth century Catholics and Huguenots had generally been buried together in the old parish cemeteries. In 1598 the Edict of Nantes decreed that Catholics and Huguenots were to be buried in separate cemeteries. Contrary to the edict, the old practice persisted for a time in many communities. Problems raising the funds to buy a new Huguenot cemetery accounted for some of these cases; others reflected good relations between the confessions. In 1609, for example, the inhabitants of Castelmoron (Agenais) agreed that, for the sake of amity and peace, all could bury their dead in the parish cemetery, "each family in the tomb of its ancestors, as much one religion as the other, just as has been done up to now."[23] As a compromise solution, royal commissioners encouraged many towns to divide their old parish cemeteries into Catholic and Huguenot sections, separated by a wall or ditch. This segregated the confessions but gave both a place in the ancestral burial ground at the heart of the community; in short, it made them separate but equal. Over the following decades, though, Catholics increasingly forced Huguenots to bury their dead in separate, new cemeteries located outside city walls. The symbolism and stigma of the move were patent, and Huguenot scholar Isaac Casaubon sensed them immediately when he attended a funeral outside Paris: "It was the first time I had seen the place reserved for our burials. We are banished from the city; we are thrown out like rubbish in I don't know what sort of place."[24] It is hardly surprising that Huguenots resisted the move.

To the very eve of the revocation of the edict, education remained in France a sphere of much interconfessional contact. In Germany, by contrast, the trend toward segregation was marked. There, many schools that had been attended by both Protestants and Catholics in the sixteenth century were subsequently split into separate ones, and confessional schools that originally attracted cross-over students ceased to do so. This change can be traced closely in Augsburg, where the Lutheran-dominated municipal gymnasium at first accommodated Catholic students, restricting religious instruction to classes where the Lutheran catechism was propounded. From 1581 the gymnasium had a rival in the local Jesuit college, which accommodated Protestant students in a similar way, attracting them especially because it was free. As late as the 1640s the college had a few Protestant students. In the wake of the Peace of Westphalia, though, secondary education in Augsburg was strictly segregated, with Catholic and Protestant institutions receiving equal funds, regardless of student numbers. Biberach also ended up with separate, parallel school systems for Catholics and Lutherans, as did Erfurt, Hildesheim, Regensburg, Maastricht (the one Dutch parity city), and the biconfessional Swiss town of Glarus. In Transylvania, with its multiple establishment of faiths, all four received religions had their own schools by the late sixteenth century.

Even in the Netherlands, the easy mixing of people of different faiths that characterized the early years of the Republic may have given way by the eighteenth century to a degree of segregation, at least in some spheres. In the province of Friesland, such a trend has been documented in charity. Beginning around 1675, municipal authorities there abdicated responsibility for those poor who were not members or at least "sympathizers" of the Reformed Church. Instead, they prodded the dissenting churches to care for their own poor, and in the 1750s the provincial government passed key legislation requiring them to do so. Each confession was to establish its own hospitals, orphanages, and old-age homes, and to distribute alms to the needy from its own funds. Mennonites took up the challenge quickly and eagerly, Catholics and Lutherans only slowly and reluctantly. To make the task easier, magistrates granted these groups certain tax exemptions, and in a crucial move the provincial government allowed dissenting congregations to accept charitable bequests. This amounted to a very limited form of legal recognition (received by Catholics only in 1776), so that one could say Friesland was moving in the direction of a multiple establishment. Here again we see, as our second model led us to expect, a correspondence between multiple establishments and segregation.

A parallel long-term trend was for religious groups to develop distinct subcultures. This is what patterns of book ownership reveal in the German cities of Speyer, Tübingen, and Frankfurt. While Lutheran and Reformed book collections differed only modestly from one another in eighteenth-century Speyer, both differed profoundly from Catholic ones. Whereas Lutherans typically owned Bibles, psalmbooks, sermons, and works of devotion that encouraged an interiorized, mystical piety—most of this literature quite old, dating from the sixteenth and seventeenth centuries, passed down in families and used by them in their household devotions—Catholics owned works on the life of Christ and on the cult of the Virgin and saints, and a profusion of images and devotional objects. Rich and poor Lutherans owned the same kinds of materials, only in different quantities; so did rich and poor Catholics. In these cities, religion was the single most important determinant of book culture.

In the French city of Metz, by contrast, there was a difference in the kind of books owned by elites and non-elites in the seventeenth century (prior to the revocation of the Edict of Nantes), and the difference cut across confessional lines. Whether Catholic or Protestant, those who received a Latin education in France tended to own secular as well as religious books. They retained a strong interest in the learned culture to which they were exposed in their colleges and academies, and their libraries typically included works by such classical authors as Cicero, Plutarch, and Seneca, as well as lesser quantities of Erasmus, Montaigne, and other modern authors. Whether or not they studied together, Catholic and Protestant urban elites in France imbibed as youths a culture that gave them common knowledge and tastes. For some, this culture remained a lifelong preoccupation, spurring them to join academies and attend salons, where Catholics and Protestants mingled. The most learned took an active role in that international, cross-confessional community of scholars known as the "Republic of Letters." For others, this culture was merely a social code—part of what it meant to be a gentleman. The very ethos of gentility, though, could unite Christians of different faiths, providing a common identity and set of values to people of a certain elevated social rank. Courtiers and landed elites had similarly, each amongst themselves, a common ethos. Class solidarity was a major factor in the toleration Polish gentry practiced—not toward their serfs but toward one another. This toleration was fed by the ideology of "Sarmatism," which hung a mythical, arcadian aura around the lifestyle of the Polish gentry and attributed a unique virtue to its members. In England similarly, Catholic and Protestant gentry (and aristocrats) shared "the same leisured lifestyle, the same interests and pleasures: estate management, the stable, the race-meeting, the chase."[25]

Much the same could be said about craftsmen or peasants: among these groups, too, Christians of different faiths shared many common values. They prized honor and neighborliness, recognized obligations of hospitality and friendship, and largely agreed on which forms of behavior were moral and which immoral. They shared many strands of popular culture, such as proverbs and jokes. Except in the most segregated communities, they participated in common recreations. In France, Calvinist clergy vainly reprimanded Huguenots who joined Catholics in dances, cabarets, hunting parties, fairs, Carnival celebrations, and saint's day festivals. In England, all but the puritanical attended football matches, horse races, and cockfights. And despite the polarization of politics that sometimes occurred along confessional lines, Christians of different faiths shared many civic loyalties. A striking example comes from the Irish town of Derry, where Catholics joined Protestants in annual festivities celebrating the Glorious Revolution of 1688. Such a thing would be unimaginable today, but in the mid-eighteenth century Irish Catholics saw the Revolution not as a defeat for their faith but as a victory for constitutional liberty over the tyrannical, absolutist pretensions of the Stuart kings.

In short, where Christians of different faiths were indeed one "people," sharing the same language, ancestors, customs, and laws, they continued, despite a trend toward segregation and subcultures, to have much in common. This was not simply a case of secular forces overpowering religious ones, uniting people whom faith divided. In the first place, secular and religious cannot be distinguished so neatly in early modern culture; almost no value or loyalty lacked some religious sanction. That was famously the case for obedience to the law and to one's rulers, who were regarded as "ordained by God" to wield authority on his behalf. It was obviously the case for moral codes that Christians based on the Ten Commandments and other biblical passages. And as we have seen, it was also the case for such values as charity and neighborliness.

In the second place, specifically religious values and ideas were shared by people of different faiths. Even the most confessional Christians shared with one another a rich religious heritage from antiquity and the Middle Ages. This heritage included common forms of theological reasoning; common forms of mysticism; common scriptural references (especially among Protestants); a common vocabulary—however differently employed—of sacrifice and forgiveness, sin and sanctity, providence and salvation, faith and communion; and much common wisdom about the relation between our mundane world and the invisible, spiritual realm that encompassed it. This heritage created common ground on which Christians of different confessions could sometimes meet. A wonderful example is the friendship that two Dutch scholars, Arnoldus Buchelius and Caspar Barlaeus, maintained in the 1620 and 1630s. Buchelius was then a militant Calvinist: after a long spiritual odyssey away from the Catholicism of his childhood, he ended up an elder of the Dutch Reformed Church in Utrecht and an ally of Gisbertus Voetius, the most polemical, "precisionist" Calvinist theologian in the Netherlands. A leading Remonstrant, Barlaeus had taught at the University of Leiden until Calvinists stripped him of his position in 1619; Voetius later waged a campaign against him. These men belonged to churches that were bitter enemies, yet after being introduced in 1626 they developed a firm friendship. In their elegant, Latin correspondence, the two men took care never to mention contentious points of doctrine or church politics, but that did not prevent them from speaking constantly to one another of God. When Buchelius, contemplating his sins, sank into melancholy, Barlaeus wrote a *Hymnus in Christum* to lighten his sadness and remind him that "there is no condemnation for those who are in Christ." Buchelius responded positively: "The words of Him who cannot deceive bring consolation: 'I do not desire the death of the sinner, but that he be converted and live'. I acknowledge my frailty and recognise the hardness of my heart. I seek and await a remedy from the One God and know that He will not reject the supplicant. The spectacles and crimes of human life which I see urge me more towards the thought of eternal matters. . . . I have now rightly come to despise this vile age and to hanker after the coming joys of blessedness. May the greatest Knower of Hearts grant these to us, He who will preserve you and me and all good men for salvation."[26] Despite their differences, Buchelius and Barlaeus perceived in one another the most precious of all qualities: "piety." Each thought the other a good Christian and likely to be saved.

Buchelius had many friends of different faiths, Catholic and Mennonite as well as Remonstrant. On the surface this seems inconsistent for a man who in his private journals reviled Catholics as stupid idolaters, was convinced Remonstrants were undermining the Christian character of Dutch society, and as elder lobbied for magistrates to act against these groups. Buchelius's personal toleration was not based on a lack of confessional ardor. Clearly, though, he had a sense about where, when, and how it was appropriate to express that ardor. This amounted to an unwritten code about how one should interact with people of other faiths. One of the key rules was that one should distinguish between rival confessions as entities—their dogmas, rituals, institutions, and political networks—and the people who belonged to them. One did not identify the individuals whom one knew personally—neighbors, relatives, fellow citizens, friends—with the remorseless, faceless ideologues who (one imagined) marched under the banner of those confessions. Perhaps this dissociation was expected and encouraged socially, but it seems also to have met a very personal, psychological need for people to reconcile their abstract confessional commitments with their concrete social experiences. By virtue of this dissociation people could wage war on the entity without it affecting their personal relationships. This rule was not unique to Buchelius—on the contrary, it seems to have informed relations generally between people of different faiths in Dutch society. Nor was it confined to the Dutch. A Polish adage captured the rule perfectly: "A friend to the person, yet an enemy to the cause." In England, Puritan vicar Joseph Bentham recommended in 1630 a "charitable Christian hatred": one should "hate knowingly, loving the person, [but] loathing his evil properties." A century and a half later, the rule found an echo in the confused reaction of a group of Protestant rioters who, in 1780, were "called upon to go to such a house, as there were Catholics there. They replied, 'What are Catholics to us? We are only against Popery!'" In Ireland, a Protestant, Lord Middleton, advocated in the early eighteenth century that the government take firm steps to combat Catholicism. Yet he thought well of a Catholic with whom he had close dealings, Standish Barry, whom he declared "a Papist, but the best of the kind I ever knew."[27] So the bigoted have always made exceptions without abandoning their beliefs.

Historians have done only limited research on patterns of social interaction between people of different faiths in the many parts of early modern Europe that were religiously mixed. These patterns were finely textured, subtle things that must have varied enormously among communities, and they certainly had many more dimensions than the ones sketched above. Our two models are merely heuristic tools, but they do have the advantage of setting in sharp relief the contrast between integration and segregation. Was there a general trend from the one to the other between the sixteenth and eighteenth centuries? What is clear is that, at least in bi- and multiconfessional communities, certain forms of separation were implemented in the expectation that they would help reduce conflict. These forms varied and in no case amounted to a strict segregation of confessional groups, especially not by place of residence. Still, the segregation of the dead in France was quite explicitly an attempt to resolve an issue that had triggered violent clashes in the sixteenth century. The new cemetery arrangements in seventeenth-century France exemplified an evolution in relations generally between Catholics and Huguenots. Likewise, Thurgauers erected physical partitions dividing the choir and nave of their shared churches to reduce strife. Catholics and Lutherans in the parity cities of the Holy Roman Empire showed over time a preference for their own institutions over shared ones. In such communities, religious groups were powerful, cohesive, and, in some respects, increasingly separate bodies.

Even in eighteenth-century Augsburg, people of opposing faiths inevitably interacted and, yes, cooperated with one another in many venues— neighborhood, marketplace, city hall. The more integrated a community, the more mixed venues there were. In the young Dutch Republic, it was common for people of opposing faiths to work together, socialize, have friendships, and, as we shall see, even marry. How they could do so without compromising their faith or being less than devout is at first glance not clear. But the friendships of Arnoldus Buchelius suggest one way they reconciled their antagonisms with their friendships: by distinguishing between the cause and the person, the group and the individual. This distinction helps explain the "Janus face" of religious toleration—the way in which people could be, and commonly were, both tolerant and intolerant.[28] Buchelius's life also illustrates the freedom individuals enjoyed as members of a fluid, integrated society. Raised a Catholic, Buchelius first joined the "Libertine" congregation founded in Utrecht by Hubert Duifhuis, with its emphasis on morality and mystical piety. Later in life he embraced the dogmatism and discipline of Dutch Calvinism. Such spiritual pilgrimages were anything but rare in the Dutch Republic.

For groups, though, as opposed to individuals, integration had a darker side. The Dutch Mennonite Thieleman van Braght pointed out some of its dangers in the great martyrology he compiled, *The Martyrs' Mirror* (1660). Van Braght actually felt some nostalgia for the days of the sixteenth century when his forebears had been persecuted more harshly than any other religious group. He viewed as a very mixed blessing the acceptance Mennonites subsequently had gained in Dutch society and the affluence that had come with it. Ease, in his view, had brought a "pernicious worldly-mindedness"—a decline in morals and religious ardor.[29] For this reason, Van Braght regarded toleration as a greater threat to the soul than persecution, and worried about the future. He had good reason: the integration of Mennonites in his day paved the way for their assimilation in the eighteenth century, when many ceased to find significant the differences between their own faith and that of other Dutch Protestants. Scores of Mennonite congregations collapsed and others shrank dramatically as their members abandoned them, joining the Reformed Church or marrying Reformed spouses and allowing their children to be raised as Reformed Protestants. The Mennonite congregations to survive were mostly the ones that had segregated themselves from the mainstream of Dutch society, opting for a simple rural lifestyle and enforcing a rigorous system of communal discipline that kept individual members in line.

In the latter decades of the eighteenth century, the Frenchman J. Hector St. John de Crèvecoeur observed among the inhabitants of North America an incredible religious variety. All the churches and sects of Europe, it seemed to him, had been transplanted to the New World. Some had settled in the new land as groups, but in most places Christians of different stripes lived side by side as neighbors. Such integration, Crèvecoeur felt certain, would have drastic consequences: "If the sectaries are not settled close together, if they are mixed with other denominations, their zeal will cool for want of fuel, and will be extinguished in a little time. Then the Americans become as to religion, what they are as to country, allied to all. In them the name of Englishman, Frenchman, and European is lost, and in like manner, the strict modes of Christianity as practised in Europe are lost also. . . . Thus all sects are mixed as well as all nations; thus religious indifference is imperceptibly disseminated from one end of the continent to the other."[30] In light of America's subsequent history, there is good reason to doubt the logic of Crèvecoeur's prediction. Integration does not always lead to indifference or even to complete assimilation; not all ingredients lose their distinctive flavor in the melting pot. That said, there is a tension, in religion as in other aspects of human society, between individual freedom and group cohesion, integration and diversity. Postmodern theorists have pointed it out in the process of questioning Enlightenment ideals; the current flare-up of religious conflicts around the globe has made us even more aware of it. As individuals, large parts of our culture and identity are rooted in the groups to which we belong—religious, ethnic, national, racial. How substantive is the toleration we enjoy, if it undermines these groups and effaces the differences between them? What is the cost of our modern, integrationist model of toleration, and what are the alternatives?

TEN

Transgressions

Jubilee in Gap

In 1628 the Catholic children of Gap, a small town nestled beneath the French Alps, could barely contain their excitement: to celebrate a jubilee, the local parish was organizing a procession and they were to take part in it. Mothers made costumes for boys to appear as angels, girls as virgins. The children of Huguenot families were intensely jealous, and on the day of the procession they wailed and pleaded that they wanted to be angels and virgins too. Eventually their parents gave in, fashioning costumes for them, and the Huguenot children gleefully joined their Catholic friends as they marched and sang. When the town's priests realized that "heretics" had joined the procession, they were scandalized and began to chase the children out of the cortège. Thus began a disturbance that attracted the attention of Gap's bishop. With canny insight, this prelate ordered his priests to leave the Huguenot children alone and let them march. That evening, returning elated to their homes, the Huguenot boys and girls told their parents, "We too, we are Catholics!"[1] According to the Capuchin missionaries who recounted the event, Gap's Calvinist parents could not dissuade their children even by beating them; many young converts had been won that day to the Church.

Not that the Capuchins' testimony can be taken at face value. For them, the story of the jubilee proved a broader point: that the pomp and splendor of Catholic ritual attracted potential converts, adults as well as children. Contrasting sharply to the austerity of Calvinism, with its whitewashed churches and stripped-back ceremonies, these aspects of Catholicism, believed the missionaries, were powerful weapons in the struggle for Christian souls. And on this point the Capuchins were surely right: in the age of the baroque, when tastes ran toward the grand and ornate, toward ceremony and drama, Catholicism had an aesthetic appeal no Protestant confession could match. Catholicism was also simply more fun; it offered more conviviality, more play. To a degree Protestantism never matched—indeed, purposefully avoided—it blended religious ritual with popular festivity. And when a town such as Gap, with its large Catholic majority, celebrated a jubilee, saint's day, or Carnival, the event took on yet another dimension, as it encompassed, spatially and symbolically, the entire community. Such an event presented Protestants with an acute question of conscience: Did they have to abstain from the fun, shun the camaraderie, and withdraw from the broader community to avoid betraying their faith? If so, that was a sacrifice not all would be prepared to make, or even understand—certainly not children.

Catholicism may have had special qualities that made it, in Protestant eyes, especially seductive, but the bottom line was that all religious groups living alongside others ran risks. Coexistence exposed the members of each group to rival beliefs and practices, and with that exposure came temptations, pressures, knowledge of alternatives, and the possibility of choice. Beyond the loss of fervor feared by Van Braght, toleration might encourage assimilation, even conversion. From our perspective, this is the most important lesson of Gap's jubilee: that life in a mixed society presented rival groups with both opportunities and perils—the opportunity of gaining members, the peril of losing them—and that church leaders faced a strategic choice between accepting integration and demanding segregation. Like many other clergy, Gap's priests favored segregation, and Gap's Calvinist parents must surely have wished, after the event, that the priests had had their way. In a moment of insight, though, Gap's bishop realized the potential of integration to make converts.

The most extreme form of integration was interfaith marriage, known in early modern Europe as "mixed" marriage. More than any other relationship or interaction, it threatened to break down whatever social barriers divided religious groups from one another. Mixed marriage brought people of different faiths together around the same hearth and in the same bed. It turned the religious "other" (or at least one such person) into a familiar, even beloved, human being on whose well-being your own depended. Requiring intimate accommodations in a couple's private, domestic life, it exposed each spouse to the other's religious views. And most importantly, it exposed children from their earliest, most formative years to two faiths, in the process giving two churches a claim to them. Conversion and mixed marriage have been called "the two greatest taboos" in early modern religious life, and the two were closely linked, for it was through mixed marriage that a great deal of the movement between faiths occurred.[2] Yet in every part of Europe that was religiously mixed, the taboos were broken, and in fluid, integrated societies like the young Dutch Republic, conversion and mixed marriage were too frequent to be called taboos at all. They constituted at once the greatest threat to Europe's churches and their greatest hope.

The War for Souls

To say that conversion was a sensitive affair in early modern Europe is an understatement: as occasions when the most personal convictions of an individual became matters of intense public concern, conversions were the ultimate "scandal." To the group losing a member, they were a betrayal of God, truth, church, friends, and family—Lutherans in Alsace, fusing the sacred and the social, called them "blasphemy against father and mother."[3] Those perpetrating such a betrayal were hated and sometimes physically attacked. In Janville, a small jurisdiction in northern France, a lawyer named Le Normand who converted in the 1660s to Protestantism "would not dare appear in the streets, because people would immediately congregate and pursue him throwing stones, going so far one time that, having followed him to his house, they pillaged it and tore to pieces everything they could not carry away."[4] Le Normand fled his village, never to return. In Weinheim, in the Palatinate, it was complained in 1719 that "if a person becomes Catholic, they are abused and reviled, even to the point that they are driven out of the village."[5] A year later, in the Scottish village of

Fochabers, a group of Catholics attacked one Thomas Miller, a convert to Protestantism, and his family in their home, stealing or destroying their possessions.

In Christian teaching, proselytizing was an act of Christian love, performed not only "for the greater glory of God" but for "the salvation of souls" that were otherwise damned.[6] In the confessional age, proselytizing was also understood as a direct attack by one confession on another. Indeed, it was viewed as a form of spiritual warfare, and in France, where in the seventeenth century the Catholic Church waged an open and bitter struggle for converts, Catholic clergy portrayed the situation as one of two armies, one composed of themselves, the other of Calvinist ministers, ranged against one another, fighting over the simple lay folk, who were the terrain of combat. Protestant leaders tended not to portray the laity as being so passive, but they too attributed frightening powers to Catholic missionaries. Above all, they demonized the Jesuits, whose foremost objective in Europe was to win Protestants back for the Catholic Church. For Protestants—as for eighteenth-century philosophes—Jesuits epitomized what they saw as the inherently aggressive, intolerant character of Catholicism. "To demand of the Catholics," wrote Hamburg's Lutheran minister Johann Adrian Bolten in 1790, "that they should not be concerned with the spread of their Church, in all places and by whatever means, would be tantamount to demanding that they should cease to be Catholics."[7] Like Bolten, most Europeans regarded proselytizing as incompatible with peaceful coexistence.

Not surprisingly, those attacked sometimes responded with violence. In Nîmes, for example, the conversion to Catholicism of a thirteen-year-old orphan named Pierre Coutelle triggered in 1650 a riot. From an eminent Huguenot family, the boy apparently came under Jesuit influence as a student at the local college, which at the time was a parity institution, shared by the two faiths. As soon as Pierre converted, Catholics whisked him away, lodging him first with a friend's family and subsequently at the palace of the local bishop. This protected him from the pressure that his Protestant guardians would have put on him. From the Protestant perspective, this was nothing less than kidnapping, and legally they had a point: precisely to forestall such battles over children, the Edict of Nantes stipulated that boys could not convert until they were fourteen years old, girls twelve. Coutelle's relatives and guardians demanded that the bishop return the boy, but in vain. Thus on September 4 (not coincidentally, a day of devotion for both Protestants and Catholics), a crowd of some five hundred Protestants, mostly wool and leather craftsmen, stormed the bishop's palace and seized the child. Their violence was terrible: three of the bishop's servants were mortally wounded; one of them, the porter, was struck with hammer blows, dragged a distance, and stoned. This "affaire Coutelle" was one of the precipitants that led to the division of the Nîmes college into two separate institutions.

Uproars over conversion were especially frequent in France, but violent incidents also occurred elsewhere, as in County Fermanagh, Ireland, where a gentry family led a crowd of a hundred to besiege a house where lodged two Methodist preachers who had converted their daughter. When John Butler, bishop of Cork, converted in 1787, the "populace were so shocked at it, that they gathered round his carriage and pelted him with all that came to their hands."[8] In Augsburg in 1661, Lutherans attacked a procession in which several local girls who had converted to Catholicism were marching. From the Lutherans' perspective, the girls were being purposefully paraded before their eyes in an act of "pure provocation."[9] It was hardly unique: converts made powerful propaganda and were commonly exploited as such to the hilt. Celebrating conversions as triumphs of divine truth, clergy took them as occasions to deliver polemical sermons, while pamphlet writers trumpeted them in print. Some churches cast the act of conversion itself as an elaborate ritual, enacted with great pomp before the entire local community, in performances comparable to modern-day political "show trials." In any case, churches always insisted that converts abjure their former beliefs publicly.[10]

It is difficult to exaggerate the jubilation on one side and anguish on the other that conversions occasioned. So powerful a testimony were they considered to the truth of one faith and falsehood of another that Catholic missionaries in France faked them, or so claimed Huguenots (the accusation being as significant as the possible act), parading as new converts people who had always been Catholics. By the same token, rumors of conversions performed privately—for example, by people on their deathbed—were eagerly spread and angrily denied. Huguenots scored a great victory in 1647 when a Jesuit named Pierre Jarrige converted, but they had it snatched from them three years later when Jarrige apparently returned to Catholicism. At least, an account of his return was published under his name; the man's actual whereabouts were unclear. Jesuits claimed that Jarrige had returned to their order and retreated from the world in repentance; Huguenots preferred to believe the Jesuits had abducted and taken their secret vengeance on him. Of all conversions, clerical ones were the most sensitive, for who could better attest to the falsehood of a faith than those expert in its teachings? Who could repudiate it with more devastating effectiveness than its previous champions? It is hardly surprising, then, that churches winning clerical converts often had them write pamphlets and preach against their former faith, creating a genre of "revocation sermons." Twice, in 1718 and 1727, such preaching triggered riots in the German city of Hildesheim.

Pamphlets and revocation sermons were meant to encourage further conversions, as lay folk followed their clerical leaders—the Catholic Church was hardly the only institution to imagine such a scenario. But in general, the scenario remained just that, imaginary. To be sure, in every part of Europe that embraced Protestantism, the conversion of clergy played a crucial role in the course of the Reformation itself, as did the flood of anti-Catholic polemics that accompanied it. In later periods, though, it is unclear how much effect clerical conversions or polemics had on laypeople. It can be expected that they swayed ever fewer hearts and minds from the late sixteenth to the early eighteenth century, as confessional mentalities grew more entrenched and ecclesiastic loyalties more stable and firm. Without further research, though, it is impossible to delineate any pattern with certainty. According to a study of Biberach, Catholic controversy sermons were responsible in the eighteenth century for "relatively frequent" conversions from Lutheranism.[11] By contrast, in Augsburg such sermons convinced almost no one: in the late seventeenth century, each year less than 0.1 percent, on average, of the city's adult population converted to Catholicism, despite a large number of clerical conversions. On the surface this seems to suggest that controversy sermons were utterly ineffectual in Augsburg. Yet there is another possibility: perhaps the true purpose of such sermons was different from their ostensible one. Perhaps, rather than trying to convince Protestants to convert to Catholicism, as they seemed to do, the sermons were motivated at heart by a desire to prevent the opposite, the apostasy of Catholics. By attacking Protestant teachings and drawing black-and-white contrasts between the two confessions, the sermons strengthened the faith and ecclesiastic loyalty of Catholic laity. Hence the

concern expressed in them for "simple" Catholics who were confused by
the coexistence of two faiths, and for the "lazy" (confessionally indifferent)
who thought both faiths were acceptable and just wanted everyone to live
in peace. If this view is correct, the sermons were actually intended to reinforce, not undermine, the boundary between confessions, rendering it less,
not more, porous.[12]

Some missionary efforts were similarly directed more toward those
whose confessional allegiances were loose and uncertain than toward the
committed adherents of rival faiths. That is to say, the efforts were more
pastoral than evangelical. This was so, for example, in Elizabethan England, where Catholic missionaries focused their efforts on "church papists,"
who considered themselves Catholic but attended parish services. It was
the case too in the Dutch Republic, where the confessions competed for the
huge number of people who were members of no church. In fact, the very
concepts of "mission" and "conversion" did not distinguish between a
change in confession and a change in manner of living—in other words,
between the conversion of heretics and the "conversion" of sinners. In both
cases, the goal of the missionary was to spark a change of heart and bring a
person to accept church teachings. St. Francis de Sales linked the two types
of conversion directly, believing that by converting Catholics to an exemplary life of piety he would succeed in winning the good will of Protestants
(remember the idea that the true faith could be recognized as the one that
inspired true piety). Both he and the Capuchins, who launched great missionary campaigns into the French countryside, took as their first goal the
incitement of Catholics to a more fervent devotion.

If, despite appearances, polemics and missionary campaigns often had
a defensive, consolidatory purpose, how were converts (in the modern
sense) gained, and among whom? The Catholic Church targeted lay elites,
especially princes and nobles. Just as it had looked to medieval rulers to
help spread Christianity in the first place, so in the post-Reformation era it
looked to those with worldly power to reimpose the true faith on their subjects and dependents. From Henri IV of France to James II of England, and
from the great Lithuanian magnate Radziwill the Orphan to the French aristocrat Turenne, eminent conversions had a powerful impact, not only—or
even primarily, in many cases—through the coercive power that could be
harnessed, but through examples set, atmospheres created, and patronage
extended or denied. In this regard, the Catholic Church may have been

most systematic, but it was hardly alone: perhaps the heaviest pressure ever put on a lay elite was in Ireland, where Catholic aristocrats and gentry were stripped in the seventeenth century of most of their lands. Under the penal code that held force in the eighteenth century, an eldest son who conformed to the Protestant Church of Ireland could claim immediately the entire family estate, which would otherwise be split into pieces upon his parents' death. Though Catholic elites might retain status and wealth by serving Protestant landlords as tenants and middlemen, Ireland's penal code induced most remaining Catholic landowners in some regions, notably Ulster, to conform.

Other groups, like the elderly and sick, were targeted for conversion because they were vulnerable. Just as fear of death—and the judgment that would follow it—was regarded as a salutary spur to godly behavior, so it was exploited to encourage people to reconsider their choice of faith, lest it prove to be the wrong one. Confrontation with death was regarded as the supreme test of a person's faith, a moment when faith had to overcome doubt, but also a last chance to repent. As represented in drama, print, sermon, and picture, the deathbed was the scene of a cosmic struggle for the soul of the dying, whose salvation hung in the balance. Family and friends played roles in this drama, and in many a personal testimony the prospect of a loved one dying in the wrong faith, destined for hell, was the cause of painful tears and urgent pleas. For clergy, offering comfort, and in the Catholic case last rites, to the dying was part of their pastoral duties. When plague struck religiously mixed cities, such as Nîmes in the 1640s, a competition of sorts would break out between the clergy of different confessions; those who risked infection by ministering most boldly to the sick gained in popular esteem and might be rewarded with deathbed conversions.

Young people, too—children, adolescents, bachelors, and maidens—showed a special susceptibility to proselytizing. The story of Gap's jubilee suggests as much, and studies of two French cities (Layrac and Lyon), a German city (Augsburg), and an English county (Cambridgeshire) offer corroboration, showing that the young accounted for a disproportionate number of converts. In Lyon, the typical convert to Catholicism was an immigrant in his or her twenties, and a striking number had lost one or both parents. Such uprooted, isolated youths were targeted from 1659 by the Company for the Propagation of the Faith, an organization that brought together priests and devout lay notables in a concerted effort to convert

Protestants. With local chapters in Paris, Rouen, Grenoble, Marseilles, and
other French cities, the Company provided the young with lodgings, ap-
prenticeship money, college tuition, dowries—whatever they needed—on
condition they embraced Catholicism and remained faithful to it. In exchange for faith, it offered security and support. To counter this threat,
Lyon's Calvinist consistory offered financial aid. Other Calvinist churches
did the same, but over time Huguenots found it increasingly difficult to
match Catholic resources: in 1652 another Catholic organization, the Company of the Holy Sacrament, created its own fund for converts, and in 1676
the French crown established a national "Caisse des Economats."

Wooing converts with financial and other incentives was a common
part of proselytizing in early modern Europe. The poor were offered charity, the elites land and government offices, the middling sorts debt annul-
ments, tax exemptions, and freedom from the obligation to quarter soldiers. Not all churches or governments engaged in the practice actively, but
none rejected it entirely. Lest we condemn it out of hand as a rank buying
of souls (which sometimes it was), we should note the observation of Sam-
uel Chandler, a Protestant dissenting minister who, even as he complained
about Catholic charity in England, cast its effect in a positive light: "And
being subdued by the kindness of those who minister to them in their ne-
cessities, How can they [the poor] think ill of a religion that thus prompts
men to acts of goodness[?]"[13] We should note also that conversion entailed
a change not only of faith but of community. Children, the poor, and other
vulnerable members of society needed care from their new co-religionists
if they were to give up the company of their old. As for nobles and patricians, while they were not vulnerable in the conventional sense, they did
have the most to win or lose—power, status, wealth—depending on their
religious allegiance. Perhaps that is why they bowed to pressure as often as
they did.

For of course the flip side of inducements was threats. It went without
saying in early modern Europe that different groups enjoyed different
rights and privileges. So it was normal for religious dissenters to suffer certain disabilities—exclusion from government office, at the very least (not
to mention restrictions on worship). Even this might prompt a certain
number of conversions among elite families. Needless to say, the penalties
for dissent could be immeasurably heavier and more painful. If we want to
sympathize with the persecuted, we should show some understanding for

those who converted under pressure. Not everyone is made of martyr's material, nor is it always necessary to be a martyr to be true to one's faith. Consider, for example, England's "church papists" under Queen Elizabeth. They conformed to the Church of England to the extent the law required, that is, by attending Sabbath services in their parish church. They made their Catholic faith clear to everyone, though, by their pointed absence from church when the Lord's Supper was administered. These men could even turn their Sunday appearances into forms of protest by ignoring the service and reading a Catholic prayer book. And it *was* predominantly men—the gender imbalance is significant. As heads of household, enfranchised subjects, and potential jurors or officeholders (some of them), English men came under much greater pressure to conform than did women or children. It was therefore a common pattern to find Catholic men conforming to the Church of England, while other members of their families did not. One could say these men were buckling under pressure, but their conformity was the gesture of submission authorities required to leave their families alone. By it, men purchased for their wives and children the freedom, in effect, to be recusants. Family members thus played different roles in a strategy that reconciled their Catholic allegiance with their need to survive in a repressive environment. Aristocratic and gentry families took the strategy a step further. By avoiding the heavy fines for recusancy and the possibility of having their lands confiscated, they preserved their wealth and power, which they then used to protect and promote Catholicism. Many such families, with church papists at their head, sheltered priests and ran house chapels. Above all, it was the mistresses of these households who actively championed the Catholic faith, raising their children in it and propagating it among their servants and tenants.

This gendered division of labor could be found in various parts of Europe, regardless of which faith was official and which dissenting. It perhaps had special utility in situations of severe repression, which may be why it was common among Protestants in Alsace after that region was "reunited" with Louis XIV's France, and likewise among elite Catholic families in eighteenth-century Ireland. Even in the Dutch Republic, though, anecdotal reports suggest that some male patricians in the early seventeenth century attended services in the Reformed Church while aiding and abetting their wives and children as they practiced Catholicism. The religious beliefs of such couples seem more mixed than in fact they were, and one should probably not count them as proper "mixed marriages," in which husband and wife held different beliefs. In these, no attempt was made to maintain appearances in public, but the accommodations necessary in private were much harder.

These Detestable Unions

In the modern world, especially in America, where the myth of the melting pot is a crucial component of national identity, intermarriage—whether of religious, ethnic, or racial groups—is commonly associated with tolerance and pluralism. So too it was in the early modern world, and the country most famous then for its toleration, the Dutch Republic, was reputed to have high rates of religiously mixed marriage. Natives and foreign visitors alike remarked on their frequency, and all agreed that they had a major impact on the Republic's religious climate. Bernard Dwinglo, a Reformed minister, observed in 1602 that "Heromnes," the Dutch everyman, "would not stand for the burning of heretics." "For [what] if one man saw his niece, another his uncle, a third his son, [and] yes, some their wives, flesh of their flesh [*uyt haer arm*], who are dearer to them than their own souls, suffer unto death? . . . What do you think, sirs, would it succeed? What joy would there be, do you think?"[14] According to the Dutch, the love they felt, despite all religious differences, for those closest to them made persecution a repugnant prospect. They commonly cited religiously mixed families, above all mixed marriages, not just as symptom but as cause of the toleration that prevailed in their society.

It is a bit surprising, therefore, to find that even in the Republic such marriages were frequently and forcefully condemned. No churchgoer could have escaped the message that they were dangerous and reprehensible. The Calvinist consistory of Amsterdam described mixed marriages as "improper," "offensive," and a sin against God.[15] Delft's consistory warned church members not to let their children marry persons of other faiths. Drawing the difference between faiths in black-and-white contrasts, it explained that Reformed Christians should not marry others because "light has nothing in common with darkness."[16] Catholic authorities condemned mixed marriages in equally sharp terms, regarding them as a form of sacrilege. Those who entered into them committed "a very grave mortal sin," warned Christianus Molina in a popular Dutch-language tract. Philip Rovenius, who as apostolic vicar headed the Holland Mission of the Catholic Church, wrote in 1648 that "entering into a marriage with unbelievers is nothing other than the prostitution of a member of Christ to the devil."[17] As late as 1741 a papal pronouncement, the Declaratio Benedictina, condemned Catholics who, "driven shamefully mad by an insane love, do not abhor in their souls . . . these detestable unions, which Holy Mother Church has always damned and forbidden." Such was the language the Curia used when, for the first time, it officially relaxed the rules concerning mixed marriage in the Netherlands.[18]

Churches discouraged mixed marriages also by disciplining those who contracted them. Practice here varied considerably. One of the earliest Dutch Reformed synods advised consistories to handle cases "according to the circumstances of the matter, either with a confession of guilt before the consistory or publicly, or by keeping them from the Lord's Supper for a while, or by proceeding with the steps of excommunication."[19] Most commonly, consistories suspended the offending church member from taking Communion until they had shown remorse and been reconciled to the congregation. Sometimes they also suspended parents who permitted their children to enter into such marriages. For its part, the Catholic Church had the weapon of the confessional. Weak, disorganized, and intermittently persecuted in the wake of the Revolt against Spain, the Church geared up only gradually to combat mixed marriages. In 1656, though, the Congregation for the Propagation of the Faith, the Roman office that supervised missionary activity, ordered the priests of the Holland Mission to refuse absolution to anyone who entered into such a union, unless and until their partner converted to Catholicism. Such a refusal barred Catholics also from taking Communion. As we shall see, it is not clear how many clergy obeyed this stern decree. In general, secular clergy operating in missionary territory were more accommodating than ones in bishoprics, while Jesuits, Dominicans, and other regulars were more accommodating still. At the end of the seventeenth century, even the pastors of Bergen op Zoom, a city that lay within the bishopric of Antwerp, were rather lax.

Strictest of all were certain Mennonite groups. How "marriage outside" (*buitentrouw*), as they called it, should be treated was in fact one of the principal points dividing different branches of the Mennonite movement from one another. At one end of the spectrum, Waterlanders believed that mixed marriage should not be punished so long as the Mennonite spouse remained an active and upright member of the congregation. Moderate groups such as the Young Frisians imposed at least a temporary ban, until the offender had demonstrated repentance. At the other extreme, Old Frisians and Old Flemings regarded marriage to other sorts of Mennonites, as well as to non-Mennonites, as a species of *buitentrouw*. Originally, they punished mixed marriage with the "full ban," that is, expulsion from the congregation and an ostracism so rigorous that even offenders' family members were supposed to avoid them. Those expelled could be readmitted only upon the conversion or death of their spouse. Old Frisians softened this punishment in the mid-seventeenth century, Old Flemings only in 1739.

Outside the Dutch Republic, churches were at least as harsh in their condemnations and censures of mixed marriage. Yet none of them denied that such marriage was an "honorable state of matrimony."[20] No Christian confession denied the validity of mixed marriages (between Christians) or the binding character of the union they created. This remarkable fact demands explanation.

One reason, clearly, was the deep respect all had for the sanctity of marriage. Protestant churches had broken with Catholicism by permitting divorce, but in practice they rarely granted it. Even though they celebrated the companionship a husband and wife could expect from one another, they never made emotional or spiritual intimacy a requirement for marriage, or lack of it sufficient grounds for divorce. A second factor was the authority of the New Testament, which explicitly declared marriages between Christians and pagans to be valid. In First Corinthians, the Apostle Paul had ruled that such marriages could be dissolved only if the pagan refused to live with the Christian spouse. In the post-Reformation era this sanction for divorce was known as the "Pauline privilege," and Protestant leaders debated whether it applied to marriages between orthodox Christians and heretics. In any event, the privilege did not extend in the other direction: Christians could not abandon or divorce their pagan—or heretical—spouse because of religious difference. Only if a woman was being persecuted so severely by her husband that "there is imminent peril to her life" might she abandon him, counseled John Calvin; otherwise she was "not to deviate from the duty which she has before God to please her husband, but to be faithful [to him] whatever happens."[21] In practice, it was indeed wives being pressured by their husbands for whom religious authorities were usually concerned. Yet, as Calvin's words suggest, their concern clashed with another imperative, to maintain patriarchal authority. Social stability and orderliness rested, all agreed, on the integrity of the family and the clear lines of authority and obedience maintained within it. This was a third reason why all Europe's churches accepted the binding force of mixed marriages. In England, preacher William Gouge used the example of wives who had "infidel husbands" as the very model of subjection wives generally owed their husbands. "If Infidels carry not the divels image, and are not, so long as they are Infidels, vassals of Satan, who are? yet wives must bee subject to them, and feare them."[22] How much more so, Gouge concluded, must they be subject to lewd, profane, drunken, and impious husbands.

In the Dutch Republic and other religiously mixed lands, clergy not only recognized mixed marriages, they performed mixed-marriage weddings. That is, they joined members of their church to nonmembers, issuing (if their church had official standing in their locale) the banns that publicly announced the union, and performing the ceremony that solemnized it. In some parts of the Republic, couples enjoyed an option to be found nowhere else in Europe: they could be married in a civil ceremony conducted by magistrates. But even here, Reformed ministers were willing to perform weddings for mixed couples—and for dissenting ones, too—on the grounds that "public marriage" was primarily a "civil" matter.[23] Protestant ministers found it easier to adopt this view than did Catholic priests, since their churches did not regard matrimony as a sacrament. They often worked closely with magistrates to regulate marital affairs, but they happily left ultimate authority over such affairs in the magistrates' hands.

As for the Catholic Church, its decree *Tametsi* in 1563 implicitly prohibited priests from marrying Catholics to heretics, or heretics to one another. The decree had no force, though, where it had not been properly promulgated, as was clearly the case in parts of the Netherlands, amidst the tumults of the Revolt. Even where it had been, many priests and some bishops were willing to violate the decree. An attempt at enforcement suggests why. In 1656 the Congregation in Rome ordered priests in the Republic to stop performing mixed-marriage weddings, unless the non-Catholic converted beforehand. Antonius Peerkens, a Franciscan stationed on the border between Friesland and Overijssel, reported to his superior how deeply this order disturbed his flock. If a non-Catholic refused to convert, the Catholic was left with the painful choice of abandoning the intended match or forgoing priestly blessing (after being married legally by a minister or magistrate, Dutch Catholics were commonly "remarried" by a cleric of their own confession). If the Catholic chose the latter and went ahead with the union, in the eyes of the church he or she was guilty of fornication and concubinage and, unless absolved for these mortal sins, was doomed to damnation. But the same order forbade absolution. Who would accept so bitter a condemnation, so hopeless a fate? Far from promoting the conversion of non-Catholics, Peerkens feared Rome's decree would lead many Catholics to abjure their faith. Peerkens realized, as did other priests with direct pastoral experience, that the Catholic Church risked losing far more than it would gain by adopting such a hard line. Odds were far better that Catholics in mixed marriages would remain true to their faith, that they would continue to practice it, and that they would raise their children in it if their wedding was performed by a priest rather than (or in addition to) a Protestant minister or magistrate. Indeed, the involvement of a priest at that crucial moment gave the church an invaluable entrée into the future life of the new family. Deafened by a chorus of protests, Apostolic Vicar Johannes van Neercassel asked the Congregation to reconsider its policy, which it did in 1671.

Across Europe, Calvinist, Catholic, Lutheran, and Anglican clergy performed the same calculation of potential loss and gain. It led them to perform mixed-marriage weddings and made them wary of chastising too harshly church members who entered into such marriages. Priests in the diocese of Strasbourg, in Alsace, warned their superiors: if they did not solemnize mixed marriages themselves, couples would simply ask a minister to do so, and then the odds would rise that the Catholic spouse would be lost to the church. A Scottish student noted a similar discrepancy between the rules of the French Reformed Churches and the practice he observed in the mid-1660s in Moyen-Poitou: "It is not permitted for a man or a woman to marry a papist. If they do, they have to come before the entire church and make a public confession of their error and of the scandal they have caused. Experience [though] teaches that this strictness should be used rarely, or gently. For if one came to enforce this rule, one would lose a believer who preferred to become a papist [than submit to the rule]."[24]

To be sure, clergy in some religiously mixed communities did refuse to solemnize mixed marriages. Catholic priests in the southern French city of Nîmes, for example, required all Protestants who wished to marry a Catholic partner in a Catholic Church to convert. Between 1609 and early 1621, a quarter of all the weddings they performed in the Nîmes cathedral involved one partner (almost always the woman) converting to Catholicism in the preceding months. The pattern that emerged in Nîmes, though, illustrates another danger, besides the loss of church members, that ensued if clergy refused to solemnize mixed marriages: the gain of hypocritical, insincere ones. Two or three times a year, on average, a Protestant woman who had converted to marry a Catholic approached the Nîmes consistory, asking it to pardon and readmit her to the Calvinist congregation. Invariably, after showing proper contrition, she was granted her request. Truthfully or not, she often blamed her parents for forcing the marriage upon her. Clearly, though, her maneuver required the connivance of several parties, including the Catholic clergy, who did not demand that such converts "pro matrimonio" undergo a very thorough course of instruction in the Catholic faith or show great proof of sincerity. This "sacrilegious sham," as one bishop of Nîmes called it, continued for decades, until in 1663 Louis XIV's government outlawed abjurations of Catholicism on pain of banishment and confiscation of property.[25]

Laws against mixed marriage could be equally counterproductive. When Augsburg's magistrates issued such a law in 1635, the number of conversions pro matrimonio shot up. The States of Holland expected a similar response when in 1755 they established the first legal impediments to mixed marriage in their province. They felt obliged to set a probationary period of a year in which converts had to prove their sincerity before they would be regarded as adherents of their new faith. Otherwise, the States feared, couples would simply evade the new penalties for mixed marriage through feigned conversions.

Of course, not all conversions pro matrimonio were prompted by pressure from authorities. Aside from any institutional obstacles, those who wished to enter into a mixed marriage had to grapple with the convictions of friends, family, neighbors, and above all their prospective spouse. One of Amsterdam's countless painters who did not achieve fame was Guilliaume Gardijn, a Catholic who converted to Calvinism in order to win a certain Anna Formiau as his wife. He later told the Amsterdam consistory bluntly that he had converted only "to get this woman."[26] Eventually

This pattern of trade-offs is widely paralleled in the experience of minorities outside the Netherlands. One of the most clear-cut examples comes from the German city of Ulm, where between 1570 and 1624 the number of Catholics declined by almost half. In that same period, the percentage of Ulm Catholics who married non-natives more than doubled. In the Luberon region of Provence, Protestants and Catholics were mixed relatively evenly. Mixed marriages were quite rare there, but whichever group formed the religious minority in a particular town had to find spouses elsewhere. Almost all geographically exogamous marriages were religiously endogamous; apparently there was no need or point to marrying a person who was both a "foreigner" *and* of a different faith. In Poitou, as in Friesland, the need to avoid marrying within the prohibited degrees of kinship (which extended much farther for Catholics than for Protestants) increased the rate of religiously mixed marriages.

For religious minorities to survive, they had to ensure that most of their members married endogamously. This they did through values they passed from one generation to the next as much as through sanctions. All were aware that failure could have drastic consequences, for mixed marriage was indeed one of the chief ways churches lost members.

For They Will Turn Away Thy Sons

Every mixed marriage presented Europe's competing confessions with both opportunities and perils. On the one hand, clergy and laity could hope to win a "heretical" spouse for the "true" faith. Indeed, the prospect of saving a soul offered one of the few positive legitimations for marrying outside the group. When the national synod held in 1578 gave permission for Dutch Calvinists to marry their children to non-church-members, it made its approval conditional on the intended spouses' being "not opposed to the [Reformed] religion" and giving "good hope that they shall grow in knowledge of the truth."[30] Such unions as the synod had chiefly in mind, however, were not mixed marriages in the strictest sense, but rather unions that joined a Reformed member to someone who had only a loose ecclesiastic affiliation or none at all. These people were the principal focus of competition in the Republic, and hope of winning them was indeed realistic: many eventually joined one church or another. Winning a convert from a different confession was another matter. On this point the Dutch churches did not differ from their counterparts elsewhere: they feared mixed marriages might produce losses as readily as gains. In 1595 the Delft consistory admonished church members that they should not "deceive themselves with a vain hope of winning over the person of contrary faith," for often "the evil gains the upperhand."[31] The Calvinist moralizer Jacob Cats, whose writings reached a huge Dutch audience, offered maidens the same advice: "Should someone fresh and healthy// Kiss a sick one's mouth,// She'll rather catch the ill// Than make the sick one well." To which he added the warning: "is it not certain that the man// Can push the matter harder than ever the maiden can?"[32] But while wives were particularly vulnerable to pressure from their husbands, in practice religious influence could flow in either direction. Every mixed marriage brought two churches into direct competition with one another, and there were no guarantees for either that it would emerge victorious. Typically, churches preferred to sacrifice the opportunity of gain if by doing so they could avoid the risk of loss.

Of course, much more was at stake than just one spouse per mixed marriage. It was the fate of the couple's children that aroused most concern among not only church leaders but also friends, relatives, and secular authorities. The possibility of losing them for Christ was the ultimate, and oldest, argument against marrying nonbelievers: "For they will turn away thy sons from following me, that they may serve other Gods" (Deuteronomy 7:4).[33] From birth, warned Molina, the children of mixed marriages are subjected to evil influences; "they suck in heresy with [mother's] milk." They are taught to despise pope, bishops, and priests, and to say heretical prayers and catechisms; later, they are matched with non-Catholic partners; "and so this cancer spreads insidiously to the children, children's children, nieces [and] nephews in the 3rd, 4th, 5th, . . . [and] 10th degrees."[34] With the children went the family's future generations. More tenaciously than any other, the Catholic Church fought to prevent such loss. Its bishops granted dispensations for mixed marriages on the condition that non-Catholic partners promise to allow their children to be raised as Catholics. Many priests demanded the same promise before they would solemnize a mixed marriage.

Yet many children of Protestant–Catholic marriages were not raised as Catholics. Ignoring church strictures, lay society developed its own practices in this regard. In some parts of Europe, such as the Enzie district of northeastern Scotland, patriarchal authority prevailed and children were raised in the faith of their fathers. This was the practice as well in Strasbourg and the small French town of Mauvezin in the seventeenth century, and in the Palatinate in the eighteenth. An even more extraordinary testimony to male authority, if true, is a report that in the French province of Poitou parents kept their daughters religiously ignorant, or at least neutral, until they married, at which point they were expected to adopt their husband's faith, whichever that was. On the other hand, it was mothers, not fathers, who generally had responsibility for the instruction of young children. In at least a couple of French locales—La Rochelle, the village of Sauve—the children of mixed marriages were often raised in their mothers' faith.

The offspring of mixed marriages, however, did not have to be raised all in the same faith. In Friesland, some couples alternated, baptizing their first child Catholic, their second Reformed, and so on, or vice versa. Alternation in birth order was the most common practice in eighteenth-century Utrecht as well. Other Frisian couples agreed "that, of the children who were born, the boys would be baptized in the Reformed church and the girls in the papist, or vice versa."[35] In the latter case, the parents' religious affiliation set the pattern for their progeny: boys would be raised in their father's faith, girls in their mother's. In this way the correspondence between gender and faith was replicated from one generation to the next. Forty percent of mixed-marriage couples followed this practice in Bergen op Zoom. In fact, this may have been the most common practice in early modern Europe, attested to in lands as diverse as Transylvania, Prussia, France, Scotland, and Ireland, as well as the Netherlands. In one case, in the German city of Augsburg, it was even applied to twins, the boy being raised Lutheran, the girl Catholic.

Why was this practice adopted so widely? Without contemporary explanations, we can only hypothesize. Clearly it encouraged sons to identify with their fathers, daughters with their mothers, the children taking on their parents' religious identities as they would their gender identities and, commonly, their social roles. As part of their training, daughters normally accompanied mothers in their day-to-day activities, including going to church. A second reason seems at least as important: when followed by many families, the practice froze into place the demographic balance between faiths. True, children could in theory choose their own faith when they reached the "age of discretion," commonly set at around twelve or fourteen. Yet as everyone knew, most adults remained loyal to the faith they were reared in. Thus unless an equal number of children, in the aggregate, were raised in each faith, a couple of generations could suffice to produce a massive shift in the number of adherents each church could claim. Such a shift would have challenged the stability of religiously mixed communities. Churches with dwindling memberships would likely have felt threatened; those with expanding ones might have tried to assert their new strength. The practice described above removed both threat and temptation. Whatever current relations were between the faiths, it tended to perpetuate them. Whether by law, custom, or prenuptial contract, it was lay society that embraced this practice; no church ever enjoined or officially encouraged it. Yet once again, in practice, Europe's confessions were opting for the safety of the status quo, for the consolidation of their positions, over the prospect of potential gain.

Arrangements for the religious upbringing of mixed-marriage children were always precarious, though, given early modern mortality rates. Many children lost one of their parents before reaching the age of discretion. When that happened, death destroyed the religious balance within the family, putting authority over the children in the surviving parent's hands. Some widows and widowers did not abide by the agreements they had made with their spouses. Such violations of trust were common enough that some communities, like the German city of Worms, issued regulations banning them. In other communities, authorities intervened on a case-by-case basis, leaving a rich record of confessional strife. In Bergen op Zoom, for example, detailed information has survived about children whose Protestant parent had died. Between the 1630s and 1760s, Bergen's Reformed ministers, elders, and magistrates mobilized repeatedly to prevent such children from being raised as Catholics. So did Protestant relatives and guardians. Indeed, a veritable tug-of-war for control of the children sometimes broke out between family and friends of the Protestant spouse, on the one hand, and those of the Catholic, on the other. In some cases, Bergen's Protestants placed children in the municipal orphanage rather than leave them in the hands of a Catholic parent or guardian. A common Catholic strategy was to send the children away to school or relatives in the nearby Southern Netherlands, a move Protestants regarded as a form of kidnapping.

These "kidnapping" incidents had intriguing parallels in seventeenth-century France, where Huguenots accused Catholics of abducting many children—the Coutelle affair mentioned earlier is but one example. Ten such accusations, involving seventeen children, were leveled in Montpellier in the early 1680s. In nine out of ten cases, the children were the offspring of a mixed marriage and one of their parents had recently died. In the French cases, though, unlike their Dutch counterparts, it was the Catholic parent's death that set off a struggle. In five instances, a close relative of the deceased Catholic parent did the actual "kidnapping," removing the children from the Protestant parent's home to prevent their being raised as Protestants. In two other cases, Catholic relatives brought legal suit against a Protestant guardian.[36] Such relatives could count on the support of France's Catholic authorities. Indeed, in 1681 a royal *arrêt* granted them a veritable license to act by reducing to seven the "age of discretion." Thereafter, even seven- and eight-year-olds who purportedly wished to convert to Catholicism could legally be whisked away. Elie Benoist's chronicle of the fortunes and misfortunes of the Reformed Churches of France is filled with "kidnapping" stories meant to curdle the blood and evoke the sympathy of any parent. By his account, Catholics stooped to trickery, pressure, and worse, inducing little children, for example, to make the sign of the cross. That sufficed for Catholics to place them in a monastery or convent.[37]

What seemed darkly sinister to Huguenots, though, made common sense to many French Catholics. They deemed a bit of coercion entirely appropriate to make children convert, just as it was to make them behave; in both instances, they believed, force had a pedagogic function and was for the children's own good. Besides, children would scarcely be able to embrace the "true" faith as long as they were immersed in Protestant society and dependent on Protestant parents. Hence the need for organizations like the Company for the Propagation of the Faith, which saw to their welfare.

If the death of one spouse in a mixed marriage invited the intervention of outsiders, the death of both spouses guaranteed it. When children were orphaned, either relatives, or family friends acting as legal guardians, or in the last instance local government had to step in to provide them with new homes. Throughout early modern Europe, orphans were classified among the most deserving of the poor, and an increasing number of cities founded orphanages to care for them. Invariably, those orphanages raised children in the city's official faith. Naturally, religious dissenters did what they could to keep children out of such institutions, placing them with families or founding separate orphanages of their own, as many Dutch ones did from the second half of the seventeenth century. Still, most orphanages were public institutions, and it was the fate of many mixed-marriage orphans to be raised in them.

If seemingly mixed marriages were sometimes a disguise for men's religious dissent, and if some conversions pro matrimonio were anything but heartfelt, it is not surprising that a whiff of uncertainty hung over the confessional allegiance of all who married outside their faith. There was something ambiguous about the status of mixed couples and their children. This is not to say that people who entered into mixed marriages were necessarily any less committed to their church, that their faith was weaker, or that religion was less central to their lives than it was for other people. But if "light and darkness" had "nothing in common," mixed marriages did seem to, well, mix them, casting a grey pall over couple and family. The first thing churches (and some secular authorities, like Utrecht's) anxiously demanded of mixed couples was that the spouse who confessed the "true" faith would not be pressured or seduced into abandoning it. They perceived that anyone who entered into a mixed marriage would inevitably be subject to baleful influences. Concern about the fate of mixed-marriage children was well founded, as we have seen, and no parental promises on this score could provide against all contingencies.

Similar anxieties surrounded converts, over whose heads a question always hovered: Was their conversion sincere and complete? In the case of forced conversions, the answer was obviously no. Castellio and other advocates of toleration illustrated this point by reference to the Jews of Spain, whose conversion in the late fourteenth and fifteenth centuries had produced so many dissembling, nominal Christians. Many popes doubted the value of such conversions, among them Pope Innocent XI, who condemned for this reason the revocation of the Edict of Nantes. But what about conversions performed under milder forms of pressure—what Louis XIV's government called "les douces violences"—or ones that brought material advantage?[38] The very practices of proselytizing in early modern Europe cast doubt on the value of the results. Even when the conversions were more than nominal, they produced people who by virtue of their origins and ties constituted an ambiguous middle group. In eighteenth-century Ireland, for example, converts to Protestantism from the aristocracy and gentry showed continued sympathy and support for their former co-religionists. They sat in parliament, practiced law, and functioned as justices of the peace, mediating between Protestant regime and Catholic population. They could not be counted on to enforce the penal laws. As one member of the Irish parliament remarked in 1714, "Can he [a convert] immediately forget all his friends and relations? Can he be so deaf to the ties of relationship as to give up a priest, his cousin or perhaps brother, to be prosecuted?"[39] Skepticism was justified.

Converts caused concern on another score too: Having violated a sacred taboo, could they ever be trusted entirely not to violate it again—not to convert back to the faith of their childhood? In fact, a significant number of converts did "relapse" sooner or later. In Augsburg, almost 20 percent did so; one of the more common patterns was for widows and widowers who had converted pro matrimonio to relapse upon the death of their spouse. In Nîmes, eight out of twenty-eight converts to Catholicism in 1661 relapsed. There were even people who relapsed twice, like Henri-Charles de La Trémouille, Prince of Tarente, born a Protestant, converted to Catholicism, returned to Protestantism, spent most of his adult life as a Protestant, but then in his old age returned to Catholicism (not coincidentally, Tarente was the child of a mixed marriage). Such cases stoked the fires of anxiety. Laws against relapsing were correspondingly severe: a 1663 French law decreed banishment and confiscation of property for Protestants who converted and then relapsed. As late as 1734 the government of the Southern Netherlands (then under Austrian rule) decreed that Protestants who converted and then relapsed were to be burned at the stake. Such was the penalty laid down in canon law for relapsed heretics, even if they returned to the bosom of the Catholic Church. For as Aquinas had long ago explained, the Church had to presume "that those who relapse after being once received, are not sincere in their return."[40] It is little wonder, then, that some converts had a chip on their shoulders and behaved as if they continually had to prove their loyalty to their adopted faith. One who perhaps deserves special mention was the French nobleman Gaspard de Calvière, Baron of Saint-Cosme. A Huguenot who became a "New Catholic" with the revocation of the Edict of Nantes, he went on to mercilessly pursue

Huguenots in the Vaunage region who refused to conform. His assassination in August 1702 was the spark that set off the War of the Cévennes, one of the least known but most vicious religious wars in European history.

Mixed marriage and conversion were unsettling phenomena in the confessional age. Both highlighted the existence of people whose confessional allegiance was not entirely certain or stable. Both showed that the boundaries between confessions were not as sharp or impermeable as the teachings of Europe's churches made them out to be. This was the hidden secret, the lurking demon that clergy sought to exorcise by their polemics. Remember the conversion of Jean Gesse, magistrate in Mauvezin, who saw good people among both Calvinists and Catholics and who saw the difference in faiths as relative, a matter of better or worse, not divine versus satanic: mixed marriage and conversions—even ones that involved a gain of followers—threatened to undermine the black-and-white, us-versus-them mentality that clergy propagated and that countless Christians embraced in their longing for security and order in a fragmented world.

Whether anyone liked it or not, the boundaries between confessions were always somewhat grey and porous. But they could be more or less so. Certainly when it came to mixed marriage, clergy showed a clear preference: rather than risk losing church members, they were prepared to sacrifice opportunities for expansion. To be sure, they wished to see their faith spread and triumph around the world, in fulfillment of God's plan. By some point in the seventeenth century, though, most clergy showed a clear preference for segregation over integration, and over the long run the force of their preference may have contributed to a heightening of the social and cultural walls dividing Protestants from Catholics. Those walls were by no means incompatible with toleration. On the contrary, as we have seen, in communities with dual or multiple establishments they may even have improved relations between religious groups. High rates of mixed marriage and conversion, then, should not be equated with toleration per se. They are indicators, rather, of a certain type of toleration, a pattern of interaction between people of different faiths that involved high degrees of integration and assimilation. To individuals such toleration offered great freedom. To groups, especially small minorities, trying to preserve their coherence and identity, it posed a very real threat.

ELEVEN

Infidels

The Invention of the Ghetto

From sunset, or a little after, to the ringing of the Maronga bell at dawn, the gates of the Venetian ghetto were locked shut. Paid by the very Jews whose confinement they secured, Christian guards kept a close and constant watch over the gates that gave access to the city's renowned Jewish quarter—not quite the first ghetto in European history, but the paradigmatic one, the one that gave us the word *ghetto*. In Venetian dialect, *ghet* meant "foundry," which is what formerly had stood on the little island, a peripheral bit of industrial brownland, onto which several hundred Jews were corralled in 1516 and forced to live. Harsh as this sounds, for Venice the creation of the ghetto was a liberalization of policy toward Jews, who in the fifteenth century had not been permitted to reside in the city. In 1509, though, the Venetian government, la Serenissima, had honored an obligation to give refuge to Jews who resided in the Veneto, the city's subject territories on *terraferma,* when the territories were invaded by a hostile army. Horrified friars thundered from the pulpits against this innovation, blaming it for bringing down God's wrath on the city and causing its military defeats. "It would be good," argued a magistrate, "to expel [the Jews] from the whole world, and God would prosper this Republic as he did the King of Portugal, who, on expelling them, discovered the new route to India, and God made him the King of Gold."[1] But the Jews were useful; indeed, the city's poor could scarcely do without their small loans, while its military machine needed all the tax revenues that could be squeezed out of them. And so the ghetto was created, a compromise between allowing the Jews to live freely in Venice and expelling them. Its purpose: to make a Jewish presence acceptable to the Christian community.

The sine qua non of this presence was segregation. Jews were allowed to come and go freely in daytime so they could engage in those activities from which the city benefited. For the "German" Jews who formed the original core of ghetto inhabitants—Ashkenazim, many of whose ancestors had lived for generations in Italy—that was lending money. Ashkenazim also traded in "strazzaria," secondhand clothes and household goods. From the 1540s this group was joined by "Levantines" from the Ottoman Empire and "Ponentines" from Spain and Portugal—both Sephardic Jews with Iberian roots. They engaged in long-distance trade, some of it very lucrative, and by the 1590s most of Venice's trade with the Balkans and Constantinople passed through their hands. To the Sephardim an additional parcel of land was allocated, and in 1633 yet another parcel was appended. With each addition, the ghetto's gates were moved and buildings were adapted to block all other access. Even visual access was blocked to some extent, so Christians could not see Jews or vice versa. Whenever they left the ghetto, Jews had to wear special headgear, so they could be immediately recognized: Levantines, who dressed in Turkish mode, wore a yellow turban; other Jews wore a yellow, later red, hat. Above all, they were forbidden to mix with Christians at nighttime, when the gates of the ghetto were locked shut and patrol boats cruised the dark canals to ensure that, without special permission, no Jew could get out and no Christian could get in.

This enforced nocturnal segregation was what made the European ghetto different from other residential quarters inhabited by a particular group. Jewish quarters had existed for centuries in Europe, as they had in North Africa and the Middle East. The ghetto, though, was essentially new to sixteenth-century Europe. Pioneered by Venice, ghettos multiplied in Italy from 1555, and new ones continued to be founded there to the end of the Old Regime. They were designed to prevent Christians and Jews from socializing—from mingling during those hours given over not to labor and business but to eating and drinking, amusements and conviviality, sleeping

ment: shoppers to buy strazzaria, landlords to collect rents (Jews not being allowed to own outright any real estate), the poor to take out loans or, if fortune smiled on them, redeem pledges, porters, street cleaners, water carriers, attendants of stalls and pitches, wandering vendors, lackeys of the magistrates, laborers employed by Jewish printers and jewelers. Christian children entered the ghetto to work and perhaps also play, until authorities forbade them in the early eighteenth century. Christian tourists visited the ghetto just to look. Leon Modena taught Hebrew to Christian as well as Jewish students, some of them foreigners who came to Venice to master the biblical tongue. His sermons attracted local friars, with whom he engaged in scholarly dialogue, and foreign dignitaries like the brother of the French king, whose attendance Modena proudly recorded in his autobiography. With shame he recorded also his compulsive gambling, which often took place in religiously mixed company.

In fact, the Venetian ghetto saw considerable coming and going even at

Figure 11.1. Portrait of Venetian rabbi Leon Modena. In an extraordinary accommodation to his Christian audience, the rabbi has himself portrayed bareheaded. Detail from the title page of his *Historia de' riti hebraici* (Venice, 1638). Courtesy of the Governing Body of Christ Church, Oxford, CHC Spec. Coll. AF.8.12(1).

night. Christian lawyers entered it to attend Jewish courts, Christian couriers to fetch Jewish letters. In 1628 the multi-talented Modena organized an unusual service for Simhat Torah featuring choral singing. It must have attracted a crowd of Christians, since "many captains and police-officers had to be stationed at the gates so that they could pass through peacefully."[7] Jewish musicians enjoyed a high reputation, and a singer named Rachel was granted special dispensation to leave the ghetto at nights to perform in the homes of "nobles, citizens, and other honorable persons."[8] Jewish doctors also were much in demand, and despite the intimacy of the doctor–patient relationship, which made authorities nervous, they were allowed to make house calls on Christian patients at night. As a mark of special eminence, some were even allowed to wear the black hat of a Christian. Even the Jewish poor were allowed out of the ghetto to purchase oil and other essential goods.

The ghetto, then, did anything but cut off relations between Christians and Jews. To the contrary, it put those relations on a new footing that made them in some respects easier and freer than they had been before. The walls and gates of the ghetto gave powerful form, at once physical and symbolic, to the separateness of the Christian and Jewish peoples. In the process, it quelled some of the anxieties Christians had about the presence of Jews in their midst. In this way, it established a new set of terms on which Christian–Jewish relations in Italy would henceforth be conducted.

The invention of the ghetto came at a turning point in the history of Christian–Jewish relations generally. For more than a century, Europe's Jews had been subjected to persecution fiercer than they had ever previously experienced. In Spain, where earlier they had achieved an unmatched prosperity and cultural brilliance, tens of thousands had been converted to Christianity at swordpoint. Those who had persisted in their faith had finally been expelled in 1492. Jews had been driven out of one land after another, until by the middle of the sixteenth century few Jews remained in western or central Europe. At that juncture, Christian communities both north and south of the Alps began to insist on new arrangements as a precondition for continuing to tolerate, or for tolerating once again, a Jewish presence in their midst. These arrangements articulated in new ways, and in some respects enhanced, the separateness of the Jewish people from the Christian communities that hosted them. From a modern perspective, these arrangements seem at best profoundly discriminatory, and let me be clear that I am not endorsing them as a solution to modern religious conflicts. From the perspective, though, of the preceding period, they brought advantages and even improvements in the conditions of Jewish life. The alternative to them at the time was not emancipation and integration, but rather pogroms, expulsions, and forced baptism.

If Muslims had been allowed to live in early modern Europe on the same terms that Jews were, they would have been far more numerous and comfortable than they were. Venice created for Muslim merchants a walled compound not altogether unlike its Jewish ghetto. Known as the Fondaco dei Turchi, it too had a guard who locked its doors at night and opened them at dawn. But whereas the Venetian ghetto became a model for Jewish communities elsewhere, the Fondaco remained exceptional. Few Muslims ventured voluntarily into what they called *dar al-Harb*, the territory of war. In Lithuania and Spain, on Europe's periphery, there lived Muslims whose communities predated the Christianization or re-Christianization, respectively, of those lands. But Spanish Muslims suffered one of the most notorious episodes of persecution in early modern history, and by 1614 their descendants, the Moriscos, had been expelled from Christendom. Elsewhere, Muslims were slaves or isolated individuals. No arrangement sufficed to make an organized presence of these other infidels acceptable in most parts of Christian Europe.

God's Scourge

Whereas the Jews of the diaspora were a scattered people, a vulnerable, weaponless minority without a land or state of their own, Muslims had a civilization and empire that, from the fifteenth to the end of the seventeenth century, represented a powerful rival to Christian Europe. Above all, the conquest of Constantinople by the Ottomans in 1453 turned "the Turk" into "the normative foe of Christendom."[9] Sweeping away the remnants of the Byzantine Empire, it left no buffer between Western Christendom and an expansionist Muslim state. On land, it presaged a struggle that was to devastate central Hungary and bring Ottoman armies twice, in 1529 and 1683, to the gates of Vienna. Until they were decisively driven back in the 1680s and 1690s, Ottoman armies would threaten central Europe directly, generating a fear that pervaded the region. At sea the Ottomans emerged as a major naval power, by the 1530s winning dominance over the eastern Mediterranean. Venice was forced to yield most of its seaborne empire and pay tribute to the Ottoman sultan. On both these fronts, emperors and popes had to rally the forces of Christendom to repel the infidel.

Farther west, Muslim forces of a different sort had a powerful presence. Almost as epochal as the Muslim conquest of Constantinople, the Christian conquest of Granada in 1492 abolished the last Muslim state on the Iberian peninsula. It only shifted, though, what remained an active military frontier. Thousands of Spanish Muslims fled to North Africa, where some joined the Moroccan army; others swelled the ranks of the Barbary corsairs. Embittered by the loss of their Andalusian home, these corsairs waged "holy guerrilla warfare" against Europe generally and Spain in particular.[10] For revenge and profit, they seized Christian ships, their cargos, crews, and passengers. At the height of their activity, in the first half of the seventeenth century, corsairs seized 466 English vessels in just nine years. Corsair ships ranged from Arabia to the English Channel, and in 1617 one of them gave Londoners a jolt of fright when it was caught in the River Thames. In fact, the corsairs' prime objective was often to capture Christians, whom they took back to North Africa and held for ransom or sold as slaves. Nor did the corsairs confine their attacks to the high seas: both they and the Ottoman navy raided Christian coasts, one assault on the Bay of Naples in 1544 netting no fewer than seven thousand captives. The scope of this activity and consequent dimensions of Christian slavery in North Africa have not always been recognized. A reasonable guesstimate puts the average number of slaves in Barbary at any one time at perhaps thirty-five thousand until the 1680s, when the figure drops. All in all, over the whole early modern period, more than a million European Christians may have tasted the bitterness of slavery at Muslim hands.[11]

No wonder the "Turk" and the "Moor" were fearsome figures in European culture, present on stage, in print, and in sermon. "God's scourge" is what Luther and other preachers called the Turks, a whip with which the Lord chastised his people for their sins. Until they repented and reformed, went the message, they could not expect him to stop brandishing it. No wonder also that Europeans thirsted for information about these enemies. In French travel literature of the sixteenth century, twice as many works treated the Ottoman Empire as treated the Americas. Some of these works, like *Les misères et tribulations que les Christiens tributaires & esclaves tenuz par le Turcz seuffrent* (1544) by Bartholomaus Gorgevic, published in six languages, were hot sellers. Yet while Gorgevic's heart-rending account of what he witnessed during his own years in captivity fed European fears and prejudices about the Turk's inhuman cruelty, other works such as diplomat Philippe du Fresne-Canaye's *Voyage du Levant* (1573) expressed admiration for the orderliness and sophistication of this rival state and civilization. In fact, Europeans had ambivalent feelings, and for all the captives in North Africa who lived out their lives as slaves, remaining true to their faith, no small number converted to Islam and "turned Turk," fashioning for themselves a new and often satisfying life in the Muslim world. From the Italian coast to the Baltic, Christian port communities organized funds to ransom back their men before they succumbed to this temptation. Some Europeans even chose freely for such a life, fleeing the Christian world. Those who abandoned Christianity for Islam were called "renegades."

The frontier between Christendom and Islam, then, was long and porous, encompassing the entire Mediterranean and part of the Atlantic. Sailors, fishermen, merchants, island and coastal dwellers all found themselves on its front line, as did the population of central Hungary, not to mention the Polish, German, Austrian, Italian, Spanish, and other fighting men who battled the Turks on land or sea. Along this frontier there was a certain amount of accommodation and mutual influence as well as conflict. This has not been much studied except in Hungary, where Ottomans and Habsburgs exploited the inhabitants in what amounted to a form of joint rule. Here Turks learned to imitate European military innovations such as artillery, while Christians learned to eat rice pilaf and their princes to wear Turkish caftans. Willingly or not, Europeans crossed the frontier in large numbers to reside in North Africa and the Levant, where of course they found a variety of Christians who had always lived there: Greek Orthodox principally, but also Armenians, Copts, Jacobites, and Maronites. Europeans too, known as "Franks," had had a presence in the Levant since the Crusades, and European merchants, led by the Venetians, established a whole series of trading posts there. As visitors, slaves, or resident minorities (so-called dhimmis), Christians had accepted roles in Ottoman society, and even Christian slaves were often allowed to practice their religion.

The question here is the opposite—whether Muslims lived and worshipped in Christian Europe, whether they were accommodated there, and if so, how. On this point, not a lot of research has been done. All indications suggest, though, that Muslims had only a scanty presence in the lands of Christendom.

This is somewhat surprising, given how connected the economies of Europe and the Middle East were. In the sixteenth century, Egypt and Sicily were still the granaries of the Mediterranean, and trade in heavy, bulk goods was voluminous. Also, despite the Portuguese end run around the Cape of Good Hope, some spices continued to travel from Asia to Europe via the Levant. By the late seventeenth century, it was Persian silk, coffee from Yemen and Ethiopia, mohair from Anatolia, wool, and cotton that went westward, while the Levant was emerging as a market for the products of European cottage industry. Little of this trade, though, was in Muslim hands. Initially, Venetian and Genoese merchants carried most of it; in the sixteenth century, Sephardic Jews came to play key roles, and in the seventeenth, Dutch, English, and French merchants dominated. For the most part, European merchants traveled to Muslim lands, not vice versa, and even in Aleppo, Smyrna (Izmir), and other Levantine commercial hubs, most trade was mediated by local Jewish and Christian minorities.

On occasion Muslim merchants did bring goods to European ports, either on their own ships or traveling on Christian ones. They stopped in Malta, Palermo, Livorno, Marseilles, Toulon, and Malaga. One Englishman thanked God for an Algerian merchant he encountered in 1688 in Plymouth, who promised to help the man gain his son's release from captivity. Muslim merchants ventured to Europe to buy tobacco, the smoking of which Muslim moralists denounced as a dirty European habit. Storms also occasionally cast Muslim merchants and sailors onto European shores. All this is different, though, from Muslims residing in Europe. Individual merchants must have done so for shorter or longer periods in some of the major ports; in Livorno in the late sixteenth century, one had a grand house built "in his country's style" that became a landmark.[12] In all of Europe, though, only Venice had a recognized community of Muslim merchants with corporate privileges and a communal residence.

True to their city's heritage as *emporium mundi*, Venetian magistrates welcomed "Turks" as one among many foreign nations come to trade their wares. With their turbans and grand mustaches, they were a visible and exotic presence in the city, despite their small numbers. The papal port of Ancona also attracted Turks for several decades, until in 1564 the sultan barred Ottoman subjects from trading there. Ancona's loss was gain for

Venice, which hosted as of 1570 some seventy-five Muslim merchants. Originally the Muslims lived in hostels or private residences, conducting their business on the Rialto alongside Christians. This exposed them to harassment, though, and when war broke out between Venice and the Ottomans in 1570, the Serenissima felt compelled to provide them with safer lodgings. Even after the war, the government more than once had to threaten severe punishment for anyone who "dare offend, molest, injure, use violence [against], or in any other way disturb the Turks . . . with deeds or words, by day or by night."[13] Christians accused the Turks, in turn, of "stealing, leading boys away, [and] keeping company with Christian women"; there were also complaints that they mocked the Christian religion.[14] To protect Turks from Christians and vice versa, as well as to regulate and tax their trade, the Venetian government found it desirable to house the Turks together in a single building. In 1579 an inn known as "The Angel" was designated for this purpose, but it proved too small, able to accommodate merchants from Bosnia and Albania but not the "Asiatics" whom authorities, it seems, were most concerned to segregate. After a vain search for alternatives, as well as popular protest, in 1621 a large new structure was opened: the Fondaco dei Turchi (Figure 11.2).

According to a papal nuncio, the Turks themselves wanted "for the convenience of merchants a place of their own, like the Jews have their ghetto."[15] Perhaps this comparison really occurred to the Turks, or perhaps just to the nuncio. In any event, the Fondaco had closer models. Hostelries for foreign merchants, often designed around a central courtyard, were common in the Muslim world, where they were called "fondouqs." Venetian merchants had direct experience of these, in imitation of which Venice itself had long ago established the Fondaco dei Tedeschi, where German merchants lived and traded. The Fondaco dei Turchi was an imposing structure on the Grand Canal, a former palazzo whose windows and doors were blocked or screened off to ensure that its residents had no opportunity to "commit any scandalous and indecent acts."[16] A Christian guard stood sentry at the one remaining door to prevent Christian women or boys from entering the building, or Turks from bringing arms into it. At night, he locked the building shut. Internally the Fondaco was divided in two parts, one for Balkan merchants, the other for "Asiatics and sellers of camlets" (a rich cloth made from a blend of camel's or goat's hair and silk, produced in Anatolia).[17] There were lodgings, storerooms, spaces to conduct business, and wells, which the guard was required to replenish with water as needed, clearly for the Muslims' ablutions—a practice remarked upon by Christians, who did not wash nearly as often. There was also a room used as a mosque.

The Fondaco was thoroughly exceptional: nowhere else in Christian Europe did Muslim merchants reside in sufficient numbers to warrant such a structure. Nor until the 1790s were there resident Muslim ambassadors. As in trade, so in diplomacy Muslims relied often on intermediaries, especially Sephardic Jews like the Pallache family, who served as agents in the Dutch Republic for a series of Moroccan sultans. Thanks to their knowledge of European languages and culture and their network of international contacts, Sephardim were well suited for the role. Also as in trade, Muslim rulers generally preferred Europeans to come to them, and as it happened this suited well many European princes, who did not wish to be seen honoring and befriending infidels. On this score there reigned a hypocrisy similar to that of the schuilkerk: actions outside the lands of Christendom were less

Figure 11.2. The Fondaco dei Turchi, Venice, before the restoration of 1858–1869. Venice. Photograph by Domenico Bresolin, circa 1855. Courtesy of Alinari Archives, Florence.

visible and hence less offensive than actions performed in Europe, in the glare of the public spotlight. Diplomacy conducted abroad was more discreet. Thus, by the end of the sixteenth century, Venice, France, England, and the Holy Roman Empire had representatives resident in Istanbul; in the following two centuries, other European lands followed suit. Turkish and Moroccan envoys were sent to Europe only on specific missions, and Persian envoys were rare indeed.

The matters of business that brought these visitors to Europe included the conclusion of alliances. All who counted the Habsburgs as their enemies had at least one common cause, and as early as 1536 the French King Francis I made a pact with the Ottomans, the first of several between France and the Sublime Porte. As a result of this pact, the entire Ottoman fleet, with some thirty thousand men, passed the winter of 1543–44 in Toulon (most of the city's inhabitants, including all women and children, were evacuated for the duration). Protestants and Muslims had an additional reason to ally: they shared a hatred of Catholicism, which both condemned for its "idolatry." Visiting The Hague in 1613, Moroccan envoy Ahmad ibn Qasim al-Hajari expressed genuine sympathy for the Calvinist faith of his hosts. In turn, according to him, Protestant scholars taught people "that they should not hate the Muslims because they are the sword of God on His earth against the worshippers of idols."[18] Not all Protestant scholars really felt such solidarity, but some did appreciate that it was Catholic states and rulers, above all the Habsburgs, who bore the direct brunt of Muslim assaults. Musing on the mysteries of divine providence, Englishman Thomas Fuller observed in 1651 how "all West-Christendome oweth her quiet sleep to [the King of Spain's] constant waking, who with his galleys muzzleth the mouth of Tunis and Algier. Yea, God in his providence hath so ordered it, that the Dominions of Catholick Princes (as they term them) are the case and cover on the East and South to keep and fense the Protestant countreys."[19] In an age of religious wars, Protestants and Muslims had common interests, an embarrassing truth that gave plausibility to the smears of Catholic polemicists who accused Protestant foes of "Calvino-Turkism." Emperor Charles V might have squelched the Protestant Reformation in an early phase if not for the Ottoman threat and other distractions. Later, by forcing Philip II to divert his resources, the Ottomans helped make possible the success of the Dutch Revolt against Spain.

The sight of an emissary like al-Hajari must have been the first contact many Europeans had with a real live Muslim. Such emissaries were most likely to be spotted, of course, in Europe's capitals: Paris, The Hague, London, Vienna, Berlin. Some, though, toured more widely. Ömer Agha, the first Turkish envoy to The Hague, was shown in 1614 around Leiden, Haarlem, Amsterdam, and Utrecht. On his way to Madrid in 1690, Mohammad bin abd al-Wahab al-Ghassani, the Moroccan vizier, passed through Cadiz, where "all the inhabitants of the city, along with soldiers and cavalry, came out to accompany us," proceeding next to Santa Maria, where he was greeted by "huge crowds of men, women, and children," and so it went in Cordoba too. These ambassadors were all the more visible because they came with suites, Agha's numbering no fewer than nineteen persons. Nor were contacts with envoys limited, for some Christians, to impersonal shows. In the two and a half years Al-Hajari spent in France before going to the Netherlands, he had conversations with priests and monks, dined at the home of a judge, was consulted by scholars who wished to improve their Arabic, and even had a romantic fling with the relative of a royal official with whom he lodged. Abdallah bin Aisha, who led a Moroccan delegation to France in 1699, had an intimate relationship with a lady at court, Charlotte Le Camus Melson, to whom he wrote love poems, while also developing a heartfelt friendship with a French diplomat and his family.

Apparently, then, some Christians did not find it too difficult to accept individual Muslims, nor did some individual Muslims find it too uncomfortable to visit Europe on business. Muslim communities, however, were a different matter. In eastern Europe, there were the Tatars of Lithuania. Descendants of the Golden Horde, they had been invited in the fourteenth century to settle in the vicinity of Vilnius, where in exchange for estates and privileges they fought in Lithuania's wars against Muscovy. In later centuries, too, many served as cavalry in the Polish-Lithuanian army. The original group being mostly male, Tatars were initially allowed to intermarry with Christians, a privilege revoked in 1616. By that time most Tatars had adopted the local Belorussian tongue. They remained, though, a discrete "nation" with a distinct religious and ethnic identity, and in the scores of village colonies they established they were allowed to have mosques. Estimates vary widely, but one of the more sensible ones puts their number in the sixteenth century at around one hundred thousand. This population had no counterpart in central or western Europe, where in the early modern period there were only two types of Muslim community: slaves and, until their expulsion, Moriscos.

The Muslim enslavement of Christian captives was no one-way street: Christians too enslaved Muslims captured along the frontier, both in regular military conflict and in predatory raids launched by slave traders, Knights of Malta, and Knights of St. Stephen. Their activity produced a slavery very different from that of earlier centuries, when most slaves bought by Europeans had been women and children and had been kept as domestic servants. In the sixteenth century, there were still thousands of household slaves in Italy and Spain, especially in the kingdoms of Naples and Sicily and in Andalusia. Such slaves, though, lived scattered among Christian households, and even where they were numerous, they might be forbidden, as in Madrid, to speak Arabic or follow their traditional customs, never mind practice Islam. There were at least a few Muslim slaves in northern Europe, too, where some princes kept gorgeously dressed Turkish boys on display at their courts as servants and lackeys, while others like Marie de' Medici kept Turkish embroiderers. Some European travelers, especially diplomats, brought a slave or two back with them from sojourns in the lands of Islam. In southern Europe, domestic slavery was on a different scale. Over time, though, it declined, leaving by the late seventeenth century the hard core, as it were, of early modern slaves: adult male captives, most of whom served as oarsmen on the galleys of Europe's Mediterranean naval powers: Venice, Genoa, Tuscany, the Papacy, Spain, and from the 1660s, France.

Compared to the criminals and prisoners of war who also provided manpower on Europe's galleys, "Turks" were reputed to be far and away the best rowers, their physical prowess giving birth to the French expression "fort comme un Turc." For their pains they were assigned the most arduous rowing positions and scattered among the vessels, to set an example to others. In port, though, they were housed together, much as Christian slaves in North Africa were, in buildings known in the common argot of the Mediterranean as "bagni." There they formed communities that, at their peaks, numbered as many as a thousand in Livorno, fifteen hundred to two thousand in Genoa, and two thousand in Marseilles and Toulon combined. They elected leaders who spoke on their behalf, arbitrated disputes, and organized worship. Much as the bagni of North Africa normally included a Christian chapel, in Livorno in 1680 Muslims had a place of worship in each of four bagni. In 1689 a Capuchin was shown what he called a genuine mosque in Livorno, and the label certainly seems to fit his description: "The aforesaid Capuchin fathers on one occasion had me see the mosque of the Turks, which is a small house which the Turks do not enter unless barefoot and quite clean of all filth, in which I saw there is a pulpit with two staircases, the book of their Alcoran and other books of their law; in one part I saw there is a gilded cape, in another a turban and other objects which are venerated by them and there they perform their exercises of their Mahometan law. This mosque is allowed them because even the Turks permit the Christians in their *bagni* to have their secret churches."[20] Muslim oarsmen in the French fleet established mosques in Marseilles and Toulon, where during the winter, when their ships did not venture out of port, they worked in manufacturing and set up shops along the waterfront. By 1701 Muslim slaves in the papal port of Civitavecchia had a place of worship of some sort, and by 1737 Genoese slaves had what was called a "moschea" in the city's docks. In all of these ports, as in the Spanish port of Cadiz, Muslims were permitted also a cemetery, again just as Christians were in North Africa. These cemeteries could not be tucked away, though, inside the dockland buildings where Muslims resided; they had to be on solid, dry land, and Muslims had to bring the corpses of their deceased to them. The cemeteries thus had a visible presence that Muslim places of worship lacked, and accordingly they attracted more hostility from local Christians. In 1696 the Castilian government had to threaten with punishment anyone who mistreated "moorish or turkish slaves, living or dead."[21] More than once the pasha of Tunisia and other North African authorities saved Muslim burial grounds in Europe from closure by threatening reprisals against their own Christian captives.

By far the largest and most vigorous Muslim presence in western Europe, though, until their expulsion, were Spain's Moriscos. These were the descendants of the Moors who in the Middle Ages had had their own Iberian kingdoms. In 1492 the last of these kingdoms had fallen, and eight years later its inhabitants were given the choice of baptism or exile. By 1526 Islam had been outlawed throughout Spain, and Spanish Muslims had become Christians, at least in name. They constituted a fifth of the total population of Aragon, a third of that of Valencia, and until 1568 a majority in Granada. In that year, on Christmas Eve, Moriscos in Granada took up arms to resist the suppression of their Muslim way of life. Their revolt turned into a bloody debacle, with atrocities committed on both sides. A turning point, it marked the end, in most places, of the "convivencia," or peaceful coexistence, that traditionally had characterized relations between Christians and Muslims in Spain. As punishment and to prevent further unrest, Philip II had some fifty thousand Moriscos from rebel areas enslaved and dispersed across Castile. At the same time, the Inquisition dramatically stepped up its prosecution of Moriscos. All together, between 1566 and 1609 about 250 Moriscos were condemned for practicing Islam and "relaxed," that is, given over to the secular authorities for execution at the spectacular ceremonies known as *autos-da-fé*. Over forty years, another thousand were sentenced to life service on the royal galleys, another form of death sentence. Resistance to such persecution was quashed: in 1591 Philip sent troops into Aragon to prevent its (Christian) nobles from continuing to protect their Morisco vassals. Mooted since the 1580s, the expulsion of the Moriscos was ordered in 1609 and carried out over five years. Three hundred thousand men, women, and children, the largest group of religious refugees in early modern history, were forced to leave their homeland. Most were deported or fled to North Africa; others went farther east.

But why did a Muslim presence become so unacceptable to Spanish authorities, and did it become equally so to ordinary Spanish "Old Christians" (as opposed to Moriscos and Jewish Conversos, who were "New Christians")? One must remember, first of all, that for centuries Christians had been engaged in a "reconquista" of the Iberian peninsula. The subjugation, nominal conversion, persecution, and expulsion of Spanish Muslims were the final acts of this crusade, which played a large role in shaping the culture and identity of Spain's Christian kingdoms, especially Castile. One must remember, too, that Spain was at war with foreign Muslim powers: the Ottomans until 1580 and the Barbary corsairs continually, while Morocco remained a staging area for possible invasions. Just as Christian dissenters did elsewhere in Europe, so in Spain Moriscos seemed natural allies of foreign powers who shared their faith—a fifth column of potential traitors who, if given an opportunity, would betray the state from within. Nor was this fear wholly unjustified. When the Turkish fleet sacked Minorca in 1558, Moriscos danced in the streets, and when the Portuguese army was obliterated in 1578, they held bullfights "and other rejoicings."[22] Some four thousand Turks and Berbers came from North Africa to join the fight in the revolt of the Moriscos of Granada, whom the governor of Algiers supplied with arms and ammunition. Nor were their co-religionists the Moriscos' only foreign allies: in the 1570s Moriscos contacted French Huguenots, and the Ottomans proposed to the Dutch a joint attack on Spanish forces, to coincide with a Morisco uprising. Similar ideas were floated later for a Dutch-Moroccan attack, though they too went nowhere.

All this time, Moriscos remained overwhelmingly loyal to Islam. If they accepted baptism, they did so with the understanding, confirmed by their religious leaders, that Islam itself permitted them to conform as necessary in times of persecution. After baptisms, they performed at home the *fadas,* a ritual in which they wiped off the chrism that had been daubed on their babies. The extent to which they could practice Islam and follow a Muslim way of life varied from place to place, depending largely on how segregated Moriscos and Old Christians were from one another. In Valencia, most of the villages where Moriscos lived had no Christian inhabitants. Here a full-fledged Islamic civilization continued to flourish right up to the expulsion. Moriscos here spoke only Arabic, males were circumcised (all of them until around 1580, later about half), and a few even practiced polygamy. While they did not worship in buildings that were overtly mosques, they had *alfaquís,* Muslim clerics, who performed Muslim marriage ceremonies and arbitrated disputes according to Sharia law. From 1502 to 1568, a similar situation prevailed in Granada. Christian authorities here tried repeatedly to ban Morisco customs—practices that were not dictated by Islam per se but were part of Arabic culture. They saw assimilation as the key to true conversion: the Moriscos were to forget all memory of "Moorish things and were to live and comport themselves like the Christians."[23] They were even encouraged to intermarry with Old Christian families.

In Aragon, by contrast, most Moriscos lived in settlements with mixed populations. In this integrated environment, they spoke Castilian, indicated both Christian and Muslim dates on their documents, and, with the exception of poorer women, dressed as Christians did. Ironically, Moriscos here suffered far more persecution (proportional to their numbers) than did their cousins in Valencia, for the Holy Office depended usually on Christian informants for accusations; but Moriscos did not betray other Moriscos. Thus while Moriscos in Aragon also remained fiercely committed to Islam, they could not practice their faith as fully as those in Valencia, nor could they do so publicly without incurring danger. Avoiding pork, refusing wine, even maintaining a high standard of personal hygiene sufficed to bring suspicion on a person. This was not a situation where the privacy of the family home enjoyed official sanction. Still, it was to some degree a reality: the home offered a physical and social space in which Muslim rituals and customs could be performed covertly. Thus the practice of Islam in Aragon ended up bearing some resemblance to the "domestic devotion" of dissenting Christians in some parts of Europe. And like such devotion, or the house chapels that grew out of it, it accorded an important role to women, who became in this environment the primary preservers and transmitters of Islam. Secluded in their houses, they cooked and cleaned and ordered the daily life of their families in accord with Muslim practice. They even led certain rites, such as the *fadas*, and of course they taught their children. Christian officials tried, increasingly with time, to intrude into this realm, but did so only with difficulty.

Moriscos fell under the jurisdiction of the Holy Office because, technically speaking, they were not infidels but heretics. When they followed Muslim practice, they betrayed a church that, despite many misgivings, had to regard them as members, since it considered baptism an irreversible sacrament. In reality, the categories of heretic and infidel blurred with the Moriscos, and most authorities sanguinely accepted that they were still, to all intents and purposes, Muslim. This made them at once like and unlike another Iberian group, the Conversos, who were also New Christians, but whose religious sentiments were more varied. Much more than the Moriscos, they threatened the Church religiously, with treachery and corruption from within.

Conversion, Sex, and Segregation

Conversos were baptized Jews and the descendants of such Jews.[24] Tens of thousands of them had been created in the horrific wave of pogroms that had swept Spain in 1391, when a third of Spanish Jewry had been massacred and another third "dragged forcibly to the baptismal font."[25] In following decades their ranks had swelled, and in 1492 they were joined by thousands who chose baptism over exile. Unlike Moriscos, some Conversos accepted their new faith quite sincerely, assimilated into Old Christian society, and raised their children as Christians. Paradoxically, this only fueled Old Christians' anxieties. Some of the greatest figures of Spanish Catholicism—the mystic Teresa of Avila, the humanist Juan Luis Vives, the Jesuits Salmeron and Laynez—came from families of Converso background. Many government officials similarly had Jewish ancestry, as Conversos proudly noted in the *Green Book of Aragon* (1507). So did Spain's first Grand Inquisitor, Torquemada himself. Such facts only confirmed the worst fears of Old Christians, who persisted in seeing all Conversos as Jews at heart, and Jewish influence as permeating Spanish society through them. It was to combat this nebulous threat that Old Christians issued "purity of blood" statutes. Defining Jewishness not on the basis of belief or practice but of ancestry, these statutes turned the Conversos into a hereditary caste. They made it possible to stigmatize even the assimilated as Jews and exclude them from institutions and positions of power.

Other Conversos remained true "sons and daughters of Israel."[26] After decades of toleration, in 1481 the Spanish Inquisition was set up to root out their covert "Judaizing," and for the first fifty years of its existence it concerned itself overwhelmingly with this form of heresy: 95 percent of its defendants were accused of it. This group included Conversos who actually did not practice Judaism as a religion but who held fast to Jewish customs, like cooking with olive oil rather than lard, changing their bedsheets on Friday, and giving their children Old Testament names: inquisitors made no distinction between faith and ethnic culture. A striking proportion of their defendants were women, who played crucial roles in crypto-Jewish practice, just as they did in crypto-Muslim. Indeed, the more inquisitors strained to suppress Judaizing, the more the home became "a bastion of cultural resistance" and the more women became "the central bearers of the Jewish heritage."[27]

Spanish authorities were convinced that such Judaizing was aided and abetted by openly professing Jews. Living still in the old Jewish quarters of cities, many Conversos rubbed shoulders every day with neighbors, friends, and even relatives who were Jews, who instructed them in Jewish practice and made them feel they were still part of the Jewish people; in some places, Conversos and Jews even worshipped together. As early as 1393, therefore, the Dominican Vincente Ferrer had urged the need to separate Conversos from Jews, and in the 1470s and 1480s attempts were made to do so in some locales. The primary goal of the 1492 expulsion decree was to radically segregate these two groups. To extirpate the insidious internal threat of heresy, Ferdinand and Isabella had to ensure that Jews would no longer "attract and pervert [New Christians] to their damned faith and opinion."[28]

No doubt, the expulsion of the Jews from Spain was a key event in Jewish history. In its day, though, it was just the largest in a series of expulsions that fundamentally altered the geography of European Jewry.[29] True, Jews had been excluded from England as early as 1290 and from the French kingdom since 1394, and in the wake of the Black Death they had suffered many attacks. But until the late fifteenth century there had been sizable Jewish communities in German, Austrian, Czech, Italian, and southern French, as well as Iberian, lands. Then, for reasons that are only partly understood, a protracted phase began in which Jews were brutally expelled from one city and territory after another. A first wave of expulsions, peaking in the 1490s, was driven forward in northern Europe by popular demand emanating from townspeople, especially guildsmen, and lower clergy, especially friars. In the south, it included expulsions from Sicily and Sardinia (1492) and Provence (1498), and a planned expulsion from Portugal that ended in 1497 with the forcible baptism of some seventy thousand Jews, mostly Spanish refugees. After a lull, expulsions picked up pace again in the 1530s, with Lutheran princes, popes, and other rulers taking the lead. By the 1570s there were few openly professing Jews left in western or central Europe.

Where did they go? Some to North Africa, others to Italy. But by far the largest numbers went east, Ashkenazim to Poland-Lithuania, Sephardim to Ottoman territories in the Balkans and the Levant. In both places they were welcomed. To be sure, in Poland's royal cities, Christian merchants and guildsmen resisted admitting Jews to their trades and crafts, and cities such as Warsaw that enjoyed the privilege *de non tolerandis Judaeis* tried to keep Jews out altogether. In the latter half of the seventeenth century, the crown broke down some of these barriers. From the beginning, though, the Commonwealth's nobles had the opposite attitude. Especially in the east, in Lithuania and Polish Ukraine, where magnates held vast, underpopulated, underdeveloped estates, they were happy for Jews to settle, appreciative of the commercial and industrial skills Jewish immigrants brought to a region with few native merchants or craftsmen. Jewish managers and leaseholders ran magnates' estates, arranging for the export of timber and massive grain surpluses. Jewish craftsmen developed industries such as soap making, fur processing, and distilling.

These immigrants had a different relationship to Christian society than that of earlier Jews in Poland. They were "westerners bringing western techniques and languages, and these they now adhered to in their changed milieu."[30] In the Middle Ages, while Jews had used Hebrew for religious purposes, generally they had spoken the language of the Christians among whom they dwelled. In the early modern era, the Jews of Poland-Lithuania spoke Yiddish, a dialect of German. Like the "Saxons" who had immigrated from Germany centuries earlier and who with the Reformation embraced Protestantism, or like the Orthodox peasants of Ruthenia or numerous other groups, they had neither language, culture, nor ancestry in common with Polish Catholics. As clearly as could be, they constituted a "foreign nation," and as we have seen, Europeans could often tolerate religious difference in such a group more easily than they could among their own kind. That was especially true in eastern Europe, where since the Middle Ages states had been multinational, multireligious entities. The situation was similar in the Ottoman Empire, where Sephardim spoke Ladino, a dialect of Spanish, and held fast to many Iberian customs.

By the 1570s, Italy was the chief exception to this pattern of Jews being foreigners. Here, after the expulsions, substantial Jewish communities remained in eleven cities: Rome, Ancona, Venice, Mantua, Ferrara, Verona, Padua, Casale Monferrato, Florence, Modena, and Parma. Although these communities included Sephardic refugees and Yiddish-speaking Ashkenazim, the majority of their members were Italian speakers who could trace their families' residence on the peninsula back at least several generations. It is no coincidence that ghettos were essentially an Italian invention and that they began to multiply at precisely this time.

Venice acquired its first imitator in 1555, when Paul IV issued the bull *Cum nimis absurdum* ordering the confinement of Jews in the papal states, including Rome's ancient community. One of the most militant Counter-Reformation popes, Paul did not believe in patiently awaiting the conversion of the Jews at Christ's Second Coming: he thought he could hasten that day by pressuring the Jews to convert now. In this way he hoped to eradicate Judaism more thoroughly than any expulsion could. Hope of converting the Jews was strong in mid-sixteenth-century Italy, as it was in Lutheran Germany in the late seventeenth century under the influence of Pietism. In neither case was great success achieved. In Rome, where a *domus catechumenorum* was established in 1543, some ten Jews (not all of them local inhabitants) converted on average per year. Each conversion, though, was prized as a victory, and converts from Judaism included some notable polemicists who used their intimate knowledge of Judaism to attack it, as did Johannes Pfefferkorn and Anthonius Margaritha. At the other end of the spectrum, as the reforming bishop Carlo Borromeo observed, many poor converts desperate for Christian charity proved unreliable adherents of their new faith. All the ambiguities that surrounded the status of converts from one Christian confession to another, as well as the lurking anxieties that affected the behavior of some of them, can be seen also in Jewish (and Muslim) converts to Christianity. Among them, as among Christian converts, we find "the zealot who allies aggressively with his adoptive church" and, by displaying an extraordinary fervor, "tries to win acceptance and disarm suspicion of himself and his motives."[31]

North of the Papal States, a desire to convert Jews may have been less a motivation in the erection of ghettos than a desire to segregate them. Even though this segregation was far from complete, the symbolism of it was powerful, helping to quell Christian anxieties about the effects of a Jewish presence. Those anxieties focused especially on two possibilities, one of which was sex between Christians and Jews. To prevent this possibility, the Fourth Lateran Council had introduced in 1215 the requirement that Jews wear a distinctive badge so that Christians could identify Jews and thus avoid any "abominable miscegenation."[32] This was also one of the reasons canon law had forbidden Jewish households to have live-in Christian maidservants. In fourteenth-century Aragon, nothing in Christian–Jewish relations had caused as much strife as Jewish men having sex with Christian women. Venetian magistrates expressed their fear of miscegenation repeatedly in regulations concerning their city's ghetto, implying that any cohabitation between Christians and Jews would inevitably lead to sex. The same concern filled many pages in the 1558 treatise by Marquardus de Susannis that laid out the rationale for establishing ghettos. To explain why "too much familiarity and conversation" with Jews was dangerous, he quoted Deuteronomy 7—the passage forbidding intermarriage and warning of its consequences.[33]

Christian anxiety focused also on the possibility of conversions to Judaism. This was no real social threat—the number of Christian converts to Judaism in the early modern period was tiny—except with regard to one group, Christians of Jewish ancestry. For Conversos who fled Portugal, Italy offered an opportunity no other Christian land did in the sixteenth century: to embrace openly the faith of their ancestors. Many were drawn to Venice as a center of international commerce, but upon arrival they faced some difficult decisions. For "the choice between Christianity and Judaism was not only a choice between faiths"; it was a choice between freedom and restriction, power and humiliation.[34] To embrace Judaism a male Converso might have to sacrifice inheritance, career, or occupation, while if he ever returned home he risked death. There were understandable reasons why some hesitated. Others who left Iberia had no intention of reverting to Judaism, only of escaping persecution or pursuing business opportunities. Jews could not assume that Conversos would come around on their own. First in Italy, therefore, and later also in northern Europe, Jewish scholars published an ample instructional and apologetic literature directed at this group. Ordinary Jews appealed to the bonds of family and ancestry in urging Conversos to repudiate Christianity. Efforts were even made to coax Conversos still in Iberia to leave the "lands of idolatry": the Dotar, for example, a charity established in Amsterdam in 1615, offered dowries to poor Converso girls if they would do so.

Those who came to Venice and there hesitated between faiths risked running foul of the Inquisition. In 1556 Paul IV declared that all persons born in Portugal were to be regarded as baptized Christians. That meant that if they embraced Judaism, they were guilty of apostasy. Venetian magistrates never agreed with this new policy, and from around 1590 they treated as Jews, not apostate Christians, all who, from the moment of their arrival in the city, lived as Jews. That meant donning the yellow hat and residing in the ghetto. Alternatively, arrivals could comport themselves as good Christians and avoid mingling with Jews. What authorities, both ecclesiastic and secular, could not abide was ambiguous conduct, uncertain allegiance, or any violation of the boundaries, social and physical, that divided Jews from Christians.

Good fences, they say, make good neighbors: so the erection of ghetto walls improved relations between Christians and Jews in Italy. By giving sharper, clearer form to the boundaries between the two, it eased Christian concerns about miscegenation and the "seduction" (note the sexual language) of Jewish proselytizing. It removed Jews from the body of the

Christian community, even as it allocated to them a space in the middle of the city. It thus made expulsion unnecessary, establishing conditions under which Jews could remain in a city, be readmitted, or even be allowed to settle for the first time. In medieval Spain, barring sex between Christians and Jews not only prevented immediate clashes, it "defused the tensions in other types of interaction and exchange."[35] The ghetto, one may suggest, had a similar effect: segregated at night, Jews and Christians could have better relations during the day. In the fifteenth and early sixteenth centuries, Jews had been allowed to reside in hundreds of Italian towns and villages, yet had been forced to earn a living by pawnbroking, an activity that had brought odium on their heads and fueled religious conflict. Concentrated in ghettos, they were allowed to pursue a wider range of occupations. This new economic freedom was both symptom and cause of a more varied and harmonious engagement between Christians and Jews.

Ghettoization turned out to have another advantage for Jews as well: it stimulated the development of a richer, more comprehensive, more distinctly Jewish culture. It forced Jews to spend evenings together, entertaining themselves with music, poetry, and dramatic performances. It encouraged them to form confraternities and study groups, many of which immersed themselves in the mysticism of the Kabbalah. Concentration and segregation prompted Jews to organize communal services, ranging from education and poor relief to burial and the provision of kosher meats. Jewish communities developed more elaborate and powerful institutions of self-government. "Psychologically and culturally . . . the Jews now turned in on themselves and became more distant from non-Jewish society. . . . Jewish society, indeed Jewish nationhood, as something distinct from Jewish religion, now emerged as much more definite realities than before."[36]

The ghetto was not alone in having this effect. If the internal exile it imposed stimulated Jewish culture and nationhood, so too did the external exile that drove Ashkenazic Jews to Poland and scattered Sephardic Jews in a new diaspora. In Poland, Jewish learning thrived at famous yeshivas while Jewish self-government developed into an elaborate, sophisticated system. In Palestine, study of the Kabbalah produced a new form of Jewish mysticism. Everywhere, the bitterness of exile fed hopes that a messiah would come to gather God's chosen people and lead them to the Holy Land. In exile, Jews developed a whole range of new expectations, capacities, and cultural assets. These they brought with them when they returned, gradually, to western and central Europe.

Strangers in Strange Lands

Nationhood was a complex thing for early modern Jews. On the one hand, they formed what they and Christians both called the Jewish or Hebrew "nation," a single people descended from the ancient Israelites. On the other hand, long residence in different lands gave Jews different languages, cultures, diets, dress, and liturgies, dividing them into distinct "nations." Some of these nations were Ashkenazic, others Sephardic. Even when they lived together in the same quarter or ghetto, they preferred to worship apart in separate synagogues. Then there was the legal "nation," a self-governing corporation of resident aliens. It might include multiple ethnic nations or split single ones, as in Venice where Italian and German Jews together formed the "German nation" but Jews of Iberian origin were divided into Ponentines and Levantines. Jews belonged to a web of overlapping communities, and their identities were correspondingly complex.

The Conversos who emigrated from Portugal and Spain to northwestern Europe in the sixteenth and seventeenth centuries were arguably as Iberian as they were Jewish. (Their attachment to Spain and to Portugal cannot be neatly separated: most Converso families in Portugal came originally from Spain, having fled there in 1492, while some of them returned subsequently to Spain, in a reverse flow that began in the 1540s, after a Portuguese office of the Inquisition was established, and swelled after 1580, when Portugal was annexed to the Spanish crown.) Castilian Spanish was the language they used for literary and intellectual writing, while in everyday life they spoke mostly Portuguese. Many had family members who remained in Iberia and served as their partners in commerce. Adapting the aristocratic ethos of the *hidalgo*, the emigrants took pride in their "noble" ancestry, claiming descent from the prophets, the royal tribe of Judah, the Virgin Mary, or other illustrious ancestors. Echoing the very statutes that had stigmatized them, some even boasted of the "purity" of their Jewish blood. Converso emigrants often referred to themselves as the "Portuguese nation": it was as such, not as Jews or would-be Jews, that they initially presented themselves and were allowed to settle in western France and in a string of cities farther north, most notably Antwerp, Amsterdam, Hamburg, and London.

To be sure, the Jewish ancestry and inclinations of these emigrants were widely known—the terms *Spaniard* and *Marrano* were practically synonyms in France. But nowhere in the region was Judaism officially tolerated before the 1610s. Conversos who migrated northward in this period rather than to Italy or the Muslim world were choosing to live, at least publicly, as Christians, as they had done in Iberia. For emigrants who lacked financial resources, France was simply the closest refuge, so they had to make the best of the situation there. Most Converso emigrants, though, were merchants who spotted golden opportunities in the corridor of maritime trade that ran along Europe's northwestern coasts from Iberia to the Baltic. Here they could make fortunes as purveyors of goods from Portugal and its overseas colonies—sugar, spices, precious metals and stones, brazilwood; later coffee, tea, chocolate, tobacco. They chose the north over the Mediterranean in a conscious compromise that sacrificed religious freedom for profit. That, at least, is the cynical view of their decision. A more nuanced view must take into account what it meant religiously to be a Converso. In the decades that followed the forced conversions of 1497, generations of Conversos had developed in Portugal a unique form of piety. Losing contact with rabbinic Judaism as a coherent set of beliefs and practices, they had been deeply influenced by the Christian education they received and the Christian culture in which they participated. Their beliefs had become a syncretistic hybrid that combined diverse elements, often holding fast to Jewish specifics but recasting them in a Christian light. Conversos took the biblical figure Esther, for example, as their patron saint; they celebrated the victims of the Inquisition as holy martyrs; and they came to believe that it did not matter whether they conformed to Christian practice, so long as they had "faith" in the Law of Moses. Some, like Isaac Orobio de Castro, adopted neoscholastic forms of theologizing; others, like Juan de Prado, moved in a deistic direction. Conversos were not simply would-be Jews, and even for those who left Iberia firmly resolved on returning to their ancestral religion, the transition to Judaism could be difficult. It required them, in the first place, to learn what orthodox Judaism really was. Submitting to rabbinic authority, they had to repudiate long-held beliefs and habits. Men had to undergo circumcision, a painful procedure that would mark them irreversibly as Jews and make a return trip to

Iberia even more perilous. Not all Converso emigrants were convinced that all this was necessary to achieve what, in Christian manner, they called the salvation of their souls.

The crucial difference was that in northwestern Europe there was no Inquisition to pry into what they thought or did privately. Only in the Habsburg Netherlands did Conversos have to show as much caution as in Iberia. Elsewhere, they could follow in relative safety Jewish household practices with regard to food and cleanliness, and pray and celebrate Sabbaths and holidays at home with their families. This is precisely what we find them doing in France, whose royal government invited "the merchants and other Portuguese called New Christians" to settle, offering them naturalization papers in 1550 and assurances that they "may live in freedom and security, without any enquiry being made into their lives or otherwise."[37] With this encouragement, thousands of Converso emigrants settled in western France, forming their largest, most vibrant communities in Bordeaux and Bayonne. Here we can trace an evolution in Converso religious life from crypto-Jewish household practice in the sixteenth century to semiclandestine congregational worship in the seventeenth. Such worship took place in house-synagogues similar to the ones in Hamburg and elsewhere. As long as they worshipped privately and made no public gestures rejecting Catholicism, France's Sephardic Jews (as they deserve to be called from this point) were left unmolested. So secure did they feel by the 1640s and 1650s that some began to put Hebrew inscriptions on their tombstones. Complaints later reached authorities that on Friday evenings Bayonne's Jews left their windows open, so that one could see the Sabbath candles burning in their homes. With the connivance of curés, Sephardim in France continued to register baptisms, marriages, and deaths with their local parish until around the 1720s, when they finally cast off all pretense of being Catholic. In 1723 a royal document referred to them for the first time as "Jews, recognized and established in our kingdom under the title of Portuguese, formerly New Christians."[38] To the end of the Old Regime, though, their synagogues continued to look on the outside like ordinary houses.

The Conversos who began arriving in Amsterdam in the 1590s found much greater freedom. Here there was, from the beginning, not only no Inquisition but no established church to which they were required to conform. Nor did it make sense for them to pretend to be Catholics, since the official faith of the Dutch Republic was Protestant. Indeed, as Catholics their loyalty to the Republic might be suspect—doubly so as Spanish or Portuguese Catholics, so long as the Republic was at war with Spain. Amsterdam's Sephardim thus began as those of France and Hamburg did, as a colony of Portuguese New Christian merchants, offered citizenship "on the understanding that they are Christians."[39] With scant knowledge of orthodox Judaism, they received their first instruction from an Ashkenazic rabbi who arrived in 1602. By 1616 their congregations had multiplied to three, one of which worshipped in a member's house, another in a warehouse; the third had a purpose-built house-synagogue with a hall on the upper floors and dwellings for two families on the ground floor. Like the schuilkerken of Christian dissenters, these structures did not look like places of worship. By 1639, though, Amsterdam's Sephardim felt no need to maintain a fiction of privacy: uniting in a single congregation, they had the synagogue on the Houtgracht dramatically modified and enlarged. Its new neoclassical façade announced with style and self-assurance the presence of Jews in the city. This synagogue, which received a visit from Stadholder Frederick Hendrik in 1642, was closed in 1675 only to make way for the even grander and more prominent Portuguese Esnoga (Figure 11.3), which still stands today. Thanks to religious and political circumstances, Amsterdam's Sephardim could worship publicly as Jews. In this respect, they enjoyed more freedom than did most Christian dissenters in the Republic.

Taking Venice's Ponentine congregation as their model, Amsterdam's Sephardim established an orthodox Jewish community. Their Mahamad, or governing board, enforced halakhic law. In disputes, they consulted Venetian rabbis, including Leon Modena. Their intellectuals debated with Christian scholars, wrote anti-Christian apologetics, and produced a stream of legal and devotional works, including of course Bibles and Talmuds. They proselytized among Conversos who remained in "lands of idolatry," smuggling prayer books into France and even Iberia. Through the Dotar, they offered Converso girls dowries if they would come to Amsterdam and embrace Judaism. Amsterdam's Sephardim arranged for poor brethren to emigrate to Palestine or the Caribbean. And in 1655 they sent the delegation, headed by their famous rabbi Menasseh ben Israel, that convinced Oliver Cromwell to "readmit" the Jews to England (a step that sounds more dramatic than it was: Cromwell merely allowed Sephardim in London to hold services in a house-synagogue and lease land for use as a ceme-

Figure 11.3. The Portuguese Synagogue (Esnoga), Amsterdam, dedicated in 1675. Etching entitled "'T Profil van de Kerk" by Romeijn de Hooghe, ca. 1680. Courtesy of the Amsterdam City Archives.

tery; typically for such semiclandestine arrangements, Cromwell refused to put his concession in writing).

Paradoxically, though, the same freedom that made Amsterdam the capital of the Portuguese diaspora made it also a center of dissent from Jewish orthodoxy. Converso modes of thinking did not simply disappear among those who, in a flow that continued into the early eighteenth century, left Iberia for Amsterdam. Some never embraced Judaism—nor did they have to, as membership in a synagogue was as voluntary in the Republic as was church membership for Christians. Others attempted to lead a double life as Christian and Jew; against these it was decreed in 1620 that no uncircumcised males would be admitted to synagogue. Still other former Conversos adopted a critical, independent stance toward Jewish teaching. From Juan de Prado to Spinoza, a series of heterodox thinkers challenged rabbinic orthodoxy in Amsterdam. Even propagators of that orthodoxy, though, attached to membership in "the nation" an importance that had no basis in halakhic law. That importance was reflected in the eligibility rules of the Dotar: while "poor orphans and poor maidens of this Portuguese Nation, and the Castilian," could receive dowries regardless of whether they were practicing Jews, girls from non-Sephardic families were excluded.[40] Blood, apparently, was thicker than belief.

As Iberians, members of the Portuguese diaspora were a profoundly foreign element in the Netherlands, France, Germany, and England. In other respects, though, many were quite assimilated. They dressed as Christians did, and the men conformed to Christian fashion in their facial hair. Their intellectuals participated in the learned culture of the day, reading classical and Renaissance literature, collecting art and exotica, and following developments in philosophy. Their physicians practiced the same medicine as Christian ones—hardly surprising, given that many had studied at a (Christian) university. The rich among them bought country houses, acquired titles of nobility, and played host to magistrates and princes. Their women wore low-cut dresses and let their hair show in public. Wealthy, refined, and experienced in the ways of the world, their leaders knew how to appeal to the mercantilist mindset of Christian rulers, offering them new veins of commerce and new industries in exchange for toleration.

Tribal loyalty, freethinking, and assimilation to Christian culture were characteristic features of the Portuguese diaspora. None were as strong, at least initially, among the Ashkenazim who, beginning in the late sixteenth century, also returned in rising numbers to central and northwestern Europe. These reverse migrants were never as numerous as the Jews who remained in Poland-Lithuania. The freedom that allowed Jews there to be peasants and craftsmen, engaging in occupations from which they were elsewhere barred, set off a demographic explosion: no more than 24,000 in the late fifteenth century, the Jewish population of the Commonwealth rose to perhaps 170,000 by 1648. A century later, it reached some 750,000, constituting "perhaps half the world's Jewish population."[41] As early as 1600, though, enough Jews had returned from the east to restore the communities of Prague and Frankfurt to their medieval splendor. Over the seventeenth century, the number of Jews grew rapidly in Czech, Austrian, and German lands. Not that ordinary Christians there showed a new inclination to tolerate Jews. Popular anti-Semitism, manifested in riots and demands for re-expulsion, seems if anything to have spiked again in the latter half of the century. Among imperial cities, Frankfurt and Hamburg were the only major ones to readmit Jews; the vast majority of lesser ones continued to exclude them. Local authorities in Vienna, where in 1624 a new *Judenstadt* had been founded, succeeded forty-five years later in pressuring Emperor Leopold I to dissolve it and banish its inhabitants. As in Poland, in Germany resistance to a Jewish presence remained most powerful, as always, among urban craftsmen. Along with other foreigners, Jews found themselves favored in the seventeenth century by princes who found it advantageous, both politically and economically, to weaken or circumvent the power of guilds. By princely fiat, Jews were allowed to settle in small country towns and villages and to take up a range of occupations there. They were invited to settle in many of the new cities founded by German princes, which lacked entrenched organs of Christian *communitas*. Jews were invited to settle also in garrison towns such as Philippsburg, where princes depended on them to provision their armies. German princes came to depend even more on the capital of Jewish merchants to finance their wars, which is why the Thirty Years' War proved such a boon to Jews in central Europe, who were often repaid in privileges rather than cash.

In the seventeenth century, Ashkenazic communities in most parts of Europe had, either on the local or some higher level, powerful institutions of self-government. Jewish law and customs shaped daily life, and rabbinic

herents of a religion. Even in the Middle Ages, they had been perceived
as constituting "nations," as the use of ethnic terms to denote them—
"Hebrews", "Turks", "Saracens", "Moors"—testifies. But their foreignness
had been sharply accentuated by the expulsions, after which Iberian Jews
(practicing ones) lived everywhere except in the lands whose languages
they spoke. Ashkenazim spoke Yiddish, whether they lived in Poland,
Bohemia, or the Dutch Republic. Even those who returned to German-
speaking lands were more distinct from Christians culturally than their ancestors had been. In all these settings, accentuating the foreignness of
Jews—whether as Jews or "Portuguese"—opened up possibilities, making
their presence more acceptable and suggesting new arrangements for accommodating them. In Italy, where an unbroken presence made some Jews
less foreign, a different approach was adopted, a new and extreme, though
far from absolute, form of segregation.

In the sixteenth and seventeenth centuries, the position of Jews in
Christian Europe was predicated, in ways it had never been before, on the
principle of their constituting foreign nations. Over the seventeenth and
eighteenth centuries, reality came to depart somewhat from this principle,
as economic, social, and cultural trends encouraged in many places a degree of Jewish assimilation. By the end of the eighteenth century, most intellectuals rejected the principle outright, and in the French Revolution it
was finally abolished.

The "emancipation" of the Jews that took place in France in 1790–91 and
the similar moves that followed, sooner or later, in other European lands
were part of a much broader project—a project inspired by the Enlightenment and its vision of human progress. Those who pursued it sought the
dissolution of all corporate entities and with it the abolition of all special
privileges and discrimination—in short, they sought the equality of all citizens before the law. No more than Louis XIV, though for entirely different
reasons, could they brook a "state within the state" or, as the Count of
Clermont-Tonnerre recast it, "a nation within the nation."[43] For the same
reason that nobles had to be stripped of their privileges and guildsmen of
their monopolies, and provinces uniformly governed, the Jews had to be
dissolved as a separate, autonomous people (or in France two peoples,
Sephardim in the west, Ashkenazim in Alsace). Only so could they be integrated into the modern state and assimilated as full, active citizens into

the body of the nation. "One must refuse everything to the Jews as a nation, and give everything to the Jews as individuals," declared Clermont-Tonnerre.[44] According to this line of thinking, for Jews to be freed as individuals, they had to cease to exist as a people.

The revolutionaries who championed emancipation "saw in it a liquidation of Jewish history and a termination of the existence of the Jewish community."[45] Legal integration was supposed to lead to full assimilation. Indeed, this was its chief selling point, eagerly anticipated and prematurely heralded by reformers and revolutionaries across Europe. For if there was one thing on which contemporaries agreed, it was that the Jews were a vice-ridden, degenerate people in need of what the Berlin *Aufklärer* Christian von Dohm called "civic improvement."[46] Above all, their "usurious" lending of money at interest was perceived as a dishonest, abusive, lazy way of making a living. The only question in dispute was whether the vices of the Jews were inherent traits or the product of circumstances. Those who shared the Enlightenment's optimism felt sure of the latter. They spotted the vicious circle in the accusation: barred from honest trades, how could Jews be blamed for making a living in the only way left to them? In a 1788 report, the secretary of the French Royal Society declared, "Our prejudices . . . [are] the primary cause of their vices. . . . We reduce them to the impossibility of being honest: how can we expect them to be so?"[47] If circumstances could be changed, reformers expected Jewish behavior to change. Once bars were dropped, most assumed (wrongly) that Jews would rush to become peasants and craftsmen, in the process adopting the customs and virtues of gentile society. Others thought, in a Rousseauian vein, that vicious habits sank deep roots and one might have to use coercion to reeducate Jews. The Abbé Gregoire, for one, proposed that the government forbid Jews to live together, promote intermarriage, and require Jewish children to attend Christian schools.

Opponents of emancipation, such as the Orientalist scholar Johann David Michaelis, doubted whether Jews could ever really assimilate. How, they asked, could Jews live with Christians or serve with them in the army if they would not eat the same food? How could they work with Christians if they observed a different Sabbath? And how could they give their allegiance to the state if they hoped one day to erect a state of their own in the Holy Land? How, in other words, could they be fully integrated unless they abandoned essential elements of their religion? The realities of Jewish–Christian relations in the eighteenth century in fact belied such acute skepticism. Yet with their questions, opponents did put their finger on a dilemma inherent in the modern, integrationist model of toleration. It is a dilemma that Jews have long faced, and that Muslims and Christians, in their mutual relations, are struggling with today.

IV

CHANGES

TWELVE

Enlightenment?

Notions of Progress

"Strange! All that was rough and shocking in the Manners of our Ancestors is quite worn off; to that rustick and forbidding Air of former times,
there has succeeded an universal Gentleness and exceeding Civility, all
Christendom over. Popery alone feels no Change; she alone keeps up her
antient and habitual Ferocity." So wrote Pierre Bayle in 1686, reflecting
with horror on the brutal persecutions that accompanied Louis XIV's revocation of the Edict of Nantes. To the Huguenot Bayle, that supreme act
of religious intolerance seemed more than an anomaly: it was proof that
Catholicism itself was "still savage and intractable," "still animated as much
as ever with a Spirit of Cruelty and Fraud." One could not explain it away
by blaming it on the personal animus of a lone tyrant. Yet such persecution
also seemed to Bayle an anachronism, hard to square with "the Civility and
Politeness" that had come to prevail in the Europe of his day.[1] Indeed, in
the revocation Bayle believed he was witnessing an act of persecution as
primitive as anything perpetrated during the French Wars of Religion.
Bayle thus held two somewhat contradictory ideas: that his was a more civilized age than previous ones, and that the religion practiced by a majority
of Europeans was as barbarous as ever.

Bayle's first idea corresponds to the story told today in many histories of Europe. Explicit in textbooks, implicit usually in monographs, the story draws a sharp contrast between an "age of religious wars" that ended around 1650 and a succeeding age in which religious conflict ceased. From the bloody, futile struggles of the first age, it is said, Europeans grew disillusioned with religious dogma. Rulers no longer allowed their decisions to be determined by its dictates, but instead calculated their political and economic interests, following raison d'état and enriching their lands through mercantilist policies. Intellectuals redefined toleration as a positive good instead of a grudging concession. As their ideas spread, people of different faiths came to accept one another. Reason advanced and religious passions receded as Enlightenment followed Scientific Revolution. Europe became more civilized.

Such histories accord Bayle himself an important role in this story. Recognized as a progenitor of the Enlightenment, Bayle wrote a *Historical and Critical Dictionary* from whose articles readers like Voltaire drew a deep skepticism, as well as vast amusement. Through his literary journal, the *Nouvelles de la République des Lettres*, he showed the way to a much broader circulation of "polite learning." And on the issue of toleration, he published (among other works) *Commentaire philosophique sur ces paroles de Jésus-Christ: Contrain-les d'entrer.* This treatise and John Locke's first *Letter Concerning Toleration*, published just three years later, are often hailed as providing for the first time a philosophical basis for religious toleration in the modern sense. By this is meant a recognition of a right human beings inherently possess to believe as they wish and to express their belief openly in word and worship. Bayle's contribution to this principle was a thorough rebuttal of St. Augustine's justification for persecution—a justification preached by Bishop Bossuet at the court of France in the fateful month of October 1685. To force people to practice a religion in which they did not believe, argued Bayle, was not to promote their salvation, as Augustine and Bossuet had said, but to make them sin, for "Whatever is done against the Dictates of Conscience is Sin."[2] For his part, Locke focused on the limits of state power, arguing (among other things) that governments had no jurisdiction over religious matters.

These arguments were not as novel as has sometimes been suggested. Bayle's extended the age-old dictum that faith could not be forced and that coercion only produced hypocrisy. Locke's built upon the distinction enunciated by Luther between two kingdoms, those of God and the world. The toleration propounded by Bayle and Locke also had limits that we would deem unacceptable today. Locke excluded both Catholics and atheists from its benefits, while Bayle believed in giving no quarter to those who, if they had the power, would persecute others. What is true is that generations of intellectuals took the writings of Bayle and Locke (to which some added those of Spinoza) as proving definitively the case for toleration. In this sense, we can agree with the many scholars who hold that "the [modern] principle of toleration was now firmly established."[3]

Yet discrepancies confront anyone who compares this principle to the behavior of Europeans in the century between its enunciation in the 1680s and the French Revolution, when it was finally codified in European law. These discrepancies match the one between Bayle's two ideas. Compared to the period before 1650, something fundamental undoubtedly was changing in cultural norms and expectations. Increasingly, Europeans were *supposed* to be tolerant, and in genteel society toleration was celebrated, and demanded, as a hallmark of civilized behavior. Yet the amount of religious strife Europe saw in the "age of Enlightenment" was far from negligible. Of course, modern scholars understand that they cannot simply blame Catholicism for such strife; that would be to accept the Whig interpretation of history that Bayle helped to construct. Like him, though, they tend to portray episodes of persecution and religious violence after 1650 essentially as aberrations, relics of an earlier phase in the development of European civilization. Take, for example, the notorious affair of Jean Calas, a Protestant of Toulouse executed in 1762 for purportedly murdering his son to prevent him from converting to Catholicism—an absurd accusation that Voltaire used to great effect in his campaign for toleration: it has been called an "anachronism" in its own day, since by then French Catholics found persecution "abhorrent."[4] If a majority of judges in Toulouse had really found it so, Calas would not have been executed. Enlightenment philosophes declared the case an anachronism, but that was to use notions of progress for polemical effect, to brand persecution a form of backward behavior. It was a common maneuver in the eighteenth century, and the rhetoric was not insincere: rather, it expressed the outlook of important groups, who inherited from Bayle and his generation a particular model of historical change. An evolutionary schema of progressive development, the model defined what was normal less by empirical observation than by the

time on, English men and women faced the likely prospect of a Catholic succeeding to the throne. Nothing could have provoked more acutely their perennial anxiety about their national church being subverted by domestic enemies. Fear of Catholic sedition rose to fever pitch in 1678 when Titus Oates confabulated his tale about a Jesuit-led conspiracy to kill Charles II, torch London (the Great Fire of 1666 was blamed on "the treachery and malice of the popish faction"), and slit the throats of Protestants in the city.[7] The ultimate aim of this "popish plot," of course, was purportedly to reimpose Catholicism on the entire country—the nightmare of every English Protestant, conjuring up images of the fires of Smithfield lit anew. The revelations of Oates set a ball rolling that gained terrifying momentum, leading to the execution of thirty-five men. Charles had to dissolve Parliament three times to prevent it from excluding James from the succession.

As king, James II soon alienated Anglicans by proposing abolition of the Test Act and maintenance of a standing army. The first proposal threatened to place England's government in the hands of Catholics; the second confirmed the view that Catholic rulers invariably aspired to absolute power. In the eyes of English Protestants, Catholicism was not just a religious abomination; it was a comprehensive, tyrannical system in which rulers enslaved men's bodies as its priests enslaved their souls: "From Popery came the notion of a standing Army and arbitrary power. . . . Formerly the Crown of *Spain,* and now *France,* supports this root of Popery amongst us; but lay Popery flat, and there's an end of arbitrary Government and Power. It is a meer chimaera, or notion, without Popery."[8] The birth to James of a son was what finally tipped enough Tories against him to create something that, at least briefly in the autumn of 1688, resembled a national consensus in favor of deposition. Facing the prospect of one Catholic monarch after another, Parliament violated a principle many deemed sacred, that of hereditary succession. To save England from Catholicism and tyranny, the political nation accepted William of Orange, stadholder of the Dutch Republic, and his wife, Mary, James's daughter, as king and queen.

England was not the only Protestant land whose fate seemed at that moment to hang in the balance. In 1685 the last Protestant elector of the Palatinate died, leaving his territory, the largest Calvinist territory in the Holy Roman Empire, to the Catholic dynasty of Pfalz-Neuburg. Despite his promise to maintain the status quo, the new elector began to favor his coreligionists. This was the best Protestants could hope for under the circum-

stances, as Louis XIV made a rival claim to the Palatinate. The policies
Louis favored were made crystal clear when his army invaded the Palatinate, seizing its territories on the left (west) bank of the Rhine plus some
on the right. Here Calvinists were roughly handled, pressured to convert,
and forced to give up or share use of their churches. Meanwhile, in Lower
Alsace French officials were coercing entire villages to convert to Catholicism. Formerly part of the Holy Roman Empire, this mostly Lutheran territory had been annexed by Louis under a dubious legal pretext. Villages
that remained Lutheran saw their churches partitioned. Between the Palatinate and Alsace, it seemed to alarmed Protestants that their faith might be
suppressed in large parts of the Rhineland.

Farther south, the Waldensians of Savoy met a more violent fate. Descendants of medieval heretics, these inhabitants of the Catholic duchy had
adopted, along with their brethren in adjacent regions of France, the Reformed faith. They had been persecuted many times before, but in December 1685 the Duke of Savoy took the ultimate step, prohibiting on pain of
death the exercise of their religion, condemning their churches to be demolished, ordering the banishment of their ministers, and requiring their
children to be baptized and raised as Catholics. Issued at Louis XIV's insistence, the terms of this revocation were similar to those of the revocation of the Edict of Nantes in France. When Waldensians refused to accept them, there broke out a religious war, if that is the term for such a
lopsided encounter. Lasting only three days, it led to the capture of perhaps
nine thousand men, women, and children (contemporary pamphlets claim
more), two-thirds of whom were killed, or allowed to die, in the following
months of captivity. The next winter, survivors of this atrocity were es-
corted to Switzerland. Dressed in "old tattered Coats," wasted by hunger
and disease, still more died on this forced march through ice- and snow-
covered mountains.[9]

But the greatest persecution of the age was the revocation itself. In 1679
Louis' government resumed the campaign it had begun in the 1660s against
the Huguenots. Two years later, an intendant in Poitou experimented with
a new technique of conversion: billeting soldiers in the homes of Huguenots, who were abused—anything short of rape or murder was the word
that went out to the troops—and paupered until they yielded. In 1685 the
government ordered the technique applied in other Huguenot strong-
holds. In Mme de Sévigné's words, the dragoons were "very good mission-

aries," so good that Louis could soon pretend that "inasmuch as the better and greater part of our subjects of the [Reformed religion] have embraced the Catholic faith . . . the execution of the Edict of Nantes . . . has been rendered nugatory."[10] It was, of course, a lie. At the time, there were about three-quarters of a million Huguenots. Only their ministers were permitted to go into exile: they had fifteen days to decide whether to go, and if they did they had to leave behind their children over the age of seven.[11] About two hundred thousand fled France illegally in the 1680s and 1690s; another hundred thousand fled later. Some who were caught received exemplary punishments: about fifteen hundred were condemned to row on the galleys of the French navy until they converted or died; women were imprisoned in convents. Scores who remained in France, where they were called "New Catholics," were executed for "relapsing" into heresy.

Burnet called it "one of the most violent persecutions that is to be found in history"; at any rate, it was certainly the greatest single act of official persecution suffered by Christian dissenters in early modern Europe.[12] Streaming to the Dutch Republic, England, Switzerland, and Germany (most famously to Brandenburg, whose Calvinist elector invited them), Huguenot refugees gave the tragedy a human face. Welcomed with charity, they strengthened Protestants' sense of belonging to an international brotherhood and of fighting a universal foe. Naturally, they lobbied their co-religionists not to take this defeat lying down.

William of Orange, for one, needed no persuading. Much has been written about the secular outlook of the prince, who to be sure had no compunction about allying with the Habsburgs and even the papacy against his archenemy, Louis XIV. But William understood that such alliances were essential to combat a threat that was religious as well as political. The "universal dominion" Louis aspired to impose on Europe would subject Protestants to persecution as well as tyranny: this was no cynical, propagandistic line concocted to rally support for the Nine Years' War (1688–1697), but the sincere belief of William's right-hand man, Hans Willem Bentinck, first Earl of Portland. The same belief was popular opinion in England and in the Dutch Republic, where a mass of pamphlets used the same metaphors and images—indeed, were sometimes the same pamphlets—as those issued during the Revolt against Spain. Casting William as an Old Testament hero, they portrayed Catholic persecutors as agents of the Antichrist and spied in their actions a coordinated campaign to extirpate Protestantism.

For most Protestants, the religious and political elements of the conflict could not be divorced.

The Peace of Rijswijk (1697) bitterly disappointed them. By it William and the other Protestant rulers acknowledged that Louis would never rescind the revocation. Militants were particularly infuriated by article four of the Peace, which stipulated that Catholic worship would continue in the Palatinate where the French had "restored" it. The elector of the Palatinate took advantage of the Peace to impose Simultaneum on all churches that were still in Reformed hands. Tensions came to a head in 1719 when a new elector confiscated copies of the Reformed catechism and seized Heidelberg's principal church, formerly shared, for exclusive use by himself and his co-religionists. In reprisal, Brandenburg-Prussia and other Protestant states punished their own Catholic subjects, and the incident turned into a diplomatic crisis for the empire. International alliances formed pitting Prussia, England (whose king, George I, was also ruler of Hanover), and France against Austria and Spain. For a while it seemed the issue was going to spark another European war.

In the meantime, religious civil wars erupted in Switzerland and in southern France, where furtive Huguenot resistance to Catholic authorities turned violent in 1702. The War of the Cévennes was arguably the nastiest conflict in Europe since the French Wars of Religion of the sixteenth century; certainly it involved the most violence perpetrated by civilian against civilian. Inspired by millenarian prophecies, Huguenots known as "Camisards" butchered priests and Catholic schoolmasters; pillaged and set fire to churches, châteaus, and Old Catholics' houses; and committed acts of terrible cruelty. The army responded with a campaign of extermination: regarding all New Catholics as complicit, it razed 466 villages in the High Cévennes in the autumn of 1703, putting their inhabitants to the sword. When troops grew scarce, due to the War of Spanish Succession, the government called up civil militias composed of Old Catholics, who wore white crosses, symbols of crusade (as militant Catholics did in the sixteenth-century wars), forming bands of "White Camisards" or "Cadets of the Cross." They perpetrated atrocities that were the mirror image of the regular, or "Black," Camisards'. By the spring of 1705, the back of the revolt was broken, but sporadic attempts at insurrection continued until 1711, encouraged by Dutch, English, and other members of the anti-French alliance.

Events in France gave new confirmation to the old idea that native dis-

This was obviously the case in central Europe, where the Thirty Years' War had disrupted religious life. Here the Peace of Westphalia marked the beginning of a long and sometimes difficult recovery. Churches had to be rebuilt, new generations of clergy trained and fielded, laypeople instructed, discipline restored. Over the following decades, the level of pastoral care and pedagogy rose enormously. More Germans than ever before came to understand and internalize the teachings of their confession. As they did, they increasingly expressed their beliefs in different facets of their daily life. Peace made possible the elaboration of distinct confessional cultures. And although the Peace introduced robust mechanisms to regulate and contain confessional conflict, it never resolved it. To the contrary, war left a legacy of bitter feelings—memories of persecution, each side by the other—that sharpened confessional allegiances. Protestant–Catholic tensions reached a new breaking point in the 1710s when riots erupted in several German cities. Both the commemoration by Protestants of historic triumphs and the polemics of Catholic preachers saw their heyday in Germany between the 1680s and 1730s.

For Catholics this was still the age of the baroque, whose flowering in piety, as in art, peaked around the turn of the eighteenth century. In southern Germany there was an explosion of church-building and -decoration, of new shrines that attracted pilgrims in unprecedented numbers, of processions and popular devotions. Dutch Catholics too went on more pilgrimages, and in 1715 they founded the first confraternity to organize trips to Our Lady of Kevelaer. In Austria the cult of the Virgin was stronger than ever before, the Eucharist venerated in elaborate forms. Monasteries and convents multiplied in Bohemia. In France, church leaders continued their long struggle to implement Tridentine reforms. One of their chief demands had always been that laypeople confess and take Communion at least once a year, at Easter. This practice was never more general than in these decades, and the same was true for attendance at high mass on Sundays. In Nice and Savoy, the dying left large sums to pay for masses for their souls. Funerals were elaborate, expensive affairs, their details specified in wills that began with florid invocations of God, the Virgin, and saints.

Protestantism around the turn of the eighteenth century has a reputation for complacency and rationalism. In England, the Dutch Republic, and the empire, many of its clergy consciously eschewed the fervor of earlier generations. Some continued to preach the dogmas of yesteryear, while a majority propagated their vision of Protestantism as a reasonable religion. But this description should not be overgeneralized, especially with regard to the laity. These decades also saw the spread of Pietism in Germany, millenarian prophesying among French Huguenots, and a boom in missionary activity. Meanwhile, for a majority of Europeans the parish remained a central focus of life. In villages and small towns, the parish church was more than ever the place where whole communities came together. Sunday services were the most regular and inclusive social event, the occasion for people to see and be seen, to hear news, and for the young discreetly to flirt. Parish clergy gave the community moral and intellectual leadership; parish officers administered charity and helped maintain law and order. Wherever small communities were united by a common faith, civic and sacral life continued to overlap and flow into one another.

Such was not the case everywhere. Beginning in the late seventeenth century, England in particular would see social and cultural changes that profoundly altered the place of religion within the public sphere. These changes proceeded first and most rapidly in England's cities, where, propelled by a great economic upswing, an urban renaissance began in the 1660s and continued for a full century. In provincial capitals and regional hubs, not to mention London, alternate centers of social life sprang up alongside the parish church. Coffeehouses, clubs, theaters, playhouses, assembly halls, libraries, and bookshops multiplied. So did literary and philosophical societies and, from the 1710s, Masonic lodges. Ambitious construction projects produced a new, more regular urban topography with squares and circuses. Spas and resort towns, like Bath and Tunbridge Wells, boomed. With these new forums came new forms of sociability and culture. People traveled more. The traditional religious and festive calendar yielded to an alternation of winter and summer social seasons. Cosmopolitan fashions spread and the appeal of local customs shrank. New ideas gained new audiences, as England's printing presses, scarcely restrained after 1695, churned out an unprecedented quantity of books, pamphlets, and prints.

Prosperity, population boom, and mobility, both social and geographic, were among the forces that produced these changes in England's cities and large towns. They probably had in themselves a pacifying effect on day-to-day interactions between people of different faiths. Artisans, shopkeepers, and laborers were not competing desperately among themselves for scarce

resources, and so had less reason to blame Catholics or Protestant dissenters for taking away their livelihood, or for bringing down God's wrath.
These forces also contributed to make England an individualistic society,
with few communal controls on behavior and belief. The Toleration Act of
1689 contributed to this as well. Read literally, all it did was exempt Protestant dissenters from the penalties imposed on them by the laws against
recusancy, which remained on the books. But as everyone understood, or
quickly came to see, this exemption had broad implications. By making attendance at Church of England services in effect voluntary, it turned religious observance into a matter of individual choice. In practice, almost
anyone, including Catholics, could absent themselves from parish services.
Protestant dissenters, who could obtain licenses for their chapels, could
form congregations, joining or leaving them at will. After the Dutch Republic, this was the closest thing in early modern Europe to a disestablishment of religion.

Prosperity, a broad civil society, individualism—beginning in the late
seventeenth and continuing in the eighteenth century, these forces encouraged the practice of toleration in England (they had long done the same
among the Dutch). Political stability also contributed to an environment
conducive to good interfaith relations. In this regard, a turning point came
after 1715, when Whigs established a lock-hold on government that was to
last for decades. Their victory ended some forty years of struggle in which
Whigs and Tories had championed opposing religious as well as political
opinions: Protestant dissenters and Low Church Anglicans on one side,
High Churchmen, nonjurors (who refused to swear loyalty to England's
monarchs after the Glorious Revolution), and Catholics on the other. The
"rage of party" had been in no small part a religious rage; in the 1720s it
finally subsided.

These factors must be placed alongside the Enlightenment to explain
why important segments of English society embraced toleration in the
eighteenth century. They also explain why the type of toleration that prevailed was integrationist, for in this relatively fluid society people of different faiths mixed freely with one another. To understand its influence, the
Enlightenment must be seen in this context. As a code of civility, it comple-
mented England's new urban environment, regulating the forms of sociability that developed there. Yet this context also explains why the influence
of the Enlightenment had limits. For who subscribed to this code? Who

participated actively in this civil society? To do so, one had to live in a city or at least frequent one, and one had to have good literacy skills and the financial means to avail oneself of coffeehouses, bookshops, and the like. This privileged group was larger and more diffuse in England than in any other country except the Dutch Republic. Defined more by wealth and culture than by family and rank, it included professionals, merchants, and prosperous artisans as well as gentry, and had an even wider penumbra. Still, the attainments and appearances it demanded were beyond the reach of a majority. Even in England, the Enlightenment was a phenomenon principally of the upper and upper-middling strata of urban society. When Methodism, with its fiery and unabashed religious "enthusiasm," began in the 1730s to spread, many members of these strata observed with disdain that it mostly attracted "common people." Though this description of the movement was undoubtedly exaggerated, intended as a smear, it was true enough to suggest that lower classes were more inclined than higher ones to repudiate "reasonable religion."

On the Continent, where the late seventeenth century saw no surge in prosperity equivalent to England's, the limits of Enlightenment were sharper and narrower. Here the cultural distance between certain groups widened and continued to do so in the eighteenth century. Elites, especially urban ones, withdrew from pastimes and pursuits in which people of all ranks had formerly engaged. Among those pursuits were religious ones. As rural and poorer populations held fast to traditional beliefs and practices, urbanites, the wealthy, and the educated abandoned them. It was the most highly educated—government officials, clergy, lawyers, physicians, professors—who led the way, abandoning earliest and most completely the precautions by which other Catholics still hoped to spare their souls the torments of purgatory. Old noble families were slower to change, as were merchants and manufacturers, while artisans, shopkeepers, and laborers showed even greater reluctance. Fewer women abandoned baroque practices than did men, creating a wide gender gap. The more cosmopolitan and prosperous the city, the earlier change came. Not even in Paris, though, did the content of Catholic wills begin to change before the 1720s, and in Provence there was little more than a partial, inconsistent slippage before the 1760s. Upper Austria represents the other end of the spectrum: little changed in the wills of any group before the Josephine reforms of the 1780s. Taken together, the evidence suggests that in Catholic Europe, the

From a modern perspective, they were strikingly limited in scope. None translated into practice the principle enunciated a century earlier (circumscribed, to be sure, with caveats) by Locke and repeated many times subsequently, that religious freedom was "every man's natural right" and that every man should "enjoy the same rights that are granted to others."[21] Rather, they reflected the mainstream consensus of polite society, whose members did not want Europe's religious establishments overthrown, merely liberalized. England's Catholic Relief Act of 1778 allowed Catholics to purchase land without legal subterfuge and reduced the penalties if priests and schoolmasters were apprehended. It did not allow Catholics to vote, hold public office, or take university degrees, and it granted them no freedom of worship. Similarly, the French royal edict of 1787 restored to Huguenots some civil rights, enabling them to marry legally and own land, but it failed to legalize Protestant worship. The Patents of Toleration Joseph II issued for Austria, Hungary, and Bohemia in 1781–1782 allowed Lutherans, Calvinists, and Orthodox Christians to worship, but only in schuilkerken, and before they could do that they would have to undergo six weeks of Catholic instruction intended to dissuade them. Building on the provisions of the Peace of Westphalia (which remained valid law in the Holy Roman Empire until the latter was dissolved in 1806), Prussia's edict of 1788 extended equal rights to Lutherans, Calvinists, and Catholics and granted protection to other groups. By the time it was issued, though, a reaction against the Enlightenment was already under way in Prussia. The edict tried to preserve the traditional orthodoxy of Prussia's Protestant churches by silencing deists and others who questioned their doctrines.

Not even these acts had the support of all magistrates and officials. Half the regional parlements in France opposed the 1787 royal edict, and the crown had to play its trump card, a royal *lit de justice,* to force three of them to register it. In Austria, local authorities had misgivings about the Josephine Patents, but their objections were swept aside by imperial fiat. These responses were nothing compared to the popular furor provoked by the Catholic Relief Act in Britain, where the public expected its representatives in parliament to take its views into account. Dramatic and well documented, the response to the British Act offers a precious glimpse into the attitudes of certain groups. Their protests cast doubt on any purported "rise of toleration" among a majority of Europeans.

The British government certainly did not expect such trouble, but to forestall any difficulties it pushed the Relief Act through Parliament late at night after minimal debate. Presented with a fait accompli, alarmed opponents founded an organization called the Protestant Association to lobby for repeal. Scottish opponents organized to prevent the government from extending the bill to Scotland. At the head of these forces stood the dashing aristocrat Lord George Gordon. More than seventy-five thousand people signed petitions against the Act, most signatories coming from cities, especially ones with a lot of Protestant dissenters. The Association and its Scottish allies also launched propaganda campaigns, with pamphlets, handbills, cards, broadsheets, meetings, and debates. In this way they succeeded in spreading alarm among urban laborers. In 1779 riots broke out in Edinburgh and Glasgow, while other Scottish towns saw minor incidents. This violence had its intended effect, frightening the government into dropping its plans for an equivalent Scottish bill. Protesters in the English capital were heartened by this success, and might also have remembered that in 1753 popular agitation had led to repeal of a bill for the naturalization of Jewish immigrants.

What became known as the Gordon Riots broke out in London in June 1780. Triggered by a rally and march on Westminster, they lasted a week. A majority of participants were wage earners—journeymen, apprentices, servants, laborers; others were small employers, shopkeepers, peddlers, craftsmen, soldiers, and sailors. They wrecked mass houses, embassy chapels, Catholic schools, and the homes and businesses of prominent Catholics. They also attacked officials who sought to put down the riots, as well as government ministers and MPs who were believed to favor greater toleration for Catholics. To those who perpetrated the attacks, the motivation of these individuals was highly suspect; some were denounced in the London press as being themselves papists in disguise. Four years earlier, parliament had passed the Quebec Act, granting freedom of worship to Catholics in Canada. Two years later the government had surreptitiously secured passage of the Relief Act. To the paranoid this bespoke a pattern, suggesting that Catholics had infiltrated the halls of power. Some suspected the king himself, George III, whose high-handed style of governance smacked of a tyranny that many Britons still associated with popery. To make their fears of Catholic conspiracy even more acute, Britain was at war with France and Spain.

The London crowds did not seek to extirpate Catholicism in the capital.

Like so many other religious riots, the Gordon Riots had essentially "reactionary and defensive" goals, to restore "the pre-1778 status quo."[22] As they continued, though, the rioters' aims grew more diffuse, the chaos more general, as prisons and even the Bank of England were attacked. Eventually the government called in troops to put down the unrest. The soldiers' musket volleys killed 210 rioters immediately, while another 75 died later of their wounds. Twenty-five rioters were subsequently hanged, and others received lesser punishments. It was the bloodiest episode of religious violence in London's history.

As an example of continuing intolerance, the Gordon Riots are all the more revealing because those involved were English, Protestant, and urban. This is not a group included in the rough characterization offered earlier of Europe's "unenlightened." Neither are the middle-class Protestant dissenters who, though they did not take part in violence, signed the Association's petitions and marched in its rallies. Our characterization requires a great deal of refinement, which further research will have to provide. In the meantime, though, it is clear that by 1780 a great difference in attitudes had developed in Britain. On the one hand there was the country's ruling elite, on the other Protestant dissenters and a group we will provisionally call plebeians. The first had embraced Enlightenment values and were no longer afraid to tolerate even Catholics; the second continued to nourish an anti-Catholicism deeply rooted in both Protestant religious identity and British national identity. Not only did dissenters and plebeians oppose greater toleration for Catholics, the tolerant new attitude of their rulers made them think the latter must be Catholics too. Triggering centuries-old fears of popish plots, elite initiatives to increase toleration provoked a popular backlash.

How widely the Enlightenment call for toleration was heeded, or even heard, among non-elites elsewhere in Europe is an open question. Throughout this book we have seen that toleration was more than an idea or a governmental policy, it was a practice that succeeded only if diverse groups participated. We have seen how, in thousands of communities from Ireland to Poland, people of every occupation and rank confronted the dilemmas caused by the division of Christendom into rival confessions, and how, by certain arrangements, some managed to live together peaceably despite their religious differences. The practice of toleration did not await the Enlightenment. What the latter did was change the attitude of powerful groups, who adopted in the eighteenth century a new creed, a belief in the positive value of toleration. But what of others? Did attitudes or behavior change among Catholic peasants? What about small-town craftsmen and shopkeepers? Perhaps religious conflict was like the prosecution of witches in early modern Europe. If such prosecution ended in the eighteenth century, it was not because most Europeans ceased to believe in witches. To the contrary, many ordinary people continued to accuse their neighbors of harming them by occult means. Elites, though, grew skeptical of such accusations, as they did of all claims of supernatural activity. As a result, magistrates and judges were no longer willing to try such cases. Likewise it may be that elites scorned the "primitive" emotions of the intolerant and discouraged religious conflict. Their new attitude mattered deeply, not only because it led to changes in governmental policy, but as a model that non-elites, especially the middling sorts who aspired to rise in society, might imitate. That does not mean, though, that old religious antagonisms had abated in the wider population.

To Edward Gibbon, the Gordon Riots revealed "a dark and diabolical fanaticism, which I had supposed to be extinct."[23] "Is humanity altered since the fanatical days of Cromwell?" asked a contemporary, rhetorically; "even now: now when this country has received the additional polish and improvement of almost an hundred and fifty years," the "magic cry" of "No papists, No Popery!" had the same effect on "the people" as formerly.[24]

Even as conventionally told, the story of the rise of toleration has many flaws. Europe's last religious wars were fought in the 1700s and 1710s, not the 1640s. Ruling elites in Britain, France, and Poland continued to treat certain religious dissenters as potential traitors until the middle of the eighteenth century or later. French and Austrian governments actively persecuted Protestants just as long. Only in the middle decades of the century did Voltaire and others make toleration the rallying cry par excellence of the Enlightenment, and only then did a consensus form within Europe's educated elites that laws and policies needed reform. A hundred years after the writings of Locke and Bayle, the toleration acts of the 1780s improved the position of religious dissenters, but not radically. As long as the Old Regime endured (and even longer in many lands—but this would take us beyond the limits of our study), there would be no dismantling of religious establishments, no freedom of worship for people of all faiths, no end to religious discrimination.

Even among Europe's elites, then, the "rise of toleration" in the eighteenth century came later, more suddenly, and was more limited than usually suggested. Once we turn to broader social groups, the whole idea of a rise begins to look questionable. The Gordon Riots were hardly the only episode of religious violence in that reputed model of toleration, England. On the Continent, too, instances of official toleration provoked popular backlash. Leaving aside sporadic episodes, did people behave more tolerantly in day-to-day life? *Simultaneum,* the sharing of church buildings, grew more common in Alsace and the Palatinate in the eighteenth century. That was by government fiat, though, not popular demand, and as the practice spread, the amount of petty harassment and minor conflict it occasioned increased proportionally. In the sphere of social interactions, we have seen that mixed marriage is a good indicator of at least a certain type of toleration. Rates of intermarriage between Protestants of different stripes do seem to have increased in Britain and the Netherlands in the eighteenth century. Yet for Protestants and Catholics to intermarry remained a rare thing; never was it less common, at least among the Dutch, than in the early 1700s. With baroque Catholicism at its most elaborate stage, the difference between Protestant and Catholic piety was probably never greater than in those decades.

These points do not answer adequately our basic question: Did relations between people of different faiths change in the eighteenth century? When, where, how? The fact of the matter is, we know too little to offer an unequivocal answer. Those who posit a rise of toleration should be equally cautious. Their confidence stems from a narrow focus on elite ideas that ignores popular belief and behavior—"elite" and "popular" being shorthand for all the social distinctions we drew earlier, and would draw more finely if we could. More perniciously, the story of the rise of toleration is an ideological construct that perpetuates our ignorance. It is a myth, not only in being at variance with known facts, but in being a symbolic story, with heroes and villains and a moral—a story told about the past to explain or justify a present state of affairs. According to this myth, toleration triumphed in the eighteenth century because reason triumphed over faith. It triumphed because religion lost its hold on people, and hence its importance as a historical phenomenon.

Ultimately, then, behind the story of the "rise of toleration" lies a second story, one that gives the first much of its plausibility and endurance. It is the story of the secularization of Western society. According to it, around 1650—or even earlier, by some accounts—Europe began to undergo a long-term, evolutionary process. Although it took centuries, by some point in the twentieth century its results were clear: churches lost much of their power and authority; clergy ceased to play major roles in politics, education, and social welfare; religious worship grew less universal; people stopped giving religious explanations for natural phenomena and human events; religious idioms ceased to pervade communications. From something inextricably intertwined with state, society, and culture, religion became a separate body of beliefs and practices, something reserved for Sundays. Driven from the public sphere, it was privatized and marginalized. This story is controversial among scholars, who disagree first as to which aspects of it are empirically true, and second, whether as a story it is not conceptually flawed. This is not the place to launch a comprehensive critique of the story, whose portrait of the eighteenth century we have already questioned. Let us conclude just by considering how it can hinder the practice of toleration today.

Herbert Butterfield, who demolished the old Whig interpretation of early modern history, himself believed that a rise of toleration had occurred in that era and that it had been a product of secularization and religious indifference. In this very direct sense, the secularization story was heir and successor to the Whig interpretation, and so it remains. No longer do we hail Protestantism for giving birth to religious freedom; instead we credit secular values—individualism, privacy, equality, human rights—whose rise we trace in the past and whose present triumph we celebrate. This is not all bad, for if we cherish those values, we will want to tell stories that contribute to their strength. But what if other people and cultures do not share those values? Can a nonindividualistic or hierarchic society be tolerant? Can one that denies that human beings possess innate, inalienable rights? This is the dilemma of postmodernism. If toleration depends on the adoption of certain contemporary Western values, its fate in the rest of the world, and perhaps in our own future, is uncertain.

That is even more true if toleration depends on the rejection, or at least marginalization, of religion. The secularization story suggests that religious fervor and commitment are fundamentally incompatible with toleration, and that the latter will flourish only as the former fades. It suggests that religion cannot play a prominent role in politics or public life without leading, in a diverse society, to conflict. Does that mean that devout people are necessarily intolerant? That societies whose laws, customs, institutions, and values are shaped by religion will feel obliged to persecute heretics and wage holy war against infidels? Experience proves that the answer to the first question is no. The second is equally spurious. Blinding us to the varieties of bona fide religion, the secularization story encourages us to associate religion in general with certain intolerant forms of religion. Equating religion with a destructive fanaticism, it tempts us to fear and condemn religion in general.

The history of early modern Europe suggests a different view. It demonstrates that, even in communities that did not know our modern values, people of different faiths could live together peacefully. Even in profoundly religious communities where antagonisms were sharp, religion was not a primitive, untameable force. In the centuries between Reformation and French Revolution, Europeans discovered that, in practice, they could often manage and contain confessional conflict. As limited, tension-ridden, and discriminatory as their accommodations and arrangements were, they can open our eyes to the unique qualities of the toleration we practice today and the possibility of other options.

NOTES

FURTHER READING

ACKNOWLEDGMENTS

INDEX

Notes

Unless otherwise indicated, all translations into English from works cited in other languages are my own.

Introduction

1. Barbara B. Diefendorf, *Beneath the Cross: Catholics and Huguenots in Sixteenth-Century Paris* (New York, 1991), 47.
2. Janine Garrisson, *Tocsin pour un massacre: La saison des Saint-Barthélemy* (Paris, 1968), 197; echoed by Denis Richet, "Aspects socio-culturels des conflits religieux à Paris dans la seconde moitié du XVIe siècle," *Annales: Economies, Sociétés, Civilisations* 32 (1977): 773.
3. Robert M. Kingdon, *Myths about the St. Bartholomew's Day Massacres, 1572–1576* (Cambridge, Mass., 1988), 41.
4. Joseph Lecler, *Histoire de la tolérance au siècle de la réforme,* 2 vols. (Aubier, 1954–1955), later published in English as *Toleration and the Reformation,* 2 vols., trans. T. L. Westow (London, 1960); W. K. Jordan, *The Development of Religious Toleration in England,* 4 vols. (London, 1932–1940).
5. The phrase of Eric R. Wolf in *Europe and the People without History* (Berkeley, 1982).
6. Mehdi Amin Razavi and David Ambuel, eds., *Philosophy, Religion, and the Question of Intolerance* (Albany, 1997), viii.
7. Hugh Trevor-Roper, "Toleration and Religion after 1688," in *From Persecution*

to *Toleration: The Glorious Revolution and Religion in England,* ed. Ole Peter Grell, Jonathan I. Israel, and Nicholas Tyacke, 389–408 (Oxford, 1991), 406; Joachim Whaley, "*Pouvoir sauver les apparences:* The Theory and Practice of Tolerance in 18th-Century Germany," *British Journal for Eighteenth-Century Studies* 13 (1990): 13.

8. So characterized by Alexandra Walsham in *Charitable Hatred: Tolerance and Intolerance in England, 1500–1700* (Manchester, 2006), 5.

9. The apt phrase of Judith Pollmann in *Religious Choice in the Dutch Republic: The Reformation of Arnoldus Buchelius (1565–1641)* (Manchester, 1999), 174.

10. For instance, Willem Frijhoff, "Dimensions de la coexistence confessionnelle," in *The Emergence of Tolerance in the Dutch Republic,* ed. Christiane Berkvens-Stevelinck, Jonathan Israel, and G. H. M. Posthumus Meyjes (Leiden, 1997), 213–237; Olivier Christin, *La paix de religion: L'autonomisation de la raison politique au XVIe siècle* (Paris, 1997); Keith Cameron, Mark Greengrass, and Penny Roberts, eds., *The Adventure of Religious Pluralism in Early Modern France* (Oxford, 2000).

1.   A Holy Zeal

1. Roland H. Bainton, *Hunted Heretic: The Life and Death of Michael Servetus* (Boston, 1953), 152–153.

2. The epithet coined by Bainton in *Hunted Heretic.*

3. Bainton, *Hunted Heretic,* 203.

4. Sebastian Castellio, *Concerning Heretics: Whether They Are to Be Persecuted and How They Are to Be Treated* (1554; New York, 1965), quotations on 129, 139, 273, 131, and 123.

5. Bainton, *Hunted Heretic,* 170–171.

6. Castellio, *Concerning Heretics,* 271–272.

7. Ibid., 108.

8. Ferdinand Buisson, *Sébastien Castellion, sa vie et son oeuvre (1515–1563),* 2 vols. (Paris, 1892), 2:23, 20, 21.

9. Nikolaus Paulus, *Protestantismus und Toleranz im 16. Jahrhundert* (Freiburg-im-Breisgau, 1911), 74.

10. Élisabeth Labrousse, "Note à propos de la conception de la tolérance au XVIIIe siècle," *Studies on Voltaire and the Eighteenth Century* 56 (1967): 802.

11. Leonard W. Levy, *Blasphemy: Verbal Offense against the Sacred, from Moses to Salman Rushdie* (Chapel Hill, 1993), 89–90.

12. Barbara B. Diefendorf, *Beneath the Cross: Catholics and Huguenots in Sixteenth-Century Paris* (New York, 1991), 56.

13. Martin Luther, *On Temporal Authority: To What Extent It Should be Obeyed,*

www.augustana.edu/religion/lutherproject/TemporalAuthority/
Temporalauthority.htm.

14. Luther, "Second Invocavit Sermon," in *The Protestant Reformation,* ed. Hans J. Hillerbrand (London, 1968), 29–37.

15. Joseph Lecler, "Liberté de conscience: Origines et sens divers de l'expression," *Recherches de Science Religieuse* 54 (1966): 375.

16. Heiko A. Oberman, *Luther: Man between God and the Devil* (New Haven, 1989), 204; Ernest W. Nelson, "The Theory of Persecution," in *Persecution and Liberty: Essays in Honor of George Lincoln Burr,* 3–20 (New York, 1931), 19.

17. John Calvin, *Institutes of the Christian Religion,* 2 vols., trans. Ford Lewis Battles, ed. John T. McNeill (Philadelphia, 1960), 846.

18. J. C. Davis, "Religion and the Struggle for Freedom in the English Revolution," *Historical Journal* 35 (1992): 519.

19. Benjamin J. Kaplan, *Calvinists and Libertines: Confession and Community in Utrecht, 1578–1620* (Oxford, 1995), 34–35.

20. Henry Kamen, *The Rise of Toleration* (New York, 1967), 9.

21. Augustine of Hippo, "The Correction of the Donatists," www.ccel.org/ccel/ schaff/npnf104.html; Augustine of Hippo, Letter 93, www.ccel.org/ccel/schaff/ npnf101.html.

22. Mark Goldie, "The Theory of Religious Intolerance in Restoration England," in *From Persecution to Toleration,* ed. O. Grell, J. I. Israel, and N. Tyacke, 331–368 (Oxford, 1991), 364.

23. Thomas Aquinas, *Summa Theologica,* second part of the second part, Q. 11, art. 1, English text at www.ccel.org/ccel/aquinas/summa.html.

24. Ibid., art. 3.

25. Keith Thomas, *Religion and the Decline of Magic* (New York, 1971), 76–77.

26. Alexandra Walsham, *Church Papists: Catholicism, Conformity and Confessional Polemic in Early Modern England* (London, 1993), 104.

27. Ibid., 47—Jesuit John Radford blasting statute Protestants.

28. E. Labrousse, "La conversion d'un huguenot au catholicisme en 1665," *Revue d'Histoire de l'Eglise de France* 64 (1978): 63.

29. Kaplan, *Calvinists and Libertines,* 49.

30. Walsham, *Church Papists,* 46.

31. Bodo Nischan, "Lutheran Confessionalization, Preaching, and the Devil," in his *Lutherans and Calvinists in the Age of Confessionalism* (Aldershot, 1999), reprint 7, p. 13.

32. William L. Lumpkin, ed., *Baptist Confessions of Faith* (Philadelphia, 1959), 26.

33. Irenaeus of Lyon, "*Adversus Haereses,*" bk. 5, chap. 26, English text at www .newadvent.org/fathers/.

34. The phrase of Elaine Pagels in *The Origin of Satan* (New York, 1995), 13.

35. Nischan, "Lutheran Confessionalization," pp. 2, 13.

36. Blair Worden, "Toleration and the Cromwellian Protectorate," in *Persecution and Toleration*, ed. W. J. Sheils, 199–233 (Oxford, 1984), 212.

37. Christopher Hill, *Antichrist in Seventeenth-Century England* (London, 1990), 85.

38. The argument that anti-Catholicism in England had the special added function of compensating for the "doctrinal fuzziness" of Anglicanism that made it "hard to define . . . positively" is made in Colin Haydon, *Anti-Catholicism in Eighteenth-Century England, c. 1714–80: A Political and Social Study* (Manchester, 1993), esp. 254.

39. Alexandra Walsham, "'The Fatall Vesper': Providentialism and Anti-Popery in Late Jacobean London," *Past and Present* 144 (1994): 54.

40. Bernard Dompnier, *Le venin de l'hérésie: Image du protestantisme et combat catholique au XVIIe siècle* (Paris, 1985), 170.

41. J. Reitsma and S. D. van Veen, eds., *Acta der provinciale en particuliere synoden, gehouden in de noordelijke Nederlanden gedurende de jaren 1572–1620*, 6 vols. (Groningen, 1892), 2:395.

42. Joachim Whaley, *Religious Toleration and Social Change in Hamburg, 1529–1819* (Cambridge, 1985), 56.

43. So characterized by Bodo Nischan in "The Elevation of the Host in the Age of Confessionalism: Adiaphoron or Ritual Demarcation?" in his *Lutherans and Calvinists*, reprint 5, quotations on pp. 19 and 27.

44. Bodo Nischan, "Ritual and Protestant Identity in Late Reformation Germany," in *Protestant History and Identity*, ed. Bruce Gordon, 2:142–158 (Aldershot, 1996), 145.

45. F. L. Rutgers, ed., *Acta van de Nederlandsche synoden der zestiende eeuw* (Utrecht, 1889), 9.

46. Alastair Duke, Gillian Lewis, and Andrew Pettegree, eds., *Calvinism in Europe, 1540–1610: A Collection of Documents* (Manchester, 1992), 213.

47. *Handbuch der Schweizer Geschichte*, 2 vols., 2nd ed. (Zurich, 1980), 634.

48. Worden, "Toleration," 200.

2. Corpus Christianum

1. David Cressy, *Bonfires and Bells: National Memory and the Protestant Calendar in Elizabethan and Stuart England* (Berkeley, 1989), 69.

2. "To the King. On his Birth-day, Nov. 19. 1632. An Epigram Anniversary," in Ben Jonson, *The Works of Ben Jonson . . .* (London, 1692), 572.

3. Cressy, *Bonfires and Bells*, 69.

4. Peter Burke, *Popular Culture in Early Modern Europe* (New York, 1978), 219.

5. The Elizabethan religious "Advertisements," quoted in David Cressy, *Birth, Marriage, and Death: Ritual, Religion, and the Life-Cycle in Tudor and Stuart England* (Oxford, 1999), 422.

6. So characterized by Barbara Diefendorf, referring to Paris, in *Beneath the Cross: Catholics and Huguenots in Sixteenth-Century Paris* (New York, 1991), 48.

7. The term coined by Mack Walker in *German Home Towns: Community, State, and General Estate, 1648–1871* (Ithaca, 1971).

8. Linda Colley, *Britons: Forging the Nation, 1707–1837* (New Haven, 1992), 17.

9. Bernd Roeck, *Eine Stadt in Krieg und Frieden: Studien zur Geschichte der Reichsstadt Augsburg zwischen Kalenderstreit und Parität (1584–1648)*, 2 vols. (Göttingen, 1989), 378.

10. Tertullian, "Liber ad Scapulam," in *Patrologiae Cursus Completus: Series Latina*, ed. J.-P. Migne, 1:774–784 (Paris, 1878–), 777, as translated in Henry Kamen, *The Rise of Toleration* (New York, 1967), 9.

11. So paraphrased by John Bossy in *Christianity in the West 1400–1700* (Oxford, 1985), 58.

12. Eamon Duffy, *The Stripping of the Altars: Traditional Religion in England, c.1400– c.1580* (New Haven, 1992), 143.

13. So characterized by R. Po-chia Hsia in *The World of Catholic Renewal, 1540–1770* (Cambridge, 1998), 201.

14. Martin Luther, "On the Councils and the Church," in *Luther's Works*, ed. Helmut T. Lehmann and Jaroslav Pelikan, 41:3–178 (Philadelphia, 1955–1986), 145, 166.

15. Ibid., 166.

16. August Friedrich Schott, *Sammlungen zu den deutschen Land- und Stadtrechten*, 3 vols. (Leipzig, 1772–1775), 1:204; see Walker, *German Home Towns*, 42.

17. Joachim Whaley, *Religious Toleration and Social Change in Hamburg 1529–1819* (Cambridge, 1985), 188 (paraphrased by Whaley), 194.

18. Mack Walker, *The Salzburg Transaction: Expulsion and Redemption in Eighteenth-Century Germany* (Ithaca, 1992), 202.

19. So catalogued and characterized by Christopher Hill in *Society and Puritanism in Pre-revolutionary England* (New York, 1997), 363–365.

20. Letters of St. Augustine, letter 22, chap. 1, para. 6, www.ccel.org/ccel/Schaff/npnf101.html.

21. Edward Muir, *Ritual in Early Modern Europe* (Cambridge, 1997), 56.

22. Duffy, *Stripping of the Altars*, 136–137.

23. Robert A. Schneider, *The Ceremonial City: Toulouse Observed, 1738–1780* (Princeton, 1995), 111–112.

24. Lambertus Danaeus, *Ad libellum ab anonymo quodam libertino recens editum, hoc titulo, de externa seu visibili Dei Ecclesia . . . Responsio* ([Geneva], 1582), 32.

25. John Coffey, *Persecution and Toleration in Protestant England, 1558–1689* (London, 2000), 34.

26. So characterized by David Underdown in *Fire from Heaven: Dorchester in the Seventeenth Century* (New Haven, 1992), 5.

27. Judith Pollmann, *Religious Choice in the Dutch Republic: The Reformation of Arnoldus Buchelius (1565–1641)* (Manchester, 1999), 151.

28. Thomas Jefferson, *Notes on the State of Virginia,* query 17, in Jefferson, *Writings* (New York, 1984), 285.

29. Marie Juliette Marinus, "Het verdwijnen van het protestantisme in de Zuidelijke Nederlanden," in *1648: De Vrede van Munster; Handelingen van het herdenkingscongres te Nijmegen en Kleef, 28–30 augustus 1996 . . . ,* ed. Hugo de Schepper, Christian L. Tümpel, and Jan J. V. M. de Vet, 261–271 (Hilversum, 1997), 263.

30. A. Schilling, ed., "Beiträge zur Geschichte der Einführung der Reformation in Biberach: 1. Zeitgenössische Aufzeichnungen des Weltpriesters Heinrich von Pflummern," *Freiburger Diöcesan-Archiv* 9 (1875): 379.

31. Heiko A. Oberman, "Europa Afflicta: The Reformation of the Refugees," *Archiv für Reformationsgeschichte* 83 (1992): 96.

32. P. M. Jones, "Parish, Seigneurie and the Community of Inhabitants in Southern Central France during the Eighteenth and Nineteenth Centuries," *Past and Present* 91 (1981): 102.

33. Janusz Tazbir, *A State without Stakes: Polish Religious Toleration in the Sixteenth and Seventeenth Centuries* (New York, 1973), 34.

3.   Flashpoints

1. Felix Stieve, *Der Ursprung des dreissigjährigen Krieges, 1607–1619* (Munich, 1875), 43.

2. Denis Crouzet, *La nuit de la Saint-Barthélemy: Un rêve perdu de la Renaissance* (Paris, 1994), 499.

3. Natalie Zemon Davis, "The Rites of Violence," in her *Society and Culture in Early Modern France,* 152–187 (Stanford, 1975).

4. Wiktor Weintraub, "Tolerance and Intolerance in Old Poland," *Canadian Slavonic Papers* 13 (1971): 42.

5. Davis, "The Rites of Violence," 153, emphasis hers.

6. Ibid., 174.

7. Colin Haydon, *Anti-Catholicism in Eighteenth-Century England, c. 1714–80: A Political and Social Study* (Manchester, 1993), 55. I follow Haydon's interpretation of the incident.

8. Ibid., 55.

9. Norman Davies, *God's Playground: A History of Poland,* 2 vols. (New York, 1982), 1:180.

10. Gregory Hanlon, *Confession and Community in Seventeenth-Century France: Catholic and Protestant Coexistence in Aquitaine* (Philadelphia, 1993), 232.

11. Élie Benoist, *Histoire de l'Edit de Nantes: Contenant les choses les plus remarquables qui se sont passées en France avant & après sa publication, à l'occasion de la diversité des Religions . . . jusques à l'edit de revocation, en Octobre 1685,* 3 vols. (Delft, 1693), 3:34.

12. All this ibid., 3:74–77, 253; and Élie Benoist, *The History of the Famous Edict of Nantes: Containing an Account of All the Persecutions, That have been in France From its First Publication to this Present Time,* 2 vols. (London, 1694), 1:253, and see 3:337–338 for an almost identical complaint that came from Normandy in the 1660s.

13. Gerhard Pfeiffer, "Das Ringen um die Parität in der Reichsstadt Biberach," *Blätter für württembergische Kirchengeschichte* 56 (1956): 30.

14. So characterized by Barbara Diefendorf in *Beneath the Cross: Catholics and Huguenots in Sixteenth-Century Paris* (New York, 1991), 149.

15. So characterized by A. N. Galpern in *The Religions of the People in Sixteenth-Century Champagne* (Cambridge, Mass., 1976), 158.

16. Bernd Roeck, *Eine Stadt in Krieg und Frieden: Studien zur Geschichte der Reichsstadt Augsburg zwischen Kalenderstreit und Parität (1584–1648),* 2 vols. (Göttingen, 1989), 184.

17. Gavin Langmuir, *Toward a Definition of Antisemitism* (Berkeley, 1990), 13.

18. Paul Warmbrunn, *Zwei Konfessionen in einer Stadt: Das Zusammenleben von Katholiken und Protestanten in den paritätischen Reichstädten Augsburg, Biberach, Ravensburg und Dinkelsbühl von 1548 bis 1648* (Wiesbaden, 1983), 376.

19. Bodo Nischan, *Prince, People, and Confession: The Second Reformation in Brandenburg* (Philadelphia, 1994), 186–187.

20. David Cressy, *Bonfires and Bells: National Memory and the Protestant Calendar in Elizabethan and Stuart England* (Berkeley, 1989), 32.

21. As pointed out by Cressy ibid., xii.

22. Haydon, *Anti-Catholicism,* 246.

23. Sheila Williams, "The Pope-Burning Processions of 1679, 1680 and 1681," *Journal of the Warburg and Courtauld Institutes* 21 (1958): 112, 113.

24. As pointed out by Cressy in *Bonfires and Bells,* 180.

25. Ibid., 182–183.

26. So characterized by Nicholas Rogers in "Riot and Popular Jacobitism in Early Hanoverian England," in *Ideology and Conspiracy: Aspects of Jacobitism, 1689–1759,* ed. E. Cruickshanks, 70–88 (Edinburgh, 1982), 77.

27. Patrick Fagan, "The Dublin Catholic Mob (1700–1750)," *Eighteenth-Century Ireland* 4 (1989): 133–142.

28. Benoist, *Famous Edict of Nantes*, 1:278.

29. In the words of Craig M. Koslofsky, *The Reformation of the Dead: Death and Ritual in Early Modern Germany, 1450–1700* (New York, 2000), 100.

30. Geoffrey Rowell, *The Liturgy of Christian Burial: An Introductory Survey of the Historical Development of Christian Burial Rites* (London, 1977), 82.

31. Joannes Gerobulus, *Waerachtich Verhael van de staet der Gereformeerde kercke/ die den Sone Gods/ binnen Utrecht door't Evangelium vergadert wert: Midsgaders van alle andere minder dingen/ tot hulpe ende onderhoudinge van den selven Staet/ aldaer gebruyckelijck ende in Train sijnde* (Utrecht, 1603), unpaginated.

32. James R. Farr, *Hands of Honor: Artisans and Their World in Dijon, 1550–1650* (Ithaca, 1988), 253.

33. Philip Caraman, ed., *The Years of Siege: Catholic Life from James I to Cromwell* (London, 1966), 28. Compare David Cressy, *Birth, Marriage and Death: Ritual, Religion, and the Life-Cycle in Tudor and Stuart England* (Oxford, 1999), 466.

34. Randolph C. Head, "Fragmented Dominion, Fragmented Churches: The Institutionalization of the *Landfrieden* in the Thurgau, 1531–1610," *Archiv für Reformationsgeschichte* 96 (2005): 139.

35. Benoist, *Famous Edict of Nantes*, 1:277.

36. Craig Koslofsky, "Honour and Violence in German Lutheran Funerals in the Confessional Age," *Social History* 20 (1995): 315–337, quotation on 330.

37. A point made by Olivier Christin in *La paix de religion: L'autonomisation de la raison politique au XVIe siècle* (Paris, 1997), 111.

38. Bernard Dompnier, *Le venin de l'hérésie: Image du protestantisme et combat catholique au XVIIe siècle* (Paris, 1985), 213.

39. Walter Scherzer, "Die Augsburger Konfessionsverwandten des Hochstifts Würzburg nach dem Westfälischen Frieden," *Zeitschrift für Bayerische Kirchengeschichte* 49 (1980): 32.

4. One Faith, One Law, One King

1. John Spurr, "'Virtue, Religion and Government': The Anglican Uses of Providence," in *The Politics of Religion in Restoration England*, ed. Tim Harris, Paul Seaward, and Mark Goldie (Oxford, 1990), 37.

2. Thomas Grenfield, *The Fast: As it was delivered in a Sermon at St. Margarets in Westminster, before the Honorable House of Commons . . .* (London, 1661), 19–21.

3. Josiah Woodward, *An account of the progress of the reformation of manners, in England, Scotland, and Ireland and other Parts of Europe and America*, 14th ed. (London, 1706), 50.

4. So characterized by Randolph C. Head in "Fragmented Dominion, Fragmented Churches: The Institutionalization of the *Landfrieden* in the Thurgau, 1531–1610," *Archiv für Reformationsgeschichte* 96 (2005): 119.

5. Leonard W. Levy, *The Establishment Clause: Religion and the First Amendment* (New York, 1986), ix.

6. Robert I. Moore, *The Formation of a Persecuting Society: Power and Deviance in Western Europe, 950–1250* (Oxford, 1987), 7.

7. Gerhard Pfeiffer, "Das Verhältnis von politischer und kirchlicher Gemeinde in den deutschen Reichsstädten," in *Staat und Kirche im Wandel der Jahrhunderte,* ed. Walter Peter Fuchs, 79–99 (Stuttgart, 1966), 91–92.

8. Ibid., 84.

9. Fritz Dickmann, "Das Problem der Gleichberechtigung der Konfessionen im Reich im 16. und 17. Jahrhundert," *Historische Zeitschrift* 201 (1965): 265–305, 279 n. 26.

10. Johann Valentin Andreae, *Christianopolis,* ed. and trans. Edward H. Thompson (Dordrecht, 1999), 196.

11. Scholars have caused confusion by using the term *confessionalization* (*Konfessionalisierung,* in the original German) in different ways. Some, including Wolfgang Reinhard and Heinz Schilling, who first developed the concept, reserve it for the combination of religious reform, state-building, and social discipline described here using Württemberg as an example. Others use it as a synonym for what Ernst Walter Zeeden first called "the formation of confessions" *(Konfessionsbildung),* also known as "the rise of confessionalism," a more purely religious process some of whose chief aspects are described in Chapter 1: the internalization of church teaching, the drawing of sharp dichotomies, and the quest for uniformity. To these one should add the theocratic tendency described here, and an elevation of clerical authority. The original concept has met with deserved criticism for suggesting that these religious trends were dependent on state sponsorship and elite imposition. See the reading list at the end of this book for relevant literature.

12. Alastair Duke and Rosemary L. Jones, "Towards a Reformed Polity in Holland, 1572–1578," *Tijdschrift voor geschiedenis* 89 (1976): 379.

13. The phrase of Janusz Tazbir in *A State without Stakes: Polish Religious Toleration in the Sixteenth and Seventeenth Centuries* (New York, 1973). One can agree, however, with Norman Davies that the triumph of the Counter-Reformation in Poland was an illusion to the extent that the Lutherans of Royal Prussia were never converted to Catholicism, but rather simply ceased to be counted as Polish after Poland's partition in the late eighteenth century (Davies, *God's Playground: A History of Poland,* 2 vols. [New York, 1982], 1:197–200).

14. Ambroise Jobert, *De Luther à Mohila: La Pologne dans la crise de la Chrétienté, 1517–1648* (Paris, 1974), 39.

15. Earl Morse Wilbur, *A History of Unitarianism: Socinianism and Its Antecedents* (Cambridge, Mass., 1947), 363.

16. Anna Coreth, *Pietas Austriaca: Österreichische Frömmigkeit im Barok* (Vienna, 1982), 11 n. 7.

17. Judith Pollmann, *Religious Choice in the Dutch Republic: The Reformation of Arnoldus Buchelius (1565–1641)* (Manchester, 1999), 149.

18. Blair Worden, "Toleration and the Cromwellian Protectorate," in *Persecution and Toleration,* ed. W. J. Sheils, 199–233 (Oxford, 1984), 224.

19. Colin Haydon, *Anti-Catholicism in Eighteenth-Century England, c. 1714–80: A Political and Social Study* (Manchester, 1993), 13.

20. David Cressy, *Bonfires and Bells: National Memory and the Protestant Calendar in Elizabethan and Stuart England* (Berkeley, 1989), 122, 72.

21. Carol Wiener, "This Beleaguered Isle: A Study of Elizabethan and Early Jacobean Anti-Catholicism," *Past and Present* 51 (1971): 27–62.

22. So characterized by John Miller in *Popery and Politics in England, 1660–1688* (Cambridge, 1973), 85.

23. As pointed out by Robin Clifton in "The Popular Fear of Catholics during the English Revolution," *Past and Present* 52 (1971): 55.

24. G. H. Jones, "The Irish Fright of 1688: Real Violence and Imagined Massacre," *Bulletin of the Institute of Historical Research* 55, no. 132 (1982): 149.

25. Nicholas Rogers, "Riot and Popular Jacobitism in Early Hanoverian England," in *Ideology and Conspiracy: Aspects of Jacobitism, 1689–1759,* ed. E. Cruickshanks, 70–88 (Edinburgh, 1982), 78.

26. The phrase of Benedict Anderson in *Imagined Communities: Reflections on the Origin and Spread of Nationalism,* 2nd ed. (New York, 1991).

27. Henry Kamen, *The Rise of Toleration* (New York, 1967), 35.

28. John Locke, *A Letter Concerning Toleration* (Indianapolis, 1955), 53–54. Johannes Brenz had made the same point as early as 1528 vis-à-vis the Anabaptists: "No insurrection were to be feared from these people if the civil sword were otherwise properly employed"—that is, other than in persecuting them. Sebastian Castellio, *Concerning Heretics: Whether They Are to Be Persecuted and How They Are to Be Treated* (1554; New York, 1965), 169.

5.   The Gold Coin

1. John Donne, *Poetry and Prose,* ed. Frank J. Warnke (New York, 1967), 207.

2. Thierry Wanegffelen, *L'édit de Nantes: Une histoire européenne de la tolérance du XVIe au XXe siècle* (Paris, 1998), 98.

3. Hélène Bordes, "François de Sales et la conversion des protestants: Les ser-

mons du chablais," in *La conversion au XVIIe siècle: Actes du XIIe Colloque de Marseille (janvier 1982)*, 111–122 (Marseille, 1983), 113.

4. Joseph Lecler, *Toleration and the Reformation*, 2 vols. (London, 1960), 1:238.

5. John P. Dolan, *History of the Reformation: A Conciliatory Assessment of Opposite Views* (New York, 1965), 376.

6. Lecler, *Toleration and the Reformation*, 1:270.

7. *Discours sur la permission de religion dite Religions-Frid* (n.p., 1579), unpag.

8. Thierry Wanegffelen, *Ni Rome ni Genève: Des fidèles entre deux chaires en France au XVIe siècle* (Paris, 1997), 455.

9. Sebastian Castellio, *Concerning Heretics: Whether They Are to Be Persecuted and How They Are to Be Treated* (1554; New York, 1965), 129–130.

10. Maurice Cranston, *John Locke: A Biography* (London, 1957), 314.

11. Benjamin J. Kaplan, *Calvinists and Libertines: Confession and Community in Utrecht, 1578–1620* (Oxford, 1995), 27; Kaplan, "'Remnants of the Papal Yoke': Apathy and Opposition in the Dutch Reformation," *Sixteenth Century Journal* 25 (1994): 651–667.

12. "Elizabeth I," www.royal.gov.uk/output/Page46.asp.

13. Peter Lake, "The Laudian Style: Order, Uniformity and the Pursuit of the Beauty of Holiness in the 1630s," in *The Early Stuart Church, 1603–1642*, ed. Kenneth Fincham, 161–185 (Stanford, 1993).

14. Paul Eisenkopf, *Leibniz und die Einigung der Christenheit: Überlegungen zur Reunion der evangelischen und katholischen Kirche* (Munich, 1975), 157–158.

15. Ambroise Jobert, *De Luther à Mohila: La Pologne dans la crise de la Chrétienté, 1517–1648* (Paris, 1974), 393.

16. Alexandra Walsham, *Church Papists: Catholicism, Conformity and Confessional Polemic in Early Modern England* (London, 1993).

17. Tim Harris, Paul Seaward, and Mark Goldie, eds., *The Politics of Religion in Restoration England* (Oxford, 1990), 18.

18. Geoffrey S. Holmes, *The Trial of Doctor Sacheverell* (London, 1973), 40; Alexandra Walsham, *Charitable Hatred: Tolerance and Intolerance in England, 1500–1700* (Manchester, 2006), 193.

19. Richard L. Goodbar, ed., *The Edict of Nantes: Five Essays and a New Translation* (Bloomington, Minn., 1998), 42.

20. Mario Turchetti, "Henri IV entre la concorde et la tolérance," in *Henri IV, le roi et la reconstruction du royaume: Volumes des actes du colloque Pau-Nérac, 14–17 septembre 1989*, 277–299 (Pau, 1990), 296.

21. Konrad Müller, ed., *Instrumenta pacis Westphalicae—Die Westfälischen Friedensverträge: Vollst. lateinischer Text mit Übers. der wichtigsten Teile und Regesten* (Bern, 1975), 24, 113.

22. H. Raab, "Der 'Discrete Catholische' des Landgrafen Ernst von Hessen-

Rheinfels (1623–1693): Ein Beitrag zur Geschichte der Reunionsbemühungen und Toleranzbestrebungen im 17. Jahrhundert," *Archiv für mittelrheinische Kirchengeschichte* 12 (1960): 187.

6. Crossing Borders

1. Gustav Reingrabner, *Adel und Reformation: Beiträge zur Geschichte des protestantischen Adels im Lande unter der Enns während des 16. und 17. Jahrhunderts* (Vienna, 1976), 59.

2. K. Kuzmány, ed., *Urkundenbuch zum österreichisch-evangelischen Kirchenrecht* (Vienna, 1856), 4–5.

3. Grete Mecenseffy, *Geschichte des Protestantismus in Österreich* (Graz, 1956), 140.

4. Josef Karl Mayr, "Wiener Protestantengeschichte im 16. und 17. Jahrhundert," *Jahrbuch der Gesellschaft für die Geschichte des Protestantismus in Österreich* 70 (1954): 103.

5. Liselotte Westmüller, "Helmhard Jörger und die protestantische Gemeinde zu Hernals," *Jahrbuch der Gesellschaft für die Geschichte des Protestantismus in Österreich* 81 (1965): 185.

6. The apt phrase of R. J. W. Evans in *The Making of the Habsburg Monarchy, 1550–1700: An Interpretation* (Oxford, 1979), 190.

7. The phrase of Robert Muchembled in his introduction to *Frontiers of Faith: Religious Exchange and the Constitution of Religious Identities, 1400–1750,* ed. Eszter Andor and István György Tóth (Budapest, 2001), 4.

8. Ernst Walder, ed., *Religionsvergleiche des 16. Jahrhunderts* (Bern, 1974), 7–8.

9. Ferdinand Elsener, "Das Majoritätsprinzip in konfessionellen Angelegenheiten und die Religionsverträge der schweizerischen Eigenossenschaft vom 16. bis 18. Jahrhundert," *Zeitschrift der Savigny-Stiftung für Rechtsgeschichte,* canon law section 86 (1969): 279.

10. R. Fischer, W. Schläpfer, and F. Stark, *Appenzeller Geschichte,* 2 vols. (Appenzell, 1964–1972), 1: 338.

11. Martin Luther, *Werke: Kritische Gesamtausgabe* (Weimar, 1883–), section 4, vol. 6, p. 353; as translated in Mack Walker, *The Salzburg Transaction: Expulsion and Redemption in Eighteenth-Century Germany* (Ithaca, 1992), 18.

12. Élisabeth Labrousse, "Plaidoyer pour le nicodémisme," *Revue d'histoire ecclésiastique* 82 (1987): 267.

13. So put by Alexandra Walsham in *Charitable Hatred: Tolerance and Intolerance in England, 1500–1700* (Manchester, 2006), 166.

14. John Toland, *Reasons for naturalizing the Jews in Great Britain and Ireland, on the same foot with all other nations . . .* (London, 1714), 6.

15. As pointed out by Walker in *The Salzburg Transaction,* 18.

16. Henry Kamen, *The Spanish Inquisition: A Historical Revision* (New Haven, 1997), 8.

17. Ernst Walter Zeeden, "Ein landesherrliches Toleranzedikt aus dem 17. Jahrhundert: Der Gnadenbrief Johann Philipps von Schönborn für die Stadt Kitzingen (1650)," *Historisches Jahrbuch* 103 (1983): 150.

18. The phrase of Penny Roberts in "The Most Crucial Battle of the Wars of Religion? The Conflict over Sites for Reformed Worship in Sixteenth-Century France," *Archiv für Reformationsgeschichte* 89 (1998): 247–267.

19. "Erhalt uns, Herr, bei denem Wort// und steur des Papsts und Türken Mord," translation by Z. Philip Ambrose at www.uvm.edu/~classics/faculty/bach.

7. Fictions of Privacy

1. *Bijdragen voor de Geschiedenis van het Bisdom Haarlem* 1 (1873): 319.

2. H. A. Enno van Gelder, *Getemperde vrijheid: Een verhandeling over de verhouding van Kerk en Staat in de Republiek der Verenigde Nederlanden en de vrijheid van meningsuiting in zake godsdienst, drukpers en onderwijs, gedurende de 17e eeuw* (Groningen, 1972), 113.

3. Ibid., 118.

4. Gemeentearchief Amsterdam, 5024, inv. nr. 2: Resolutiën van Burgemeesters 1649–1698, fol. 279r–v (1691).

5. Christian Gellinek, ed., *Europas erster Baedeker: Filip von Zesens Amsterdam 1664* (New York, 1988), 180, 191–195, 293–295, 359–361; Jan Wagenaar, *Amsterdam in zijne opkomst, aanwas, geschiedenissen, vorregten, koophandel, gebouwen, kerkenstaat, schoolen, schutterye, gilden en regeeringe* (Amsterdam, 1760), vol. 3, bk. 3. Von Zesen included synagogues and Protestant schuilkerken, but not Catholic ones.

6. Leo Schwering, "Die religiöse und wirtschaftliche Entwicklung des Protestantismus in Köln während des 17. Jahrhunderts: Ein Versuch," *Annalen des historischen Vereins für den Niederrhein* 85 (1908): 14.

7. Clemens von Looz-Corswarem, "Köln und Mülheim am Rhein im 18. Jahrhundert: Reichsstadt und Flecken als wirtschaftliche Rivalen," in *Civitatum Communitas: Studien zum europäischen Städtewesen*, ed. Helmut Jäger, Franz Petri, and Heinz Quinn (Cologne, 1984), 548. "Blainville" was probably a pseudonym.

8. E. Heinen, "Der Kölner Toleranzstreit (1787–1789)," *Jahrbuch des kölnischen Geschichtsvereins* 44 (1973): 70.

9. Walter Grossmann, "Städtisches Wachstum und religiöse Toleranzpolitik am Beispiel Neuwied," *Archiv für Kulturgeschichte* 62/63 (1980–1981): 221; Erich Randt, *Die Mennoniten in Ostpreussen und Litauen bis zum Jahre 1772* (Königsberg, 1912), 18.

10. C. Litton Falkiner, *Illustrations of Irish History and Topography, Mainly of the Seventeenth Century* (London, 1904), 382.

11. "Report on the State of Popery, Ireland 1731," *Archivium Hibernicum* 1–4 (1912–1915): 2 (1913): 127; and 4 (1915): 159.

12. English translation in Roland Mousnier, *The Assassination of Henry IV: The Tyrannicide Problem and the Consolidation of the French Absolute Monarchy in the Early Seventeenth Century* (London, 1973), 353, 362, 320, 321.

13. Konrad Müller, ed., *Instrumenta pacis Westphalicae—Die Westfälischen Friedensverträge: Vollst. lateinischer Text mit Übers. der wichtigsten Teile und Regesten* (Bern, 1975), 47 Latin, 133 German.

14. As paraphrased in Paul Friedrich Stälin, "Das Rechtsverhältnis der religiösen Gemeinschaften und der fremden Religionsverwandten in Württemberg nach seiner geschichtlichen Entwicklung," *Württembergische Jahrbücher für Statistik und Landeskunde* (1868), 160.

15. Joachim Whaley, *Religious Toleration and Social Change in Hamburg, 1529–1819* (Cambridge, 1985), 54.

16. The phrases of Garrett Mattingly, *Renaissance Diplomacy* (Boston, 1971), 272, 280–281; and E. A. Adair, *The Exterritoriality of Ambassadors in the Sixteenth and Seventeenth Centuries* (New York, 1929).

17. Freddy Raphaël and Robert Weyl, *Juifs en Alsace: Culture, société, histoire* (Toulouse, 1977), 134.

18. Ibid., 135–137.

19. Whaley, *Hamburg*, 92.

20. Roger Williams, *The bloudy tenent, of persecution, for cause of conscience, discussed* . . . (London, 1644), 25.

21. George Hay, *The Architecture of Scottish Post-Reformation Churches, 1560–1843* (Oxford, 1957), 154.

22. Peter F. Barton, ed., "'Das' Toleranzpatent von 1781: Edition der wichtigsten Fassungen," in *Im Zeichen der Toleranz: Aufsätze zur Toleranzgesetzgebung des 18. Jahrhunderts in den Reichen Joseph II., ihren Voraussetzungen und ihren Folgen; Eine Festschrift*, ed. Peter F. Barton (Vienna, 1981), 165, also 168, 170.

23. Müller, *Instrumenta Pacis Westphalicae*, German text 149, Latin 37.

24. "In aedibus propriis aut alienis ei rei destinatis," in Müller, *Instrumenta Pacis Westphalicae*, Latin text 18, German 107.

25. Jürgen Habermas, *The Structural Transformation of the Public Sphere: An Inquiry into a Category of Bourgeois Society*, trans. Thomas Berger (Cambridge, 1989).

26. Ibid., 5.

27. So described by James Van Horn Melton in *The Rise of the Public in Enlightenment Europe* (Cambridge, 2001), 15.

8. Sharing Churches, Sharing Power

1. Ernst Walder, ed., *Religionsvergleiche des 16. Jahrhunderts* (Bern, 1974), 53 (art. 27).

2. This outcome had one important medieval precedent: Bohemia after the Hussite uprising of 1419–1436. This was the one case, prior to the reformations, where a heretical movement had grown too powerful for Catholic forces to suppress it or drive it underground. After five crusades failed to crush the followers of Jan Hus, an agreement known as the Basel Compacts brought in 1436 a measure of peace by granting "Utraquists," who formed the larger, more moderate branch of the Hussite movement, permission to take Communion "sub utraque specie." The Council of Basel, which approved it, envisaged the concession as only a temporary one to a group *within* the Catholic church. What developed in the kingdom instead were separate, rival churches. Renewed warfare from 1465 to 1478 again left power in Bohemia divided between adherents of the two. Finally, in 1485 Catholic and Utraquist members of Bohemia's estates concluded the Peace of Kutna Hora, the first legal document to provide for the peaceful coexistence of Catholic and non-Catholic Christians within a state.

   Not by conscious imitation—no one, so far as I know, subsequently took the Bohemian treaty as a model—but by force of parallel circumstances, Kutna Hora anticipated post-Reformation treaties in crucial respects: it was intended originally to be merely temporary; it was a purely political arrangement that suffered from an essential, spiritual illegitimacy; it did not separate church from state but rather gave Bohemia two official faiths; it granted no protection to other faiths—namely, that of the Bohemian Brethren, the more radical branch of the Hussite movement—leaving their practice wholly illegal; it attempted to establish peace in part by freezing the status quo; and it provided for the establishment (though this never transpired) of a special court, half of whose judges would be Catholic, half Utraquist, to decide future disputes between the two confessions. See Winfried Eberhard, "Entstehungsbedingungen für öffentliche Toleranz am Beispiel des Kuttenberger Religionsfriedens von 1485," *Communio viatorum* 29 (1986): 129–154; Eberhard, "Zu den politischen und ideologischen Bedingungen öffentlicher Toleranz: Der Kuttenberger Religionsfrieden 1485," *Studia Germano-Polonica* 1 (1992): 101–118.

3. W. A. J. Munier, *De beginfase van het z.g. simultaneum in de kerk van de H. H. Nicolaas en Barbara te Valkenburg (1632–1687): Katholieken en protestanten in strijd om het bezit van een kerkgebouw* (Valkenburg, 1985), 40.

4. Kurt Rosendorn, *Die rheinhessischen Simultankirchen bis zum Beginn des 18. Jahrhunderts: Eine rechtsgeschichtliche Untersuchung* (Mainz, 1958), 4.

5. Munier, *De beginfase,* 40.

6. Gerhard Pfeiffer, "Das Ringen um die Parität in der Reichsstadt Biberach," *Blätter für württembergische Kirchengeschichte* 56 (1956): 24.

7. Peter G. Wallace, "Hostility, Rivalry, and Resistance: *Simultaneum* Churches and Confessional Politics in Eighteenth-Century Alsace" (unpublished essay, Department of History, Hartwick College), p. 29. My thanks to the author for sharing this material with me.

8. Andrea Riotte, "Die paritätische Stadt: Biberach, 1649–1806," in *Geschichte der Stadt Biberach,* ed. Dieter Stievermann, Volker Press, and Kurt Diemer, 309–366 (Stuttgart, 1991), 333.

9. As pointed out by David Nirenberg in *Communities of Violence: Persecution of Minorities in the Middle Ages* (Princeton, 1995), 228.

10. Étienne François, *Die unsichtbare Grenze: Protestanten und Katholiken in Augsburg, 1648–1806* (Sigmaringen, 1991), 230 n. 12.

11. So characterized by François ibid., title and 60.

12. Olivier Christin, *La paix de religion: L'autonomisation de la raison politique au XVIe siècle* (Paris, 1997), 312 (the wording used in Montélimar).

13. As pointed out by Christin ibid., 92.

14. Hermann Conrad, "Religionsbann, Toleranz und Parität am Ende des alten Reiches," *Römische Quartalschrift für christliche Altertumskunde und Kirchengeschichte* 56 (1961): 172.

15. Christin, *La paix de religion,* 140.

16. Ferdinand Elsener, "Das Majoritätsprinzip in konfessionellen Angelegenheiten und die Religionsverträge der schweizerischen Eigenossenschaft vom 16. bis 18. Jahrhundert," *Zeitschrift der Savigny-Stiftung für Rechtsgeschichte,* canon law section 86 (1969): 270, 279.

17. Fritz Fleiner, "Die Entwicklung der Parität in der Schweiz," in Fleiner, *Ausgewählte Schriften und Reden,* 81–100 (Zurich, 1941), 85.

18. Raymond A. Mentzer, "Bipartisan Justice and the Pacification of Late Sixteenth-Century Languedoc," in *Regnum, Religio et Ratio: Essays Presented to Robert M. Kingdon,* ed. Jerome Friedman, 125–132 (Kirksville, Mo., 1987).

19. Walder, *Religionsvergleiche,* 54.

20. Christin calls them "federalist" state structures in *La paix de religion,* 203–204.

21. Rosendorn, *Die rheinhessischen Simultankirchen,* 4.

9. A Friend to the Person

1. William Temple, *Observations upon the United Provinces of the Netherlands* (London, 1673), 182.

2. Ibid., 183.

3. So characterized by Barbara Diefendorf in *Beneath the Cross: Catholics and Huguenots in Sixteenth-Century Paris* (New York, 1991), 134.

4. Will Kymlicka, "Two Models of Pluralism and Tolerance," in *Toleration: An Elusive Virtue,* ed. David Heyd, 81–105 (Princeton, 1996).

5. Étienne François, *Die unsichtbare Grenze: Protestanten und Katholiken in Augsburg, 1648–1806* (Sigmaringen, 1991).

6. Giovanni Boccaccio, *The decameron containing an hundred pleasant nouels: Wittily discoursed, betweene seauen honourable ladies, and three noble gentlemen* (London, 1620), 16v (first Day, third Nouell).

7. Brian Pullan, *The Jews of Europe and the Inquisition of Venice, 1550–1670* (London, 1997), 160–161; Carlo Ginzburg, *The Cheese and the Worms: The Cosmos of a Sixteenth-Century Miller,* trans. John and Anne Tedeschi (New York, 1980), 106, 47.

8. Stuart B. Schwartz, "Hispanic Doubts and American Dreams: The Roots of Toleration in Early Modern Latin America," www.mtholyoke.edu/acad/latam/ schomburgmoreno/schwartz.htm.

9. As pointed out in Pullan, *Jews of Europe,* 153.

10. Janusz Tazbir, *A State without Stakes: Polish Religious Toleration in the Sixteenth and Seventeenth Centuries* (New York, 1973), 35.

11. Benjamin J. Kaplan, *Calvinists and Libertines: Confession and Community in Utrecht, 1578–1620* (Oxford, 1995), 280 (both quotations).

12. Wiktor Weintraub, "Tolerance and Intolerance in Old Poland," *Canadian Slavonic Papers* 13 (1971): 42.

13. Élie Benoist, *The History of the Famous Edict of Nantes: Containing an Account of All the Persecutions, That have been in France From its First Publication to this Present Time,* 2 vols. (London, 1694), 2:326 (vol. 2, bk. 8).

14. Christian Gottfried Oertel, ed., *Vollständiges Corpus Gravaminum Evangelicorum* (Regensburg, 1775), fifth section, 2:1780–81.

15. Bill Stevenson, "The Social Integration of Post-Restoration Dissenters, 1660–1725," in *The World of the Rural Dissenters, 1520–1795,* ed. Margaret Spufford, 360–387 (Cambridge, 1995), 373.

16. David Underdown, *Fire from Heaven: Dorchester in the Seventeenth Century* (New Haven, 1992), 262.

17. Odile Martin, *La Conversion protestante à Lyon (1659–1687)* (Geneva, 1986), 71.

18. Élie Benoist, *Histoire de l'Edit de Nantes: Contenant les choses les plus remarquables qui se sont passées en France avant & après sa publication, à l'occasion de la diversité des Religions . . . jusques à l'edit de revocation, en Octobre 1685,* 3 vols. (Delft, 1693), vol. 3, pt. 1, 401.

19. W. P. C. Knuttel, ed., *Acta der particuliere synoden van Zuid-Holland, 1621–1700,* 6 vols. (The Hague, 1908–1916), 3:295.

20. Robert Sauzet, *Contre-réforme et réforme catholique en Bas-Languedoc: Le diocèse de Nîmes au XVIIe siècle* (Paris, 1979), 186.

21. Jean Quéniart, *La Révocation de l'Edit de Nantes: Protestants et catholiques en France de 1598 à 1685* (Paris, 1985), 74.

22. Peter Martyr Vermigli, *A Treatise of the Cohabitacyon of the Faithfull with the Unfaithfull* (Strasbourg, 1555), A2r.

23. Keith Luria, "Separated by Death? Burials, Cemeteries, and Confessional Boundaries in Seventeenth-Century France," *French Historical Studies* 24 (2001): 207.

24. Ibid., 218; quoted also in Charles Read, "Cimetières et inhumations des huguenots principalement à Paris aux XVIe, XVIIe, et XVIIIe siècles, 1563–1792," *Bulletin de la Société d'histoire du protestantisme français* 11 (1862): 134.

25. As pointed out by John Miller in *Popery and Politics in England, 1660–1688* (Cambridge, 1973), 16.

26. Judith Pollmann, *Religious Choice in the Dutch Republic: The Reformation of Arnoldus Buchelius (1565–1641)* (Manchester, 1999), 171–172.

27. Johann Junius Brutus Polonus [pseud. for Johann Crell], *A Learned and exceeding well compiled Vindication of Liberty of Religion* (Vindiciae pro religionis libertate), trans. John Dury ([London], 1646), 39; Alexandra Walsham, *Charitable Hatred: Tolerance and Intolerance in England, 1500–1700* (Manchester, 2006), 148; Colin Haydon, *Anti-Catholicism in Eighteenth-Century England, c. 1714–80: A Political and Social Study* (Manchester, 1993), 13; S. J. Connolly, *Religion, Law, and Power: The Making of Protestant Ireland, 1660–1760* (Oxford, 1992), 127.

28. The apt phrase of Pollmann in *Religious Choice*, 174.

29. Thieleman J. van Braght, *The Bloody Theater or Martyrs Mirror of the Defenseless Christians . . .* , trans. Joseph F. Sohm (Waterloo, Ontario, 1999), 8. In *Pilgrim's Progress*, John Bunyan warned of the same danger: having passed through Vanity Fair and survived persecution, Christian and his companion Faithful reach "a delicate Plain, called Ease" where they face Lucre and other temptations (Bunyan, *Pilgrim's Progress* [1678], pt. 1, at gateway.proquest.com/).

30. J. Hector St. John de Crèvecoeur, *Letters from an American Farmer* (New York, 1904), 62–66.

10. Transgressions

1. René Debon, "Religion et vie quotidienne à Gap (1657–1685)," in *Le Protestantisme en Dauphiné au XVIIe siècle*, ed. Pierre Bolle, 90–169 (Curandera, 1983), 136–137; Charles Charronnet, *Les Guerres de religion et la société protestante dans les Hautes-Alpes, 1560–1789* (Gap, 1861), 354–355.

2. Étienne François, *Die unsichtbare Grenze: Protestanten und Katholiken in Augsburg, 1648–1806* (Sigmaringen, 1991), pt. 3, title of chap. 3.

3. Louis Châtellier, *Tradition chrétienne et renouveau catholique dans le cadre de l'ancien diocèse de Strasbourg (1650–1770)* (Paris, 1981), 350.

4. Élie Benoist, *Histoire de l'Edit de Nantes: Contenant les choses les plus remarquables qui se sont passées en France avant & après sa publication, à l'occasion de la diversité des Religions . . . jusques à l'edit de revocation, en Octobre 1685,* 3 vols. (Delft, 1693), vol. 3, pt. 1, 449–450.

5. Meinrad Schaab, "Die Wiederherstellung des Katholizismus in der Kurpfalz im 17. und 18. Jahrhundert," *Zeitschrift für Geschichte des Oberrheins* 114 (1966): 170.

6. Odile Martin, *La Conversion protestante à Lyon (1659–1687)* (Geneva, 1986), 89.

7. Joachim Whaley, *Religious Toleration and Social Change in Hamburg, 1529–1819* (Cambridge, 1985), 46–47.

8. John Brady and Patrick J. Corish, *The Church under the Penal Code* (Dublin, 1971), 49–50.

9. François, *Die unsichtbare Grenze,* 216 n. 159 (François's phrase).

10. As pointed out by Colin Haydon in *Anti-Catholicism in Eighteenth-Century England, c. 1714–80: A Political and Social Study* (Manchester, 1993), 254.

11. Andrea Riotte, "Die paritätische Stadt: Biberach, 1649–1806," in *Geschichte der Stadt Biberach,* ed. Dieter Stievermann, Volker Press, and Kurt Diemer, 309–366 (Stuttgart, 1991), 337.

12. This argument is made by Étienne François in *Die unsichtbare Grenze,* 144–153.

13. Eamon Duffy, "'Poor Protestant Flies': Conversion to Catholicism in Early Eighteenth-Century England," in *Religious Motivation: Biographical and Sociological Problems for the Church Historian,* ed. Derek Baker, 292–304 (Oxford, 1978), 297.

14. Wiebe Bergsma, *Tussen Gideonsbende en publieke kerk: Een studie over het gereformeerd protestantisme in Friesland, 1580–1650* (Hilversum, 1999), 96 n. 1.

15. Herman Roodenburg, *Onder censuur: De kerkelijke tucht in de gereformeerde gemeente van Amsterdam, 1578–1700* (Hilversum, 1990), 152, 168.

16. A. Ph. F. Wouters and P. H. A. M. Abels, *Nieuw en ongezien: Kerk en samenleving in de classis Delft en Delfland, 1572–1621,* 2 vols. (Delft, 1994), 2:202.

17. C. Molina [Christianus Vermeulen], *Den Oprechten Schriftuerlijcken Roomsch-Catholycken Mondt-Stopper,* 15th ed. (Antwerp, 1745), 178; P. Rovenius, *Reipublicae christianae libri duo, tractantes de variis hominum statibus, gradibus, officiis et functionibus in ecclesia Christi, et quae in singulis amplect[a]nda, quae fugienda sint* (Antwerp, 1648), 386.

18. Church of Rome, *Declaratio SSmi D. N. Benedicti PP. XIV. super matrimoniis*

Hollandiae et Foederati Belgii: Et Acta in Sacra Congregatione . . . Cardinalium Sacri Concilii Tridentini Interpretum, coram SS. D.N. 13. Maii 1741. exhibita. (Louvain, 1742), 7–8; see H. F. W. D. Fischer, "De gemengde huwelijken tussen katholieken en protestanten in de Nederlanden van de XVIe tot de XVIIIe eeuw," *Tijdschrift voor rechtsgeschiedenis* 31 (1963): 471. Henceforth, the church recognized as valid Protestant-Catholic and Protestant-Protestant marriages that had been solemnized by a magistrate or Reformed minister in the United Provinces or one of the "barrier cities" manned by Dutch troops.

19. J. Reitsma and S. D. van Veen, eds., *Acta der provinciale en particuliere synoden, gehouden in de noordelijke Nederlanden gedurende de jaren 1572–1620,* 6 vols. (Groningen, 1892), 2:147.

20. S. Zijlstra, *Om de ware gemeente en de oude gronden: Geschiedenis van de dopersen in de Nederlanden, 1531–1675* (Hilversum, 2000), 307.

21. Philip E. Hughes, ed. and trans., *The Register of the Company of Pastors of Geneva in the Time of Calvin* (Grand Rapids, 1966), 345. Theodore Beza counseled similarly in *Tractatus de Repudiis et Divortiis . . .* (Leiden, 1651), 246.

22. William Gouge, *Of domesticall duties,* 2nd ed. (London, 1634), 275.

23. F. L. Rutgers, ed., *Acta van de Nederlandsche synoden der zestiende eeuw* (Utrecht, 1889), 161; Reitsma and Veen, *Acta der provinciale en particuliere synoden,* 2:439–440, 3:446.

24. André Benoist, "Catholiques et protestants en 'Moyen-Poitou' jusqu'à la Révocation de l'Édit de Nantes (1534–1685)," *Bulletin de la Société historique et scientifique des Deux-Sevres* 2, no. 16 (1983): 329.

25. Robert Sauzet, *Contre-réforme et réforme catholique en Bas-Languedoc: Le diocèse de Nîmes au XVIIe siècle* (Paris, 1979), 165–167, 266–269.

26. Roodenburg, *Onder censuur,* 158–159.

27. As noted by Kevin Herlihy in *The Irish Dissenting Tradition, 1650–1750* (Dublin, 1995), 94.

28. *Archief voor de geschiedenis van het Aartsbisdom Utrecht* 33 (1907): 50.

29. Fr. Marcellinus a Civetia and Fr. Theophilus Domenichelli, eds., *Epistolae missionariorum ordinis S. Francisci ex Frisia et Hollandia* (Quaracchi, 1888), 244 (#425, 5 May 1660).

30. Rutgers, *Acta van de Nederlandsche synoden,* 273.

31. Wouters and Abels, *Nieuw en ongezien,* 1:245.

32. Jacob Cats, *Houwelyck, dat is De gantsche gelegentheyt des Echten-Staets* (Middelburg, 1625), *Vrijster,* 2:33.

33. Quoted by, among others, Franciscus Duysseldorpius, *Reverendi . . . F. D. L. [Francisci Duysseldorpii Lugdunensis] tractatus de matrimonio non ineundo cum his, qui extra ecclesiam sunt* (Antwerp, 1636), 353, 362; Christianus Catholicus [Johannes Watelaar], *Korte ende waere uytvaert, Van alle oncatholijcke*

religien: Dienende tot eeuwige welvaert van alle Christelijcke zielen . . . Toe-ge-eygent aen alle de Catholijcken, die aen oncatholijcken getrouwt syn (Roermond, 1651), 9; rebutted in Ben Israels [Yeme de Ringh], *Tractaet Teghen het straffen der Buyten-getrouden, sonder onderscheydt: Dat is: Verantwoordinge, op eenen Brief, geschreven (van een Dienaer van Lenaert Klock: of Jan Schellinghwous* [sic] *ghezinde) aen een Broeder der Vereenighde Gemeente. aengaende het bannen over den buyten-ghetrouden* (Amsterdam, 1628), 11, 15–16. Cited also in Ireland: Alan Ford, "The Protestant Reformation in Ireland," in *Natives and New-comers: Essay on the Making of Irish Colonial Society, 1534–1641,* ed. Ciaran Brady and Raymond Gillespie, 50–74 (Dublin, 1986), 70.

34. Molina, *Mondt-Stopper,* 180.

35. Bergsma, *Tussen gideonsbende en publieke kerk,* 337.

36. Jean-Paul Pittion, "L'affaire Paulet (Montpellier 1680–83) et les conversions forcées d'enfants," in *La conversion au XVIIe siècle: Actes du XIIe Colloque de Marseille (janvier 1982),* 209–229 (Marseille, 1983).

37. Benoist, *Histoire de L'Edit de Nantes,* vol. 3, pt. 1, 142–144, 188, 250, 296, 547; vol. 3, pt. 2, 19, 20, 71–73, 174, 229–230, 243–247, 299, 334, 338–339, 445, 449–452, 510–511; vol. 3, pt. 3, 1003.

38. Châtellier, *Tradition chrétienne et renouveau catholique,* 278.

39. William P. Burke, *The Irish Priests in the Penal Times (1660–1760)* (Waterford, 1914), 194.

40. Aquinas, *Summa Theologica,* second part of the second part, Q. 11, art. 4. See Ernest W. Nelson, "The Theory of Persecution," in *Persecution and Liberty: Essays in Honor of George Lincoln Burr,* 3–20 (New York, 1931), 13.

11. Infidels

1. Brian Pullan, *Rich and Poor in Renaissance Venice: The Social Institutions of a Catholic State, to 1620* (Oxford, 1971), 489. The magistrate's argument was inaccurate in representing the events of 1497 as an expulsion.

2. Paraphrasing Brian Pullan, *The Jews of Europe and the Inquisition of Venice, 1550–1670* (London, 1997), 153.

3. Marquardus de Susannis, *De Iudaeis et aliis infidelibus, circa concernentia originem contractuum, bella, foedera, vltimas voluntates, iudicia, & delicta Iudaeorum & aliorum infidelium, & eorum conuersiones ad fidem* (Venice, 1558), 8r.

4. Hugo de Groot, *Remonstrantie nopende de ordre dije in de landen van Hollandt ende Westvrieslandt dijent gestelt op de joden,* ed. J. Meijer (Amsterdam, 1949), 110.

5. Leon Poliakov, *The History of Anti-Semitism,* vol. 1: *From Roman Times to the Court Jews* (London, 1974), 201.

6. Leon Modena, *Leo Modenas Briefe und Schriftstücke: Ein Beitrag zur Geschichte*

der Juden in Italien und zur Geschichte des hebräischen Privatstiles, ed. Ludwig Blau (Budapest, 1905), 151.

7. Benjamin Ravid, "Curfew Time in the Ghetto of Venice," in his *Studies on the Jews of Venice, 1382–1797* (Aldershot, 2003), 251.

8. Ibid., 247.

9. So characterized by Norman Housley in *Religious Warfare in Europe, 1400–1536* (Oxford, 2002), 131.

10. The phrase of Pullan in *Jews of Europe,* 192.

11. Robert C. Davis, *Christian Slaves, Muslim Masters: White Slavery in the Mediterranean, the Barbary Coast, and Italy, 1500–1800* (Basingstoke, 2003), 3–26.

12. Cemal Kafadar, "A Death in Venice (1575): Anatolian Muslim Merchants Trading in the Serenissima," in *Merchant Networks in the Early Modern World,* ed. Sanjay Subrahmanyam, 97–124 (Brookfield, Vt., 1996), 103.

13. Giorgio Vercellin, "Mercanti Turchi e Sensali a Venezia," *Studi Veneziani,* n.s. 4 (1980): 48 (a 1622 ordinance).

14. Paolo Preto, *Venezia e i Turchi* (Florence, 1975), 130, as translated in Kafadar, "A Death in Venice," 108.

15. Kafadar, "A Death in Venice," 130.

16. Ugo Tucci, "Tra Venezia e mondo turco: I mercanti," in *Venezia e i Turchi: Scontri e confronti di due civiltà,* 38–55 (Milan, 1985), 52.

17. Kafadar, "A Death in Venice," 108.

18. Ahmad ibn Qasim al-Hajari, *Kitab nasir al-din 'ala 'lqawm al-kafirin* (The Supporter of Religion against the Infidel), ed. and trans. P. S. van Koningsveld, Q. al-Samarrai, and G. A. Wiegers (Madrid, 1997), 195.

19. Thomas Fuller, *The History of the Holy Warre,* 4th ed. (Cambridge, 1651), 281.

20. Salvatore Bono, *Schiavi musulmani nell'Italia moderna: Galeotti, vu' cumprà, domestici* (Naples, 1999), 243.

21. Alessandro Stella, *Histoires d'esclaves dans la péninsule ibérique* (Paris, 2000), 56–57.

22. E. William Monter, *Frontiers of Heresy: The Spanish Inquisition from the Basque Lands to Sicily* (New York, 1990), 215.

23. Catherine Gaignard, *Maures et chrétiens à Grenade, 1492–1570* (Paris, 1997), 265.

24. Like many historians currently, I use the term *Converso* rather than *Marrano* because the latter implies a crypto-Judaizing that was not common to all of them.

25. According to Jonathan I. Israel in *European Jewry in the Age of Mercantilism, 1550–1750* (Oxford, 1989), 6.

26. Phrase adapted from Renee Levine Melammed, *Heretics or Daughters of Israel? The Crypto-Jewish Women of Castile* (New York, 1999).

27. As characterized by Melammed, ibid., 168, the first phrase being a quotation from Mary Perry, who was speaking of Moriscas.

28. Haim Beinart, "The Expulsion from Spain: Causes and Results," in *The Sephardi Legacy*, 2 vols., ed. Haim Beinart, vol. 2, pp. 11–42 (Jerusalem, 1992), 2:29.

29. On the geography and demography of Europe's Jewish population, I follow closely Israel, *European Jewry*.

30. According to Israel, ibid., 31, speaking of Jewish immigrants to both Polish and Ottoman lands.

31. As described by Brian Pullan in *Jews of Europe*, 245.

32. "Nefarie commiscentur"—from Honorius III's bull *Ad nostram noveritis* (1221), ordering the enforcement of the council's decree in the province of Burdegalen. Antonius Flavius de Sanctis, Church of Rome, and Carlo Cocquelines, eds., *Bullarium privilegiorum ac diplomatum Romanorum Pontificum amplissima collectio . . . [Bullarium Romanum]*, 6 vols. (Rome, 1739), vol. 3, pt. 1, p. 221.

33. Susannis, *De Iudaeis*, 14v.

34. So described by Pullan in his *Jews of Europe*, 168.

35. As pointed out by David Nirenberg in *Communities of Violence: Persecution of Minorities in the Middle Ages* (Princeton, 1995), 158.

36. According to Israel in *European Jewry*, 31, 71.

37. Gérard Nahon, "From New Christians to the Portuguese Jewish Nation in France," in *The Sephardi Legacy*, ed. Haim Beinart, vol. 2, pp. 336–364 (Jerusalem, 1992), 338.

38. Ibid., 338.

39. R. G. Fuks-Mansfeld, *De Sefardim in Amsterdam tot 1795* (Hilversum, 1989), 39.

40. Miriam Bodian, *Hebrews of the Portuguese Nation: Conversos and Community in Early Modern Amsterdam* (Bloomington, 1997), 134.

41. So estimated by Anthony Polonsky in his introduction to *The Jews in Old Poland: Jewish Community in the Poland-Lithuania Commonwealth, 1000–1795,* ed. Anthony Polonsky, Jakub Basista, and Andrzej Link-Lenczkowski (London, 1993), 5.

42. De Groot, *Remonstrantie*, 113 (adages from Tacitus and Seneca).

43. Lynn Hunt, ed. and trans., *The French Revolution and Human Rights: A Brief Documentary History* (New York, 1996), 88.

44. Gary Kates, "Jews into Frenchmen: Nationality and Representation in Revolutionary France," in *The French Revolution and the Birth of Modernity*, ed. Ferenc Feher, 103–116 (Berkeley, 1990), 113.

45. The conclusion of Jacob Katz in his *Out of the Ghetto: The Social Background of Jewish Emancipation, 1770–1870* (Cambridge, Mass., 1973), 208.

46. C. K. W. von Dohm, *Über die bürgerliche Verbesserung der Juden* (Berlin, 1781).
47. Paul Meyer, "The Attitude of the Enlightenment towards the Jews," *Studies on Voltaire and the Eighteenth Century* 26 (1963): 1198.

12. Enlightenment?

1. Pierre Bayle, *A Philosophical Commentary on these words of the Gospel, Luke XIV. 23: Compel them to come in, that my house may be full . . .* , 2 vols. (London, 1708; orig. French ed. 1686), 1:7.
2. Ibid., 1: 273.
3. J. W. Gough, "The Development of John Locke's Belief in Toleration," in *John Locke: A Letter Concerning Toleration in Focus,* ed. John Horton and Susan Mendus (London, 1991), 74, speaking of Locke's treatise.
4. David D. Bien, *The Calas Affair: Persecution, Toleration, and Heresy in Eighteenth-Century Toulouse* (Westport, 1979), 3, 5.
5. Bernard Lewis, *Cultures in Conflict: Christians, Muslims, and Jews in the Age of Discovery* (New York, 1995), 17.
6. Gilbert Burnet, *Bishop Burnet's History of his own time,* 3 vols. (London, 1725), 3:1120.
7. J. P. Kenyon, *The Popish Plot* (London, 1972), 13.
8. Sir Henry Capel, in Anchitell Grey, ed., *Debates of the House of Commons, from the year 1667 to the year 1694,* 10 vols. (London, 1769), 7:149 (27 April 1679).
9. Gilbert Burnet, *The History of the Persecution of the Valleys of Piedmont . . .* (London, 1688), 42.
10. Jean Quéniart, *La Révocation de l'Edit de Nantes: Protestants et catholiques en France de 1598 à 1685* (Paris, 1985), 123; "Revocation of the Edict of Nantes," history.hanover.edu/texts/nonantes.html.
11. This most despicable practice, the separation of children from parents, became at this time a common part of religious persecution, especially in Austria. In 1684 Protestants driven from Defereggental, in Eastern Tyrol, were required to leave children under age fifteen behind, to be raised as Catholics. Protestants forced to leave Dürrnberg around the same time faced the same order. In the so-called transmigration, a.k.a. deportation, of Austrian Protestants to Transylvania in the eighteenth century, authorities held back Protestant children, founding in 1752 four "conversion houses" for them to be raised in. The last of these deportations took place in 1774.
12. Burnet, *Bishop Burnet's History,* 3:1126.
13. John Locke, *Letter Concerning Toleration* (Indianapolis, 1955), 51.
14. *The Spectator,* 8 vols. (Dublin, 1755), 6:23 (no. 399); classiclit.about.com/library/bl=etexts/apope/.

15. John Locke, *The reasonableness of Christianity as delivered in the Scriptures* (London, 1695), 266.

16. As accused by Peter Gay in *The Enlightenment: An Interpretation*, 2 vols. (New York, 1969), 1:343.

17. Ole Peter Grell and Roy Porter, eds., *Toleration in Enlightenment Europe* (Cambridge, 2000), 14–15.

18. Slingsby Bethel, *The present interest of England stated* (London, 1671), 13.

19. Voltaire, *A treatise on religious toleration: Occasioned by the execution of the unfortunate John Calas* . . . (London, 1764; orig. French ed., 1763), 47.

20. As paraphrased by Marisa Linton, "Citizenship and Religious Toleration in France," in Grell and Porter, *Toleration in Enlightenment Europe*, 170–171.

21. Locke, *Letter Concerning Toleration*, 52, 55.

22. In the words of Colin Haydon, *Anti-Catholicism in Eighteenth-Century England, c. 1714–80: A Political and Social Study* (Manchester, 1993), 224.

23. Haydon, *Anti-Catholicism*, 240.

24. "A real friend to religion and to Britain," *Fanaticism and Treason; or, a dispassionate history of the rise, progress, and suppression, of the rebellious insurrections in June, 1780*, 3rd ed. (London, 1781), 4, 7.

Further Reading

Our story begins and ends with the Enlightenment—the concept of progress it has bequeathed to us and the role of toleration in its historical schema. Studies of the Enlightenment invariably discuss these topics, and good ones, such as Dorinda Outram's *The Enlightenment* (Cambridge, 1995) and Peter Gay's outdated but still classic *The Enlightenment: An Interpretation*, 2 vols. (New York, 1969), do not fail to point out that the utopian optimism of a Condorcet or Turgot was not universally shared. By the mid-nineteenth century, though, confidence had spread, at least in the Anglo-American world, that religious freedom, along with political freedom, had at long last been fully achieved. At that point, narratives of the "rise of toleration" took on a triumphal tone, as can be sampled in Thomas Babington Macaulay, *The History of England from the Accession of James II*, 2 vols. (1849–1861; London, 1985); John Lothrop Motley, *The Rise of the Dutch Republic* (London, 1868); and W. E. H. Lecky, *History of the Rise and Influence of the Spirit of Rationalism in Europe*, 2 vols. (London, 1865). These works put forth what later came to be called the "Whig" interpretation of history, which in the twentieth century was expounded and elaborated in such works as Wilbur K. Jordan, *The Development of Religious Toleration in England*, 4 vols. (Cambridge, Mass., 1932–1940); William Haller, *Liberty and Reformation in the Puritan Revolution* (New York, 1955); and

Roland Herbert Bainton, *The Travail of Religious Liberty: Nine Biographical Studies* (Hamden, Conn., 1971). In 1950 Herbert Butterfield, in *The Whig Interpretation of History* (London, 1950), published his damning critique of this interpretation and the assumptions on which it was based. Butterfield exposed the fallacies inherent in all "whiggish" versions of the past that construct history as a struggle between progressives and reactionaries, persons whose ideas were analogous to our own and those who opposed such ideas. On an empirical level, Joseph Lecler argued a few years later, in a magisterial study that is still required reading, *Toleration and the Reformation*, 2 vols. (London, 1960) (orig. French edition 1955), that Catholic, not Protestant, states had the best records for toleration in the sixteenth century. Lecler's study was a classic combination of intellectual and political history. In *The Rise of Toleration* (New York, 1967), Henry Kamen expanded the focus to include economic and social forces, crediting free trade along with rationalism for increases in toleration, which he conceded were contingent and limited, not the inevitable consequence of certain ideas. By the 1980s a broad consensus had emerged among scholars and nonscholars that rationalism and secularization, not Protestantism, had brought about a long-term rise of toleration in the West. The original Whig interpretation was as good as dead, but whiggish schemas were as prevalent as ever.

Further challenges to the "rise of toleration" narrative awaited the 1990s, taking then the somewhat hesitant form of essay collections: Ole Peter Grell, Jonathan I. Israel, and Nicholas Tyacke, eds., *From Persecution to Toleration: The Glorious Revolution and Religion in England* (Oxford, 1991); Ole Peter Grell and Bob Scribner, eds., *Tolerance and Intolerance in the European Reformation* (Cambridge, 1996); John Christian Laursen and Cary J. Nederman, eds., *Beyond the Persecuting Society: Religious Toleration before the Enlightenment* (Philadelphia, 1998); Ole Peter Grell and Roy Porter, eds., *Toleration in Enlightenment Europe* (Cambridge, 2000). These volumes are inconsistent and piecemeal in their revisionism, but include many important essays. The quatercentenary in 1998 of the French Edict of Nantes inspired a great outpouring of works. Some, like Thierry Wanegffelen's *L'édit de Nantes: Une histoire européenne de la tolérance du XVIe au XXe siècle* (Paris, 1998), told a traditional story, while others, again especially essay collections (the fruit often of conferences), were informed by new methodologies and self-critical reflections: see especially Richard L. Goodbar, ed., *The Edict of Nantes: Five Essays and a New Translation*

(Bloomington, Minn., 1998); Keith Cameron, Mark Greengrass, and Penny Roberts, eds., *The Adventure of Religious Pluralism in Early Modern France: Papers from the Exeter Conference, April 1999* (Oxford, 2000); Ruth Whelan and Carol Baxter, eds., *Toleration and Religious Identity: The Edict of Nantes and Its Implications in France, Britain and Ireland* (Dublin, 2003); and Michel Grandjean and Bernard Roussel, eds., *Coexister dans l'intolérance: L'édit de Nantes (1598)* (Geneva, 1998). Revisionism provoked in turn a minor backlash: the Whig interpretation appears in something close to its original form in John Coffey, *Persecution and Toleration in Protestant England 1558–1689* (London, 2000), while Perez Zagorin, in *How the Idea of Religious Toleration Came to the West* (Princeton, 2003), offers a roundup of the usual heroes and their ideas. Most books and articles devoted to the history of toleration are still primarily studies in intellectual history; some of the more provocative recent ones have been written by political theorists: Cary J. Nederman, *Worlds of Difference: European Discourses of Toleration, c. 1100–c. 1550* (University Park, Pa., 2000); Andrew R. Murphy, *Conscience and Community: Revisiting Toleration and Religious Dissent in Early Modern England and America* (University Park, Pa., 2001); Ingrid Creppell, *Toleration and Identity: Foundations in Early Modern Thought* (New York, 2003). John Locke, who holds a preeminent place in genealogies of liberalism, remains a key figure for both historians and theorists. John Marshall, in *John Locke, Toleration and Early Enlightenment Culture* (Cambridge, 2006), situates his ideas in their full context, surveying practices as well as theories of intolerance and toleration in western Europe in the late seventeenth century. For philosophical analyses of toleration and its place in liberal political theory, see, among others, David Heyd, ed., *Toleration: An Elusive Virtue* (Princeton, 1996); Susan Mendus, *Toleration and the Limits of Liberalism* (Atlantic Highlands, 1993); Will Kymlicka, *Liberalism, Community and Culture* (Oxford, 1989). Political theorist Michael Walzer has taken a different tack, analyzing in a short and stimulating book, *On Toleration* (New Haven, 1997), the sorts of political "regimes" conducive to toleration.

Those interested in exploring the history of toleration in particular countries will find the essays in Grell and Scribner, *Tolerance and Intolerance in the European Reformation,* and Grell and Porter, *Toleration in Enlightenment Europe,* good starting points. For England, they could not have a better introduction than Alexandra Walsham, *Charitable Hatred: Toler-*

ance and Intolerance in England, 1500–1700 (Manchester, 2006), which only appeared when most of the work for this book was completed; its readers will find in it many points of agreement with this book. Keith P. Luria, *Sacred Boundaries: Religious Coexistence and Conflict in Early-Modern France* (Washington, D.C., 2005), is an innovative study of France inspired by cultural anthropology; Philip Benedict, *The Faith and Fortunes of France's Huguenots, 1600–85* (Aldershot, 2001), contains important essays. Readers of French naturally have more choices, including Jean Quéniart, *La Révocation de l'Édit de Nantes: Protestants et catholiques en France de 1598 à 1685* (Paris, 1985); and Elisabeth Labrousse, *"Une foi, une loi, un roi?" Essai sur la Revocation de l'Édit de Nantes* (Geneva, 1985). An important work on the sixteenth century, with a comparative perspective, is Olivier Christin, *La paix de religion: L'autonomisation de la raison politique au XVIe siècle* (Paris, 1997). For an overview of the Holy Roman Empire (if such a thing is possible), readers of English will find only scattered articles: Anton Schindling, "Neighbours of a Different Faith: Confessional Coexistence and Parity in the Territorial States and Towns of the Empire," in *1648: War and Peace in Europe*, ed. Klaus Bussmann and Heinz Schilling, 1:465–473 (Munich, 1998); Walter Grossmann, "Religious Toleration in Germany, 1684 [1648]–1750," *Studies on Voltaire and the Eighteenth Century* 201 (1982): 115–141; Joachim Whaley, *"Pouvoir sauver les apparences:* The Theory and Practice of Tolerance in 18th-Century Germany," *British Journal for Eighteenth Century Studies* 13 (1990): 1–18. Étienne François, "De l'uniformité à la tolérance: Confession et société urbaine en Allemagne, 1650–1800," *Annales: Économies, sociétés, civilisations* 37 (1982): 783–800, offers a useful typology of German cities, and readers of German will find Anton Schindling and Walter Ziegler, eds., *Die Territorien des Reichs im Zeitalter der Reformation und Konfessionalisierung: Land und Konfession 1500–1650,* 7 vols. (Münster, 1989–1997), an invaluable reference work. An assemblage of political narratives, Jean Bérenger, *Tolérance ou paix de religion en Europe centrale (1415–1792)* (Paris, 2000), offers a traditional but accessible overview of the Holy Roman Empire, Austria, Poland, Hungary, and the Czech lands. For Poland there is—outdated but still not replaced—Janusz Tazbir, *A State without Stakes: Polish Religious Toleration in the Sixteenth and Seventeenth Centuries* (New York, 1973); for Hungary the closest thing to a book on religious toleration (and conflict) is Márta Fata, *Ungarn, das Reich der Stephanskrone, im Zeitalter der Reformation und Konfessionalisierung:*

Multiethnizität, Land und Konfession 1500 bis 1700 (Münster, 2000). For a survey of east central Europe, see E. William Monter, "Toleration and Its Discontents in East-Central Europe," in his *Ritual, Myth and Magic in Early Modern Europe* (Athens, Ohio, 1983), 130–147. *Toleration* is not a word usually applied to Ireland, though it should be, especially for the eighteenth century; see C. D. A. Leighton, *Catholicism in a Protestant Kingdom: A Study of the Irish Ancien Régime* (New York, 1994). For the Netherlands there are two essay collections in English: R. Po-chia Hsia and H. F. K. van Nierop, eds., *Calvinism and Religious Toleration in the Dutch Golden Age* (Cambridge, 2002); and Christiane Berkvens-Stevelinck, Jonathan Irvine Israel, and G. H. M Posthumus Meyjes, eds., *The Emergence of Tolerance in the Dutch Republic* (Leiden, 1997).

Histories of Europe's religious minorities offer crucial insights into issues of toleration. Among the best are John Bossy, *The English Catholic Community, 1570–1850* (New York, 1976); and Michael R. Watts, *The Dissenters*, 2 vols. (Oxford, 1978–1995). Until the 1970s, though, and in many cases even later, the history of minorities tended to be written by members of those minorities. Religious groups had their own historiographic traditions, through which they formulated and expressed key aspects of their identity. Much of the resulting scholarship had deeply embedded biases; often, too, it had an antiquarian character. Some of it, nevertheless, was of outstanding quality and remains a point of orientation for current debates as well as a source of information—see, for example, L. J. Rogier, *Geschiedenis van het katholicisme in Noord-Nederland in de zestiende en zeventiende eeuw*, 2 vols. (Amsterdam, 1946); Mihály Bucsay, *Der Protestantismus in Ungarn, 1521–1978: Ungarns Reformkirchen in Geschichte und Gegenwart*, 2 vols. (Vienna, 1977–1979); and the monumental Salo Wittmayer Baron, *A Social and Religious History of the Jews*, 16 vols. (New York, 1952–1976). The confessional impetus led also to the publication of many primary sources. A portion of these materials, primary and secondary, appeared in proprietary journals such as *Recusant History, Archivium Hibernicum* for Ireland, *Bulletin de la Société de l'histoire du protestantisme français, Jahrbuch der Gesellschaft für die Geschichte des Protestantismus in Österreich, Archief voor de Geschiedenis van het Aartsbisdom Utrecht, Bijdragen voor de Geschiedenis van het Bisdom Haarlem, Revue des études juives,* and *Studia Rosenthaliana.* Much information relevant to the history of toleration can be gleaned from the pages of these publications.

Among primary sources, treaties such as the Peace of Westphalia and laws such as the English Toleration Act of 1689 are of course very important. Printed editions of them can be found in André Stegmann, ed., *Édits des guerres de religion* (Paris, 1979); Goodbar, *The Edict of Nantes;* Ernst Walder, ed., *Religionsvergleiche des 16. Jahrhunderts* (Bern, 1974); Konrad Müller, ed., *Instrumenta pacis Westphalicae—Die Westfälischen Friedens-verträge: Vollständiger lateinischer Text mit Übersetzung der wichtigsten Teile und Regesten* (Bern, 1949); K. Kuzmány, ed., *Urkundenbuch zum österreichisch-evangelischen Kirchenrecht* (Vienna, 1856) (for Austria and Hungary); Peter F. Barton, ed., *Im Zeichen der Toleranz: Aufsätze zur Toler-anzgesetzgebung des 18. Jahrhunderts in den Reichen Joseph II., ihren Voraus-setzungen und ihren Folgen; Eine Festschrift* (Vienna, 1981) (the 1781 *Toler-anzpatent*); Geoffrey R. Elton, ed., *The Tudor Constitution: Documents and Commentary* (Cambridge, 1960); J. P. Kenyon, ed., *The Stuart Constitution, 1603–1688: Documents and Commentary* (Cambridge, 1966); Grell, Israel, and Tyacke, *From Persecution to Toleration* (facsimile of the 1689 Act); G. M. von Knonau et al., eds., *Ämtliche Sammlung der ältern eidgenössischen Abschiede,* 8 in 23 vols. (Lucern, 1839–1986).

To understand the practice of toleration on the local level, however, no source is as important as modern case studies of religious life in local communities. The following are among the most revealing. For France, Louis Pérouas, *Le diocèse de La Rochelle de 1648 à 1724: Sociologie et pastorale* (Paris, 1964); Robert Sauzet, *Contre-réforme et réforme catholique en Bas-Languedoc: Le diocèse de Nîmes au XVIIe siècle* (Paris, 1979); Louis Châtellier, *Tradition chrétienne et renouveau catholique dans le cadre de l'ancien diocèse de Strasbourg (1650–1770)* (Paris, 1981); Barbara B. Diefendorf, *Beneath the Cross: Catholics and Huguenots in Sixteenth-Century Paris* (New York, 1991); Gregory Hanlon, *Confession and Community in Seventeenth-Century France: Catholic and Protestant Coexistence in Aqui-taine* (Philadelphia, 1993); and Mark W. Konnert, *Civic Agendas and Re-ligious Passion: Châlons-sur-Marne during the French Wars of Religion* (Kirksville, 1997). For Germany, Gerald Lyman Soliday, *A Community in Conflict: Frankfurt Society in the Seventeenth and Early Eighteenth Cen-turies* (Hanover, N.H., 1974); Peter Lang, *Die Ulmer Katholiken im Zeitalter der Glaubenskämpfe: Lebensbedingungen einer konfessionellen Minderheit* (Frankfurt am Main, 1977); Paul Warmbrunn, *Zwei Konfessionen in einer Stadt: Das Zusammenleben von Katholiken und Protestanten in den paritätischen Reichstädten Augsburg, Biberach, Ravensburg und Dinkelsbühl von 1548 bis 1648* (Wiesbaden, 1983); Peter Zschunke, *Konfession und Alltag in Oppenheim: Beiträge zur Geschichte von Bevölkerung und Gesellschaft einer gemischtkonfessionellen Kleinstadt in der frühen Neuzeit* (Wiesbaden, 1984); Joachim Whaley, *Religious Toleration and Social Change in Hamburg 1529–1819* (Cambridge, 1985); Bernd Roeck, *Eine Stadt in Krieg und Frieden: Studien zur Geschichte der Reichsstadt Augsburg zwischen Kalenderstreit und Parität (1584–1648)*, 2 vols. (Göttingen, 1989); Marc R. Forster, *The Counter-Reformation in the Villages: Religion and Reform in the Bishopric of Speyer, 1560–1720* (Ithaca, 1992); Stefan Ehrenpreis, *"Wir sind mit blutigen Köpfen davongelaufen . . .": Lokale Konfessionskonflikte im Herzogtum Berg 1550–1700* (Bochum, 1993); and Peter G. Wallace, *Communities and Conflict in Early Modern Colmar, 1575–1730* (Atlantic Highlands, 1995). For the Netherlands, Joke Spaans, *Haarlem na de Reformatie: Stedelijke cultuur en kerkelijk leven, 1577–1620* (The Hague, 1989); Benjamin J. Kaplan, *Calvinists and Libertines: Confession and Community in Utrecht, 1578–1620* (Oxford, 1995); and Charles de Mooij, *Geloof kan bergen verzetten: Reformatie en katholieke herleving te Bergen op Zoom 1577–1795* (Hilversum, 1998). For Switzerland, Randolph C. Head, "Religious Coexistence and Confessional Conflict in the *Vier Dörfer:* Practices of Toleration in Eastern Switzerland, 1525–1615," in Laursen and Nederman, *Beyond the Persecuting Society,* 145–165; and Frauke Volkland, *Konfession und Selbstverständnis: Reformierte Rituale in der gemischtkonfessionellen Kleinstadt Bischofszell im 17. Jahrhundert* (Göttingen, 2005). For the British Isles, Daniel C. Beaver, *Parish Communities and Religious Conflict in the Vale of Gloucester, 1590–1690* (Cambridge, Mass., 1998); Muriel C. McClendon, *The Quiet Reformation: Magistrates and the Emergence of Protestantism in Tudor Norwich* (Stanford, 1999); Gordon DesBrisay, "Catholics, Quakers and Religious Persecution in Restoration Aberdeen," *Innes Review* 47 (1996): 136–168; and Kevin Whelan, "The Catholic Community in Eighteenth-Century Wexford," in *Endurance and Emergence: Catholics in Ireland in the Eighteenth Century,* ed. T. P. Power and Kevin Whelan, 129–170 (Blackrock, Co. Dublin, 1990). For Hungary, Franz Galambos, ed. and trans., *Glaube und Kirche in der Schwäbischen Türkei des 18. Jahrhunderts: Aufzeichnungen von Michael Winkler in den Pfarrchroniken von Szakadát, Bonyhád und Gödre* (Munich, 1987). For the cities of Poland there is a series of crucial articles by Gottfried Schramm published disparately in *Jahrbücher für Geschichte*

Osteuropas, Zeitschrift für Ostforschung, and elsewhere. Though the scale of its terrain is different, this book derives much of its approach, as well as countless facts, from such local studies, above all from Étienne François's outstanding study of Augsburg, *Die unsichtbare Grenze: Protestanten und Katholiken in Augsburg, 1648–1806* (Sigmaringen, 1991), available in French translation as *Protestants et catholiques en Allemagne: Identités et pluralisme, Augsbourg, 1648–1806* (Paris, 1993).

Several other bodies of recent literature have helped cast the history of toleration in a new light. One treats the phenomenon known as confessionalization, which has become the reigning paradigm in studies of German religious life after the Reformation, and has been extended to the rest of Europe as well. Implicit in my discussion in Chapter 1 of confessionalism as a form of religious culture is a critique of Heinz Schilling and other scholars who connect it inseparably to state-building and social discipline. For an initial orientation, see Wolfgang Reinhard, "Reformation, Counter-Reformation, and the Early Modern State: A Reassessment," *Catholic Historical Review* 75 (1989): 383–401; Heinz Schilling, "Confessionalisation in Europe: Causes and Effects for Church, State, Society, and Culture," in Bussmann and Schilling, *1648,* 1:219–228; R. Po-chia Hsia, *Social Discipline in the Reformation: Central Europe, 1550–1750* (London, 1989); Kaplan, *Calvinists and Libertines,* intro. and chap. 1; Andrew Pettegree, "Confessionalization in North Western Europe," in *Konfessionalisierung in Ostmitteleuropa: Wirkungen des religiösen Wandels im 16. und 17. Jahrhundert in Staat, Gesellschaft und Kultur,* ed. Joachim Bahlcke and Arno Strohmeyer, 105–120 (Stuttgart, 1999); and Philip Benedict, "Confessionalization in France? Critical Reflections and New Evidence," in *Society and Culture in the Huguenot World, 1559–1685,* ed. Raymond A. Mentzer and Andrew Spicer, 44–61 (Cambridge, 2002). Another related body of work is the literature on religious violence, a subject explored most profoundly, for tragic reasons, by historians of France. On the religious rioting that accompanied the French Wars of Religion, see first and foremost Natalie Zemon Davis, "The Rites of Violence," in her *Society and Culture in Early Modern France,* 152–187 (Stanford, 1975). Mark Greengrass, "The Psychology of Religious Violence," *French History* 5 (1991): 467–474, and Mack P. Holt, "Putting Religion Back into the Wars of Religion," *French Historical Studies* 18 (1993): 524–551, are useful review articles; readers of French will find compelling and sometimes disturbing the *grande oeuvre* of Denis Crouzet,

Les guerriers de Dieu: La violence au temps des troubles de religion (vers 1525–vers 1610), 2 vols. (Seyssel, 1990). Historians of England have come to recognize the power of anti-Catholic sentiment and the central role it played in the development of English national identity; these are illuminated in Robin Clifton, "The Popular Fear of Catholics during the English Revolution," *Past and Present* 52 (1971): 23–55; Carol Wiener, "This Beleaguered Isle: A Study of Elizabethan and Early Jacobean Anti-Catholicism," *Past and Present* 51 (1971): 27–62; John Miller, *Popery and Politics in England, 1660–1688* (Cambridge, 1973); Peter Lake, "Anti-Popery: The Structure of a Prejudice," in *Conflict in Early Stuart England: Studies in Religion and Politics, 1603–1642*, ed. Richard Cust and Ann Hughes, 72–106 (London, 1989); Linda Colley, *Britons: Forging the Nation, 1707–1837* (New Haven, 1992), chap. 1; Colin Haydon, *Anti-Catholicism in Eighteenth-Century England, c. 1714–80: A Political and Social Study* (Manchester, 1993); and Tony Claydon and Ian McBride, eds., *Protestantism and National Identity: Britain and Ireland, c. 1650–c. 1850* (Cambridge, 1998). Finally, the historiography of Judaism has undergone in recent years a veritable revolution. My treatment of early modern Jewish history in Chapter 11, especially my description of the ghetto, echoes the revisionism that commands a broad consensus among current specialists, who reject the "lachrymose" view of Jewish history as a tale of perpetual, ever-worse suffering. For an introduction to their work, see Robert Bonfil, *Jewish Life in Renaissance Italy* (Berkeley, 1994); David B. Ruderman, ed., *Essential Papers on Jewish Culture in Renaissance and Baroque Italy* (New York, 1992); Mark R. Cohen, ed., *The Autobiography of a Seventeenth-Century Venetian Rabbi: Leon Modena's Life of Judah* (Princeton, 1988); R. Po-chia Hsia and Hartmut Lehmann, eds., *In and Out of the Ghetto: Jewish–Gentile Relations in Late Medieval and Early Modern Germany* (Washington, D.C., 1995); and a book on which I rely at numerous points, Jonathan I. Israel, *European Jewry in the Age of Mercantilism, 1550–1750* (Oxford, 1989).

As will be clear by now, this book is eclectic in its methodology. In addition to the debts mentioned above and many others that remain unmentioned, it draws heavily on the demographic approach to religious history found in Philip Benedict, *The Huguenot Population of France, 1600–1685: The Demographic Fate and Customs of a Religious Minority* (Philadelphia, 1991); on the anthropological approaches of Natalie Zemon Davis, "The Sacred and the Body Social in Sixteenth-Century Lyon," *Past and Present*

90 (1981): 40–70; and David Nirenberg, *Communities of Violence: Persecution of Minorities in the Middle Ages* (Princeton, 1995); on studies of memory and commemoration, in particular David Cressy, *Bonfires and Bells: National Memory and the Protestant Calendar in Elizabethan and Stuart England* (Berkeley, 1989); and on studies of religious culture and identity, including Alexandra Walsham, *Church Papists: Catholicism, Conformity and Confessional Polemic in Early Modern England* (London, 1993); Miriam Bodian, *Hebrews of the Portuguese Nation: Conversos and Community in Early Modern Amsterdam* (Bloomington, 1997); Judith Pollmann, *Religious Choice in the Dutch Republic: The Reformation of Arnoldus Buchelius (1565–1641)* (Manchester, 1999); and Willem Frijhoff, *Embodied Belief: Ten Essays on Religious Culture in Dutch History* (Hilversum, 2002).

Acknowledgments

Writing a book that covers so wide a terrain has been a tremendous learning experience. It has required me to expand my expertise far beyond the Netherlands, my area of geographic specialization, to learn the history of lands I had scarcely studied before and deepen my understanding of ones I had. Such an undertaking would have been impossible if various institutions had not given me the precious gift of time. I am grateful to the Frederick Burckhardt program of the American Council of Learned Societies; the National Endowment for the Humanities; the Folger Shakespeare Library; the Institute for Research in the Humanities in Madison, Wisconsin; the Woodrow Wilson International Center for Scholars; the University of Iowa; and University College London for fellowships, grants, and other financial support that made this project possible. I am grateful also to the scholars and friends who assisted me in this learning process, sharing with me their understanding of different parts of Europe: Kurt Diemer, Randolph Head, Henry Horwitz, Georg Michels, Alexandra Walsham, and Gillian Weiss.

Portions of this book, in earlier forms, were presented at the University of Amsterdam, the Catholic University of America, Harvard University, the University of Maryland, Miami University, Oxford University, the University of St. Andrews, University College London, the University of Virginia, Yale University, the research institutes mentioned above, and numerous conferences. I wish to thank the colleagues and students who gave me feedback on those occasions. I am indebted also to Laura Hein and others who provided feedback on draft chapters. When a draft of the book was complete, Philip Benedict, Steven Jaffe, and Judith Pollmann did me the enormous favor of reading it and making suggestions for improvement. This is a better book thanks to them, and to my editor, Joyce Seltzer, whose enthusiasm, gentle admonitions, and incisive feedback have done much to shape the book and help bring it to completion. I wish also to express my appreciation for the comments provided by Steven Ozment and two other readers for Harvard University Press, and for the work of mapmaker Philip Schwartzberg. Finally, I wish to express my profound gratitude to my parents, Fred and Gloria, my brother, Noah, and sister, Julia, and my dear friends Marten Jan Bok and Kitty Kilian for the love and support they have given me over the years. Without it I would not be the same person and my work on this book would never have been possible. To them, and to my beloved Katy, whom I am so lucky to have found, I dedicate this book.

An earlier version of Chapter 7 was published in *The American Historical Review* 7, no. 4 (October 2002): 1031–1064; my thanks to the editors of the journal for permission to republish it. Some material in Chapter 10 is reprinted by permission of the publishers from "'For They Will Turn Away Thy Sons': The Practice and Perils of Mixed Marriage in the Dutch Golden Age," in *Piety and Family in Early Modern Europe: Essays in Honour of Steven Ozment,* ed. Benjamin J. Kaplan and Marc R. Forster (Aldershot: Ashgate, 2005), pp. 115–133 (copyright © 2005). Some material in Chapter 12 has appeared previously in Benjamin J. Kaplan, *Muslims in the Dutch Golden Age: Representations and Realities of Religious Toleration* (Amsterdam, 2007), and appears here by permission of the Amsterdams Centrum voor de Studie van de Gouden Eeuw. With the permission of Blackwell Publishers, I have also incorporated material that appeared previously in my essay "Coexistence, Conflict, and the Practice of Toleration," published as chapter 29 of *A Companion to the Reformation World,* ed. R. Po-chia Hsia (Blackwell Publishers, 2003), pp. 486–505.

To cite all the books and articles on which this work of synthesis and interpretation draws would have made the notes massive and unwieldy. The

publisher and I have opted instead to indicate the source of all direct quotations, keep the notes otherwise to a minimum, and provide at the end
a brief bibliographic essay. Intended as a guide to further reading, the latter makes clear my greatest debts but leaves unmentioned many scholars
whose research has informed this study. To them I express here my apolo-
gies and thanks.

Index